Economics for Everyone

Economics for Everyone
website: www.economicsforeveryone.com
e-mail Jim Stanford: author@economicsforeveryone.com

Economics for Everyone

A Short Guide to the Economics of Capitalism

Second edition

Jim Stanford

Illustrations by Tony Biddle

C C P A
CANADIAN CENTRE
for POLICY ALTERNATIVES
CENTRE CANADIEN
de POLITIQUES ALTERNATIVES

PlutoPress
www.plutobooks.com

First published 2008.
Second edition published 2015 by Pluto Press
345 Archway Road, London N6 5AA
www.plutobooks.com

and

Published in Canada by Canadian Centre for Policy Alternatives
Suite 500, 251 Bank Street, Ottawa, ON, K2P 1X3, Canada
www.policyalternatives.ca

ISBN 978 0 7453 3578 0   Hardback
ISBN 978 0 7453 3577 3   Paperback (Pluto)
ISBN 978 1 7837 1326 4   PDF eBook
ISBN 978 1 7837 1328 8   Kindle eBook
ISBN 978 1 7837 1327 1   EPUB eBook

This book is printed on paper suitable for recycling and made from fully managed and
sustained forest sources. Logging, pulping and manufacturing processes are expected to
conform to the environmental standards of the country of origin.

10   9   8   7   6   5   4   3   2   1

Typeset by Stanford DTP Services, Northampton, England
Text design by Melanie Patrick
Printed in Canada

Dedicated to the hard-working people who produce the wealth
– in hopes that by better understanding the economy,
we can be more successful in changing it.

All author royalties generated from the sale of this book are donated
to the Canadian Centre for Policy Alternatives.

Contents

Part Five: Challenging Capitalism

Acknowledgements

The first edition of this book had its genesis in an on-line course in economics for trade union members jointly developed by my union at the time (the Canadian Auto Workers, CAW) and Mcmaster University in Hamilton, Canada. That sparked my efforts to develop teaching resources with broader applications in trade union and social change settings, culminating in Economics for Everyone. I thank my colleagues David Robertson (formerly of CAW) and Wayne Lewchuk (at McMaster) for that initial inspiration, and for their own outstanding efforts to develop worker-friendly pedagogy.

The support of other colleagues at CAW and subsequently Unifor (formed in 2013 through the merger of the CAW and the Communications, Energy and Paperworkers' Union) has also been essential to the first edition, its subsequent use, and now the publication of this second edition. I am very grateful to our leaders over that time (Buzz Hargrove, Jim O'Neil, Ken Lewenza, Peter Kennedy, and Jerry Dias) for their support not only of this book, but more generally of my role as a union economist; they allow me to take on issues and projects that go well beyond the immediate bread-and-butter needs of the union. My colleagues in the union's outstanding research and education departments have provided consistent and generous support for the book and its application in popular education (including through Unifor's own world-renowned Paid Educational Leave program). I have received first-rate administrative, research, and technical support from Kristine Vendrame, Kathy Bennett, Linda McCrorie, and Shahmez Khimji and his technical team.

Consistent enthusiasm from Bruce Campbell and his team at the Canadian Centre for Policy Alternatives (CCPA) has been crucial to the Economics for Everyone project from the outset. Equally enthusiastic and ongoing support from Pluto Press (under the leadership of Roger van Zwanenberg and now David Shulman) allowed me to reach a wider, international audience for this work. I am grateful to the five international publishers who undertook translations of the first edition.

Special mention in this regard is due to the outstanding and energetic team at Lux Éditeur in Montréal, who did much more than just republish the book in French; they created an entirely customized and exciting book in its own right (Petit Cours d'Autodéfense en Économie). Sadly there is a tragic footnote to that fine project: the outstanding original cartoons for Petit Cours were created by Charb (Stéphane Charbonnier), who also published the French satirical newspaper Charlie

Hebdo. Charb was assassinated in the Charlie Hebdo attacks of January 2015; his commitment to social justice and free expression is gratefully acknowledged and very deeply missed.

The first edition received a generous response from many reviewers, and I thank them for their support and their suggestions for improvements (many of which are reflected in this second edition). These reviewers include Andrew Allentuck, Fletcher Baragar, Amit Basole, Simon Black, Nick Bonokoski, Bill Burgess, Damien Cahill, Tristan Ewins, Travis Fast, Larry French, Stephen LaRose, Roger Lever, Bruce Little, Heather Mallick, Margaret Ann McHugh, Ron Miller, Don Nicholls, Sue Hui Ong, Véronique Parenteau, Tom Sandborn, Larry Savage, Frank Stilwell, and Mel Watkins. Just as important has been the feedback received from the many educators (in both formal educational institutions, and in social movement and trade union settings) who used the book in their teaching, and from students in those courses. The students I personally taught using the book (in courses sponsored by Unifor, the Canadian Labour College, the Australian Manufacturing Workers Union, the New Zealand Amalgamated Engineering, Printing & Manufacturing Union, the New Zealand Council of Trade Unions, and the International Transport Federation) consistently impressed me with their hunger to learn and their excitement to apply economic knowledge in their social justice activism.

For this second edition, excellent comments on draft chapters were provided to me by many people, including Donna Baines, Jordan Brennan, John Cartwright, Bill Dunn, John King, Peter Kriesler, Marc Lavoie, Marc Lee, Eric Miller, Adam David Morton, Laurell Ritchie, Vinay Sharma, Frank Stilwell, Ross Teppett, and Nurzhan Zhambekov.

Tony Biddle's accessible, humorous illustrations and road maps have added immeasurably to the educational and entertainment value of this book. I thank Tony for his interest in this project, for his timely and innovative work, and for all the other ways he devotes his considerable artistic and political talents to the cause of social justice.

Much of the research and writing on this second edition took place while I was a visiting scholar at the Department of Political Economy at the University of Sydney, Australia. I thank that department for their hospitable, collegial welcome. That program is a unique and globally important meeting point for critical, high-quality research and instruction in critical economics and political economy.

Nobody develops their ideas in a vacuum, and I owe an intellectual debt to the many passionate, principled, and rigorous economists who have taught and influenced me over the years: my free-thinking professors at the University of Calgary, Cambridge, and the New School; my colleagues in the Progressive Economics Forum (Canada's network of progressive economists); and my soulmates in the broader heterodox community (with special mention to Dean

Baker, the late Andrew Glyn, the late David M. Gordon, Steve Keen, Marc Lavoie, Kari Polanyi Levitt, John Loxley, Tom Palley, Robert Pollin, Malcolm Sawyer, and Mel Watkins).

My most passionate gratitude goes to my immediate family: Donna Baines, Ché Baines, and Thea Baines. Their support while working on the book and its associated activities over the last several years has been generous and essential. But I am even more thankful that they continue to share with me their energy, hope, and passion for life, and their determination to build a better world.

In the seven years since the first edition of Economics for Everyone was published, capitalism has continued to evolve – in often surprising, usually harmful ways. The core principles that I outlined in that first edition for understanding this dynamic, flexible, and infuriating economic system have mostly remained relevant and valid. In particular, my emphasis on the waste and fragility of financialization was ratified by the global meltdown that ensued within months of the first edition's publication. This new edition updates the description and analysis of trends in capitalism (including a whole new chapter on the global crisis of 2008–09 and its aftermath, and another new chapter on the causes and consequences of inequality). But my overall story remains the same. Capitalism is a powerful, resilient, at times productive, but always exploitive and often inhumane method for organizing our economic affairs and activity. And there is no doubt in my mind that humanity can do better.

Introduction
Why Study Economics?

Never trust an economist with your job

Most people think economics is a technical, confusing, and even mysterious subject. It's a field best left to the experts: namely, the economists.

But in reality, economics should be quite straightforward. Ultimately economics is simply about how we work. What we produce. And how we distribute and ultimately use what we've produced. Economics is about who does what, who gets what, and what they do with it.

At that simplest, grass-roots level, we all know something about the economy. And so we should all have something to say about economics.

Moreover, because we interact, cooperate, and clash with each other in the economy (even Robinson Crusoe didn't work alone – he had Friday around to help), economics is inherently a *social* subject. It's not just technical forces like technology and productivity that matter. It's also the interactions and relationships between *people* that make the economy go around.

So you don't need to be an economist to know a lot about economics. Everyone experiences the economy. Everyone contributes to it, one way or another. Everyone has an interest in the economy: in *how* it functions, how *well* it functions, and in *whose interests* it functions. And everyone has a grass-roots sense of where they personally fit into the big economic picture, and how well they are doing (compared to others, compared to the past, and compared to their expectations). This is the stuff economics should be made of.

Unfortunately, most professional economists don't think about economics in this common-sense, grass-roots context. To the contrary, they tend to adopt a rather superior attitude in their dealings with the untrained masses. They invoke complicated technical mumbo-jumbo – usually utterly unnecessary to their arguments – to make their case. They claim to know what's good for the people, even better than the people themselves do. They take great pleasure in expounding theories that are counter-intuitive and puzzling to the rest of us. They present themselves as interpreters of a mysterious realm which average people cannot hope to comprehend. And since they study things that are measured in billions or even trillions of dollars, their sense of importance grows – in their own eyes, and in others'.

That's why we see economists on the television news every night. We almost never see educators, social workers, nutritionists, or architects on the nightly news. Perhaps we should hear more from those other professions, and less from the economists. Their advice might actually be more important to our long-term economic well-being than that of the economists.

Nothing better exemplifies economists' know-it-all attitude than debates over free trade. Conventionally trained economists take it as a *proven fact* that free trade between two countries always makes both sides better off. People who question or oppose free trade – trade unionists, social activists, nationalists – must either be acting from ignorance, or else are pursuing some narrow vested interest that conflicts with the broader good. These troublesome people should be lectured to (and economists love nothing better than expounding their beautiful theory of COMPARATIVE ADVANTAGE*), or simply ignored. And that's exactly what most governments do. (Ironically, even some conventional economists now recognize that traditional free trade theory is wrong, for many reasons – some of which we'll discuss in Chapter 22 of this book. But that hasn't affected the profession's near-religious devotion to free trade policies.)

Most economists are wedded to a particular, peculiar version of economics – called NEOCLASSICAL ECONOMICS. This kind of economics is as ideological as it is scientific. It was developed in the late nineteenth century to *defend* capitalism, not just explain it. And it still goes to great lengths to try to "prove" a whole portfolio of bizarre, politically loaded, and obviously untrue propositions: like claiming that merely owning financial wealth is itself productive, or that everyone is paid according to their productivity, or that unemployment doesn't even actually exist.

And the arrogance of economists is not neutral. Outside the academic world, the vast majority of professional economists work for organizations with a deep vested interest in the status quo: banks, brokerages, corporations, industry associations, and governments. Inside academia, too, the ideological influence of business and wealth is increasingly apparent over curriculum and research in economics – enforced partly through corporate and major donor funding of economics and business schools. Whether in universities or in the real world, therefore, most economists accept that competition, inequality, and the accumulation of private wealth are inevitable, natural, and even desirable features of a vibrant, efficient economy. This value system infuses their analysis and their recommendations.

I think we need a more democratic economics, a more grass-roots approach. I think we need an economics that's not based on abstract assumptions (like the other-worldly theory of PERFECT COMPETITION, which we'll explain in

---

*   Terms appearing in BOLD SMALL CAPITALS are defined in the on-line glossary provided at www. economicsforeveryone.com.

Chapter 11), but instead starts from the concrete circumstances of average people's lives. We need an economics for everyone.

My approach is not motivated by an "anti-expert" mentality. I would not want to be operated on by an untrained medical student. And people who make important economic decisions, and give important economic advice, should be formally trained in economics.

But debates over economic issues are not technical debates, where expertise alone settles the day. They are always *political* debates, in the broad sense of that word: distinct groups of people have distinct interests, they know their interests, and they naturally work to promote them. This occurs everywhere in the economy – and economics shouldn't pretend that it doesn't.

A hard-working labourer has very different economic interests from a red-suspendered currency trader. And the labourer has as much to say about economics as the trader. (In fact, in hard economic terms, the labourer produces far more real value than the currency trader – despite the enormous sums of money passing through the trader's computer every business day.) But the elitism of economics disempowers and silences the voices of non-experts, and devalues the economic contributions of working people.

My main goal with this book, and throughout my career as an economist, has been to encourage non-experts – workers, union members, activists, consumers, neighbours – to develop their natural, grass-roots interest in economics, by:

- Studying the economy, and learning more about how it functions.
- Thinking concretely about their personal role and stake in the economy (rather than abstract indicators like gross domestic product, stock markets, or foreign exchange).
- Recognizing that the economy embodies distinct groups of people with distinct and often conflicting interests, and that economics itself reflects those distinctions and conflicts. Economics is not a neutral, technical discipline.
- Being ready to challenge, when necessary, the way "expert" economists explain the economy and (even more dangerously) tell us how to change it.

The economy is too important to be left to the economists. Ordinary people have valuable economic knowledge – knowledge that's usually ignored by the experts. More importantly, the analysis and advice of the experts is all too often compromised by their position in the economy they are telling us how to manage. Everyone has a stake in the economy. Everyone has economic interests they need to identify and protect. Learning about economics will help them understand where they fit into the bigger system, and help them fight for a better deal.

An economist may tell you that your job depends on the central bank raising interest rates to control inflation (in the long run, anyway). An economist may

I once attended a dinner speech given by the then-Secretary-General of the Organization for Economic Cooperation and Development (OECD), which is an international association of developed capitalist countries. He was promoting the concept of "economic literacy." He argued that if more people in society understood the fundamentals of economic theory (like supply and demand, competition, and free trade), then they would more readily accept policy "reforms" implemented by their governments – even if those reforms were painful.

As an example, he referred to the dramatic (and successful) protests that occurred in France in the mid-2000s against government efforts to weaken labour protections. These changes would have made it easier for employers to fire workers, especially young workers. If the French understood that these seemingly painful "reforms" actually make the labour market function more "efficiently," he argued, they wouldn't have protested.

This kind of "literacy" sounds to me more like brainwashing than education.

During the question period, I took issue with the OECD chief's assertion that the French do not understand economics. Compare France to the US – usually held up as the prototype of an efficient, flexible, market-driven system. On average, a French worker works 300 hours per year fewer than an American (that's seven extra weeks off per year). Yet they produce nearly as much value added with each hour of labour as Americans. Unemployment is higher in France – yet most unemployed French receive more income (from social benefits) than millions of *employed* low-wage Americans. As a result, the French have enough money, and lots of time, to eat in restaurants, make love, and attend protest demonstrations (and not necessarily in that order!)

In America, meanwhile, there were almost 11 million *employed workers* in 2013, aged 18 to 64, whose incomes left them below the official poverty line (a standard which is still based on the standard of living in 1964) – and that does not include their children and other dependents.* Their hard work is not taking them far. Economic mobility between income groups in the US is much less common than in other countries (where income is distributed more evenly), yet the ideology that anyone can get ahead In life as long as they work hard still exercises incredible sway. For example, one survey found that 39 percent of Americans believed either that they already ranked within the wealthiest 1 percent of society, or else soon would make it there.† The mathematical impossibility of this bizarre worldview has not (yet) undermined the American mythology of "upward mobility" – a myth which inhibits hard-working, poor people from standing up and demanding a better deal here and now, rather than waiting for the day they finally make it rich (or else win the lottery).

Ironically, the OECD itself subsequently published abundant economic evidence indicating that employment protection laws (like those French regulations) actually have no visible impact whatsoever on unemployment rates.‡

So who really understands economics? I think it's the protestors in France.

* United States Census Bureau, "Current Population Survey, Annual Social and Economic Supplement" (2014).

† Survey conducted by Time/CNN, cited in Andrew Glyn, *Capitalism Unleashed: Finance, Globalization and Welfare* (Oxford: Oxford University Press, 2006, p. 179).

‡ Organization for Economic Cooperation and Development, "Reassessing the Role of Policies and Institutions for Labour Market Performance," *OECD Employment Outlook*, Chapter 7 (2006).

tell you that free trade will increase productivity and hence increase incomes (although you may lose your job in the process). An economist may tell you that eliminating unions and minimum wages will make society richer (although, just as with aerobic exercise, it might hurt at first … no pain, no gain!).

> ## Watch Out!
>
> "The purpose of studying economics is not to acquire a set of ready-made answers to economic questions, but to learn how to avoid being deceived by economists."
>
> Joan Robinson, British economist (1960).

Never trust an economist with your job. Learn about economics yourself. And make up your own mind about what might protect your job – and what might destroy it.

A society in which ordinary people know more about economics, and recognize the often conflicting interests at stake in the economy, is a society in which more people will feel confident deciding for themselves what's best – instead of trusting the experts. It will be a more democratic society.

Capitalism: the economy we know

So far, we've been speaking very broadly about "the economy." But in fact, this book is about the workings of a particular kind of economy, called capitalism. "Capitalism" and "the economy" are not the same thing – even though many economists pretend capitalism is a natural, permanent state of affairs, and hence the *only* economy. However, there were other economies that existed before capitalism. And I tend to think there will be other economies that come after capitalism, too.

Capitalism has particular features and forces that need to be identified, just to understand how it works. This is true regardless of how you feel about capitalism. Just to understand what's happening in capitalism, we need to identify and study its crucial facts:

- Most people have to work for others, in return for a wage or salary.
- A small proportion of society owns the bulk of wealth, and use that wealth in an effort to generate still more wealth.
- Competition between companies, each trying to maximize its own profits, forces them to behave in particular, sometimes perverse ways.

It seems bizarre, but conventional economists mostly ignore these central facts (with the partial exception of the third). They don't even use the word "capitalism." Instead, they call our system a "market economy." The fact that a few people own immense wealth, while most people own almost nothing, is considered accidental or even irrelevant. They claim, incredibly, that the economy would be exactly the same whether capitalists hired workers, or workers hired capitalists.

> ### Let's be Honest
>
> "Capitalism [is] a word that has gone largely out of fashion. The approved reference now is to the market system. This shift minimizes - indeed, deletes - the role of wealth in the economic and social system. And it sheds the adverse connotation going back to Marx. Instead of the owners of capital or their attendants in control, we have the admirably impersonal role of market forces. It would be hard to think of a change in terminology more in the interest of those to whom money accords power. They have now a functional anonymity."
>
> John Kenneth Galbraith, Canadian-American economist (1999).

These central and unique features of capitalism impart particular kinds of behaviour and motion to the economy. They explain why capitalism is *dynamic*: flexible, creative, and always changing. They explain why capitalism is *conflictual*: marked by ongoing struggle and conflict between different groups of people. They explain why capitalism is *unstable*: exhibiting periods of growth and prosperity, followed by periods of stagnation, recession, and even breakdown.

Economists who ignore the key features of capitalism will be less able to understand and explain how capitalism actually works. So purely from a scientific perspective, it's important to be frank about what we are dealing with.

Of course, economists of all political stripes carry political baggage. I certainly do. It's impossible to name and analyze capitalism without passing judgement on it. (Conventional economists pretend that the "positive" science of describing the economy can be separated from the "normative" practice of evaluating and trying to improve the economy - but this phony distinction has never been very convincing.)

Capitalism has been immensely successful, on many criteria. It ushered in the industrial era, and the prosperity (for some people, but not everyone) that came with it. It ruthlessly undermines old-fashioned restrictions and taboos, and probes endlessly to find new ways of generating private profit (some of which are socially useful, some of which are not). It harnesses immense energy, creativity, and discipline from many of its participants.

On the other hand, capitalism has patently failed to live up to many of its promises. Billions of the world's people endure hardship, poverty, and premature death, even though humanity possesses abundant wealth to abolish these afflictions. Vast resources - like the talent and energy of hundreds of millions of unemployed and underemployed individuals - are chronically misused or wasted. The natural environment is being deeply, perhaps critically damaged by the profit-maximizing, cost-shifting imperatives of private profit; global climate change is just the most catastrophic symptom of this failure. And even on its own terms – the rapid investment of private capital to generate profit – capitalism may be running out of steam (something we will discuss in Chapter 12).

I am critical of capitalism's failings – but I am also respectful of its flexibility and its staying power. I am utterly convinced that there are many obvious changes that would help the economy meet human and environmental needs, without breaking fundamentally from the underlying logic which drives the whole system. I also believe that it is ultimately possible to build an alternative economic system guided directly by our desire to improve the human condition, rather than by a hunger for private profit. (Exactly what that alternative system would look like, however, is not at all clear today.) We'll consider these criticisms of capitalism, and alternative visions, in the last chapters of this book.

But quite apart from whether you think capitalism is good or bad, capitalism is something we must study. It's the economy we live in, the economy we know. And the more ordinary people understand about capitalism, the better is the economic "deal" they'll be able to extract from it.

The organization of this book

This book has five major parts, which cover the following subject areas:

1. **Preliminaries**   The first part of the book defines the economy, and identifies the unique features of a capitalist economy. It also provides some historical background. We discuss how capitalism emerged and evolved, and also how the study of *economics* emerged and evolved. In both cases, we highlight the conflicts and controversies encountered en route to the present day. I believe that studying economic history and the history of economic thought is an inherently subversive undertaking. It refutes the assumption that capitalism is "natural" and hence ever-lasting, and the related claim that economics is the neutral, technical study of that natural, ever-lasting system.

2. **The Basics of Capitalism**   This part of the book studies the core activities and relationships that make up capitalism. First we discuss *work*. Broadly defined, work (or human effort) is the essential ingredient that drives everything in the economy. But we don't work with our bare hands; we must work with tools. We have to make those tools, and (in capitalism, anyway) someone owns them. Most work in capitalism is undertaken by employees who are paid wages or salaries for their efforts. But much work also occurs without any payment, inside households, as people care for themselves and their family members. We describe this basic economic "circle," in which profit-seeking investment

initiates production, generates employment, and allows people (supplemented by unpaid work at home) to support themselves.

3. **Capitalism as a System**   After introducing these basic, core relationships, Part Three describes how the capitalist economy functions as an overall system. It describes competition between firms; the determination of overall investment; the determination of overall employment; the distribution of income; the pervasive inequality that is pervasive in capitalism; and the fundamental relationship between the economy and the natural environment.

4. **The Complexity of Capitalism**   Apart from the basic relationships between private companies, their workers, and households, there are other important players in modern capitalism. We introduce these players and what they do in Part Four. We start with the monetary and financial system. The financial industry itself is not inherently productive, but it plays a crucial role in facilitating investment and distributing profits. We also introduce government and its diverse, often contradictory economic functions. And we start to describe capitalism on a global level: globalization, foreign trade, capital flows, and economic development. The smaller, simple "circle" we described in Part Two of the book now becomes a lot bigger and more complex. We also consider the boom-and-bust instability that seems endemic to capitalism – including a detailed review of the causes and consequences of the 2008 GLOBAL FINANCIAL CRISIS.

5. **Challenging Capitalism**   Once we've described capitalism as a complete, global economic system, the final part of the book evaluates capitalism: both its successes, and its failures. It considers ways in which capitalism could be reformed, to more effectively meet human needs and protect the natural environment. And it starts to imagine completely different ways of organizing the economy in the future.

Building an economic "map"

The book describes an economy of gradually increasing complexity – starting with the simplest relationships between employers and workers, shifting our focus to the interaction between companies, and then considering the roles of the environment, the financial industry, government, and globalization.

To portray these increasingly complex relationships, we provide a series of economic "road maps," illustrated by Tony Biddle. The maps use simple visual icons to identify the major players, and connect the dots between them. By the time we've explained our "big circle" at the conclusion of Part Four, this map will be a very handy tool for finding your way around capitalism. Like any map, it will help you figure out where you are, where you want to go – and how to get there.

The Economics for Everyone website

The overarching goal of this book is to make economics accessible and even entertaining for non-specialist readers. That's why we've kept the book short, used plain language, illustrated it with Tony Biddle's awesome cartoons, and avoided (wherever possible) the use of academic-style citations and references.

For those who want to continue their study of grass-roots economics, however, we have provided additional information and resources. These are posted, free of charge, at a special Economics for Everyone website, generously hosted by the Canadian Centre for Policy Alternatives (Canada's major progressive think tank, and the co-publisher of this book):

www.economicsforeveryone.com

The following materials are available at the website (direct links and supplementary content are also provided in the e-book version of this book):

- **Instructor resources**   Dozens of unions, community groups, schools and colleges, and other organizations have been using Economics for Everyone as a teaching resource for grass-roots economics instruction. To this end, the website includes a sample course outline (based on material in this book), lecture slides, and a set of hands-on, entertaining student exercises – all free. The book and the web-based materials thus constitute a ready-made teaching resource. With them, any progressive organization can undertake to offer basic instruction in economics to its members, without any formal prerequisites. (We also encourage instructors to supplement these materials with local information, resources, and guest speakers.)
- **Glossary**   Every term in this book highlighted in BOLD SMALL CAPITALS is defined in an on-line glossary that can be accessed from the website (or through direct links in the e-book).
- **"How-to" guides**   The website includes short guides to help readers locate and interpret key economic data and statistics, such as GDP statistics, labour market data, and corporate financial reports
- **"You Write the Book"**   In several places I invite readers to provide their own ideas, illustrations, or examples of phenomena described in the text. For example, in Chapter 7 I explain why just because an activity is profitable for a private company, does not ensure it is useful from the standpoint of society or human well-being. At that point I invite readers to help "write the book": send your examples of profitable activities that are useless, annoying, or downright destructive – and I will publish the best of them

(with acknowledgment) on the Economics for Everyone website. Submit your ideas to author@economicsforeveryone.com.

- **"Jimbo Talks"** You've heard of "Ted Talks": short on-line lectures dealing with fascinating subjects. The Economics for Everyone website has links to several "Jimbo Talks" (Jimbo has been my nickname ever since I was a kid!). These short videos aim to illustrate key themes in the book through often humorous examples or applications. They can also be used in teaching and popular education.

- **Other supplementary materials** The website also provides a list of suggestions for further reading (including links to organizations which undertake progressive economic research and education), and a complete list of sources for the data and citations included in the book.

- **Social media** Follow me on Twitter (@jimbostanford) or Facebook (jimbo.stanford) for updates on current economic events and controversies, commentary, reports on public events related to the book, and reactions to the book.

It's up to you

Your impressions, responses, questions, and suggestions are invited and appreciated. They will help to refine and improve this work for future editions and applications. Send your feedback to author@economicsforeveryone.com. I will endeavour to respond to every query.

If there's a simple, overarching theme running through this book, it's the idea that people have to fight for whatever they get from the economy. Nothing comes automatically, via the magical workings of supply and demand. Rather, it comes to them through education and awareness, organizational strength, action, and power. Knowing this basic fact of economic life, and identifying where and how

---

A Note on Sources and Citations

To keep this book as readable and uncluttered as possible, we have dispensed with most of the formal references, source notes, and citations common in academic books. Most of the statistical information contained in the book (including graphs and tables) was obtained from standard public sources (national statistical agencies, or international organizations like the United Nations and the Organization for Economic Cooperation and Development). Where I have referred to data collected or analyzed originally by other researchers (rather than data from standard public sources), or where I have repeated quotations from a secondary source (when another researcher located and reported the original quotation), more complete references are provided in a footnote.

to fight for a fairer share of the pie, will allow you and your fellow workmates, activists, and neighbours to make the most of economics.

In this sense, it really is up to you: to take your grass-roots knowledge of the economy, and translate it into economic action, and economic change.

Part One

Preliminaries

1

The Economy and Economics

Take a walk

The economy must be a very complicated, volatile thing. At least that's how it seems in the business pages of the newspaper. Mind-boggling stock market tables. Charts and graphs. GDP statistics. Foreign exchange rates. It's little wonder the media turn to economists, the high priests of this mysterious world, to tell us what it means, and why it's important. And we hear from them several times each day – usually via monotonous "market updates" that interrupt the hourly news broadcasts. Company X's shares are up two points; Company Y's are down two points; the analysts are "bullish"; the analysts are "bearish."

But is all that financial hyperactivity really what the economy is about? Is economics really so complex and unintelligible? Should we trust the "experts" and analysts at all? Maybe we should find out what's going on for ourselves.

Forget the market updates. Here's a better way to find out about the economy – *your* economy. Take a walk. And ask some questions.

Start at the front door of your own household. How many people live there? What generations? Who works outside the household, and how much do they earn? How long have they been working there? How long do they plan to keep working, and how will they support themselves when they retire? What kind of work goes on inside the household? How many hours? Is it paid or unpaid, and who does it? Who does which chores? Are there any children? Who cares for them? Does anyone else in your home require care? Do you own your house or apartment, or do you rent it? If you rent it, from whom? If you own it, how did you pay for it? What shape is it in?

Now walk through your neighbourhood, and the next neighbourhood. Are the homes or apartments all roughly the same, or different? Does everyone have a home? Are the homes well-cared-for, or falling apart? Do most people have jobs? What sorts of jobs? Are they well off? Can they comfortably pay for the things they and their families need?

Watch your neighbours going off to work, school, or other destinations. How are they travelling? In their own cars? On public transport? Walking? How much money, time, and physical space is devoted in your neighbourhood to "getting around"?

Is there a school in your neighbourhood? A hospital? A library? Who pays for those buildings? Who works there? How do those public facilities compare with the private homes and businesses around them? Are they newer, or older? Nicer, or shabbier? Is there anywhere a person can go inside in your neighbourhood (other than their own home) without having to pay money or buy something?

Are the streets clean? If so, who cleaned them? Is the air fresh or smoggy? Are there any parks in your neighbourhood? Is there anywhere to play? Can people in your neighbourhood safely drink the water from their taps? How much do they pay for that water? And to whom?

Walk through the nearest shopping district. What kinds of products are displayed in the windows? Were any of them produced locally (say, within 100 miles of your home)? Elsewhere in your country? In another country? Can your neighbours afford what they buy? Are they usually happy with their purchases, or disappointed? Do they pay with cash, bank cards, or credit cards?

Now walk to a local bank branch and see what's happening inside. Compare what you see (deposits, withdrawals, home loans) with the activities you read about in the business pages of the newspaper (leveraged buyouts, financial speculation, foreign exchange). Which matters more to day-to-day life in your neighbourhood?

This is a good time to stop at a café. Pull out a pencil and paper. List your approximate monthly income. Then list how much of it goes to the following categories: rent or mortgage (including utilities); income taxes; car payments or public transport; groceries; other "stuff" (merchandise); and going out (entertainment). Can you comfortably pay your bills each month? Do you regularly save? Is your income higher than it was five years ago, lower, or about the same? Has your income increased faster than the prices of the things you buy? If you had a little more income, what would you do with it? If you walked back to that bank and asked for a loan, would they give you one?

Apart from the places we've mentioned (schools, stores, and banks), what other workplaces are visible in your neighbourhood? Any factories? What do they produce, and what shape are they in? Any professional or government offices? Other services? Can you see any office buildings from your neighbourhood? Who works there? Can you guess what they do? Imagine the conditions in those offices (spaciousness, quality of furnishings, security, caretaking), and compare them to conditions inside your local school. Which would be a nicer place to spend time?

Have any new workplaces opened up recently in your neighbourhood? If so, what do they do? Or did you see any businesses that have closed down? Did you see any "help wanted" signs posted in local workplaces? What kinds of jobs were they advertising for?

Now you can return home. Congratulations! You've done a lot more than just take a stroll. You've conducted a composite economic profile of your own community. It has no statistics, charts, or graphs (though you could add those if you wish, with a bit of work at the local library). Nevertheless, just by walking around your neighbourhood, asking questions, and taking notes, you have identified the crucial factors determining economic affairs in your community:

- **Work** Who works? Who works inside the home, and works outside the home? Are they employed by someone else (and if so, who?), or do they work for themselves? Do they get paid, and if so, how much? What tools do they use? Are they productive and efficient? Is it hard to find a job?
- **Consumption** What do people need to buy, in order to stay alive? What do they wish for, to make their lives better? Can they afford it all?
- **Capital and Investment** What kinds of tools and technology do people use in their work? And who buys them? Private companies and public agencies must spend money maintaining and expanding their facilities and workplaces (this is called investment), or else the economy (and your neighbourhood) goes quickly downhill. Is that happening? Or is the state of these different "tools" being run down?

- **Finance** Most economic activity (but not all) requires money. Where do people get money? How is it created and controlled? Who gets to spend it? What do they spend it on?
- **Environment** Everything we do in the economy requires space, air, and inputs of natural materials. What's the state of the natural environment in your neighbourhood? Is it valued by the community, or taken for granted? Are there strict rules regarding pollution, dumping, and land use? Or can people and businesses treat the environment as they please?

These are the building blocks from which the most complicated economic theories are constructed: work, consumption, capital (or "tools"), finance, and the environment. And they are all visible, right there in your neighbourhood. As we go through this book, we will build a simple but informative economic "map" that includes all of these elements.

Don't ever believe that economics is a subject only for "experts." The essence of economics is visible to everyone, right there in your own 'hood. Economics is about life – *your* life.

What is the economy?

The economy is simultaneously mystifying and straightforward. Everyone has experience with the economy. Everyone participates in it. Everyone knows something about it – long before the pinstripe-wearing economist appears on TV to tell you about it.

The forces and relationships you investigated on your walk are far more important to economic life than the pointless ups and downs of the stock market. Yet our local economic lives are nevertheless affected (and disrupted) by the bigger and more complex developments reported in the business pages.

At its simplest, the "economy" simply consists of all the work that human beings perform, in order to produce the things we need and use in our lives. (By work, we mean all productive human activity, not just employment; we'll discuss that distinction later.) We need to organize and perform our work (economists call that **PRODUCTION**). And then we need to divide up the fruits of our work (economists call that **DISTRIBUTION**), and use it.

What kind of work are we talking about? Any kind of work is part of the economy, as long as it's aimed at producing something we need or want. Factory workers, office workers. Executives, farmers. Teachers, nurses. Homemakers, homebuilders. All of these people perform productive work, and all of that work is part of the economy.

What do we produce when we work? Production involves both goods and services. **GOODS** are tangible items that we can see and touch: food and clothes, houses and buildings, electronics and automobiles, machines and toys. SERVICES are tasks that one or several people perform for others: cutting hair and preparing restaurant meals, classroom instruction and brain surgery, transportation and auditing.

Where do we perform this work? Productive work occurs almost everywhere: in private companies, in government departments and public agencies. Work also occurs in the home. In cities, in towns, on farms, and in forests.

Why do we work? We must survive, and hence we require the basic material needs of life: food, clothing, shelter, education, medical care. Beyond that, we want to get the most out of our lives, and hence we aim for more than bare-bones subsistence. We want a greater quantity, and a greater variety, of goods and services: for entertainment, for travel, for cultural and personal enrichment, for comfort, for meaning, for security. We may also work because we enjoy it. Perversely for economists (most of whom view work solely as a "disutility"), most people are happier when they have work to do – thanks to the social interaction, financial well-being, and self-esteem that good work provides.

How do we distribute, and eventually use, the economic pie we have baked together? In many different ways. Some things are produced directly for our own use (like food grown in a garden, and then cooked in a household kitchen). Most things we must buy with money. We are entitled to consume certain products – like walking down a paved street, listening to the radio, or going to a public school – without directly paying anything. Importantly, some of what we produce must be re-invested (rather than consumed), in order to allow for more economic activity in the future.

So when you think about the "economy," just think about work. What work do we do? What do we produce? And what do we do with what we've produced?

The economy and society

The economy is a fundamentally *social* activity. Nobody does it all by themselves (unless you are a hermit). We rely on each other, and we interact with each other, in the course of our work.

It is common to equate the economy with private or individual wealth, profit, and self-interest, and hence it may seem strange to describe it as something "social." Indeed, free-market economists adopt the starting premise that human beings are inherently selfish (even though this assumption has been proven false by sociobiologists and anthropologists alike).

In fact, the capitalist economy is not individualistic at all. It is social, and in many ways it is cooperative. The richest billionaire in the world couldn't have earned a dollar without the supporting roles played by his or her workers, suppliers, and customers. There's no such thing as a "self-made" millionaire or

---

Economics Matters

"The mode of production of material life determines the social, political and intellectual life process in general."

Karl Marx, German philosopher and economist (1859).

"It's the economy, stupid."

James Carville, political advisor to US President Bill Clinton (1992).

---

billionaire: every one of them needed other people to play their required roles (as workers, suppliers, or customers) in order for them to become so rich. Indeed, our economic lives are increasingly intertwined with each other, as we each play our own little roles in a much bigger picture. That's why most of us live in cities (where the specialized, collective nature of the economy is especially visible). And that's how we can interact economically with people in other countries, thousands of miles away.

So the economy is about work: organizing it, doing it, and dividing up and making use of its final output. And in our work, one way or another, we always work (directly or indirectly) with other people.

The link between the economy and society goes two ways. The economy is a fundamentally social arena. But society as a whole depends strongly on the state of the economy. Politics, culture, religion, and international affairs are all deeply influenced by the progress of the economy. Governments are re-elected or turfed from office depending on the state of the economy. Family life is organized around the demands of work (both inside and outside the home). Being able to comfortably support oneself and one's family is a central determinant of happiness.

So the economy is an important, perhaps even dominant, force in human development. That doesn't mean that we should make "sacrifices" for the sake of the economy – since the whole point of the economy is to meet our material needs, not the other way around. And it certainly doesn't mean that we should grant undue attention or influence to economists. But it does mean that we will understand a great deal about human history, current social reality, and our future evolution as a species, when we understand more about economics.

What is economics?

Economics is the study of human economic behaviour: the production and distribution of the goods and services we need and want. Hence, economics is a social science, not a physical science. (Unfortunately, many economists are confused on this point! They foolishly try to describe human economic activity with as much mechanical precision as physicists describe the behaviour of atoms.)

Economics encompasses several sub-disciplines. Economic history; money and finance; household economics; labour studies and labour relations; business economics and management; international economics; environmental economics; and others. A broad (and rather artificial) division is often made between **MICROECONOMICS** (the study of the economic behaviour of individual consumers, workers, and companies) and **MACROECONOMICS** (the study of how the economy functions at the aggregate level).

This all seems relatively straightforward. Unfortunately, the dominant stream in modern economics (**NEOCLASSICAL ECONOMICS**, which we'll discuss more in Chapter 4) makes it more complicated than it needs to be. Instead of addressing broad questions of production and distribution, neoclassical economics focuses narrowly on *markets* and *exchange*. The purpose of economics, in the neoclassical mindset, was defined by one of its founders (Lord Lionel Robbins) back in 1932, in a definition that is still taught in universities today:

"Economics is the science which studies human behaviour as a relationship between given ends and scarce means which have alternative uses."

Embedded in this definition is a very peculiar (and rather dismal) interpretation of economic life. Scarcity is a normal condition. Humans are "endowed" with arbitrary amounts of useful resources. By trading through markets, they can extract maximum well-being from that arbitrary endowment – just like school kids are happier when they can trade their duplicate superhero cards with one another in the playground. An "efficient" economy is one which maximizes, through exchange, the usefulness of that initial endowment – regardless of how output is distributed, what kinds of things are produced, or how rich or poor people are at the end of the day. (This curious and narrow concept of efficiency is called **ALLOCATIVE EFFICIENCY.**)

As we'll learn later in this book, by defining the fundamental economic "question" in this particular way, neoclassical economics misses many important economic issues related to production, innovation, development, and fairness. Its dour emphasis on scarcity as a natural and permanent condition also leads to an inherent receptiveness to policies of **AUSTERITY** and belt-tightening.

I prefer to keep economics more simple, immediate, and concrete. We'll stick with a much broader definition of economics: the study of how humans work, and what we do with the fruits of our labour. Part of this involves studying markets and exchange – but only part. Economics also involves studying many other things: history, technology, tradition, family, power, and conflict.

Economics and politics

Economics and politics have always gone hand-in-hand. Indeed, the first economists called their discipline "political economy." The connections between economics and politics reflect, in part, the importance of economic conditions to political conditions. The well-being of the economy can influence the rise and fall of politicians and governments, even entire social systems.

But here, too, the influence goes both ways. Politics also affects the economy – and economics itself. The economy is a realm of competing, often conflicting interests. Determining whose interests prevail, and how conflicts are managed, is a deeply political process. (Neoclassical economists claim that anonymous "market forces" determine all these outcomes, but don't be fooled: what they call the "market" is itself a social institution in which some people's interests are enhanced at the expense of others'.) Different economic actors use their political influence and power to advance their respective economic interests. The extent to which groups of people tolerate economic outcomes (even unfavourable ones) also depends on political factors: such as whether or not they believe those outcomes are "natural" or "inevitable," and whether or not they feel they have any power to bring about change.

Finally, the social science which aims to interpret and explain all this scrabbling, teeming behaviour – economics – has its own political assumptions and biases. In Chapter 4 we'll review how most economic theories over the years have been motivated by political considerations. Modern economics (including this book!) is no different: economics is always a deeply political subject.

Measuring the economy

GROSS DOMESTIC PRODUCT (GDP) is the most common way to measure the economy. But beware: it is a deeply flawed measure. GDP adds up the value of all the different goods and services that are produced *for money* in the economy. GDP is thus one measure of the total value of the work we do – but only the work we do for money.

In the private sector of the economy, GDP adds up the market prices of everything that's bought and sold. In the public and non-profit sectors, it is based on the cost of everything that's produced. In both cases, statisticians must deduct the costs of the many inputs and supplies purchased in any particular industry, from the total output produced by that industry. (This is so that we don't double-count the work that went into all those inputs.) In this way, GDP is designed to only include the VALUE ADDED by new work at each stage of production.

An obvious drawback of GDP is that it excludes the value of work that is *not* performed for money. This is a highly arbitrary and misleading exclusion. For example, most people perform unpaid chores in their households, and many must care for other family members (especially children and elders). Some of this household work can be "outsourced" to paid help: cleaners, nannies, and restaurants (the richer you are, the more you can outsource). In this case it is included in GDP. But if you "do it yourself," then it doesn't count! Volunteer work and community participation are other forms of valuable, productive work excluded from GDP.

This phony distinction has big consequences for how we measure the economy. Unfortunately, things that we measure often take on extra importance (with the media, and with policy-makers), purely because they *can* be measured. GDP underestimates the total value of work performed in the economy, and hence misjudges our productivity. It undervalues the unpaid work done within our homes and our communities. Because of sexism at home and in the workplace, most of that unpaid work is done by women; hence, GDP underestimates the economic contribution of women.

It's especially misguided to interpret GDP as a measure of human well-being. We've seen that there are many valuable things that are not included in GDP. On the other hand, many of the goods and services that *are* counted in GDP are utterly useless, annoying, or even destructive to human well-being – like dinner-hour telephone solicitations, many pharmaceuticals, excess consumer packaging, and armaments production. Moreover, just because a society produces more GDP is never a guarantee that most members of society will ever receive a bigger amount of it.

So we must be cautious in our use of GDP statistics, and we must never equate GDP with prosperity or well-being.

Despite these caveats, GDP is still an important and relevant measure. It indicates the value of all production that occurs for money. This is an important, appropriate piece of information for many purposes. (For example, the ability of governments to collect taxes depends directly on the money value of GDP.) We need to understand the weaknesses of GDP, and supplement it with other measures. Above all, we must remember that expanding GDP is never an end in itself. At best, properly managed, it can be a means to an end (the goal of improving human well-being). Indeed, there is a positive but imperfect relationship between GDP and human welfare (see box). This suggests that we need to be concerned with how much we produce, but just as concerned with what we use it for.

To be meaningful, GDP figures must take several additional factors into account. If the apparent value of our work grows purely because of **INFLATION** (which is a general increase in the prices of *all* goods and services), then there hasn't been any actual improvement in the economy. Therefore we distinguish between **NOMINAL** GDP (measured in dollars, pounds, or euros) and **REAL** GDP (which deducts the effect of inflation). There are many other economic variables (such as wages and interest rates) for which this distinction between nominal and real values is also

GDP and Human Well-Being

The United Nations Development Program produces an annual ranking of countries according to their "human development." The UN defines human development on the basis of three key indicators: GDP per capita, life expectancy, and educational attainment. We've already seen that GDP is a highly misleading measure. The UN approach tries to broaden that by including two other criteria (health and education), but it is still far from perfect. It attaches value to GDP, but attaches no value to social equity, leisure time, and other important human goals.

Nevertheless, it is interesting to compare the ranking of countries according to human development, with their ranking according to GDP. In general, countries with high human development also have high levels of GDP per capita (partly because GDP is itself one of the three variables used to calculate the index, but also because higher GDP allows a society to devote more resources to health and education). This indicates that economic development (increasing both the amount and the quality of production over time) is indeed very important to standard of living.

However, the link between GDP and human development is not perfect. Some countries rank higher in the UN list than they do on the basis of GDP alone. This indicates they are more efficient at translating GDP into genuine human welfare (usually thanks to extensive public services, financed with high taxes). On the other hand, countries which rank lower on the UN list than in the GDP standings are relatively ineffective at translating GDP into well-being; many of these countries have relatively low taxes, weak public programs, and large gaps between rich and poor (reflected In low living standards for most people).

Table 1.1 summarizes the key human development statistics for selected countries, from the UN's 2014 report. High-tax Norway (where government spends over 50 percent of GDP on public programs) ranks first. Low-tax America ranks fifth (despite having the third-highest GDP in the world); its life expectancy is the lowest of any developed country. For each country, the difference between its GDP rank and its human development rank is an indicator of its success at translating GDP into genuine well-being; this difference is reported in the fourth column. A positive score in this column indicates that a country makes the most of its GDP; a negative score indicates the opposite. Tiny Georgia – which ranks 106th according to income, but 70th according to human development – does more, given its GDP, to improve human welfare than any other country in the world. Sri Lanka, Argentina, and Poland are other countries which "punch above their weight" according to human development. On the other hand, oil-rich Equatorial Guinea does the worst job of any country at channelling GDP into well-being: it ranks 34th according to income, but only 138th for human development. Iraq and South Africa also have very low human development rankings, despite relatively high GDP, primarily because of low life expectancy and a very unequal distribution of income.

Table 1.1 GDP and Human Well-Being

Country	Human Development Index Rank* (HDI)	Income Rank*	Income Rank – HDI Rank†	Income per Capita (US$)	Life Expectancy (years)
Norway	1	1	0	$63,909	81.5
Australia	2	11	9	$41,524	82.5
Switzerland	3	2	-1	$53,762	82.6
Netherlands	4	8	4	$42,397	81.0
United States	5	3	-2	$52,308	78.9
Germany	6	5	-1	$43,049	80.7
New Zealand	7	20	13	$32,569	81.1
Canada	8	10	2	$41,887	81.5
China	81	78	-3	$11,477	75.3
India	125	120	-5	$5,150	66.4
Selected Human Development "Over-Achievers"					
Georgia	70	106	36	$6,890	74.3
Sri Lanka	73	93	20	$9,250	74.3
Argentina	39	53	14	$17,297	76.3
Poland	29	41	12	$21,487	76.4
Selected Human Development "Under-Achievers"					
Equatorial Guinea	134	38	-96	$21,972	53.1
Gabon	102	55	-47	$16,977	63.5
Iraq	110	67	-43	$14,007	69.4
South Africa	108	74	-34	$11,788	56.9

* Excluding city states and oil-producing monarchies.
† A positive score indicates better HDI ranking than GDP ranking.
Source: United Nations Development Program, *Human Development Report* (2014).

important. **ECONOMIC GROWTH** is usually measured by the expansion of real GDP. Economic growth usually consists of two components: an increase in the amount of work that is performed, and improvements in efficiency or **PRODUCTIVITY** (that is, increases in the amount of output produced by each hour of that work).

A country's GDP could expand simply because its population was growing – but this does not imply the country is becoming more prosperous. This is important when comparing growth rates across countries. For example, in countries with near-zero population growth (such as Europe and Japan), even the slow growth of real GDP can translate into improved living standards; this is not the case where population is growing more quickly. Therefore, economists often divide GDP by population, to get a measure called **GDP PER CAPITA**. This, too, can be expressed in both nominal and real terms. Real GDP per capita is often used as a rough indicator of prosperity (and its growth over time) – although we must always remember that GDP excludes many valuable types of work, and says nothing about how production is distributed.

Growth: good or bad?

GDP equals the total value of all the goods and services produced for money in the economy, and increases in real GDP (adjusted to strip out the effects of inflation) are an indication of economic growth. Newspaper headlines report breathlessly on the latest GDP statistics, as if they were a bellwether for our overall economic health. But growth for growth's sake cannot be the end-goal of our economic activity. As we have seen, simply producing more GDP does not imply that we are producing the right stuff, dividing it fairly, or using it wisely.

Politicians like to boast about strong GDP growth. But the economy is not actually managed to maximize growth … far from it. In fact, as we will learn in coming chapters, it has been a central, deliberate goal of economic policy in recent decades to tightly restrict growth (in order to maintain a "healthy" pool of unemployed people, and thus keep a lid on wages). Economic growth since the late 1970s has been anemic at best across most advanced economies – and since the **GLOBAL FINANCIAL CRISIS** of 2008–09, it has been virtually nonexistent. While individual companies always strive to expand their sales and profits (to satisfy shareholders and boost executive bonuses), whether this translates into economy-wide growth depends on the overall state of affairs (including whether governments and their agencies, like **CENTRAL BANKS**, actually want more growth).

And while some commentators pretend that growth is somehow our overarching economic goal, others have concluded that economic growth itself is actually the enemy. Particularly among those rightly concerned with the environmental side-effects of economic activity, there is a common view that if we restrict or even halt economic growth, then pollution, climate change, and other environmental problems would be abated. We will discuss the relationships between the economy and the environment in detail in Chapter 16. But in general I think it is misplaced to blame economic growth, in and of itself, for environmental problems. Some types of economic activity clearly harm the environment, but some do not – and some types of work, obviously, are good for the environment (like building green energy and public transit systems, cleaning up toxic waste sites, and others). The issue is not how much work we are collectively performing, but what we are doing, how, and what our output is used for.

Moreover, while growth in its own right does not necessarily make us better off, many economic and social problems clearly get worse when the economy stops growing. Unemployment rises, since there is not enough work for everyone who needs it. (Due to ongoing productivity growth, even a stable level of real GDP over time will translate into ever-fewer jobs.) Incomes fall for many in society, making it harder to make ends meet. And inequality gets worse. In fact, whenever economic growth rates are low relative to the rates of profit generated on financial wealth, there is a powerful tendency for more wealth to become concentrated in the hands of very rich households. (This mechanism was effectively highlighted by the French economist Thomas Piketty in his important 2014 book, *Capital in the Twenty-First Century*.) Even from an environmental perspective, it is not clear that stopping growth (at least under the current rules of the game) makes things better.

The growth rates reported in quarterly GDP statistics are ultimately a by-product of decisions made by powerful economic players: mostly private companies in our economy, influenced by governments and (somewhat) by worker attitudes and public opinion. Our economic system today is not managed to maximize growth: if it was, it would look very different than it does today, and everyone who wanted a job could have one. In reality, the economy is managed to maximize the profits and power of private companies, and the well-off people who own them. Our goal is to find ways to challenge that power, and in so doing alter the criteria on which all economic activity is undertaken. We should be performing work not because it is profitable, but because it is useful. And there is plenty of useful work that needs to be done in our society: caring for each other, caring for the environment, producing the goods and services necessary for us all to lead a rich, full life (and ensuring we have enough leisure time to enjoy the fruits of our labour). Performing all that necessary work would add to our GDP, no doubt about it. But so long as we are doing more good things with our work, and fewer destructive, that should be beneficial, both socially and environmentally.

For those reasons, this book does not generally talk about economic growth as either a goal, or as something to be avoided. What shows up as economic growth in the GDP statistics is merely a consequence of other decisions made across the economy (and in the present economy, those decisions are made by companies and governments concerned mostly with maximizing profits). Instead of focusing on growth (good or bad), I prefer to focus on work, quality of life, and sustainability. There is much work to be done, and billions of people who desperately need work to support themselves. So let's connect those dots – and design an economy that puts people to work, doing important things, in a way that benefits both human society and the natural environment.

What is a good economy?

Economics tries to explain how the economy works. But economists naturally wonder how to make it work *better*. This inherently requires the economist (and every citizen) to make value judgements about what kind of economy is more desirable. Most economists, unfortunately, are not honest about those value judgements; they try to pretend that their profession is "scientific" and hence value-free, but this is a charade.

Deciding what economic goals to pursue will reflect the priorities and interests of different individuals, communities, and classes. It is an inherently subjective, political choice.

You Write the Book: Economic Value Judgments

There is no objective or neutral way to evaluate the performance of an economy. Whether an economy works well depends on the goals and interests of the people it is supposed to serve. In addition to or instead of the seven criteria suggested in this chapter, specify one or more additional goals that you think an effective economic system should meet. In your judgment, what is a "good" economy? Send your ideas to author@economicsforeveryone. com. We'll post several examples at www.economicsforeveryone.com.

Here is my list of key economic goals. In my view, the more of these goals an economy achieves, the better off people will be:

1. **Prosperity**   An economy should produce enough goods and services to support its citizens and allow them to enjoy life to the fullest. Prosperity does not just mean having more "stuff." It means enjoying a good balance between private consumption, public services, and leisure time. (Incidentally, leisure time is another valuable thing that doesn't appear in GDP statistics.)

2. **Security**   People should be confident that their economic conditions are reasonably stable. They shouldn't have to worry about being able to support themselves, to keep their homes, and to pass on decent economic opportunities to their children. The economic insecurity faced by billions of people today undermines their quality of life in concrete ways. Even people who may never lose their job or home, spend a great deal of time and energy worrying that they might. That fear is costly, and may lead to decisions that undermine economic performance and social well-being. By the same token, economic security – being able to sleep at night without worrying about your livelihood – is valuable in its own right.

3. **Innovation**   Economic progress requires us to think continuously about how to make our work more effective and useful. This continuous improvement is called "innovation"; it includes imagining new goods and services (products), and better ways of producing them (processes). An economy should be organized in a way that promotes and facilitates innovative behaviour, or else it will eventually run out of creative energy and forward momentum.

4. **Choice**   Individuals have different preferences, hopes, and dreams (although those preferences are strongly shaped by social pressures). They should have reasonable ability to make economic decisions – including the sort of work they do, where they live, and what they consume – in line with those preferences. There is a gigantic, ideological myth that only free-market economies truly respect individual "choice." This is obviously wrong: the choices of billions of human beings are brutally suppressed by the economic hardship and social divisions which are a natural outcome of global capitalism. Moreover, the services offered by the public sector (schools, health care, culture, parks) substantially expand the choices available to people (especially those with lower incomes) – certainly more so than being able to choose among a dozen different brands of toothpaste at the supermarket. I accept that individual choice is an important economic goal – and I argue there are better ways to enhance true choice than through free-market capitalism.

5. **Equality**   Inequality is harmful if it means that large numbers of people are deprived of the ability to work and enjoy their lives. In this sense, the goal of equality is bound up with the goal of prosperity (so long as we define "prosperity" correctly, as widespread well-being, rather than equating it with the growth of GDP). But inequality is also inherently negative in its own right. Even if those at the bottom of the economic spectrum still enjoyed some decent minimal standard of living, a concentration of wealth at the top will nevertheless undermine social cohesion, well-being, and democracy. Researchers from many disciplines (including psychology, criminology, epidemiology, and physiology) have confirmed that people's emotional well-being is negatively influenced by unfavourable self-comparisons to the lifestyles of others who are much better off than they are. In this way, inequality produces distinct negative consequences, quite apart from the consequences of poverty. (We will consider these consequences in more detail in Chapter 14.) Therefore, limiting the economic distance between rich and poor is an important economic goal.

6. **Sustainability**   Humans depend on their natural environment. It directly enhances our quality of life (through the air we breathe, the water we drink, and the spaces we inhabit). And it provides needed inputs that are essential to the work we do in every single industry. As we will learn, all production involves the application of human work to "add value" to resources and materials we get from nature. Of course, maintaining the environment is important in its own right (all the more so if we accept that humans have some responsibility to the other species which inhabit our planet). It is also important in a more narrowly economic sense, since our ability to keep producing goods and services in the future will depend on finding sustainable ways to harvest (without continuously depleting or polluting) the natural inputs we need.

7. **Democracy and accountability**   We've seen that the economy is an inherently social undertaking. Different people perform different functions. Some individuals and organizations have great decision-making power, while others have very little. How do we ensure that economic decisions, and the overall evolution of the economy, reflect our collective desires and preferences? And how do we monitor and ensure that people and institutions are doing the work they are supposed to? Modern capitalism has a well-developed but narrow notion of private-sector accountability, through which corporations are guided carefully to maximize the wealth of their shareholders. Competitive markets also impose another narrow form of accountability, enforced through the threat of lost sales and ultimate bankruptcy for companies which produce shoddy or unduly expensive products. Democratic elections allow citizens to exert some influence (through their governments) over economic trends – although the ability of elected governments to steer a capitalist economy is fundamentally constrained by the unelected power of businesses and investors. None of these limited forms of accountability provide for thorough or consistent channels of democratic control over the economy. Yet given the overarching importance of the economy to our general social condition, we are entitled to more genuine and far-reaching forms of economic democracy and accountability.

Is our present economy a good economy? In some ways, modern capitalism has done better than any previous arrangement in advancing many of these goals. In other ways, it fails the "good economy" test miserably. The rest of this book will endeavour to explain how the capitalist economy functions, the extent to which it meets (and fails to meet) these goals – and whether or not there are any better ways to do the job.

2

Capitalism

Capitalism: one kind of economy

This book focuses mostly on describing one very particular kind of economy: capitalism.

There, I've said it: the "C-word." Just mentioning that term sounds almost subversive. Even talking about "capitalism" makes it sound like you're a dangerous radical of some kind. But we live in a capitalist economy, and we might as well name it. More importantly, we need to understand what we are dealing with.

Curiously, even though capitalism dominates the world economy, the term "capitalism" is not commonly used. Even more curiously, this word is almost *never* used by economists. Neoclassical economics is dedicated to the study of capitalism; in fact, other kinds of economies (that existed in the past, or that may exist in the future) are not even contemplated. Yet the term "capitalism" does not appear in neoclassical economics textbooks.

Instead, economists refer simply to "the economy" – as if there is only one kind of economy, and hence no need to name or define it. This is wrong. As we have already seen, "the economy" is simply where people work to produce the things we need and want. There are different ways to organize that work. Capitalism is just one of them.

Homo sapiens have existed on this planet for approximately 100,000 years. They had an economy all of that time. Humans have always had to work to meet the material needs of their survival (food, clothing, and shelter) – not to mention, when possible, to enjoy the "finer things" in life. Capitalism, in contrast, has existed for around 250 years. If the entire history of Homo sapiens to date was a 24-hour day, then capitalism has existed for three-and-a-half minutes.

What we call "the economy" went through many different stages en route to capitalism. (We'll study more of this economic history in Chapter 3.) Even today, different kinds of economies exist. Some entire countries are non-capitalist. And within capitalist economies, there are important non-capitalist parts (although most capitalist economies are becoming *more* capitalist as time goes by).

I think it's a pretty safe bet that human beings will eventually find other, better ways to organize work in the future – maybe sooner, maybe later. It's almost inconceivable that the major features of what we call "capitalism" will exist for the rest of human history (unless, of course, we drive ourselves to extinction in the near future through war, pollution, or other self-inflicted injuries).

So we should never understand "the economy" and "capitalism" as identical. They are two different things; the latter is just one specific example of the former. In this book we will study capitalism, as the dominant current form of economic organization. But we must always distinguish between what is *general* to all types of economy, and what is *specific* to capitalism.

What is capitalism?

There are two key features that make an economy capitalist:

1. Most production of goods and services is undertaken by privately-owned companies, which produce and sell their output in hopes of making a profit. This is called **PRODUCTION FOR PROFIT**.
2. Most work in the economy is performed by people who do not own their company or their output, but are hired by someone else to work in return for a money wage or salary. This is called **WAGE LABOUR**.

An economy in which private, profit-seeking companies undertake most production, and in which wage-earning employees do most of the work, is a capitalist economy. We will see that these twin features (profit-driven production and wage labour) create particular patterns and relationships, which in turn shape the overall functioning of capitalism as a system.

Any economy driven by these two features – production for profit and wage labour – tends to replicate the following trends and patterns, over and over again:

- Fierce *competition* between private companies for markets, sales, and profit.
- *Innovation*, as companies constantly experiment with new technologies, new products, and new forms of organization – in order to succeed in that competition.
- An inherent tendency to *growth,* resulting from the desire of each individual company to make more profit.
- Deep *inequality* between those who own successful companies, and the rest of society who do not own companies.
- A general *conflict* of interest between those who work for wages, and the employers who hire them.
- Economic *cycles* or "rollercoasters," with periods of strong growth followed by periods of stagnation or depression; sometimes these cycles even produce dramatic economic and social crises.

Some of these patterns and outcomes are positive, and help to explain why capitalism has been so successful. But some of these patterns and outcomes are negative, and explain why capitalism tends to be economically (and sometimes politically) unstable. The rest of this book will explain why these patterns develop under capitalism, and what (if anything) can be done to make the economy work better.

Capitalism began in Europe in the mid-1700s. Until then, these twin features – production for profit and wage labour – were rare. In pre-capitalist societies, most people worked for themselves, one way or another. Where people worked for someone else, that relationship was based on something other than monetary payment (like a sense of obligation, or the power of brute force). And most production occurred to meet some direct need or desire (on the part of an individual, a community, or a government), not to generate a money profit.

Capitalism and markets

Even when economists bother to "name" the economy they are studying, they usually use a euphemism instead of the "C-word." They don't call it capitalism. They call it a "market economy." This implies that what is unique about capitalism is its reliance on markets and market signals (like supply, demand, and prices) to organize the economy. But that is wrong, too.

Markets of various kinds do indeed play a major role in capitalism. A market is simply a "place" where various buyers and sellers meet to haggle over price and agree on sales of a good, a service, or an asset. (By "place," I do not mean that a market has to have an actual physical location – it just needs to provide a way in which buyers and sellers can communicate and strike deals. In the internet era, markets can exist in cyberspace, not just in a town square or at a stock exchange.)

Markets usually (but not always) imply some kind of competition, in which different buyers and sellers compete with each other to get the best deal. We will study the particular nature of competition under capitalism in detail in Chapter 11.

But capitalism is not the only economic system which uses markets. Pre-capitalist economies also had markets – where producers could sell excess supplies of agricultural goods or handicrafts, and where exotic commodities (like spices or fabrics) from far-off lands could be purchased. Most forms of socialism also rely on markets to distribute end products and even, in some cases, to organize investment and production. So markets are not unique to capitalism, and there is nothing inherently capitalist about a market.

Just as important, there are many aspects of modern capitalism that have nothing to do with markets. Within large companies, for example, very few decisions are made through market mechanisms. Instead, relationships of command, control, and planning reign supreme. (Remember, some corporations are economically larger than many countries, so these internal non-market relationships are important.) And there are other ways in which capitalism reflects powerful *non-market* forces and motivations – like tradition, habit, politeness, reciprocity, altruism, coercion, even (sometimes) brute force.

The Centrally Planned Corporation

The biggest corporations are larger than many countries. They operate thousands of facilities around the world, employ millions of workers, and deal with thousands of different suppliers. And the success of these giant, complex firms is not really a testimony to the virtues of the free market. A more important factor in corporate success has been the astounding ability of corporate managers to deliberately *plan*.

Wal-Mart Wal-Mart operates a fantastically complicated logistics and delivery system, distributing merchandise to its far-flung stores in the most cost-efficient manner. It also maintains an immense database on sales patterns, which it uses to centrally determine the precise layout of every Wal-Mart store – right down to which socks are displayed next to which pantyhose, all in order to maximize sales, reduce inventory turnover times, and enhance profits. The immense productivity of this central planning has been the key force behind Wal-Mart's success. The poverty-level wages it pays its workers are just icing on the cake for the company's owners.

Toyota The world's most successful automaker has a legendary reputation for effective central planning, right down to the tiniest nut and bolt. Toyota produces over 60 models of vehicles (9 million units a year), in over 50 major manufacturing operations (and dozens of smaller factories), in 27 different countries. Yet all this manufacturing activity is centrally planned and coordinated through a complex manufacturing and logistics strategy called the Toyota Production System. Corporate planners standardize engineering and design (to allow parts to be transferred across vehicles). Relations with suppliers are minutely planned, so that specific parts are produced and delivered to assembly plants "just in time" for installation on a Toyota car. Other manufacturing companies have been trying to imitate Toyota's model for decades.

ExxonMobil This global behemoth is the most profitable company in the world: it recorded a $45 billion annual profit in 2012, and has surpassed $40 billion in annual profits five times in total. Its profitability is carefully monitored and managed through an incredibly detailed and centralized system of financial control, through which core directors oversee over 100 business divisions and subsidiaries, operating in almost every country in the world. Divisional leaders present regular business plans, including proposals for new investment spending, which are reviewed and ranked by the company's central financial authorities. New capital is then carefully allocated to what are deemed to be the most promising initiatives from across this worldwide menu of options.

▶

These and other successful corporations have raised the art of deliberate economic planning to heights that former Soviet planners could never have imagined – utilizing both their dictatorial control over the internal activities of the company, and new technological tools for collecting and managing information. To be sure, even megacorps operate within an unplanned, competitive market environment. They must sell their output; market conditions affect what they must pay for their inputs; and they must generate a competitive profit for their investors. However, their fantastic ability to plan and coordinate is the crucial reason why corporations have emerged as the most effective institutional tool for generating private profit. That's completely opposite from the neoclassical stereotype of capitalism as a system rooted in individualism and decentralization.

By pretending that capitalism is a system of "markets," economists imply that it is based on relationships between essentially equal parties. Neoclassical economists study two main kinds of markets: markets for **FACTORS OF PRODUCTION** (things that are used in production, like labour, land, and natural resources), and markets for the final products (**GOODS** and **SERVICES**) produced with those factors. Neoclassical economists even describe the relationship between a large company and its workers as a form of market exchange: the workers sell their capacity to work, and the employer buys it. Everyone comes to the "market" with something to sell, and in theory they're all better off (than they were in the first place) as a result of trading in that marketplace.

Imagine a bustling bazaar, to represent the whole economy. In one corner of the hall is General Electric, one of the largest and most complex corporations in the world, which brings US$650 billion worth of capital assets to the market. In the other corner are some workers, with only their brains and brawn – their intelligence and their physical strength – to sell. Will a "trade" between these two sides be equal or voluntary, in any meaningful sense of those words? Not at all. And neoclassical economics doesn't bother explaining the historical process by which one stall at the bazaar is stocked with US$650 billion in capital, while another is stocked only with hard-working human bodies.

By pretending that capitalism is just a system of "markets," neoclassical economics deliberately blurs the real power relationships, and the often-violent historical processes, which explain the economic system we actually live in. Yes, we must study markets when we study capitalism – their flaws, as well as their virtues. But markets are not the idealized institutions portrayed in economics textbooks. And capitalism is equally shaped by other, non-market forces and structures, too.

So capitalism is not a "market economy." Capitalism is a system in which most production occurs for private profit, and most work is performed by wage labour.

Is capitalism still capitalism?

Of course, capitalism can change its "look" a lot, while still preserving its core, underlying features. Indeed, one of the most impressive features of capitalism is its flexibility: its capacity to change and adapt. Many economists and commentators have argued that capitalism today is not at all like capitalism in its early days (back in the soot and grime of the Industrial Revolution). Here are some of the terms used to describe modern capitalism, implying (falsely) that it's a whole "new" system:

1. **The "post-industrial" economy**   As discussed in Chapter 1, every economy produces both goods and services. Over time, a growing share of total value added in advanced capitalist countries consists of services. Today, services account for about 70 percent of GDP in advanced economies – and an even larger share, if we count work that is not performed for money, like housework. The shrinking importance of goods is partly because technology and globalization have reduced their costs compared to services, and partly because most consumers prefer to buy a greater proportion of services (especially "luxuries" such as restaurant meals and tourism) as their incomes rise. As large-scale industry becomes less important in the big economic picture, some economists argue that capitalism has changed, and that old stereotypes about "workers and bosses" no longer apply in this "post-industrial" system.

2. **The "information" economy**   A related argument suggests that the advent of computer technology and the internet have created a fundamentally new economy – one centred on information, rather than commodities. Some pundits call this the "new economy," or the "knowledge economy." Possessing valuable skills, rather than owning wealth, is supposedly the new key to prosperity. Some even argue this "information" economy is immune to the traditional boom-and-bust cycles of earlier times.

3. **The "shareholder" economy**   Some commentators have focused on the role played by pension funds, mutual funds, and other so-called "institutional" investors in modern stock markets. They argue that capitalism is fairer than it used to be, since more individuals can own shares and other forms of financial wealth (either directly, or indirectly through mutual and pension funds). They claim that this new "shareholder" system has somehow "solved" the age-old conflict between workers and capitalists. Former US President George W. Bush famously celebrated this idea as the "ownership society."

There is a grain of truth in each of these portrayals – but only a grain. And in no case is it reasonable to conclude that capitalism has *fundamentally* changed.

Yes, services are increasingly important as a share of total output. But the production of goods (including food, housing, and manufactured products) will always be central to any economy, because of the simple reality that we live in a material, tangible world, and need material goods for our survival. And don't forget that many services are produced in large-scale, factory-like workplaces. Think of a long-distance call centre, with hundreds of workers sitting in small cubicles, their work electronically paced and constantly monitored. That work is as regimented and deadening as any assembly line job. And the services sector of the economy is still dominated (just like goods-producing industries) by profit-seeking private companies, many of them very large – and very profitable. That still sounds like capitalism.

Yes, information is more important and faster-flowing than ever. But people cannot "eat" information. It is economically useful mostly as an input in the production of other, traditional goods and services industries. And far from ushering in a new era of decentralization and supposed economic "participation," computer-related industries are still dominated by huge, profit-hungry companies (like Microsoft, Google, and Amazon). That's still capitalism.

Yes, pension and mutual funds are important players in stock markets. But the vast majority of financial wealth is still owned the old-fashioned way: by a surprisingly small elite of very wealthy families. In fact, in most capitalist countries financial wealth has become *more* concentrated among the rich, not less (we will discuss this in more detail in Chapter 7). That's definitely capitalism.

So while capitalism produces more services and less goods than it used to; while companies rely on sophisticated information technology to manage their affairs; and while pension funds and mutual funds are important players in financial markets, the core features of capitalism are still very much in place. Most production is undertaken by profit-seeking private companies. And most work is performed by people who do not own those companies, but who instead must work for wages. There is still incredible inequality, and an inherent conflict of interest, between the people who own successful companies, and the rest of us.

Capitalism hasn't really changed its stripes at all.

Capitalism and human nature

Many defenders of capitalism claim that human beings are inherently "selfish," and hence a system rooted in profit maximization and greed is merely consistent with our human nature. By the same token, any efforts to build an economic system based on "sharing" are doomed to failure, defeated by this perhaps lamentable but inevitable self-interest.

Indeed, this assumption that people are motivated solely by individualized self-interest is a starting point of neoclassical economic theory. Neoclassical theories start with a crucial, initial assumption that each individual cares about maximizing their own "utility," and nothing else. This species of greed-fueled maximizers has been nicknamed "Homo economicus." And while the assumption of natural greed is mathematically convenient for neoclassical theory (without it, their theoretical models do not work), it is ridiculed by social scientists from other disciplines – who immediately recognize its shortcomings as a misguided caricature of actual human social behaviour.

In fact, if real-world Homo sapiens actually behaved like Homo economicus, there is no possibility we could have survived when we first descended from the trees somewhere in East Africa. Human beings are the only species of animals where unrelated individuals cooperate in performing complex tasks. This unique social intelligence and ability to cooperate is precisely what allowed us to survive harsh conditions, outperform other species of primates, and eventually proliferate to inhabit most of the planet. To support this essential cooperation over millenia of human evolution, deeply-rooted traditions and instincts of mutual recognition and reciprocity took hold, that social biologists and geneticists are now beginning to understand.

All for One, or One for All?

"The first principle of economics is that every agent is actuated only by self-interest."

F.Y. Edgeworth, Irish economist, and a founder of neoclassical economics (1881).

"In no other species but Homo sapiens do thousands of unrelated individuals work together to accomplish a common project."

Samuel Bowles, Richard Edwards, and Frank Roosevelt, US economists (2005).

There are many plausible scenarios in which competition and self-interest can leave all sides worse off. And using new experimental techniques (such as **BEHAVIOURAL ECONOMICS** and **GAME THEORY**), modern economists have shown that cooperative economic strategies (in which social behaviour is reciprocated, but selfish behaviour is punished) beat out purely selfish or competitive strategies in evolutionary competition.

One famous behavioural experiment is called the "ultimatum game." In it, participants are paired off, and each given a sum of real money (say, $10) which they actually get to keep if they succeed in the game. One partner in each pair is instructed to propose a one-time split of the $10 with the other partner. It's a take-it-or-leave-it offer; no bargaining is allowed. If the partner accepts the proposed deal, then both participants get to keep their respective shares according to the offer. If the partner refuses, then neither partner gets anything. A member of Homo economicus should propose the following split, every time: they keep $9.99, and their partner gets one penny. And in the world of Homo economicus, that ridiculous offer should be accepted every time. Why? Because even the short-changed partner is still better off (by one penny) than if they had rejected the offer – and that's all they care about. So there is no rational reason for the offer to be rejected.

In practice, of course, anyone with the gall to propose such a lopsided bargain would face certain rejection. Experiments with real money have shown that splits as lopsided as 75–25 are almost always rejected (even though a partner rejecting that split forgoes a real $2.50 gain). And the most common offer proposed is a 50–50 split. That won't surprise many people – but it does, strangely, surprise neoclassical economists! In short, the real-world behaviour of humans is not remotely consistent with the assumption of blind, individualistic greed.

This experiment (and other more complex research) confirms that human beings have a deep concern with perceived fairness and reciprocity, and will go out of their way (even incurring significant personal costs) to enforce those norms. Scientists now believe that these instincts arose because of the evolutionary necessity of cooperation for survival. For example, to reinforce that instinct, our bodies actually release pleasure-causing endorphins when we cooperate successfully with others. And our unique social intelligence has been identified with the relatively larger size of certain parts of our brains (relative to other primates). In fact, the early mutations which contributed to that social intelligence were among the defining features that made us "human" in the first place (along with our flexible vocal chords, our opposable thumbs, and the ability to walk upright). Far from being innately selfish, therefore, our unique capacity to cooperate is actually a core feature of our very humanity.

Of course, we just have to look around to recognize that the most important and powerful human actions are motivated by something very different than greed. The firefighter entering a burning building is not doing it "for the money." Neither are the impoverished grandmothers in Africa who've taken on raising orphans who lost their parents to HIV-AIDS. Even salaried scientists spending 60-hour weeks seeking a cure for cancer are not motivated by profit; they are driven by a desire to improve the human condition. And the quiet, hidden heroism of everyday people who devote uncounted hours to caring for children and elders, after performing a full day's work in the paid labour market, reflects the powerful motivation of love, not money.

To be sure, economic incentives are important, in any kind of society. People want to be rewarded for their work and their sacrifices, and they want to know that they personally will be treated fairly in any division of the economic pie. But if everyone you encountered in daily life was truly and solely out to maximize their immediate self-interest (at your expense), life would resemble the chaos of some failed anarchic state (like postwar Iraq), not a civilized society. Every person would be perpetually "on guard" against risk, theft, and danger. And the simplest economic transaction would be immensely complicated by mutual fear that the other party was planning to exploit, steal, or assault. Investment, collective work, and production would become impossible. Modern economists have developed a theory called **SOCIAL CAPITAL** to explain how intangible values like trust, reciprocity, and familiarity are actually crucial ingredients in economic production.

In reality, any practical economic system (even capitalism) requires a level of mutual trust, safety, honesty, and morality that is not consistent with the assumption of overarching individual selfishness. So as we think about how to change capitalism, or replace it entirely, we should be confident that finding better ways for humans to work together, and fairly share the fruits of our joint labour, does not at all violate human nature. And our alternative economic vision does not actually depend on "sharing" or "charity," anyway. Instead, we can advance a vision of collective self-interest, in which we're all better off when we work together, cooperate, enforce norms of mutual and fair behaviour, and all receive a fair share of the pie we produce together. That's much closer to "human nature" than the cartoonish stereotype of Homo economicus.

3

Economic History

A short history of the economy

In the early days of human civilization, the "economy" was a pretty simple affair. Our work consisted of hunting animals for meat, fur, and bones; gathering wild produce (like berries); and constructing simple shelters. These hunter-gatherer economies were often nomadic (moving in tune with the weather or animal migrations). They were cooperative, in that everyone in a family or clan grouping worked together (with some division of tasks across genders and ages). And they were mostly non-hierarchical: no-one "owned" anything or "hired" anyone. (While priests, chiefs, or other leaders had special authority, that authority did not derive from their economic position.) In general, these economies produced just enough to keep their members alive from one year to the next.

Eventually humans learned they could deliberately cultivate useful plants, and agriculture began. This caused corresponding social and economic changes. First, it allowed for permanent settlements (with the opportunity to build better homes and other structures). Second, the greater productivity of agriculture allowed society to generate an economic **SURPLUS**: production beyond what was required just to keep the producers alive. Third, with that surplus came the task of deciding how to use it. The existence of a surplus allowed some members of society, for the first time, not to work. This opened up a whole new can of worms. Who would get to avoid working on the farm? What would they do instead? And how would they keep the rest of society – those who had to keep working – in line?

With permanent settlements and a growing economic surplus, therefore, came the first **CLASS** divisions within society – in which different groups of people fulfilled fundamentally different economic roles, depending on their status and their relationship to work. Different economic systems handled this fundamental issue in different ways. For example, under monarchist systems, a powerful elite controlled the surplus and its allocation based on inherited birthright. The monarch needed the acceptance or at least acquiescence of his or her subjects, which generally needed to be imposed (from time to time, anyway) by brute force.

Many of these societies also relied on **SLAVERY**, in which entire groups of people (often designated by race or caste) were forced to work through brute force. In case this sounds like ancient history, remember that the US economy (the most powerful capitalist country in the world) was based significantly on slavery until fewer than 150 years ago, and coerced labour of different kinds still effectively forcibly enslaves millions of people around the world today (see box). The resulting economic surplus produced by the slaves was used in various ways: luxury consumption of the ruling elite; the construction of impressive buildings and monuments; the financing of exploration, war, and conquest; the work of non-agricultural artisans and scholars; and re-investment into new and improved economic techniques.

Modern Slavery

Unfortunately, slavery and other forms of forced labour are not just a problem for the history books. History has proven that it's usually more flexible and efficient to elicit hard work and loyalty from workers through wage labour. But bosses are not averse to using old-fashioned compulsion and servitude, when necessary. The International Labour Organization estimates that there are at least 21 million people around the world who still experience forced labour in one form or another.* These include:

- Over 5 million children.
- Over 10 million migrants.
- Over 14 million people in forced labour with private businesses.
- Over 2 million forced labourers in state prisons.

* International Labour Organization, "Profits and Poverty: The Economics of Forced Labour" (2014).

While slavery and direct authoritarian rule were certainly powerful and straightforward ways for elites to control the economy and the resulting surplus, they had their drawbacks, too. Slaves and subjects often revolted. Their work ethic was not always the best: slaves tend to be grudging and bitter (for obvious reasons), requiring "active supervision" (often with a whip!) to elicit their effort and productivity.

Eventually a more subtle and ultimately more effective economic system evolved, called **FEUDALISM**. In this system, a more complex and flexible web of mutual obligations and rights was used to organize work and control the surplus. Peasants were permitted to farm on land that was governed by members of a higher class (gentry, landlords, or royalty). They could support themselves and their families, but in return had to transfer most of their surplus production to the gentry (in the form of annual payments or tithes). The gentry used this surplus to finance their own (luxury) consumption, the construction of castles, the work of artisans and priests, maintenance of a simple state apparatus, wars, and other "extras." In return, they were supposed to protect the peasantry on their land (from attack by competing landlords), and ensure their security.

Agriculture became steadily more productive (with the invention of techniques such as crop rotation, the use of livestock, and horticulture). The surplus became larger, allowing the development of more complex and ambitious non-agricultural activities – including the emergence of a more powerful and well-resourced central government, more ambitious non-agricultural production (including the emergence of small early manufacturing workshops), and farther-reaching exploration and conquest. More effective transportation (like ocean-going ships) allowed the development of long-range trade (bringing in specialty goods from far-flung colonies and trading partners). Later in the Middle Ages, this trade sparked the emergence of a whole new class: merchants, who earned an often-lucrative slice of the surplus by facilitating this growing trade. These merchants would play an important transitional role in the subsequent development of capitalism.

Figure 3.1 Economic Evolution

This is a ridiculously condensed review of economic history. Yet it still conveys some crucial lessons that are relevant today:

- Human beings learn by doing. As they work at something for a while, they identify and implement ways to do it better. In economic terms, this leads to improvements in technology and productivity over time – sometimes very slowly, sometimes very quickly.
- These ongoing changes in productivity and technology tend to require corresponding changes in how work is organized, and indeed how society is organized. The evolution of workplaces, class structure, markets, even politics has occurred hand-in-hand with the ongoing evolution of the economy.
- Economic systems come, and economic systems go. No economic system lasts forever. Capitalism is not likely to last forever, either.

Where did capitalism come from?

Capitalism first emerged in Western Europe, especially Britain, in the mid-1700s. It evolved from relatively advanced feudal monarchies, in which non-agricultural production and long-distance trade had become important economic activities, and in which central state power was relatively strong. Historians have spent a lot of time trying to determine the causes of this incredible economic and social transformation, and arguing about why it occurred in Europe instead of elsewhere in the world. (During the Middle Ages, China and India had been about as wealthy as Europe – but for various reasons, the social and technological changes which led to capitalism did not occur there.)

There is broad agreement on at least these key factors which contributed to the rise of capitalism:

- **New technology** The invention of steam power, semi-automated spinning and weaving machines, and other early industrial technologies dramatically increased productivity. Also, these technologies needed completely new ways of organizing work: in larger-scale factories which required more complex (and expensive) equipment. And they implied new structures of ownership: the machinery (and associated costs of raw materials and other necessary inputs) was too expensive for individuals or small groups of workers to finance on their own. An owner was needed to finance the large up-front investments necessary to get the factories working.
- **Empire** The fact that Britain (and, to a lesser extent, other European colonial powers) possessed the organizational and military ability to conquer and dominate far-off lands contributed to the development of capitalism

in many ways. It fostered the emergence of a class of merchants – which eventually evolved into a class of industrial capitalists. It provided raw materials and exotic goods, including cheap imported foodstuffs to feed the growing non-agricultural workforce. It extracted wealth from the colonies by brute force (including good old-fashioned slavery, in many instances) to support the growth of capitalism at home. It provided an inflow of precious metals to serve as money and lubricate commerce. And empire also provided captive markets for the impressive output of the new factories.

- **Government** In addition to the role of colonialism, the centralized state power that existed in Britain, France, and Holland was crucial to the emergence of capitalism. A strong government provided a reliable currency, standardization of commerce, and protection of the private property of the ambitious new capitalists. It could also help to keep peasants and workers in line, as they endured the painful shift from feudalism to capitalism. As we will discuss in Chapter 20, a strong central state was also crucial to the successful spread of capitalism to other countries, too (including Germany, America and Japan).

- **Resources** Conveniently, Britain had ample supplies of coal and iron needed for the new industries. Water-power in rural areas was also important in the early days of the Industrial Revolution. The availability of resources shouldn't be over-emphasized, however: many countries with abundant resources failed to develop quickly, while some countries (like Japan) successfully developed with very few resources.

The birth of capitalism was not pretty. Wages and conditions in the early factories were hellish. How did the first capitalists recruit workers? They were former feudal peasants, driven off their former lands (which they never formally owned) by a process called the ENCLOSURES. Lands which were once held in common and worked under feudal rules were fenced in and assigned as formal private property to landlords – whose status became legal rather than traditional in nature. This also facilitated the depopulation of rural areas – necessary in light of tremendous increases in the productivity of agriculture (far fewer farmers were needed to produce all the food the whole country needed). In this way, capitalism produced two entirely new economic classes: a group of industrial capitalists who owned the new factories, and a group of workers who possessed nothing other than their ability to work in those factories.

The evolution of capitalism

The "birth" of capitalism, amidst the smoke and soot of the Industrial Revolution, was a painful and in many ways violent process. Workers were forced off their

land and driven into cities, where they suffered horrendous exploitation and
conditions that would be considered intolerable today: seven-day working weeks,
twelve-hour working days, child labour, frequent injury, early death. Vast profits
were earned by the new class of capitalists, most of which they ploughed back
into new investment, technology, and growth – but some of which they used to
finance their own luxurious consumption. The early capitalist societies were not at
all democratic: the right to vote was limited to property owners, and basic rights to
speak out and organize (including to organize unions) were routinely (and often
violently) trampled.

Needless to say, this state of affairs was not socially sustainable. Working people
and others fought hard for better conditions, a fairer share of the incredible wealth
they were producing, and democratic rights. Under this pressure, capitalism
evolved, unevenly, toward a more balanced and democratic system. Labour laws
established minimum standards; unions won higher wages; governments became
more active in regulating the economy and providing public services. But this
progress was not "natural" or inevitable; it reflected decades of social struggle and
conflict. And that progress could be reversed if and when circumstances changed –
such as during times of war or recession. Indeed, the history of capitalism has been
dominated by a rollercoaster pattern of boom, followed by bust.

Perhaps the greatest bust of all, the Great Depression of the 1930s, spurred
more changes. New banking regulations were aimed at preventing financial chaos.
Government income-support and make-work projects tried to put people back
to work. To some extent, these projects were influenced by the economic ideas
of John Maynard Keynes (more on him in the next chapter). The greatest (and
deadliest) make-work project was World War II. The war spurred massive military
spending which suddenly kicked all the major economies back into high gear, and
eliminated unemployment.

After World War II, a unique set of circumstances combined to create the most
vibrant and in many ways most optimistic chapter in the history of capitalism
– what is now often called the "Golden Age." This postwar boom lasted for
about three decades, during which wages and living standards in the developed
capitalist world more than doubled. Strong business investment (motivated in
part by postwar recovery and rebuilding) was reinforced by a rapid expansion
of government spending in most capitalist economies. Unemployment was low,
productivity grew rapidly, yet profits (initially at least) were strong. This was also
the era of the "Cold War" between capitalism (led by the US) and communism
(led by the former Soviet Union). In this context, business leaders and Western
governments felt all the more pressure to accept demands for greater equality and
security, since they were forced by global geopolitics to defend the virtues of the
capitalist system.

Neoliberalism

Beginning in the late 1970s, this "Golden Age" drew to a close, and global capitalism entered a distinct and more aggressive phase. The previous willingness of business owners and governments to tolerate taxes, social programs, unions, and regulations petered out. Businesses and financial investors rebelled against shrinking profits, high inflation, lousy financial returns, militant workers, and international "instability" (represented most frighteningly by the success of left-wing revolutions in several countries in Asia, Africa, and Latin America in the 1970s). They began to agitate for a new, harder-line approach – and eventually they got it.

The Gloves are Off

"Neoliberalism is capitalism with the gloves off and back on the offensive."

Adolph Reed Jr., American Political Scientist (2013).

In retrospect, there were two clear "cannon shots" that signaled the beginning of this new chapter in the history of capitalism:

1. Paul Volcker became the head of the US Federal Reserve (America's **CENTRAL BANK**) in 1979. He immediately implemented very strict **MONETARY POLICY**, heavily influenced by the ideas of Milton Friedman and the **MONETARIST** school (we'll discuss them more in Chapters 17 and 18). Interest rates rose dramatically, and economic growth slowed. Volcker claimed this high-interest-rate policy was necessary to control and reduce inflation. But it quickly became clear that a deeper shift had occurred. Instead of promoting full employment as their top priority (as during the Golden Age), central bankers would now focus on strictly controlling inflation, protecting the value of financial wealth, and keeping labour markets (and labour movements) strictly in check.

2. Margaret Thatcher was elected as UK Prime Minister in 1979, followed by the election of Ronald Reagan as US President a year later. Both advocated an aggressive new approach to managing the economy (and all of society) in the interests of private business. They fully endorsed the hard-line taken by Volcker (and his central bank counterparts in other countries). They were even tougher in attacking unions and undermining labour law and social policies (Reagan crushed the US air traffic controllers' union in 1981, while Thatcher defeated the strong British miners' union in 1985). Reagan and Thatcher shattered the broad Golden Age consensus, under which even conservative governments grudgingly accepted relatively generous social benefits and extensive government management of the economy. Despite forceful opposition, both

leaders prevailed (supported by business interests) and became role models for hard-right conservatives in many other countries. Thatcher justified her initiatives with the now-classic (but false) slogan: "There is no alternative."

It gradually became clear that capitalism had fundamentally changed. The "kinder, gentler" improvements of the Golden Age era came under sustained attack, and would gradually (over the next quarter-century) be rolled back – though not without stubborn resistance by workers and communities. Some argued that capitalism could no longer afford those Golden Age programs; in my view, this is invalid, although there is no doubt that the Golden Age recipe did encounter significant economic problems. Others argued that with the decline of communism and the weakening of left-wing parties, capitalism no longer *needed* to mollify its critics with compassionate policies (since it no longer faced a serious challenge to its continued existence).

This new era in capitalism has gone by several different names: neoconservativism, the "corporate agenda," economic rationalism, and others. The most common term now used around the world is NEOLIBERALISM. This term is confusing, since in some countries "liberal" refers to a centre or centre-left political ideology which still supports some Golden Age-style policies. In economics, however, "liberal" means something quite different: it means *an absence of government interference*. In this sense, "neoliberalism" implies going back to a more rough-and-tumble kind of capitalism, in which governments play a smaller role in regulating the economy and pursuing social goals. But even this definition is not quite accurate: in fact, government and the state still wield decisive economic power under neoliberal capitalism (we will discuss this further in later chapters). What has changed is *how*, and in *whose interests*, that power is now exercised.

The main goals of neoliberalism, and the tools used to achieve those goals, are listed in Table 3.1. They include controlling inflation; disciplining labour; downsizing and focusing government; and reinforcing business leadership – over the economy and all of society. The broadest but perhaps most important goal is the last one listed in the first part of Table 3.1: ratcheting down popular expectations. There has been a deliberate and multidimensional effort since the early 1980s to construct a whole new cultural mindset, in which people stop demanding much from the economy, and accept insecurity and vulnerability as permanent, "natural" features of life. In the 1970s workers in most capitalist countries were uppity and feisty, ready to demand a better deal from their employers and their society. Today, more than three decades after neoliberalism began, many are tempted to bow down in thanks that they still have a job. Overturning this passive, defeatist mindset will be crucial in motivating people to challenge the inequality and exploitation that typify the economy today.

Table 3.1 Key Goals and Tools of Neoliberalism

Key Goals:
- Reduce and control inflation; protect the value of financial wealth
- Restore insecurity and "discipline" to labour markets
- Eliminate "entitlements"; force families to fend for themselves
- Roll back and refocus government activities to meet business needs; cut taxes
- Generally restore the economic and social dominance of private business and wealth
- Claw back expectations; foster a sense of resignation to insecurity and hardship

Key Tools:
- Use interest rates aggressively to regulate inflation and control labour markets
- Privatize and deregulate more industries
- Provide special freedoms and benefits for the financial industry
- Reform the governance of corporations so that maximizing shareholder wealth always guides executive decisions
- Scale back social security programs (especially for working-age adults)
- Restructure labour markets by weakening labour standards, attacking unions, and more
- Use free-trade agreements to expand markets and constrain government interventions

Kinds of capitalism

Even under neoliberalism, and despite the pressures for conformity that arise from globalization, there are still clear differences between different capitalist economies – even those at similar levels of development. (There are even bigger differences, of course, between richer capitalist countries and poor ones.) So it would be a dangerous mistake to imply that all capitalist economies must now follow exactly the same set of policies. And those differences produce very different outcomes for the people who live and work in those economies.

Table 3.2 identifies four broad "types" of capitalism among the most developed countries in the world. They operate very differently in terms of how workers are treated, how active is government, and sectoral make-up. The "Anglo-Saxon" variant of capitalism is, by most indicators, the most unequal of all. It is characterized by a small role for government, an overdeveloped financial sector, and the largest inequalities in income. Other variants of capitalism – like the Nordic, the continental, or the Asian variants – offer generally better outcomes for working people.

Clearly, different societies still have considerable leeway to put their own stamp on the economy, even when the fundamental features of capitalism (namely a reliance on production for profit and wage labour) remain in place. Working for incremental improvements in capitalism, making it a little bit fairer and less degrading, is clearly important. On the other hand, it is also true that powerful forces in global capitalism (including competition for trade and investment) have

Table 3.2 Types of Capitalism (in the advanced countries)

Type of Capitalism	Role of Government: Taxes as Share GDP	Role of Government: Economic Regulation	Financial Sector (Banks, Stock Market)	Income Distribution	Managing Income Distribution	Union Coverage as % Workforce
Anglo-Saxon (US, UK, Canada, Australia)	30–35%	Weak	Very Large	Very Unequal	Market Power	10–30%
Continental (France, Germany, Italy)	35–45%	Moderate	Moderate	Somewhat Equal	Mild Corporatist¶	50–90%
Asian (Japan, Korea, China)	25–35%	Strong†	Relatively Small	Somewhat Equal	Paternalist Corporatist¶	10–20%
Nordic (Sweden, Norway, Denmark, others*)	45–55%	Strong	Relatively Small	Very Equal	Strong Corporatist¶	50–80%

* Some other European countries (like Austria and the Netherlands) have features similar to the Nordic type.

† The state is especially active in the Asian model in stimulating capital investment and managing the sectoral make-up of the economy.

¶ CORPORATISM refers to a system of centralized negotiation between business, labour, and government.

created some harmonizing tendencies across countries. Even the Nordic countries have faced economic and political challenges to their more inclusive, egalitarian version of capitalism in recent years, typically justified by the same old claim that "there is no alternative" to neoliberalism. In Sweden, for example, the poverty rate has doubled in the last decade – from one of the lowest in the world, to one that is only typical of European economies – as a result of more conservative labour market and social policies.

After capitalism?

At the same time as we fight for positive reforms in capitalism, we may also want to consider whether it's possible to move completely *beyond* the fundamental rules and structures of the system. After all, capitalism represents just one phase (and a relatively short phase, so far) in the evolution of human economic activity. That long process of evolution is not going to suddenly stop. We haven't arrived at some kind of economic "nirvana": a perfect system which can't possibly be improved. Collectively, we will continue developing new technologies, new goods and services, and new ways of organizing work. And it is almost certain that we will ultimately find new forms of ownership, and new forms of economic management, to make the most of those new tools – and, hopefully, to do a better job of meeting our human and environmental needs in the process. Sooner or later, I suspect we'll end up with something quite different from capitalism: some system in which most production is no longer undertaken by private, profit-seeking companies, and most work is no longer undertaken solely in return for a money wage.

The world has some experience with "life after capitalism," but that experience has been difficult and in most cases unsuccessful. Communist-led economies were built in Eastern Europe, China, and some developing countries in the mid-twentieth century; most of these failed in the face of economic stagnation and/or political breakdown. A few countries (like Cuba) have tried to preserve aspects of that system, and others (like Bolivia, Ecuador, and Venezuela) are trying to build new forms of socialism. Successful smaller-scale experiments in non-capitalist economic development have taken place on a regional basis in some countries – like the Basque region of Spain, the Emilia-Romagna region of Italy, or the Indian state of Kerala – with encouraging results.

We will discuss the problems and prospects of post-capitalist society in the last part of this book. We don't know what will come after capitalism, or when or how it will happen. But it would be folly to expect capitalism to last forever.

4

The Politics of Economics

Early economics

In earlier eras, human economic activity was pretty straightforward. You worked hard to produce the things you needed to survive. Powerful people (slave owners or feudal lords) took some of what you produced. You kept what was left, and tried to get by. End of story.

As the economy became more complex, however, the relationships between different economic players became more indirect and harder to decipher. Economics was born, as the social science which aimed to explain those increasingly complex links. The first economists were called "political economists," in recognition of the close ties between economics and politics. They began to theorize about the nature of work, production, value, and growth just as Europe's economy was evolving from feudalism toward capitalism.

The first identifiable school of economics was the **MERCANTILISTS**, based mostly in Britain in the 1600s. Their theories paralleled the growing economic power of the British empire, so not surprisingly they emphasized the importance of international trade to national economic development. In particular, they believed that a country's national wealth would grow if it generated large trade surpluses: that is, if it exported more than it imported. Mercantilists were also forceful advocates of strong central government, in part to strengthen colonial power and hence boost the trade surplus. Even today, the mercantilist spirit lives on (in modified form) in modern-day theories of "export-led growth" – followed in recent years by countries like Germany, Korea, and China.

Across the English Channel and a century later, a group of French thinkers called the **PHYSIOCRATS** developed a very different approach to economics – one that also lives on in modern economics. They focused on the relationship between agricultural and non-agricultural industries (such as early artisans and workshops), and traced the flow of money between those different sectors. They likened this flow to the circulation of blood through the human body; indeed, the most famous Physiocrat was François Quesnay, a physician to the French king. Their early efforts to trace the relationships between different sectors of the economy inspired modern theories of monetary circulation (which we will consider in Part Four). And they were the first school of economics to analyze the economy in terms of **CLASS**.

The Scottish writer Adam Smith is often viewed as the "father" of free-market economics. (This stereotype is not quite accurate; in many ways Smith's theories are very different from modern-day neoclassical economics.) And his famous *Wealth of Nations* (published in 1776, the same year as American independence) came to symbolize (like America itself) the dynamism and opportunity of capitalism. Smith identified the productivity gains from large-scale factory production and its more sophisticated division of labour (whereby different workers or groups of workers are assigned to different specialized tasks). To support this new system, he advocated deregulation of markets, the expansion of trade, and policies to protect the profits and property rights of the early capitalists (who Smith celebrated as virtuous innovators and accumulators). He argued that free-market forces (which he called the "invisible hand") and the pursuit of self-interest would best stimulate innovation and growth. However, his social analysis (building on the Physiocrats) was rooted more in *class* than in individuals: he favoured policies to undermine the vested interests of rural landlords (who he thought were unproductive) in favour of the more dynamic new class of capitalists.

Defunct Economists

"The ideas of economists and political philosophers, both when they are right and when they are wrong, are more powerful than is commonly understood. Indeed the world is ruled by little else. Practical men, who believe themselves to be quite exempt from any intellectual influence, are usually the slaves of some defunct economist."

John Maynard Keynes, British economist (1936).

Smith's work founded what is now known as **CLASSICAL ECONOMICS**. This school of thought focused on the dynamic processes of growth and change in capitalism, and analyzed the often conflictual relationship between different classes. In general, classical economists accepted the idea that the value of a product was determined by the amount of work required to produce it (what became known as the "labour theory of value"). After Smith, the most famous classical theorists were David Ricardo and Thomas Malthus. Ricardo developed a hugely influential theory of free trade known as **COMPARATIVE ADVANTAGE**. It claims that every country will be better off through free trade, even if *all* its industries are inefficient. (The theory is true, but only under very restrictive assumptions; we'll discuss it further in Chapter 21.) Meanwhile, Ricardo's friend Thomas Malthus developed an infamous theory of population growth which justified keeping wages very low. He argued that if wages were raised above bare subsistence levels, workers would simply procreate until their growing population absorbed all the new income.

Therefore, wages should naturally settle at subsistence levels. Malthus was dead wrong: in fact, birth rates *decline* as living standards improve. Nevertheless, the classical economists (and Karl Marx after them) did accept the broad idea that workers' wages tended to stagnate in the long term (rather than rising automatically with economic growth).

Needless to say, the oppressive working and living conditions of the Industrial Revolution, and the glaring contrast between the poverty of the new working class and the wealth of the new capitalist class, sparked regular economic and political turmoil. Workers formed unions and political parties to fight for a better deal, often encountering violent responses from employers and governments. An economic foundation for this fightback was provided by Karl Marx. Like the classical economists, he focused on the dynamic evolution of capitalism as a system, and the turbulent relationships between different classes. He argued that the payment of profit on private investments did not constitute a true economic return, but rather reflected the *social* power and status of the capitalists. Profit represented a new, more subtle form of **EXPLOITATION**: an indirect, effective way of capturing economic surplus from those (the workers) who truly do the work. Marx tried (unsuccessfully) to explain how money prices in capitalism (which include the payment of profit) could still be based on the true underlying "labour values" of different commodities. And he predicted the ultimate breakdown of capitalism, in the face of both economic instability (the ongoing boom-and-bust cycle) and political revolution. Marx's ideas were very influential in the later development of labour and socialist movements around the world.

Neoclassical economics

Following Marx, the capitalist economies of Europe continued to be disrupted by regular interludes of revolutionary fervour. Gradual economic and political reforms were achieved through the nineteenth century in response to these upheavals: limited social programs and union rights were introduced to moderate the worst inequalities of industry, and democracy was gradually expanded (at first, workers were not even allowed to vote since they didn't own property). It was in the context of these conflicts that a whole new school of economics arose.

Following an especially strident wave of revolutionary struggles in Europe (including the world's first, but short-lived, attempt to establish a socialist society, in the Paris Commune of 1871), **NEOCLASSICAL ECONOMICS** strove to justify the economic efficiency and moral superiority of the capitalist (or "free market") system. The neoclassical pioneers included Léon Walras (in Switzerland), Carl Menger (in Austria), and Stanley Jevons (in Britain); Walras was ultimately the most influential.

These theorists seemed to start from the precepts of their market-friendly classical predecessors: after all, "neoclassical" simply means "new classical". But in fact they made important changes to the classical approach. First, they focused on individuals, not classes. Second, they focused on the existence of market EQUILIBRIUM at any particular point in time – like a snapshot of the economy – rather than on the evolution and development of an economy over time. Third, they began to apply mathematical techniques to economic questions. Finally, they adopted a much more abstract approach to theory: instead of studying concrete, visible realities in the economy, neoclassical theory uses abstract logic to build complex economic theories on the basis of a few starting assumptions, or "axioms."

Neoclassical theory dominates the teaching of economics in developed countries, although there are many cracks in its walls. The key premises of the neoclassical approach include:

- Every individual starts life with some initial "endowment" of one or more of the FACTORS OF PRODUCTION (labour power, skill, wealth, or other resources). The theory does not concern itself with explaining how that initial endowment came about.
- Every individual also has a set of PREFERENCES which determine what goods and services they like to consume. Again, the theory does not concern itself with explaining where those preferences came from.
- Technology determines how those various factors of production can be converted into useable goods and services, through the process of production. Initially, neoclassical theory did not try to explain technology; more recent neoclassical writers have begun to study how and why technology evolves.
- Through extensive market trading (in both factors of production and produced goods and services), the economic system will ensure that all factors of production are used (including all labour being employed) in a manner which best satisfies the preferences of consumers. Important and unrealistic assumptions about the nature of markets and competition are required to reach this optimal equilibrium (or resting point) – a market-determined economic nirvana.

If supply equals demand in all markets (both for factors of production and for final goods and services), then the system is considered to be in GENERAL EQUILIBRIUM. Walras was the first to describe this situation, and the theory came to be known as *Walrasian general equilibrium*. Modern neoclassical thinkers have tried to prove mathematically that this general equilibrium is in fact possible; they have failed repeatedly, and today general equilibrium theory has fallen out of favour with many academic economists. Even in theory, the model depends on incredibly extreme and unrealistic assumptions (regarding perfect competition, perfect information, and perfect rationality). The theory has almost no practical applications. Nevertheless, the policy conclusions of the Walrasian view remain very influential, even though their logical underpinning is weak. Here are the key neoclassical conclusions:

- Left to its own devices, the economy will settle at a position of full employment, in which all potential economic resources (including labour) are used efficiently. For this reason, the economy is **SUPPLY-CONSTRAINED**: only the supply of productive factors limits what the economy can produce.
- This works best when private markets are allowed maximum leeway to operate. Attempts to regulate market outcomes (such as by imposing minimum wages, other regulations, or taxes) will reduce economic well-being by interfering with market forces. Governments should limit their role to providing essential infrastructure and protecting private property rights.
- Expanding trade (including international trade) will always expand the total economic pie, and this creates the *potential* for improving the economic outcomes of everyone in society.
- Workers' wages reflect the actual productivity of their labour (although this productivity is measured in a very odd way, by a theory called **MARGINAL PRODUCTIVITY**, in which wages are determined by the productivity of the very last person hired in a workplace). If workers are poor, therefore, it must be because they are not very productive. In other words, it's their own fault.
- In the same way, the profit received by investors also reflects the real "productivity" of the capital that they own, and hence profit is both legitimate and economically efficient. Proving that profit is economically and morally legitimate, rather than the result of exploitation (as Marx claimed), has been a central preoccupation of neoclassical economics.

Economics after Keynes

The development of neoclassical theory reflected the debates and conflicts of industrial capitalism. The capitalist economy continued to develop through the nineteenth and twentieth centuries in fits and starts, with periods of vibrant growth interspersed with periods of sustained stagnation and recession. But with the Great Depression of the 1930s, it became very obvious that neoclassical faith in the economy's self-adjusting, full-employment equilibrium was painfully misplaced. In reality, capitalism was clearly unable to ensure that all resources (especially labour) were indeed employed.

A new era of thinkers arose to explain both the failure of capitalism to employ all available labour, and advise what could be done about it. The most famous was John Maynard Keynes, who worked in Britain between the two world wars. Just as important but lesser known was Michal Kalecki, who was born in Poland but also worked in Britain. Working separately, they developed (at about the same time) the theory of EFFECTIVE DEMAND. In general, they found, an economy's output and employment were not usually limited by the supply of productive factors (as believed in neoclassical theory). More often, the economy is DEMAND-CONSTRAINED, limited by the amount of aggregate purchasing power. If purchasing power is weak for some reason (due to financial or banking problems, pessimism among consumers or investors, or other factors), then unemployment will exist. Worse yet, there is no natural tendency for that unemployment to resolve itself.

To deal with this problem, Keynes advocated proactive government policies to adjust taxes, government spending, and interest rates in order to attain full employment. Kalecki went further than Keynes, and showed that effective demand conditions also depend on the distribution of income (and the distribution of power) between classes; he advocated socialism as the ultimate solution to the problem of unemployment.

As it turned out, massive government military spending during World War II did indeed "solve" the Great Depression. Then, during the vibrant postwar expansion that followed, neoclassical economics tried (uncomfortably) to digest a watered-down version of Keynesian ideas. The leading economists of this era (such as America's Paul Samuelson and Britain's John Hicks) tried to construct a "synthesis" of neoclassical and Keynesian approaches. They concluded that unemployment and depression could only occur under very particular conditions. In most cases, however, they argued that the basic neoclassical model was still valid.

Eventually even this limited departure from key neoclassical commandments was abandoned. Global capitalism experienced growing instability and stagnation in the 1970s, as the Golden Age drew to a close. A new group of hard-nosed neoclassical thinkers – led by Milton Friedman and his colleagues at the University of Chicago – attributed this instability to misplaced government intervention. They resuscitated the core neoclassical policy framework (according to which government should provide a stable, market-friendly environment, and then just get out of the way), and hence provided the intellectual foundation for neoliberalism. This renewed neoclassical thinking is once again dominant in economics in most countries.

There is still much debate and controversy within economics today – although not nearly as much as there should be. Economics instruction in most English-speaking countries conforms especially narrowly to neoclassical doctrine; there is more diversity in economics in continental Europe, Latin America, and a few other countries.

Several alternative schools of economic thought have developed on the basis of non-neoclassical assumptions and methodology. For example, POST-KEYNESIANS have emphasized and developed the more non-neoclassical aspects of Keynes' work – emphasizing the economic importance of uncertainty and the peculiar nature of money. (Keynes himself never fundamentally broke from neoclassical thinking, and this has caused great confusion and controversy in subsequent years about what he "really" meant.) Other economists, known as radical or **STRUCTURALIST** thinkers, have branched out from Kalecki's work, emphasizing the connections between power, class, demand, and growth. Some economists continue to work within the Marxian tradition, and others in a broad stream of thought known as **INSTITUTIONALIST** economics (which emphasizes the evolution of economic and social institutions).

It will be very important in coming years to nurture all of these "heterodox" streams within economics ("heterodox" refers here to any economist who breaks away from neoclassical orthodoxy). That will be essential to provide some badly-needed diversity and balance within the profession.

Impure Science

"Economics has three functions – to try to understand how an economy operates, to make proposals for improving it, and to justify the criterion by which improvement is judged. The criterion of what is desirable necessarily involves moral and political judgements. Economics can never be a perfectly 'pure' science, unmixed with human values."

Joan Robinson and John Eatwell, British economists (1973).

The economy, economics, and politics

This extremely condensed history of economics reveals a couple of important lessons:

- The development of economics has paralleled the development of the economy itself. Economists have tried to keep up with real-world economic problems, challenges, and conflicts. The theories of some economists have supported those seeking to change the economy; the theories of others have justified the status quo.
- Consequently, economics is not a "pure" science; it never has been. Economists have worked to try to understand the economy and how it functions. But they have also had views – usually very strong ones, and often hidden – about how the economy *should* function. In the jargon of economics, the pure study of the economy is called "positive" economics; it is supposed to be separate from the advocacy of particular policies, called "normative" economics. But in practice, these two functions get mixed up all the time.

- The theories of economists have always been spurred by real world debates, politics, and interests (see Table 4.1). The Mercantilists celebrated the power and reach of empire. The Physiocrats tried to protect farmers against undue expropriation of their produce. The classical writers were concerned to celebrate (and hence justify) the innovative and growth-inducing behaviour of the new capitalist class. Marx's analysis of conflicts in capitalism was tied up with his vision of radical political change. Neoclassical economics tried to justify the payment of private profit and the dominance of markets. Keynes grappled with the destruction and lost potential of the Depression, while the subsequent resurgence of neoclassical doctrine both reflected and assisted the parallel reassertion of business power under neoliberalism.

Table 4.1 Economics and Politics Through the Ages

Theory	Time	Economic Context	Political Context
Mercantilists	Seventeenth century	Expansion of European colonial empires	Support for centralized state political and military power
Physiocrats	Early eighteenth century	Expansion of non-agricultural industries	Defend agricultural surplus against undue expropriation
Classical	Late eighteenth century, early nineteenth century	Birth of industrial capitalism	Favour ascendant capitalists over landlords; promote expansion of markets
Marx	Mid-nineteenth century	Consolidation, expansion of capitalism	Explain and criticize exploitation of workers; describe socialist alternative
Neoclassical	Late nineteenth century, early twentieth century	Consolidation, expansion of capitalism; democratic and social reforms	Reaction against European revolutions; provide justification for private profit
Keynes/ Kalecki	Post-1930s	Great Depression; WWII; advent of "Golden Age"	Policies to restore full employment, expand social security
Monetarism, neoclassical resurgence	1970s to today	Breakdown of "Golden Age," birth of neoliberalism	Describe failure of "Golden Age" policies; intellectual justification for neoliberalism
Modern heterodox*	Today	Consolidation of neoliberalism	Describe failures of neoliberalism; advance alternative policies

* Includes Post-Keynesian, structuralist, institutionalist, Marxian.

Today, economics continues to display its inherently political character. There is no economic policy debate which does not involve trade-offs and conflicting interests; discussions of economic "efficiency" and "rationalism" are never neutral. When a blue-suited bank economist appears on TV to interpret the latest GDP numbers, the reporter never mentions that this "expert" is ultimately paid to enhance the wealth of the shareholders of the bank. (On the rare occasions when a *union* economist is interviewed, the bias is usually presumed, by both the reporter and the audience, to be closer to the surface.)

And when economists invoke seemingly scientific and neutral terms like "efficiency," "growth," and "productivity," we must always ask: "Efficiency for whom? What kind of growth? And who will reap the benefits of productivity?"

Part Two

The Basics of Capitalism: Work, Tools, and Profit

5

Work, Production, and Value

What is work?

As we defined it earlier, the economy is no more and no less than the amalgamation of our collective work – all the work that is necessary to produce the goods and services we need and want. And once we've produced those things, we need to decide how to distribute and use them.

By "work," we refer to any productive human activity. Most obviously, this includes work in a paid job. Indeed, in modern capitalism, wage labour is so widespread that many people wrongly equate "work" with "employment." A frustrated parent is likely to tell their lazy teenager to "Get a job!" when what they really mean is "Get up and do some work!" Under capitalism, *most* work consists of wage labour, but not all. There is other important work that we must also consider.

Life's Work

"Far and away the best prize that life offers is the chance to work hard at work worth doing."

Theodore Roosevelt, former US President (1903).

Most modern jobs and careers fall into the category of wage labour – whether they are in private companies or public agencies, blue-collar or white-collar, producing tangible goods or intangible services. The stereotype of a "worker" as someone who performs menial tasks on an assembly line is badly outdated. Workers today perform a wide variety of functions, many of them requiring advanced skills. But they are still workers, so long as they perform that work for someone else, under their direction, in return for a wage or salary. Scientists in a research laboratory; surgeons in a large hospital; engineers in a construction firm – these are all workers (although culturally, they may not define themselves as such). They perform their labour in return for a salary, they are employed only when their employer desires, and they do not own or significantly control either the organization they work for, or the produce of their labour.

Some workers assume that if they are paid a monthly salary, rather than an hourly wage, then they must belong to a higher "class." This is wishful thinking.

They are still paid (although usually at a higher rate) to perform labour. They are still utterly dependent on the decisions of their employer (including the decision to hire them in the first place). And in some ways, they may be *more* exploited than hourly wage-labourers, despite their professional incomes. Most salaried employees do not have strictly fixed hours of work, and hence must perform overtime when required (usually unpaid) to finish their assigned tasks. Their self-identification as "professionals" (and their associated willingness to tolerate unpaid overtime and hectic conditions) assists employers to extract maximum work effort for minimum compensation.

Similarly, private companies need supervisors and managers to oversee production, keep the workforce in line, and make minor business decisions. But most of these so-called "management" jobs (especially lower-level supervisors and technicians) are just glorified forms of wage labour. These employees follow orders given by more senior executives, they do not meaningfully control or direct the activities of the company (despite their ability to boss around underlings), their compensation consists solely of a salary, and they are as easily dispensable as any assembly-line worker when their services are no longer needed.

In recent years, employers in many industries have expanded their use of part-time, temporary, and contract workers – reducing their reliance on full-time, permanent staff. This form of labour is called **PRECARIOUS WORK**, since the workers have little security or predictability regarding when their services will be required. Wages tend to be lower, hours of work unpredictable, and employment benefits (like pensions or supplementary health insurance) are rare. In some cases, these precarious positions hardly seem like a traditional "job" at all. In fact, some don't pay any money at all: many companies have expanded their use of unpaid "interns" in recent years, taking advantage of young workers' desperation for any "foot in the door" of a depressing labour market. But make no mistake: workers in precarious jobs are still workers. They still sell their labour to an employer, in hopes of earning enough to live on. It's just that their conditions and compensation are clearly inferior to those in more permanent, stable jobs. Employers often favour precarious, "non-standard" work arrangements because they allow companies to adjust employment flexibly and costlessly to the level of demand. For workers, however, the risk and uncertainty of never knowing when you will work, and how much income you will earn, is a costly, painful burden.

So most work in capitalism consists of wage labour, in a variety of forms. And most people in society have to perform wage labour, in order to support themselves and their families over their lifecycle. In developed capitalist economies, around 85 percent or more of the population fits this category – and that share has grown over time. (This includes people who are too young or too old to work, are unemployed, or have a disability. But their ultimate well-being in life still depends on wage labour performed by themselves, or by someone in their family who supports them.) Despite the many significant differences between workers (in the nature of work they do, their relative security, and their pay), 85 percent of the population share this fundamental economic characteristic: they must work for someone else, to earn money to support themselves.

Of course, having a job is not only useful as a way to financially support oneself. Human beings also enjoy the creative activity and social interaction that comes with work – especially if working conditions are comfortable and safe, and the work itself allows for some variety and creativity. Lots of evidence shows that individuals' self-esteem and mental health can also benefit from being employed. However, it is ultimately economic compulsion that drives wage labour under capitalism: namely, the hard reality, for most members of society, that you have to work if you want to eat.

It's for the Money, Dude

Employers can ask the most patronizing, demeaning questions during a job interview:

"Where do you see yourself in five years?"
"Tell us about a situation where you really used your initiative."
"What is your greatest weakness?"

But perhaps the most offensive interview question is this one: "Why do you want this job?"

Isn't it obvious? The vast majority of people need paid employment just to pay for the essentials of life, for themselves and their family. It's no more complicated (or meaningful) than that.

In addition to wage labour, there are other kinds of work that also add real value to the economy. Consider, for example, the very top managers or executives of a company or agency. These senior managers do, indeed, perform work – typically very long, hard hours. Their work is essential to the performance of their companies, and to the whole economy. They enjoy a unique degree of control over the operations of their enterprises: they may be owners or partners of those companies, or they may be hired by the company's shareholders to make the most important decisions. And their income depends on the profit of the company. True, they may receive a salary (and usually an extremely high salary, at that). But their income also always includes a substantial profit-related component: either a direct share of the profits (when top managers are also owners or partners of the company), or else stock options and other bonuses which depend directly on the company's financial performance. Companies like this system of executive compensation, because it better inspires managers to focus ruthlessly on maximizing the wealth of shareholders.

Their direct and substantial economic stake in the profits of the enterprise, and their unique control over its activity, fundamentally distinguish these top managers from other, less powerful staff (including most salaried staff). In part, their abundant compensation reflects their *work*. But it also reflects – directly or indirectly – a meaningful share in the enterprise's *profit*, which is a very different thing. (Some clever companies have taken to offering small profit-sharing bonuses to lower-level staff, too, as a way of strengthening employee loyalty and discouraging unionization; but these largely token payments do not imply that the workers have somehow become "owners.") Nevertheless, top managers do perform useful, productive, important work, and this work must be considered in any complete description of the economy. Some owners of businesses, meanwhile, don't perform any direct labour in the companies they own; instead, they hire top managers to take care of the dirty work. Only a small proportion of individuals in society belong to this category of owners or top managers of companies (perhaps 2 percent of the total population).

Another significant proportion of the population (between 10 and 15 percent in most developed capitalist economies) is self-employed: they work, nominally "for themselves," in a small business or on a farm. (Individuals who own a company which employs other people to do most of the work would fall into the category of "top managers" defined above.) In most capitalist countries, self-employment has declined over time as a result of agricultural depopulation and the rise of large corporations. At the same time, however, there has been an expansion of self-employment in some other parts of the economy (such as smaller-scale services companies).

For example, modern corporations have often found it profitable to shift (or "outsource") many peripheral service functions to outside contractors, who may be nominally self-employed. Instead of hiring someone to make photocopies, companies may outsource this work to a small photocopy shop. They may do the same with other subsidiary functions, from cleaning to accounting. But are these contractors really any different from workers performing the same function, but on the company's payroll? They still fundamentally depend on the large company for work and income; indeed, their total compensation (considering pensions and benefits, which contractors don't usually receive) is often lower than for standard employees. Realistically, these "self-employed" people are still workers. (Technically, they may be termed "dependent contractors.") Many of them clearly fit into the category of PRECARIOUS WORK, defined above.

Even for self-employed individuals who sell their services into a broader "market," rather than to one or a few corporate customers, the dictates of competition typically force them to accept incomes and working conditions below those attained by paid employees. Indeed, the per capita income of most proprietors of small businesses and farms in the major Anglo-Saxon economies falls below the average income of paid workers. It's safe to conclude, then, that most of the income received by these individuals reflects their ongoing *work*; very little of that income, if any, reflects their status as *owners* of their farms or businesses.

Many market-friendly economists and politicians celebrate self-employment as a sign of initiative and self-reliance. And most countries provide various subsidies and supports for small business formation (including lower company tax rates and various tax loopholes). In terms of real economic output, productivity, and income, however, self-employment is generally inferior to paid employment. And many people who start a small business ae driven less by the freedom of "being your own boss," and more by desperation arising from their inability to find a paid job.

So far, therefore, we have defined three broad categories of work: those who perform wage labour, those who control and direct the activities of companies (in which most work is performed by other paid employees), and those who work in small businesses or farms (which operate mostly on the basis of work by the owner and members of his or her family). We call these broad categories CLASSES, and we have now identified three major ones: workers, top managers and major owners, and proprietors of small businesses and farms. This approach recognizes that members of each class, despite differences among them, share a fundamental economic feature: namely, they all support themselves in a similar way.

In addition to these categories of money-generating work, however, don't forget that most individuals also perform significant amounts of unpaid work to operate their household, care for family members, and participate in their community. This work is not included in the GDP statistics, yet it is essential to our individual and collective well-being. A disproportionate share of this work is performed by women. We will discuss the unpaid work that occurs in families and communities further in Chapter 9.

To sum up, here is a breakdown of the main classes in a developed capitalist economy, and their approximate share of the total population:

- Employees (wage labourers) and their families: about 85 percent.
- Top managers and major owners: under 2 percent.
- Proprietors of small businesses and farms: 10–15 percent.

Most paid work under capitalism, but not all, consists of wage labour, or employment. And the share of wage labour in total paid work has grown over the history of capitalism. Unpaid work is another large category of productive work. But as we'll discuss in Chapter 9, most unpaid work can be interpreted as a "cost of producing workers": that is, it's an input to the ongoing re-creation of a willing and able labour force (feeding, clothing, and caring for people, in order to send them back into paid work the next day). Therefore, the vast majority of work in our economy consists either of working for someone else, or *getting ready* to work for someone else.

Only a small proportion of total work occurs outside of this central employment relationship that is a defining feature of capitalism. Some consists of people working (at least nominally) for "themselves," in a small business or farm. And a very small share of total work consists of directing the operation of larger companies, in which most work is performed by other people who work for wages or salaries.

Work and value

Just about everything we need or want in our lives requires human effort to produce it. In other words, almost nothing comes without work. The exception to this general rule is what the classical economists called "free gifts of nature": useful things that are readily and abundantly available in the natural environment, just waiting to be "picked." Plucking ripe fruit from a wild blackberry bush; fishing for trout in a clear stream; drinking fresh water from a spring. As we all know, there aren't many "free gifts of nature" left anymore (and you should never drink water from a spring unless it's been tested!). And even the previous examples required *some* work: picking, fishing, carrying. Perhaps the air we breathe is the only free gift of nature left – and even that is questionable, in many parts of the world.

Ultimately, all production involves the application of human work to various materials which we gather from the natural environment in order to make them more useful. This is obviously true of **GOODS**: every tangible product consists of natural materials which have been transformed or manipulated in some way to make them more useable. (Even "synthetic" products, like polyester shirts or edible petroleum coffee whitener, began life as some substance in our natural environment.) But this is also true of **SERVICES**. No-one produces a service solely with their bare hands – except perhaps a masseur (and even they need massage oil and a massage table!). So service-producing industries, too, require inputs of goods, which in turn consist of transformed natural substances. Therefore, work and the natural environment are the ultimate sources of everything produced in our economy; in this sense, they are the source of all "value." And work is the only thing that *adds* value to the things we collect from nature.

But this term, "value," is notoriously difficult to define, and economists have been debating the nature of value, and how to measure it, for centuries. Today, economists mean various things by "value," and the term is used in many different contexts. The value of a product may refer to its price, in comparison to the prices of other products. Value can also refer to the total value created in a particular industry, or in the economy as a whole. For the purposes of GDP statistics, **VALUE ADDED** in the *private* sector is the sum of all goods and services produced, evaluated at their prices. In the *public* sector, in contrast, value added is usually defined as the cost of producing a public service (like education or health care) – since these services don't usually carry a "price."

The payment of private profit greatly complicates the definition and measurement of value. In a capitalist economy, the owners of private capital receive a rate of profit on their investments, even if they do no work in production. This does not imply, however, that capital is itself "productive," nor that profit is morally legitimate, nor that the owners of capital actually did anything useful. Rather, the payment of profit simply signifies that under capitalism, private ownership (and the payment of profit based on private ownership) is a fact of life. Because of the payment of profits, the price of something in a capitalist economy will *not* exactly reflect the amount of work that went into producing it. Two products which require an equal amount of labour to produce will generally have different prices, depending on the amount of profit that's paid out (and hence built into the price) in the course of producing each product. Similarly, GDP includes not just the value of all paid work (of various sorts, including self-employment and the work of top managers) performed in an economy. GDP also includes other forms of income paid out in the economy – like profits.

For simplicity, the classical economists adopted a **LABOUR THEORY OF VALUE**. In this theory, the prices of producible commodities are held to reflect the total amount of labour required to produce them (including both immediate or direct labour in that industry, and the indirect labour required to produce the tools, machines, and raw materials used in production – a complication we'll discuss in the next chapter). Marx realized this simplified theory was wrong: prices under capitalism must also reflect the payment of profit. But he was politically committed to explaining prices on the basis of their "underlying" labour values, so he undertook a complicated (and ultimately unsuccessful) attempt to explain prices on the basis of labour values. Neoclassical economists, responding to Marx, tried to provide an intellectual and moral justification for the fact that profits *are* paid on capital investments by attempting to show that capital itself is actually productive. These efforts, too, were unsuccessful.

Ultimately, this long historical debate about profit and value was more about politics, than economics. Productive human effort ("work," broadly defined) is clearly the only way to transform the things we harvest from our natural environment into useful goods and services. In this sense, work is the source of all value added. For society as a whole, just as for that lazy teenager, if we don't work, we don't eat. Nothing else – not alien landings, not divine intervention, and not some mystical property of "capital" – is genuinely productive. Under capitalism, profits are paid on capital investments. These profits reflect a social institution called "private ownership," not any real productive activity or function. (In fact, as we'll see, it's not even possible to clearly *measure* capital, let alone to prove that it is productive!) Because of this social structure called private ownership, profits are built into the prices of various goods and services (and hence also into the measurement of GDP). Neoclassical economics has been preoccupied since its inception with justifying the payment of profit on the basis of economic principles like "productivity" and "thrift." But in the end, profits are explained by power, privilege, tradition – and sometimes by brute force. Not actual work.

Exploitation and Algebra

Here's an interesting historical note regarding the endless controversies in economics over how to measure "value." Piero Sraffa was an Italian economist who worked in Cambridge, England in the mid-twentieth century (alongside Keynes, Kalecki, and the other famous heterodox economists based there). He developed a technique for explaining relative prices on the basis of the amount of direct labour involved in production, the indirect labour embodied in inputs of raw materials and machinery, and (under capitalism) the payment of profit on invested capital. He showed  (with a little modern algebra) that Marx didn't need to worry about trying to "transform" labour values into prices. In fact, without any labour theory of value, Sraffa still proved that an inverse relationship must exist between wages and profits: if one is higher, the other must be lower. This was utterly contrary to the conclusion of neoclassical economists that labour and capital have complementary interests, rather than conflicting interests. Throw in appropriate political terminology (if desired), and Sraffa's theories prove that labour is the ultimate engine of production, and that the payment of profit represents the capture (or "exploitation") of a share of the surplus that workers produce.

Work, scarcity, and value

Economics is known as the "dismal science," and many neoclassical thinkers take great pleasure in living up to that reputation. They are obsessed with the concept of scarcity: the idea that human existence is perpetually and fundamentally constrained by economic shortage. This mind-set overlaps nicely with the dour, moralizing prescriptions of neoclassical writers – emphasizing thrift, self-sacrifice, deferred gratification, and immutable budget constraints. Indeed, the concept of scarcity takes modern form in the painful policies of AUSTERITY implemented in so many countries after the 2008 GLOBAL FINANCIAL CRISIS (more on this in Chapter 26).

This concept of permanent scarcity fits nicely with the emphasis that neoclassical economists place on exchange (or the "forces of supply and demand"). Remember, the neoclassical nirvana – a lovely place called GENERAL EQUILIBRIUM – features a balance between supply and demand in every market in the economy. This includes not just markets for produced goods and services, but also the markets for factors of production (inputs used in production, including labour and "capital"). Scarcity plays a crucial role in this theory. Since factors of production are available (or "endowed") in arbitrary and largely fixed amounts, equilibrium prices for each factor (and hence the prices of everything made from that factor) will depend directly on the amount that is available. At the macroeconomic level, total output is ultimately held back only by available quantities of scarce factor inputs: free markets then ensure that all available inputs are employed efficiently in production. In neoclassical theory, as a result, the economy is SUPPLY-CONSTRAINED. The only thing limiting total output is the scarcity of productive inputs. Mutually beneficial exchange between buyers and sellers in every market is the best way to make the most of those scarce inputs, and that's why (in theory) neoclassical economists worship the free market.

But even a cursory look at the world around us confirms that the economy is not supply-constrained at all. To the contrary, the economy normally possesses enormous quantities of unutilized labour (visible in unemployment, underemployment, and non-participation). In fact, as we will see in Chapter 13, neoliberal economic policy tries to maintain unemployment at some minimum desirable level. The normal limit on total employment is therefore not the scarcity of willing and capable workers; the normal limit is inadequate demand for their services by companies and employers. Similarly, the economy is almost never held back by a scarcity of "capital" (a concept which we will define in the next chapter). The modern banking system literally creates finance out of thin air to pay for new investments in productive facilities or technology (as we will explain in Chapter 17). All that is needed is a willingness on the part of capitalists to make those investments.

Therefore, with very rare historical exceptions (such as a wartime economy, bursting at the seams to desperately support the war effort), the economy can almost always produce more. The only thing holding back total output and employment is the level of spending power required to purchase that output; capitalism, therefore, is almost always DEMAND-CONSTRAINED. Instead of focusing on trade-offs between alternative uses of presumably scarce resources, economists would do better to focus on making sure more of those resources are used in the first place: by creating new jobs for workers, and stimulating more investment by companies.

Money for Nothing

Policies implemented in several countries following the 2008 financial crisis provided a surprising twist on the whole idea of "scarcity." Several central banks (including those in the US, the UK, and Japan) embarked on an unorthodox policy called QUANTITATIVE EASING. Consumer and business spending remained weak for years after the initial downturn, despite record-low interest rates. So central banks developed alternative ways to pump spending power directly into the economy. They created trillions of dollars of new money, and used it to purchase financial securities (thus transferring huge sums into the private banking system). This policy, and its strengths and weaknesses, are explained in Chapter 26.

An unintended consequence of quantitative easing has been to expose traditional neoclassical conceptions of scarcity as unfounded. For years neoliberal governments pled poverty: shortages of funds, they claimed, necessitated cutbacks in income security, social programs, and public investments. Yet when the private financial system fell into crisis, governments (through their central banks) were able to magically create trillions of dollars of new spending power. Private banks were the main beneficiary; the rest of the economy received some indirect benefits, but not as strong as they could (or should) have been.

If trillions of dollars of new wealth can be created out of thin air to purchase financial securities and support private banks, why can't we create new wealth out of thin air to directly pay for things of value – like public services, housing, clean energy systems, or transit infrastructure? The answer is, "We can!" The only barrier to a policy of "social quantitative easing" – using credit creation to put unemployed people to work doing useful things – is political, not economic. After the financial crisis, government willingly wielded extraordinary power to protect the interests of the most powerful segments of society. But in so doing, they revealed that scarcity is an ideological myth. If we can impose different priorities on government (through political action), then equally dramatic measures could be taken to support the interests of the whole community – not just private banks.

Achieving greater abundance, rather than managing scarcity, becomes the goal. That's why heterodox economists, rejecting the neoclassical obsession with scarcity, tend to focus their analysis on employment, production, and accumulation (rather than exchange).

How does scarcity concretely affect value and prices? Generally not very much. More production does not typically imply (or require) higher prices. In fact, more output usually results in *lower* prices: that's because most goods and services can be produced more efficiently in larger quantities. So the traditional neoclassical conception that price is determined by the intensity of demand relative to scarce supply is not generally informative. Consumer tastes and other demand-side factors certainly influence the composition of final output. And temporary shortages (due to changes in demand, or problems in supply) can send prices shooting up for a while. But in normal economic times, prices are determined by the cost of production (which in our economy includes a normal rate of profit for the capitalists), not by demand and scarcity. Almost anything produced at a given quantity can usually be produced at a greater quantity – and at a lower cost, to boot. So the interaction between consumer demand and the assumed scarcity of available resources is not usually relevant.

An exception to this general rule is provided by products which are in some way unique and irreplaceable. Economists call these "non-producible" goods. In general, the value of a producible good or service will equal the cost of producing it. A non-producible item, on the other hand, possesses some special characteristic which cannot be duplicated: fine art, a rare mineral, a plot of land in a very convenient location, or a very unusual and innate skill (such as possessed by sports legends and opera stars). The prices of non-producible goods and services may deviate from their cost of production, depending on the extent to which purchasers are willing to pay a premium for those specific attributes. And hence the extra money collected by the owners of those commodities genuinely reflects their scarcity. In economics, these super-profits are often termed **RENTS**.

Therefore, it is only for non-producible goods and services that demand conditions (that is, what customers are willing to pay) enter directly into the determination of price. For producible goods and services, if customers want more of something, industry simply supplies it – and the cost of production (including a profit margin under capitalism) determines its value. By definition, producible goods and services constitute all of what we "produce" (and hence all of what is counted in GDP), so we tend to focus on them. But where scarce (and hence non-producible) inputs are required for production, then an element of scarcity and demand can indeed enter the picture.

One example of scarcity that affects many working people is the cost of housing in large cities. Urban real estate prices usually reflect the price of the land underneath a house, more than the cost of the actual building itself. (To see this, compare the market value of a house, with the amount it is insured for; the latter is usually much less than the former, since the insurance only covers the cost of rebuilding the home itself in event of fire or destruction.) The building is producible, but the land is not – and in large cities (especially those facing geographic constraints, like an ocean or mountain range) the demand for scarce space can drive up housing costs to intolerable levels. In a free market system, the resulting super-profits (or economic "rents") will accrue to land-owners and property developers. To limit these super-profits, and keep the cost of living more affordable, local governments and urban planners need to manage the allocation of scarce land using tools like zoning laws, public transit services, affordable housing programs, and rent controls.

Another way in which scarcity has genuine economic relevance is through the worrisome environmental constraints now facing the economy. Every industry requires natural resources as inputs; and humans always need land to live on, air to breathe, and water to drink. We are now painfully aware that nature's ability to supply those necessary inputs, while at the same time absorbing pollution (a side-effect of much economic activity), is limited. Some specific natural resources (like petroleum) are genuinely scarce and non-producible; their scarcity will therefore affect the prices of anything which uses that resource, and may even (in extreme cases) limit total output. Often, however, alternative sources of supply can be developed, and conservation or recycling measures may reduce resource consumption; it is rare that total economic output is constrained by a pure resource shortage. The bigger environmental risk is posed by nature's limited capacity to absorb continuing pollution without jeopardizing our quality of life and ability to work. Global **CLIMATE CHANGE**, the product of centuries of greenhouse gas emissions (mostly from fossil fuels) since the Industrial Revolution, is the most dangerous example. Coming to grips with climate change, and building a more sustainable economy, must be an overarching priority for economic policy in the years ahead. Chapter 16 will consider the environmental dimensions of economic activity in detail. Achieving sustainability will entail strict conservation of non-renewable resources, shifting economic output to products (like public services) that are less resource-intensive, and investing heavily in alternative energy systems, public transit, and pollution abatement. Note that environmental constraints do not necessarily limit our capacity to work and produce: if anything, creating a cleaner environment will require us to do more work in future, not less. But these environmental challenges will certainly change what we produce, and how we do it.

To sum up, the traditional emphasis on scarcity as a natural, even moral feature of economic life is misplaced. It reflects the ideological mission of neoclassical economics to justify hardship – rather than working to alleviate it. Our economy could produce far more than it does today, and the standard of living of most people (properly defined to include services, quality of life, and leisure time) could rise, if we organized and managed our economy differently. Instead of adjusting ourselves to assumed scarcity, we should imagine ways to improve living standards through our work, investment, and productivity – as well as through the better distribution of the fruits of our labour.

The only ultimate constraints on economic activity are our collective capacity to work, and the environment's capacity to provide the resources and inputs we need to work and live. All production consists of the application of human labour to the resources and supplies which we harvest from nature. So long as there are idle people willing and able to work, and so long as we manage our interactions with the environment in a sustainable way, then "scarcity" is a neoclassical myth, not economic reality.

You Write the Book: Work and Nature

Everything produced in our economy requires labour. And everything also requires resources and supplies obtained from the natural environment. (This is true even of service industries, like haircuts or restaurant meals or massage therapy: they depend on the direct labour of service sector workers, but they also need tools and supplies to do their work.) Any product, therefore, can be decomposed into the various flows of work and natural resources which are used in its production.

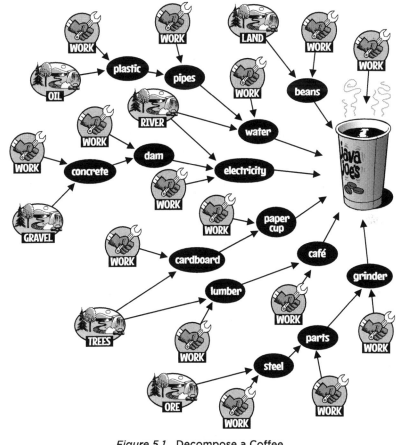

Figure 5.1 Decompose a Coffee

An example of this decomposition is provided in Figure 5.1. Start with a very simple product: a cup of coffee from your neighbourhood café. What was required to make that coffee? The direct labour of the waiter, obviously. But they didn't use their bare hands to make your coffee: they also used many tools and supplies, including coffee beans, water, a cup, a coffee grinder, electricity, and the building itself (since capital structures, the places where we work, are also "tools"). Keep going: we can then decompose each of those tools or inputs into the work and natural resources that were required to produce them, too: work and land for the beans, work and cardboard for the paper cup, work and steel for the grinder, work and water power for the electricity, work and building materials for the café, and so on. Some of those inputs in turn require another stage of production: work and trees to make the cardboard, work and ore to make the steel, and so on – as each link is added to the chain of value-added that makes up the whole economy.

Eventually we can decompose the whole process into work and the original resources and supplies which we harvested from nature. Economists thus refer to labour and natural resources as the PRIMARY FACTORS of production. All the tools and supplies used in production (including all forms of "capital") are INTERMEDIATE GOODS: produced from primary factors, in order to assist with the production of other goods and services. Note that intermediate goods cannot themselves limit the long-run productive capacity of the economy (although shortages can arise in the short-run); only the availability of labour, and the resources we need from nature, ultimately limit what we can do. INPUT-OUTPUT TABLES are complicated databases prepared by statistical agencies that describe these complex connections between different sectors of the economy.

Try drawing a similar decomposition of production in the industry where you work. Start with the final good or service that you produce. Then break it down into labour, natural resources, and intermediate goods. Then break down each of those intermediate goods into their respective inputs, and so on, until everything is decomposed into work and nature. Scan your illustration and send it to author@economicsforeveryone.com. We will post examples at www.economicsforeveryone.com.

Work and surplus

In Chapter 3 we saw that changes in economic systems over time were closely related to changes in the production and control of an economic **SURPLUS**. The surplus is the amount of excess production in an economy, above and beyond what is required to sustain the workers of that economy, and restart production over again the following year. Once a surplus is produced, two crucial questions must be addressed: Who will control it? And what will it be used for? Indeed, the control and use of the surplus is a central factor determining how economies evolve over time.

The size of the surplus depends on a couple of important variables. First is the **PRODUCTIVITY** of an economy: how much it is able to produce, relative to the amount of work that goes into producing it. Productivity is best measured as the amount of total value added per hour of labour. If workers are more productive, then it takes less working time to produce enough to keep them and their families alive for another year. Thus the surplus will be larger.

Second, however, there is no absolute standard for what we call the "necessities" of life. A subsistence standard of living may be defined as a physiological minimum: that is, what is required to prevent people from starving. More likely, however, it will be influenced by changing social norms about what is considered a "minimum" or decent standard of living. In general, those norms change over time to reflect the growing productivity of the economy and corresponding changes in social norms. (This relates to the distinction between absolute and relative measures of poverty, which we will explain in Chapter 14.)

What's left after paying for a necessary minimum standard of living for workers, and setting aside enough production (for tools, materials, and supplies) to ensure that production can start again next year, is the social surplus. Measuring that surplus is a tricky exercise. In most developed countries, workers only receive about half the total value of output produced in the economy. Some of that reflects a minimum necessary standard of living, but in most countries some also clearly reflects extra income above and beyond the subsistence minimum. Workers won that extra income over time through their successful efforts (supported by unions) to demand higher-than-subsistence wages. GDP also includes allowances for the **DEPRECIATION** (wearing out) of capital equipment; that depreciation must be covered in order to maintain the economy's ability to produce. GDP includes income received by farmers and small businesses; most of that reflects the necessary minimum standard of living for farmers and small businesses, but some reflects profit too. Corporate profit (over and above depreciation) obviously reflects a share of social surplus collected by larger businesses. Government collects a share of GDP directly through sales taxes and other revenue tools.

Table 5.1 provides a rough breakdown of the various components of GDP in the US. After deducting an estimate of minimum consumption for people who perform productive work (including farmers, small businesses, and even capitalists), the value of essential public services, and allowances to replace used-up capital equipment, the remaining value of output (over one-half of total GDP) is the economy's surplus.

The surplus can be "gathered" in various ways. In earlier societies, it was directly collected (seized from slave labour, or gathered via the tithes of feudal peasants). In modern times, it is mostly collected indirectly through corporate profits or taxes. And the surplus can be "spent" in various ways. It can be consumed (either through the luxury consumption of the well-off elite, or through mass consumption by working people who win wages over and above the subsistence level). It can be spent on other projects: paying for wars, building monuments or temples, or supporting the arts. (In economic terms, these are also forms of consumption.) Or the surplus can be invested, to allow the economy to expand over time.

Table 5.1 The "Surplus" in the US Economy, 2013

Every economy must set aside enough output to provide subsistence consumption for its workers (including essential public services), and replace wear and tear on capital equipment. These expenditures are required just for the economy to reproduce itself. In the US, those necessary expenditures use up barely half of total output. Most of the remainder – the surplus – is consumed (allowing for a higher-than-subsistence standard of living … at least for the affluent). Smaller amounts are allocated to wasteful public programs (like the military, police, and jails) and net new investment (over and above depreciation). In fact, foreign borrowing allows the US to use more output for all these uses than it actually produces. Unlike the early days of capitalism (when dynamic capitalists ploughed back most of their profits into their growing businesses), very little of the modern US surplus is reinvested in new capital projects; most is consumed.

	US$ Trillion
Estimating the Surplus:	
Gross domestic product	$16.8
"Subsistence" personal consumption*	−$4.8
Depreciation of capital	−$2.6
Necessary public services†	−$2.1
Surplus	**$7.3**
Uses of Surplus:	
"Extra" personal consumption	$6.7
Net new investment¶	$0.6
Military, police, and jails	$1.0
Foreign borrowing and other adjustments	−$1.0
Total	**$7.3**

*   Consumption equal to relative poverty income threshold (50% of median personal income) for all Americans.
†   Government services production excluding military, police, and jails.
¶   New investment after accounting for depreciation.
Source: Author's calculations from US Bureau of Economic Analysis, US Census Bureau, *Statistical Abstract of the United States.*

The advent of capitalism brought important changes in the size of the surplus (which became much larger, thanks to the impressive productivity of new technology), the way it was collected (largely through business profits, rather than forcible seizure), and what it was used for. On this score, the fact that early capitalists re-invested most of their profits (driven partly by hunger for more profits, and partly by competition from other capitalists) was crucial to the early dynamism demonstrated by the new system. Whether modern-day capitalists retain that productive urge is an open question; we will return to it in later chapters.

6

Working with Tools

Learning to work with tools

Very early in human civilization, we learned that it's much more effective to use tools instead of working with our bare hands. Indeed, even many animals are intelligent enough to grasp this essential economic fact: chimpanzees use blow-tubes to extract termites from a mound; crows use custom-cut twigs to root out grubs from the underbrush; bees and beavers build structures (which are also a kind of tool) to aid their busy work. Early human tools included simple stone cutters, weapons for hunting, and cooking implements. Later we learned to melt and forge metals to produce more complicated, expensive tools, which in turn allowed us to develop permanent agriculture, long-range transportation, and complex construction – functions which were all essential to our gradual economic evolution.

Today, of course, the "tools" we use to perform our work are fantastic: computers of all kinds, massive machinery, laser beams, satellite telecommunications, nanotechnology that operates at the molecular level, and many more. These tools are a precondition for our productivity: without them, we couldn't produce the quantity or quality of goods and services that we do. But tools also exert a critical influence on our *social* structure. The tools we use shape everything in the economy: who does what work, how our workplaces are managed, what we produce, and how the economic pie is divided up. Technology affects society, but at the same time society also influences technology: some new technology is motivated by social imperatives, not technical ones (like increasingly sophisticated surveillance technology that keeps track of how fast people are working).

There are several important economic consequences from our reliance on tools:

- We learn to use tools by experimenting. Initially that learning process took a long time: it took generations or even centuries to devise rather modest improvements in production. Today, thanks to our developed and more deliberate scientific capacities, learning is much faster. But we still "learn by doing": by working, we learn (in various incremental ways) how to work better. And those improvements almost always require more tools.
- In general, we do not "consume" our tools, and hence they do not directly contribute to our material standard of living. (A few fanatical home-handymen

might derive intrinsic enjoyment from admiring their newly purchased hardware – but they are hardly typical!) Instead, we use tools to produce other things (goods or services) that we *can* consume and that *are* inherently useful. For this reason, economists call tools INTERMEDIATE PRODUCTS: things that are needed to produce something else, not for their own sake. FINAL PRODUCTS, on the other hand, are the goods and services that we ultimately use or consume.

- In order to use tools in our work, and hence to become more productive, we must devote some initial work effort and time to the task of *producing* those tools. Then we use the tools to produce (with extra efficiency) the good or service that we ultimately desire. For simplicity, think of this as a two-stage process: first we produce the tools, then we use them to produce what we need or want. In reality, a modern economy involves a complex, overlapping network of many different industries, producing both intermediate and final products simultaneously; moreover, we need tools in order to produce tools, so the whole process takes many stages, not just two. Nevertheless, all production can be deconstructed (if you go far enough back in time) into a series of dated activities involving *first* the production of tools, and *then* the production of final goods and services.

- Tools themselves are never "productive" in their own right. Rather, we use tools in order to make our *work* more productive. No tool or machine runs by itself. Even the most automated production system needs a living person to push the "Start" button – not to mention oversee and maintain the machinery to make sure it works properly. At any rate, a more "automatic" production system is simply one in which most or nearly all of the work involved has been any devoted to the prior task of producing the tools; only a little work is then required to use the tools to produce the desired final good or service. But the whole process still depends completely on *work*. The reason we devote time and energy to producing tools is because we've learned that our overall work effort (*including* the time we spent building the tools) is much more productive when we use tools, rather than our bare hands.

Two ways to grow corn

To understand these points a bit better, let's imagine a very simple economy. It only produces one thing: corn. In pre-capitalist societies, corn was produced solely with labour, seeds left over from the previous season, and simple hand tools. Imagine that there were 100 farmers in the community, and they produced enough corn (let's say 100 bushels) to give each farmer enough corn to support them and their families at a minimal, subsistence level (one bushel per farmer).

Now suppose that the farmers discover how to make and use a tractor. A tractor (which is a sophisticated tool) allows the farmers to plough, plant, and harvest corn more quickly, with less required labour. However, they must devote some initial time and effort to producing the tractor. Let's say that ten farmers can build the tractor with one year of work. Then the same ten farmers can use that tractor to grow corn in the second year, and subsequent years. Thanks to the tractor, those ten farmers can till just as much land as 100 farmers used to work by hand. Better yet, the tractor improves the quality of seeding and harvesting, so that total corn output (from the same land) increases: it now produces 180 bushels, up from 100. Finally, suppose that a tractor lasts for five seasons; each year of farming therefore "uses up" one-fifth of the tractor. (This gradual wearing out of tractors, and other tools, is called **DEPRECIATION**.)

Table 6.1 A Corn Economy: Manual and Mechanized

	Manual	*Mechanized*
Direct labour: farming (person-years)	100	10
Indirect labour: tractor-making (person-years)	0	2*
Total labour (person-years)	100	12
Output (bushels)	100	180
Productivity (bushels per person-year)	1	15

*   It takes ten person-years to make the tractor, and the tractor lasts for five seasons, so two person-years of indirect labour are used up per season.

Table 6.1 summarizes the key economic facts of this simple corn economy – both before and after the discovery of tractors. Manual farming produced 100 bushels of corn, from 100 person-years of work. The productivity of this economy, therefore, was one bushel per person-year of farming. Mechanized farming, however, dramatically improves productivity. The community now produces 180 bushels of corn per year, with just ten farmers doing the direct work. However, we must also count the indirect work involved in this new system. It takes ten person-years to build the tractor, and it lasts for five years. So two person-years of indirect labour must also be ascribed to each year of corn production. That implies a total of twelve person-years of work for each year: ten for direct farming, and two for indirect work on inputs (namely, a proportionate share of producing the tractor). Productivity therefore equals the total output of corn (180 bushels) divided by the total input of labour (twelve person-years). Productivity is thus 15 bushels per person-year of labour – 15 times higher than in manual farming. This is actually a realistic illustration of how dramatically mechanization improves the productivity of agriculture.

There are many amazing economic and social implications from the discovery of mechanized farming, and the incredible expansion of productivity which it brought about. The preceding example, of course, is highly simplified and, in many ways, unrealistic. For example, it would be unusual to have the same group of workers both producing tractors and then using the tractors for farming (more likely, a community would assign some workers to specialize in building tractors, and others to specialize in farming – rather than expecting the same people to do both jobs). And the production of tractors itself requires the use of many types of tools and equipment; it could not simply be undertaken directly by ten workers with their bare hands.

But even this simple example highlights some crucial and complicated questions:

- Where does the extra productivity come from? Clearly, not from the tractor itself. The tractor is not magic; it cannot produce corn by itself. Work is still essential: both to build the tractor, and to use it. The great improvement in productivity is attained because the farmers learned it was more efficient to first build a tractor, and then use it in farming – rather than trying to farm with their bare hands. In other words, the productivity improved because of the *technique of production* (first build a tractor, then grow corn), not from the tractor itself. Strictly speaking, the term TECHNOLOGY refers to a technique of production, not to a particular piece of equipment or machinery. The term is often misused to refer to equipment itself ("Wow, dude, you have some awesome technology in here!"). In its correct use, though, "technology" refers to knowledge about how to produce something – not the physical *tools* we use to produce it. A new technology can be highly productive; but a tool or machine, in and of itself, is not.

- Who owns the tractor? Right now, nobody does. The members of this economy have simply discovered that it's smarter to first build a tractor, then grow the corn – rather than growing the corn manually. So they invest some of their own time to make the tractor, and then capture the benefit of improved productivity down the road. If someone did own the tractor, then they would probably charge a price (like a rental rate) for its use. They would receive income in return for their ownership rights – but that ownership is not productive in and of itself. The tractor is still useful, even if nobody owns it. Moreover, in this simplified example, it's not at all clear why the workers would *allow* anyone to charge them for the tractor, because they could simply build themselves another one. In practice, various barriers prevent workers from "building" their own equipment – such as technical know-how, start-up costs, or patents. These barriers are essential to the ability of capitalists to charge for the use of their tools. A modern example is the effort by biotechnology firms (such as the global giant Monsanto) to patent new crop seeds, legally preventing farmers from planting them unless they pay fees to the owner. Seeds are perhaps the simplest "tool" (something that is not consumed, but used to produce something else), yet even they are becoming private property – with access restricted to reinforce the economic power of the patent owner.

• Whether or not anyone owns the tractor, it takes time to build it – and the tractor workers need to eat while they are building it. If the economy actually followed the two-year process implied above, it would have to set aside enough corn one year to keep the ten tractor workers alive while they were building the tractor (until the tractor could be used in the second year to produce corn). In practice, a real economy would produce both tractors and corn simultaneously, supplying just enough tractors to replace each farm's equipment once every five years. Nevertheless, *time* is an essential element of working with tools, by virtue of the fact that we first need to build our tools, before we can use them. And because more productive technologies use more complex tools, they take more time (from start to finish).

What Came First?

"Labour Is prior to, and independent of, capital. Capital is only the fruit of labour, and could never have existed if labour had not first existed."

Abraham Lincoln, Former US President (1861).

• What happens to the extra workers? The manual corn economy required 100 workers. The mechanized corn economy requires only ten (along with the equivalent of two workers per year in factory production). The community must decide what the surplus workers should do. They could be transferred into other industries: consuming corn to stay alive, but producing non-agricultural goods and services (like construction, entertainment, simple handicrafts and manufactures, or military jobs) for the whole community (or for certain members of the community). Or all 100 workers could divide up the existing work amongst themselves (each working a small part of the year, and taking the rest of the year off as vacation). They would thus capture the benefits of higher productivity as extra leisure time. Alternatively, excess workers could just be relocated to other regions (like far-off cities) to fend for themselves, or simply left to starve. In historical practice, each of these "solutions" has been used, to differing extents, in different times and places, when new technology sharply reduced the number of workers required in a particular industry.

- What should be done with the surplus? The economy now produces far more corn than is needed to support the ten workers involved in corn production (and the two tractor workers). This opens up dramatic new possibilities for re-investment (including the expansion of non-agricultural industries); for luxurious or wasteful consumption by a small elite (including pet projects like building monuments or waging wars); or for modest improvements in consumption for the whole population. In history, economies which re-invest more of their surplus tend to grow and develop faster. At the same time, economies which allocate a hefty share of the fruits of mechanization to support increased mass consumption tend to be more socially and politically stable – since average working people get to share in the gains of new technology (and hence are more satisfied and less rebellious).

What is capital?

Without yet naming it, this discussion has introduced the concept of **CAPITAL**. "Capital" can mean many different things in economics, depending on the context. Very broadly, it refers to the various "tools" we use in our work; these tangible tools are called **PHYSICAL CAPITAL**. This category can include any tangible product used to produce something else (rather than being consumed in its own right), such as buildings (factories, mines, offices, or stores) and other structures (pipelines, electricity towers) used by private businesses or other productive enterprises. It also includes all forms of machinery and equipment, including tools, computers, machinery, robots, and transportation equipment – again, so long as they are dedicated to the production of something else. Sometimes, whether something is a "capital" good or not depends solely on what it is being used for: a motor vehicle used to deliver packages is a capital good, but the same vehicle used for personal purposes is a consumption good. (The arbitrariness of this distinction inspires all sorts of shenanigans on business tax returns!) Capital goods which last for some time and are installed in a certain place are called **FIXED CAPITAL**. But a portion of physical capital also consists, at any point in time, of inventories of supplies, partly-processed, or finished goods en route to their final productive destination.

Capitalism is an economic system in which private profit is paid to the people who own capital. In this context, capital takes on a particular *social relationship* (based on private property), not just a physical form. Without this social dimension of ownership (and all the power and privilege that goes with it), capital would be synonymous with "tools," and that would be the end of the story.

In modern times, "capital" has also come to mean a sum of money which is invested in a business, in hopes of generating profit. I prefer to call this FINANCE, rather than capital, in order to distinguish the physical and the monetary forms of investment.

The development of new technologies, and the accumulation of physical capital (that is, tools) required by those technologies, have been the dominant forces behind the stunning economic changes which have occurred in the last two centuries of human civilization. And the continued accumulation of physical capital, and development of new technologies, is a crucial driver of our future economic progress.

Theories of capital and profit

In capitalist economies, tractors and most other physical capital are owned by private companies or individuals, who receive profit for their use. Recall that a fundamental political motivation for the development of neoclassical economists was to justify the payment of profit on invested capital. Neoclassical theory attempts to do this using two different, but related, arguments:

1. Capital is inherently productive, so someone who owns capital should be paid for its use just like any other factor of production. We have already seen that a tool is simply the physical embodiment of the work required to produce it; no tool is useful separate from the work that went into making it, and the work required to operate it. But there's an even deeper, logical problem with the "capital is productive" argument. Unlike labour, land, or natural resources, capital cannot be measured in physical units. A modern economy uses thousands of different kinds of tools, and it makes no sense at all to speak broadly of capital in "tons" or "machines" or "tractors" (as we can speak of labour in hours, or land in hectares). Capital, in aggregate, is always measured in money terms – and, indeed, that's how profit is paid (as a percentage of invested money). But the prices of tools (like other prices in capitalism) themselves depend on the profit rate. We need to know the profit rate before we can even know the value of the physical capital (that is, tools) that's been invested. So how can profit reflect the amount of invested "capital" (measured in aggregate), when the amount of invested "capital" itself depends on the profit rate? This neoclassical argument collapses in circular reasoning.

2. Production with tools takes time, and profit should be paid to the owners of those tools to reflect their patience while they wait for production to occur. Capital represents real output that is reinvested in production instead of being consumed; the thrifty investor who made that choice to defer consumption should be rewarded for their patience. It is certainly true that when someone

owns something, they will indeed usually demand to be paid for lending it. This payment reflects the economic power that comes from their social status as "owners". But "waiting" is not, in itself, a productive activity. Indeed, poor and working people spend billions of hours waiting every week without ever receiving a cent for it: waiting for the bus, waiting for service in public institutions, waiting to work. It is only because someone *owns* the capital that they get paid for "waiting." In this manner, the payment of profit is inevitably tied up with the social institution of ownership, rather than any inherent characteristic of production itself. Moreover, the "compensation for waiting" argument gets caught in the same circular reasoning as the "capital is productive" argument. Whether one particular technology requires more "waiting" than another is seldom self-evident, independently of the rate of profit that is being paid out. This is because the "waiting" typically occurs in different patterns over different periods of time. A technology that involves relatively more "waiting" (and hence more paid profit) at one rate of profit could involve relatively less "waiting" (and hence less profit) at another, because the different bits of waiting must be evaluated and compared to each other (using the profit

Time is Money

One especially destructive application of the neoclassical theory of profit is a practice called DISCOUNTED CASH FLOW analysis. It is commonly used by corporations to compare the value of revenues or profits received by a company over several years. On the assumption that "time is money," and owners of money should be rewarded for deferring their access to that money, corporate financial planners discount future revenues by a certain percentage per year. This is held to reflect what companies could have earned on the money if they had invested it elsewhere, and the assumed hardship of investors who have deferred consumption in order to make an investment.

The effect of discounting is to reduce the perceived value of things received in the future – and that effect can be dramatic. Companies choose a discount rate (measured in percent per year) on the basis of assumed risk, and the profitability of alternative opportunities. Typical discount rates fall between 5 percent and 15 percent per year. Even at lower discount rates (5 percent), $100 loses 99 percent of its value over a century. At 15 percent, it loses essentially all of its value in a generation (see Table 6.2). This mode of thinking, derived directly from neoclassical economics, enforces a ruthless focus on quick profit. It dramatically devalues the importance of long-run investments in physical capital, community, and the environment. Even governments use this mode of analysis to evaluate long-run policies affecting social well-being, resource conservation, and climate change.

Table 6.2 How Much is $100 Worth in the Future?

		Discount Period					
		1 year	5 years	10 years	25 years	100 yrs	1,000 yrs
Discount rate	5%	$95	$78	$61	$30	$1	$0
	10%	$91	$62	$39	$9	$0	$0
	15%	$87	$50	$25	$3	$0	$0

Anthropologists believe that the oldest continuously surviving human societies on the planet are the Bininj and Mungguy aboriginal communities in the Kakadu region of north Australia. They have inhabited their lands for over 50,000 years. A crucial aspect of their culture is their self-perception as guardians of the rich but fragile natural environment there, and this responsibility motivates their continuing concern with careful conservation and preservation. Contrast this view of the world, with the myopia that is produced by discounted cash flow analysis. Even a huge sum of money (say, a billion dollars), discounted at a very small discount rate (even 1 percent per year) for 50,000 years, becomes valueless: worth a tiny fraction of a penny. Thankfully, the Bininj and Mungguy peoples do not make decisions this way.

In a discounted cash flow world, the long-run value of Planet Earth is worth nothing. For humans and the other species which inhabit this planet, of course, it is priceless.

rate). The measurement of "waiting" (like the measurement of the aggregate value of physical capital) cannot occur without knowing the profit being paid, and hence it cannot in turn determine the payment of profit.

By the 1960s, it was clear that both neoclassical approaches were theoretically invalid (following a long academic debate called the "capital controversy"). At that point, pure neoclassical economists began to pursue other directions in their thinking. Some developed a very strange concept called "intertemporal equilibrium," which sidesteps the problems noted above by avoiding any attempt to measure aggregate capital at all. Instead, it calculates a separate rate of profit for each specific tool, calculated at each particular point in time. The theory is internally consistent but useless for practical applications. Other economists effectively abandoned the notion of general equilibrium altogether (including its effort to explain and justify profit), and began to pursue other interests. Despite this high-level intellectual retreat, however, the broad belief that profit is a legitimate and efficient payment that reflects the real productivity of capital still rules the roost in economics instruction and economic policy-making.

There is another major approach to understanding capital and profit, which views the payment of profit as a way to collect and control the economic surplus. As we saw in Chapter 4, this view originated with the classical economists, was modified by Marx, and lives on in the theories of modern heterodox thinkers (inspired by Piero Sraffa, Michal Kalecki, and others). In this approach, profit is a residual: what's left after a company pays its bills (including wages, raw materials, depreciation on capital, and others). Therefore, profit is paid from the surplus production generated by an economy – over and above the cost required to reproduce itself (including sufficient wages to keep workers alive, and the cost of wear and tear on existing capital). Understanding profit in this way does not necessarily imply that profit is "wrong," nor that profit should be eliminated (so that workers are paid the full value of everything they produce). Indeed, if workers actually received (and consumed) everything they produced, any economy (not just a capitalist one) would soon collapse for lack of investment. Until we develop and implement a better way to organize the economy, profit is a fact of life under capitalism – and investors' demands for it shape our economic and social actions accordingly.

However, recognizing that profit is a fact of life under capitalism (and hence built into the price of everything produced and sold) is very different from accepting that profit is a natural and legitimate compensation for the real economic "productivity" of private capital. One can certainly recognize and even tolerate the power of private owners to collect profit on their investments, without accepting their self-congratulatory storyline about why it should be paid (based on mumbo-jumbo about "patience" and "productivity"). Moreover, understanding capital and profit in this way allows us to better understand how capitalism actually works.

For example, profit rates have increased substantially in most countries in the wake of the painful, pro-business policies associated with neoliberalism. According to neoclassical theory, this rise in profits must reflect some improvement in the real productivity of capital – and hence it is an outcome that's both natural and fair. But that is hard to believe. In fact, according to neoclassical theories of **DIMINISHING RETURNS**, capital should become incrementally less productive as more of it is accumulated. The surplus approach provides a more concrete and convincing explanation: higher profits under neoliberalism reflect the broad pro-business changes that have occurred under neoliberalism in economic policies and structures. They enhanced business power; reduced what companies have to pay out in wages, taxes, and other costs; and boosted the bottom-line profits left over (as a residual) at the end of each year. In this understanding, higher profits reflect a shift in social, political, and economic power, not some automatic or "natural" reward for capital's supposed productivity.

7

Companies, Owners, and Profit

The private company

One defining feature of capitalism is that most production is undertaken to generate private profit. (The other defining feature of capitalism is that most of the work required for production is performed in the form of wage labour.) In order to generate and collect that profit, a specialized institutional form has emerged: the private company. Today private firms dominate the economy: their decisions about investment, production, and employment are the most important factors determining whether and how the economy evolves, and how people work. The actions of private companies are far more important on a day-to-day basis than things that governments do. This makes it incredibly ironic to hear government officials claim credit for "good economic management," or opposition leaders berate the party in power for "bad economic management." These political debates are mostly beside the point – since in reality it is businesses, not government, that sit in the economic driver's seat.

Companies come in all shapes and sizes. A few thousand very large corporations wield decisive influence over global economic development; the largest are as big (in value added, employment, and assets) as medium-sized countries (see Table 7.1). Tens of thousands of medium-sized businesses, and millions of very small firms and partnerships, also play critical economic roles. Together, the few

Table 7.1 **The Biggest of the Big, 2013 (US dollars)***

Category	Large Corporation	Equivalent Country
Value added	ExxonMobil ($195 billion)	Finland ($195 billion)
Employment	Wal-Mart (2.3 million)	New Zealand (2.3 million)
Cash	Apple Inc. Cash & Securities ($147 billion)	US Federal Government Official Reserve Assets ($110 billion)

* Estimated corporate GDP equals revenue less product purchases.

Source: Author's calculations from company reports; Organization for Economic Cooperation and Development; US Federal Reserve Board, "Financial Accounts of the United States."

thousand huge companies produce as much as all the others put together. And since many smaller companies depend directly and indirectly on bigger companies for their own business, the actions and decisions of these megacorps are clearly the most important influence on the overall economy.

All companies have two crucial features in common:

- Somebody owns them (usually one or more private investors – but some companies are owned by governments, public agencies, or cooperatives), and hence any profits produced by the company become the property of those owners.
- The owners must ensure their company is governed and managed in accordance with their wishes. Usually the owners' goal is to maximize the company's profits, and/or maximize the company's value on the stock market. (If the stock market is working well, those two criteria should be equivalent, since the stock market is supposed to value companies on the basis of their expected future profits.)

The structure of the private firm has changed over time, as have the methods by which firms are managed and governed. In the early days of capitalism, most private companies were owned outright by well-off individuals, who also managed them on a day-to-day basis. In this case, it was easy to ensure that a company acted in the best interests of its owner, since the owner and the manager were one and the same. Today, many private companies still conform to this model – mostly very small businesses, called proprietorships. In some cases a group of proprietors will cooperate on joint endeavours, called partnerships, in order to share the costs, risks, and rewards.

The most common business form in modern times, however, is the **CORPORATION**. A corporation is a private firm which has been granted the legal rights and responsibilities of a person, but in a manner which keeps the corporation itself separate from the (real) people who own it. The main benefit of this approach is that it limits the extent to which individual owners are liable for losses or damages resulting from a corporation's activities. This is called the principle of **LIMITED LIABILITY**. It allows well-off investors to protect their total wealth: the amount put at risk in any particular business venture is limited to the assets they directly invest in that business. Even if the corporation then goes bankrupt, or incurs large legal damages, the owners' *other* wealth is protected.

As a separate, artificial entity, corporations are well-suited to the joint-stock system, whereby a company is owned by a number (possibly a large number) of different individual investors. These corporations issue **SHARES** reflecting the up-front investments made by different owners; usually, these shares can then be bought and sold on a **STOCK MARKET**. Corporations which publicly issue shares in this manner are called publicly-traded corporations (not to be confused with publicly-owned corporations, which are owned by governments or other public agencies).

Corporations are governed according to a narrow, skewed version of democracy: one share, one vote. Shareholders get direct input to management at annual general meetings (which elect corporate boards of directors), and through occasional special ballots when companies face unique and important decisions. Company directors are elected to represent shareholders on a day-to-day basis, and they keep a close watch over the regular actions of the corporation's top executives.

We will discuss the workings of stock markets in detail in Chapter 19. For now, keep in mind simply that the trading value of a company's shares depends on the expectations of investors regarding that company's future profits. If profits are high and expected to stay high, then a company's share price will also be high. Shareholders can thus get their hands on the profits of the companies they own in two ways: via direct payouts from those companies (such as interest or dividend payments – see box), or via increases in the price of their shares (which can be sold on the stock market).

The distinction between the investors who own the company and the top managers who control it on a day-to-day basis is a constant challenge facing corporations. In the 1950s and 1960s, many economists believed that corporations had become powers unto themselves. Insulated, self-interested executives ran businesses without real supervision from the shareholders.

More recently, however, legal and organizational changes ensure that even very large companies operate with a strict focus on maximizing the wealth of their shareholders. Under neoliberalism, corporate decision-making structures have been reformed by a so-called "shareholder revolution". This movement has campaigned for many changes (such as linking executive compensation to share prices, more powerful boards of directors to oversee management, and more ability to launch hostile takeovers of companies that don't meet investor expectations) that have erased any doubt about who is in charge of companies, and reinforced their focus on maximizing profits. As much as at any time in the history of capitalism, therefore, the fundamental purpose of private companies – including the very largest corporations – is clearly to generate profits for the individuals who own them.

And private firms continue to evolve, always seeking new and more effective ways to generate profits for their owners. For example, in recent years a new form of ownership called **PRIVATE EQUITY** has emerged. A private equity firm (typically financed by a small group of very wealthy investors) takes large direct ownership stakes in other companies. Typically they dramatically restructure acquired businesses to boost profitability; sometimes private equity owners even break up companies and sell off the remaining "parts." This type of ownership is faster and more ruthless in doing whatever it takes to increase profits, no matter the damage to workers and other stakeholders. And because private equity firms do not issue shares publicly, they are spared the trouble and expense of publicly reporting on their operations.

Another organizational innovation widely used by some megacorps is a system called **FRANCHISING**. In this system, each small branch of a company's operations is owned by an individual investor, who handles the day-to-day duties of hiring and firing staff, ordering supplies, dealing with customers, and so on. The franchise system is appropriate when the head company can standardize production processes and ensure each franchise meets quality standards; examples include bottlers of popular soft drinks, outlets of chain restaurants, individual stores in some retail chains, and local branches of some service chains (especially in business or household services). Franchises allow the head company to conserve on capital spending (since it is up to each franchise owner to pay for branch-level investment costs), and avoid having to deal with the minutiae of local management. It would obviously be a mistake to call a McDonald's restaurant a "small business," even though it may be owned by a single entrepreneur. Clearly, franchising is simply a cost-minimizing, risk-minimizing way for an enormous company (McDonald's) to organize its operations.

Who owns companies?

During the Industrial Revolution, it was easy to tell who was the capitalist and who were the workers. The capitalist wore a black suit and a top hat, lived in a mansion, and ran the company. The workers were the ones risking their lives in the factory, making barely enough wages to keep them and their families alive.

Capitalism has changed a lot since then, of course, and so have the dividing lines between social classes. Workers have fought for and (in some countries) won better wages and working conditions. The capitalist is harder to spot; they may not even work in the factory. But they still own the company. The distinctions between classes still very much exist. They are just a little trickier to define.

Most large corporations are owned by many different shareholders. With joint-stock corporations, investors can place bets on the success of many different companies, without having to play a central management role in any one of them. This allows investors to diversify their financial holdings, and adjust their investments gradually and conveniently. It also allows them to capture profits on their investments, without having to get involved in the dirty, troublesome business of actually running a company. (Well-paid top executives do that for them.)

And since the wealth of joint-stock companies is parceled up into bite-size chunks, anyone with a bit of spare money can get into the action – even buying

---

Play the Odds

Financial advertising pretends that everyone can now "play the markets," and that building up a personal stock market fortune is the best way for individuals to achieve financial security in retirement. However, when asked how they would most likely accumulate the hundreds of thousands of dollars of wealth required to buy a decent private pension, 38% of low-income Americans provided a refreshingly honest answer: "Win the lottery!"* The odds of winning America's biggest lottery, Powerball, are approximately 175-million-to-1 (or 0.0000006%). While this view was ridiculed by financial planners, it is perhaps surprisingly rational. After all, the chance that an average American will get rich by picking the right stocks and bonds is exceedingly remote – and hence playing the weekly lotto seems like a sensible financial strategy.

* Consumer Federation of America, "How Americans View Personal Wealth" (2009).

---

one share makes you, technically, a "part-owner" of the company. (An exception is Berkshire Hathaway, the investment company run by American billionaire Warren Buffet; its shares cost over US$200,000 each!) This seems to make it possible for anyone to become a "capitalist," in the sense of owning a little bit of a private company. Clever companies play up this seemingly "participatory" aspect of modern capitalism. Some might even give a few token shares to their workers, to make them "feel" like owners and promote closer identification with management. Financial vehicles called **MUTUAL FUNDS** (through which investors buy shares in a pooled fund, which in turn invests in many different companies) allow investors to further share the risks, and the administrative costs, associated with owning shares. On this basis, defenders of capitalism imply that anyone who owns even a single share in a company is now themselves a "capitalist."

It's easy to cut through this self-serving hype. Hard statistics on wealth ownership indicate clearly that the ownership of financial wealth (including corporate shares) is shockingly concentrated among a surprisingly small elite. Moreover, it is becoming *more* concentrated over time – not less. Table 7.2 provides some summary measures of financial wealth concentration for the largest Anglo-Saxon economies, and the whole world. In every case, the clear majority of financial wealth is owned by a group representing well under one-tenth of the population. In every case, the financial holdings of the median household – the household exactly in the middle of the income ladder – is tiny in any aggregate macroeconomic sense. In fact, most typical households own no significant wealth outside of the equity in the homes they live in. In every case, the financial holdings of median households – the households in the middle of the income ladder – are tiny in any aggregate macroeconomic sense.

Table 7.2 Concentration of Financial Wealth in Selected Capitalist Economies

Unlike data on income distribution, statistics on the distribution of financial wealth are not regularly published in most countries, so it is difficult to paint a complete portrait of who owns what. Government statistics often include the value of owner-occupied housing in wealth statistics; this is very misleading, especially during periods of rapid house price inflation (when even average families can "seem" rich purely because of a real estate bubble). Moreover, official reports badly underestimate the inequality of wealth, since they are usually based on random sampling methods that almost always miss the few ultra-rich households who make up a tiny share of the total population (but who own a substantial share of total wealth). The best indicator of the precarious concentration of business and financial ownership (and resulting imbalances in economic and political power) is provided by data on the distribution of net financial wealth. The top half of Table 7.2 summarizes some data on financial wealth distribution for selected Anglo-Saxon capitalist economies. In every case included, the richest 1% of the population owns many times more financial wealth (excluding the equity in owner-occupied residences) than the entire bottom half of the population; a clear majority of financial wealth is always owned by the richest decile (10%) of society.

Another startling indicator of wealth distribution is provided by published lists of super-wealthy individuals in various countries (assembled each year by business magazines). These data are summarized on the bottom half of Table 7.2. These reports indicate that in every country, a handful of billionaires single-handedly owns between 5% and 10% of all net financial wealth in each country: more than the entire bottom half of the population.

Country	Year	Source	Total Wealth: Findings
US	2010	Wolff (2012)	The richest 1% of adult Americans owns 42.1% of all non-home financial net worth. The richest 5% owns 71.7% of all non-home net worth, and the richest 10% own 85% of all non-home wealth. The bottom 60% of the US population holds negative financial non-home net worth (equal to −0.9% of the total).
US	2012	Saez and Zucman (2014)	Excluding housing, the richest 0.1% of Americans owns 25.2% of all net wealth. The richest 1% owns 45.9%, and the richest 10% owns 79.3%. The bottom 90% owns just over one-fifth of all wealth. Even including net housing assets, the distribution of wealth is not much more equal: the richest 1% owns 41.8%, while the bottom 90% owns only 22.8%.
US	2013	US Federal Reserve	The wealthiest 10% of households owns 75.3% of all net worth (including home equity). The lower half of all households owns just 1% of all net worth (including home equity). The lowest 25% of households has negative net worth. Financial assets are distributed much more unequally. ▶

			Total Wealth:
Country	Year	Source	Findings
UK	2008–10	HM Revenue & Customs (2014)	The UK government reports detailed wealth distribution based on inheritance taxes collected from the estates of deceased persons; these data underestimate the share of wealth owned by rich households, because very small estates (under £5,000) do not have to file estate tax reports. The richest 0.65% of estates (those with total assets exceeding £2 million each) represented 22% of all financial assets, and 27% of all net financial worth. The next richest 1.5% of estates (between £1 million and £2 million) held another 12% of net financial worth. The lowest fifth of estates had negative net financial worth. The bottom 64% of estates (with total assets under £200,000) held 13% of all net financial worth.
Canada	2005	Statistics Canada (2006)	Statistics Canada reports only very broad data regarding the distribution of household wealth and net worth, on the basis of a small occasional survey of financial security. In 2005 (most recent data), the top quintile (20%) of the population owned 69% of household net worth, and 94% of net financial wealth.
Canada	2011	Canada Revenue Agency (2013)	Income tax statistics provide an indirect indication of the concentration of financial wealth, through data on the distribution of *income* from financial wealth. In Canada the richest 0.5% of tax-filers declared a total of 38% of all income from financial investments (including dividends, interest, and capital gains). The richest 2% of tax-filers declared over 50%. The bottom 72% declared only 15% of all income from financial investments.
Australia	2011–12	Australian Bureau of Statistics (2013)	Excluding owner-occupied property and contents, the richest 20% of society owned 73% of all net worth, The poorest 20% had 0.8% of net worth, and the bottom half of households owned 11% of net worth. The bottom 60% of the population had *negative* net financial wealth, and the richest 20% owned over 100% of all net financial wealth.
Australia	2002	Heady et al. (2008)	Including home equity, the richest 5% of Australian households owns 31% of all net worth, and the richest 10% owns 45%. The bottom 50% of households owns under 9% of all new worth. Financial assets are distributed much more unequally.

Total Wealth:			
Country	Year	Source	Findings
World	2013	Credit Suisse (2014)	There are 32 million individuals in the world (0.7% of the adult global population) with net financial wealth above US$1 million, and they own 41% of all world wealth. Another 361 million individuals (7.7% of all adults) have net financial wealth between US$100,000 and $1 million, and they own another 42.3% of all wealth. The richest 8.4% of the global population thus owns 83.3% of all wealth. Over two-thirds of adults own less than US$10,000 in net financial wealth; together they own 3% of all global wealth.

Sources: Edward Wolff, "The Asset Price Meltdown and the Wealth of the Middle Class," New York University (2012); Emmanuel Saez and Gabriel Zucman, "Wealth Inequality In the United States since 1913," NBER Working Paper #20625 (2014); US Federal Reserve Board of Governors, "Survey of Consumer Finances" (2013); HM Revenue and Customs, "Distribution of Personal Wealth Statistics" (2014) ; Statistics Canada, "The Wealth of Canadians: An Overview of the Results of the Survey of Financial Security," Summary Tables (2006); Canada Revenue Agency, "Income Statistics, T1 Final Statistics" (2013); Australian Bureau of Statistics, "Household Wealth and Wealth Distribution" (2013); Bruce Heady, Diana Warren, and Mark Wooden, " The structure and distribution of household wealth in Australia: cohort differences and retirement issues," Australia Department of Families, Housing, Community Services, and Indigenous Affairs (2008); Credit Suisse, *Global Wealth Report* (2014).

The Wealth of Billionaires:					
Country	Published Source	No. of Billionaires (2014)*	Billionaire Wealth	Total Household Financial Net Worth	Billionaire Share of Total Wealth
US	*Forbes* Billionaires List	492	US$2.5 trillion	US$52.0 trillion	6%
UK	*Sunday Times* Rich List	213	£373 billion	£3.6 trillion	10%
Canada	*Canadian Business* Rich 100	78	C$211 billion	C$3.5 trillion	6%
Australia	*BRW* Rich 200	39	A$115 billion	A$2.0 trillion	6%
World	*Forbes* Billionaires List	1645	US$6.6 trillion	US$135.5 trillion	5%

* Billionaires defined as having net worth over $1 billion in national currency for the US, Canada, Australia; over US$1 billion for world; and over £500 million for UK.

Sources: Author's calculations from data in US Federal Reserve Board of Governors; UK Office of National Statistics; Statistics Canada; Australian Bureau of Statistics; *Forbes*; *Sunday Times*; *Canadian Business*; *BRW*, Boston Consulting Group.

Most business wealth is owned (and increasingly tightly controlled) by a surprisingly small minority of society. It is still meaningful, therefore, to speak of a class of "capitalists," defined as those individuals who control, and/or own a dominant stake in, the private businesses which undertake most production in modern capitalist economies.

I would include in that group of capitalists both major owners and top managers. By "top managers," I refer to those individuals who control the day-to-day actions of businesses through their positions as top managers and executives. (We exclude very small businesses, in which the owner and family members perform most of the required work.) Those top managers account for less than 2 percent of all the work done in the economy; moreover, they almost always have significant ownership stakes in the companies they work for.

There is another group of individuals who can also be considered part of the capitalist class: those who own enough business wealth to support themselves comfortably without having to work at all. The wealth of these "major owners" may be held directly through ownership of particular companies, or indirectly through large amounts of corporate shares. Let's conservatively assume an ongoing average profit rate of 5 percent (most businesses earn more than this). Then an individual owning $2 million in business and financial wealth (not counting the value of their own home) can receive an income of $100,000 per year purely from their wealth. That's enough to rank well within the top 5 percent of the income distribution, without having to do any work at all (other than go to the bank to deposit dividend cheques!). Many of these rich individuals choose to work; but the key distinction

here is that they don't *have* to work, since their business wealth is sufficient to support themselves very comfortably *without* working. Statistical surveys indicate that less than 2 percent of individuals in Anglo-Saxon economies own business and financial wealth on this scale; and there is considerable overlap between this category and the top managers.

Either way, these top managers and major owners have a substantial, direct personal stake in the profits of business. Both groups identify closely with the business community, and exert their (disproportionate) political, social, and personal influence on its behalf. Put together, this class of top managers and wealthy investors accounts for perhaps 2 percent of the population of developed capitalist economies. They are the modern capitalist class: less visible, more sophisticated, possibly even more compassionate than the capitalists of the 1700s. But they are

---

The 1% and the 99%

The terrible aftershocks of the 2008–09 GLOBAL FINANCIAL CRISIS sparked a new grass-roots movement called "Occupy." It all started in New York City in September 2011, when activists established an encampment in a public park in the Wall Street financial district. They were protesting the lopsided nature of the government's response to the meltdown: spending trillions to bail out banks and investors, even as millions of Americans were being ejected from their foreclosed homes. Occupy protests then spread quickly to cities around the world.

The movement used a powerful slogan, "We are the 99%," to highlight the contrast in economic prospects between the very richest members of society, and the rest of us. Important support came from economists (like Nobel prize winner Joseph Stiglitz*) who also focused on the 1% versus the 99% in analyzing the lopsided concentration of income and power in modern capitalism.

The Occupy movement's contrast between the 1% and the 99% almost matches the simple description of economic classes under capitalism described above. We have estimated that just over 2% of people in advanced capitalist economies are top managers of companies in which most work is performed by hired employees, and/or possess enough wealth to support themselves comfortably without working. (Most top executives also own enough financial wealth to support themselves without working, so the two categories largely overlap.) Everyone else in society must work to support themselves: most commonly in the form of wage labour (around 85% of the population), or else at small businesses or farms where they (and their family members) perform most of the work.

In my view, therefore, dividing society into the 2% and the 98% would be a slightly more accurate categorization. But that wouldn't make for nearly as catchy a slogan at protest rallies!

* Joseph E. Stiglitz, "Of the 1%, By the 1%, For the 1%," *Vanity Fair* (May 2011).

richer than ever, and their well-being still depends on the profitability of businesses they directly or indirectly own, but in which most of the productive work is done by paid help. And their actions and decisions are dominant in determining how the economy develops.

Roughly another 10–15 percent of individuals in developed capitalist economies are owners of much smaller businesses (including farms), for which they and their family members perform most of the required work. But these owner-managers are not really "capitalists," for two reasons: they must actively work (since their ownership of wealth is not sufficient to provide a comfortable living on the basis of ownership income alone), and their companies do not primarily depend on the wage labour of others.

As described in Chapter 5, the vast majority of households in capitalist societies – the remaining 85 percent or so of the population – depend almost exclusively on the wage labour they supply to employers for the income they receive over their lives. At any given point in time, not all the workers in these households are employed: some are unemployed, sick or disabled, or retired (in which case, in modern capitalism, they rely on government social programs to supplement their incomes). But over their lives, their ability to sell their labour is their only source of independent income. They do not own significant financial wealth. They are the modern working class.

Of course, there are many differences between different groups of workers: their skills and training, the nature of their work, their incomes, their relative power, and their relative security. But they all have one fundamental thing in common: they all support themselves by offering their labour to someone else in return for a wage or salary. And together they constitute the vast majority of society.

The logic of profit

The hunt for profit is the dominant driving force of a capitalist economy. And there are important consequences arising from the fact that most production is undertaken with the explicit goal of generating maximum profits for the people who own the company.

Since Adam Smith's time, most economists have emphasized the broader social benefits of "greed." They argue that the pursuit of profit will encourage people to work harder, and be more creative in developing new products and new ways of producing them. In reality, however, we've seen that at least 85 percent of people in capitalism don't actually work for profit – they work for wages and salaries. So the importance of the profit motive in eliciting work, at the level of *individual* psychology, is vastly overstated.

At the corporate level, however, profits are indeed very important. In fact, for private businesses, they are the meaning of life. Corporate managers and directors act quickly and decisively to ensure their businesses generate as much profit as possible. They closely supervise the work of their paid employees (and in this way, profits can be an *indirect* motivation for individual workers – not because they'll earn profits if they work hard, but because they'll be fired by their profit-seeking boss if they don't!). And they organize their companies' activities in line with that never-ending hunt for profit. Some profit-seeking behaviour is beneficial to the overall economy, but much is not. It is utterly invalid to assume that profit-seeking automatically leads to efficiency and productivity – especially if we define "efficiency," appropriately, as the extent to which economic activity translates into human well-being.

Creative companies can devise all sorts of different ways of earning profits. Some are useful: developing higher-quality new products, and developing better, more efficient ways of producing them. But competitive markets can also reward companies for doing things that are utterly useless, from the perspective of human welfare (see Table 7.3). And if lax laws and regulations allow them to, profit-seeking companies will do things that are downright destructive to workers, communities, customers, and innocent bystanders.

The problem arises from the distinction between the *private* costs of an economic activity, and its *social* costs. A private company aims to maximize its own private profits. It does this by maximizing its private revenues, and minimizing its private

Table 7.3 Useless and Destructive Activities that Also Happen to be Profitable

---

Activities Performed by Profit-Seeking Companies that are Socially Useless:

- Advertising
- Developing copycat products that have no real additional value
- Excess or showy packaging to attract buyer interest
- Maintaining more capacity than required, in order to "catch" new sales or supplies before a competitor does
- Producing things designed to break down or become obsolescent, forcing customers to buy new ones

Activities Performed by Profit-Seeking Companies that are Socially Destructive:

- Selling products that are harmful, unsafe or dangerous
- Tricking consumers into thinking they are buying something they're not
- Allocating resources to directly undermine competitors (through disruption, spying, or sabotage)
- Spending to prevent others from duplicating your work (such as anti-copying protections)
- Limiting production of a useful product in order to boost profits
- Shifting costs (including hidden costs like pollution) to consumers, suppliers, or the public at large
- Advertising that makes people feel inferior or inadequate if they don't purchase a product

---

costs. One way to minimize costs is to shift them to someone else. For example, pollution is a way for a company to avoid a cost of production (namely, the waste it produces) by simply dumping it into the broader environment. Alternatively, a company may do something that is socially destructive but privately profitable. Selling harmful products like cigarettes is an example of this activity. By the same token, there are things that would benefit society hugely, but which are *not* undertaken because the private benefits to companies are insufficient. A literally sickening example of this failure is the misallocation of research and marketing efforts by global pharmaceutical giants, whose priorities are guided by their own profits, not public health (see box).

Private companies are efficient and creative at maximizing their private profits and minimizing their private costs. But there's no reason to assume that those actions will maximize the social benefits and minimize the social costs

---

In Sickness and in Health

The global pharmaceutical industry provides one of the strongest illustrations of how the profit motive can misdirect human creativity and badly misallocate resources. It costs hundreds of millions of dollars to develop a new drug (including expensive trials to make sure it is safe). But once the drug is ready, companies (anxious to recoup their costs) charge very high prices (backed up by strict patent laws), thus limiting its human usefulness. That's like buying an expensive new car – but then not driving it, because it cost so much! The most deadly infectious diseases in the world (like malaria, dysentery, and measles) mostly affect poor people who cannot afford private medicines, so the global industry does not invest much in new treatments. Instead, it allocates most R&D to less pressing, but more profitable, opportunities. Pharmaceutical companies prefer drugs that require long-term use (such as heart disease, cholesterol, and arthritis medicines), for the obvious reason that those ongoing treatments create an unending, lucrative market. One of the most glaring misallocations of all: the spread of drug-resistant bacteria poses an enormous public health threat to populations around the world, with the potential to return human civilization to the death and misery of the pre-penicillin era. Yet pharmaceutical companies invest little in the search for new antibiotics, because they do not see short-term antibiotic prescriptions as an especially profitable market. A better approach, favoured by many public health experts, is to publicly fund drug research, allocating the most attention to the most dangerous diseases, and then make new drugs available to those who need them at their direct cost of production (or less). There is no evidence that scientists working in privately-owned labs invent better drugs than those working in universities, hospitals, or public institutions – and the resulting wider accessibility to new treatments would save millions of lives.

Measuring (and Paying) Profit

Profits result when a company sells what it produces for more than it cost to produce it. A company collects revenues from its sales, from which it must pay wages to its workers and cover the cost of raw materials, parts, and services used in the course of production. The company must also account for the cost of wear and tear on capital equipment (called DEPRECIATION). If some of the company's finance was borrowed from banks or other lenders, interest costs on those loans must also be deducted. The residual left at the end, after paying all those bills, is the company's profit.

In addition to measuring the mass of profit (in dollars), it is also useful to measure the *rate* of profit. This indicates how profitable a company is, relative to the amount of capital that was invested in it. This is important for comparing profitability over time, and between different companies. There are various ways to measure the profit rate. For the owners of a company, the RETURN ON EQUITY is the best measure. It is the ratio of bottom-line profits to the amount of shareholder's equity invested in the company (not including loans from banks and other lenders). Companies usually aim to generate a return on equity of at least 10 percent per year, or more. Other concepts of the profit rate include the RETURN ON ASSETS or the PROFIT MARGIN.

A company's financial performance is described in its financial statements. If the company is publicly-traded (with its shares bought and sold on the stock market), it is required to disclose those statements to the public. Quarterly or semi-annual statements provide quick updates; annual reports provide more detail; supplementary reports filed with financial regulators (such as the detailed "10-K" forms published in the US, or prospectus statements issued whenever a company issues new shares) provide the most detailed portrait of the company's overall business.

There are various ways for investors to receive the profits of the companies they own. If they have loaned capital to a company, they receive INTEREST on those loans, at a certain percentage per year. Shareholders (and some types of lenders) receive DIVIDENDS, which are fixed cash payments paid (typically every quarter or every year) to the owner of each share. Most companies store away a portion of their profits to fund future investments; these are called RETAINED EARNINGS. Another way for shareholders to realize their profits is by selling some of their shares. If a company is profitable and growing, its share price will rise. Shareholders can then convert profits into cold hard cash by selling a few shares (this is called a CAPITAL GAIN).

The tax systems of most capitalist countries are heavily biased toward company owners and financial investors (not surprising, given their political and economic influence). As a result, tax rates on dividend and capital gains income are usually much lower than tax rates on labour income. This is especially ironic since the people who receive most of that investment income are very rich.

Visit www.economicsforeveryone.com for a short "how-to" guide on how to obtain and understand company financial statistics.

of economic activity. To attain a closer match between private cost-benefit and social cost-benefit calculations requires forcing companies to respect goals other than just maximizing their private profits. In turn, this requires that corporations be constrained by government regulations, unions, and other limits – to push companies to reduce their social costs and increase the social benefits of their actions. Alternatively, we could organize production in different ways, in order to directly focus on maximum social benefits, instead of hoping that the public interest is maximized as an accidental by-product of private profit. (We will discuss some possible ways to do this in Chapter 29.)

8

Working for a Living

Why labour is different

A **COMMODITY** is anything that is bought and sold for money. With the advent of capitalism and widespread wage labour, labour itself became a commodity. And neoclassical economics analyzes labour essentially like any other commodity: there are suppliers (workers), demanders (employers), and a price (the wage rate). In theory, if governments and unions stay out of the way, fluctuations in the price of labour will supposedly ensure that everyone finds a job, in which case labour supply equals labour demand and there is no **UNEMPLOYMENT**. If unemployment exists, just let the wage fall; employers will hire more workers, eventually absorbing all the slack in the labour market.

This neoclassical story is simplistic and very inaccurate. It is true that labour is bought and sold for money (and hence is a commodity). But lurking under the surface are several crucial differences that make labour totally unique among commodities, and explain why the labour market is different from all others. They also explain why the standard neoclassical advice – cut wages to eliminate unemployment – does not often work.

Here are the most important factors that make labour unique. Most are obvious even to an untrained onlooker, yet they have been curiously difficult for many economists (with their supply-and-demand mindset) to grasp:

- Labour is alive. Labourers are living, thinking beings, who can influence their surroundings and circumstances. One important consequence of this is that they always find ways – individual or collective – to resist work arrangements or practices they believe are unfair.
- Labour itself is not produced as a commodity, for someone's profit. It is produced (or, more specifically, *reproduced*) within families, as part of the normal lifecycle of human existence. We'll discuss the economics of reproduction – but not the physiology of it! – in the next chapter.
- Labour is "produced" by households, which are economic *consumers*. Yet labour is "consumed" by private companies (and other employers), which are economic *producers*. Therefore, the production (or supply) of labour

depends on consumption, while the consumption of (or demand for) labour depends on production.

- No employer hires labour for its own sake, just to have a few more bodies around the workplace. Labour is always hired to do something: namely, to produce a good or service that is then sold to final customers. The demand for labour is thus derived from (and dependent on) the demand for whatever it is that the workers are producing.

- Unlike other commodities, the labour market almost never "clears." When labour supply equals labour demand, then everyone who wants to work can find a job (economists call this **FULL EMPLOYMENT**), and unemployment is zero. In practice, however, unemployment almost *always* exists under capitalism. (Bizarrely, despite observed reality, some neoclassical economists still claim that unemployment does not actually exist.)

- Every market exchange reflects a balance of power (economic power, and other kinds of power) between the buyer and seller, not just "pure" supply and demand forces. But the balance – or *imbalance* – of power is especially obvious and important in the case of labour. Wage labourers must sell their labour to survive. Employers, on the other hand, are much less desperate to consummate the deal. While they *need* labour to produce (and hence make profit), this need is never as immediate as a worker's need to put food on the table. And the asymmetry in size between employers (especially larger ones) and individual workers adds further to the imbalance. A large employer hardly notices the departure of any particular worker – but each worker painfully and immediately notices the disappearance of their job. For all these reasons, a clear asymmetry in power between employers and employees is a fundamental feature of the labour market. Employment is indeed an exchange (trading labour for money), but it is a very unequal exchange.

- When labour is bought, there is an important distinction between what the buyer purchases, and what they actually desire. Employers need someone to perform *work* (human effort or activity). But what they purchase, usually, is labour *time*: that is, a certain number of hours a worker agrees to be on the job. Converting time into work is a central and complicated problem of employment. Moreover, it happens *inside* the firm, in a context of hierarchical control and management authority, not through a "market."

- There is not one labour market, but many different labour markets. Different groups of workers tend to work in very different types of jobs: men and women, different racialized and cultural groups, different skills and occupations, and different regions. These large differences in jobs and wages are a normal, ongoing feature of the labour market; and various institutional, cultural, economic, and even legal barriers keep these various parts of the labour market separate. Economists call this **LABOUR MARKET**

SEGMENTATION; it differs from other markets where competition tends to produce more uniform outcomes.

Labour extraction and labour discipline

The distinction between labour time and labour effort (or actual work) gives rise to a central and fundamental challenge facing employers under capitalism, which we call the LABOUR EXTRACTION problem. It is not enough for an employer to hire a worker. They must also supervise the worker to perform the desired quantity and quality of work. LABOUR INTENSITY is the degree to which a worker performs the desired work effort during the hours they are employed.

Employees are paid for their time. They do not own the company, nor have any direct or meaningful stake in its profits. At the individual level, their personal work effort seldom has any measurable impact on whether the company succeeds or not. Therefore, once they have a job, why should they work hard? To some extent, most individuals genuinely prefer to use their time productively: it helps the time pass, and adds to one's sense of self-worth. But left on their own, most workers would not work as hard or as fast as employers want, nor follow the employer's instructions precisely – especially given the unpleasant, tiring, boring, and often unsafe nature of many jobs. Employers therefore invest vast effort and resources in a system of labour extraction, to enhance labour intensity and extract maximum effort from each hour of paid labour time.

Like a farmer trying to motivate a donkey, effective labour discipline typically requires both a carrot and a stick; both a positive incentive and a potential punishment. Why should a paid employee work hard? Perhaps they will make more money if they do. And perhaps they'll get fired if they don't. Management labour extraction strategies use both carrots and sticks.

Some jobs link compensation directly to work effort. Piece-work systems, which pay workers for each bit of work they perform, are one example of this approach; so are contract workers (hired to perform a specific task, and paid only when that task is completed). This strategy has limited application, however: usually employers want their workers to be more flexible, performing a range of hard-to-specify functions (rather than simply churning out a certain number of widgets per hour). Even in straightforward jobs, piece-work systems produce notoriously bad quality,

---

Just Enough

"Most people work just hard enough not to get fired,
and get paid just enough money not to quit."

George Carlin, US comedian (1997).

teamwork, and employee morale. Other attempts to link compensation to work effort are even less reliable – like profit-sharing bonuses, or tips paid to restaurant waiters. Here the link between an individual's work effort and their personal compensation is very indirect (since the total output of a factory, or the quality of a restaurant meal, depends on the performance of the entire organization – not just one person's effort). Of course, if you are recognized as a "good worker" you might get a promotion or a raise, but at best this is an indirect, long-term incentive.

That's why the stick, not just the carrot, must always be present, and the biggest stick of all is the threat of dismissal. Employers crave the power to fire workers whose performance is judged inferior – not just to be rid of those particular workers, but more importantly to motivate and discipline the rest of the workforce. Indeed, in the eyes of the boss, provisions limiting their power to fire indiscriminately are among the most hated features of union contracts; by the same token, winning some protection against arbitrary dismissal is one of the greatest benefits of belonging to a union. But to make the threat of job loss meaningful, several conditions must be met:

- Employers must have the legal and contractual right to fire staff. Even if they don't use that power often, it has to be there (to motivate frightened workers).
- Employers have to be able to distinguish well-performing workers from undesirable workers. So employers spend heavily on supervision and monitoring systems – everything from shop-floor supervisors looking over workers' shoulders, to sophisticated electronic monitoring technologies (which can measure the speed of cashiers and typists, spy on telephone and e-mail conversations, and track the precise location of drivers and couriers).
- Losing one's job must impose a major cost on fired workers, so that the fear of being fired elicits the desired discipline and compliance. The out-of-pocket loss that a fired worker incurs is called the COST OF JOB LOSS. It depends on several variables: how long they can expect to be unemployed (before finding another job), what (if anything) they receive in unemployment insurance benefits while they are jobless, and how the wages and benefits at their new job compare to what they earned in their old job.

If the labour market actually worked like neoclassical economists imagine (with labour supply equal to labour demand, and competition ensuring that all equivalent workers are paid the same wage), then the cost of job loss would be *zero*. There's no unemployment, and everyone makes the same wage. If someone gets fired, they simply go out the next day and find another job paying the same wage. This would make it impossible for bosses to enforce any workplace discipline whatsoever (something that radical economists, such as Michal Kalecki, have always understood well – see box).

"On Guard"

The labour extraction problem facing employers requires them to invest in often-expensive systems of monitoring, supervision, and discipline. That effort can itself consume enormous resources – and this constitutes a substantial inefficiency in the overall economic system.

US economists Arjun Jayadev and Samuel Bowles* have attempted to measure the amount of real effort required to monitor, supervise, discipline, and frighten workers in the US economy. This includes supervisors, monitors, security guards, police and military personnel, prison guards (as well as prisoners), the unemployed (who discipline other workers through their own visible hardship), and others. They come to the surprising conclusion that one-quarter of all working-age adults in the US economy are engaged in one or another of these "guard" duties. More equal societies don't need to devote as many resources to keeping the less-well-off in line; they estimate that in Switzerland, for example, only one-tenth of workers serve guard functions. Too much reliance on the stick, and not enough on the carrot, undermines real productivity and well-being.

* Arjun Jayadev and Samuel Bowles, "Guard Labor," *Journal of Development Economics* 79 (2006, pp. 328–48).

The implications of the labour extraction problem are many. First, workers and employers experience directly conflicting interests – not just over wage levels, but also over the organization and intensity of work. Second, employers' desire to enforce labour discipline will affect everything from the way compensation is paid, to the nature of workplace technology. In fact, sometimes companies will invest in particular technologies not because they are inherently more efficient, but simply because they facilitate "better" labour discipline (hence boosting *profitability*, which is quite separate from boosting *efficiency*). The dramatic expansion of workplace monitoring and surveillance technology has clearly strengthened the disciplining hand of employers. Since the "stick" (close supervision) has become cheaper and more effective, employers feel less need to use the "carrot" – and hence real wages in many occupations subject to this kind of surveillance have stagnated or declined.

Finally, it is clear that a central goal of neoliberal economic and social policy has been to alter the fundamental balance of power in the employment relationship, by recreating a broad degree of insecurity and discipline among workers. After the heady, prosperous years of the Golden Age, when workers felt economically secure and more confident in the workplace, employers longed for a more insecure, fearful workforce. And with neoliberalism, they got it.

One way to strengthen labour discipline is through legal changes making it easier for employers to fire troublesome workers. Another is to substantially increase

Capitalism's Full-Employment Sickness

Along with John Maynard Keynes, the Polish economist Michal Kalecki discovered that government spending policies could eliminate unemployment. But would capitalism even *want* to achieve this seemingly wonderful outcome? Kalecki thought not. With remarkable foresight, he explained in 1943 why full employment, while technically possible, would eventually encounter fierce resistance from employers:

"Lasting full employment is not at all to [business leaders'] liking. The workers would get 'out of hand' and the 'captains of industry' would be anxious to 'teach them a lesson.' Moreover, the price increase in the upswing is to the disadvantage of small and big rentiers [financial investors] and makes them 'boom tired.' In this situation a powerful bloc is likely to be formed between big business and the rentier interests, and they would probably find more than one economist to declare that the situation was manifestly unsound. The pressure of all of these forces, and in particular of big business, would most probably induce the government to return to the orthodox policy."

Kalecki thus remarkably predicted the economic and political U-turn that occurred with the advent of neoliberalism. Three decades of something close to full employment emboldened workers and undermined the day-to-day power of employers in the workplace, motivating shared efforts by both employers and financial investors to restore a desired, "efficient" cushion of unemployment. Kalecki concluded that new systems of wage determination and workplace decision-making (likely requiring a socialist ownership structure) would ultimately be necessary to sustain full employment.

the cost of job loss, once a worker is fired. Initially, this involved re-creating mass unemployment. Beginning in the late 1970s, interest rates were raised to deliberately create and maintain a "cushion" of unemployment. The disciplining power of unemployment was reinforced by reductions in unemployment benefits (in many countries, workers who quit or are fired are denied unemployment benefits altogether). The effect on labour discipline is obvious: now, if a worker is fired, they have nothing to fall back on. These changes undermined the bargaining power of all workers, even those who never needed unemployment benefits. The higher cost of job loss thus casts a pall over wage determination – even for workers whose jobs are relatively secure.

The widening gaps between different groups of workers, and a more intense segmentation of labour markets, also enhanced the cost of job loss and hence labour discipline. Workers in "core" jobs (those requiring especially important skills, or in highly productive industries) receive premium wages and benefits, and enjoy some long-term job security (though never fully guaranteed). On the other hand, workers in **PRECARIOUS** jobs (like part-time, temporary, or contract positions) receive much lower wages, with much less security. Some receive no income at all: like the growing army of "interns" who now work for free, in hopes of eventually landing a paying job. Even if the official unemployment rate is relatively low, therefore, the threat of being "exiled" from a high-wage core job to a low-wage precarious job still constitutes a powerful disciplining threat for workers in the higher-wage positions. (The more that wages fall in marginal jobs, however, the harder it becomes for employers in *those* industries to impose meaningful labour discipline – something that is obvious from the poor quality of service that is often delivered in those low-wage industries.)

The effectiveness of neoliberal policies in disciplining labour and reducing unit labour costs is visible in the stark shift in wage trends that occurred beginning around the early 1980s. Real wages stagnated in most countries, in the face of higher unemployment, attacks on unions, and reductions in income security and other measures that supported workers' bargaining power. Yet productivity continued to grow, thanks both to employers' renewed power in the workplace and to continued technological progress. Figure 8.1 illustrates the sharp divergence of real wages from labour productivity in the US economy that coincides perfectly with the arrival of neoliberalism. The combination of flat wages with growing productivity implies steadily falling unit labour costs, and this has been a major

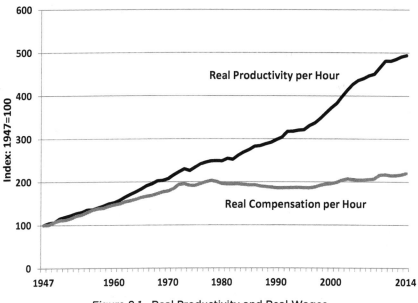

Figure 8.1 Real Productivity and Real Wages
US business sector

Source: Author's calculations from the US Bureau of Labor Statistics,
Economic Policy Institute, State of Working America.

factor in the strong increase in business profitability that has been achieved under this harsh new regime.

Workers and bosses: sites of conflict

Private employers do not hire workers as a public service. They employ people to produce something and sell it for profit. Companies constantly try to cut production costs to maximize the profit margin that remains at the bottom line. In fact, as we will see in Chapter 11, competition from other capitalists *forces* companies to ruthlessly minimize costs, on pain of being driven out of business.

Employers aim to produce the maximum possible output, for the lowest possible labour cost. They are therefore interested both in minimizing wages and in maximizing the output of hired labour. How much workers produce in a given period of work time is their **PRODUCTIVITY**. Productivity depends on many factors. Labour intensity can affect realized productivity. By eliminating rest periods and "cracking the whip" to enforce a faster pace of work, employers can boost output per hour – but only to a point. Sustained growth in productivity requires improvements in genuine efficiency: that is, how effectively a given amount of work effort translates into actual output. True efficiency depends on technology, work organization, and the nature of the product being made (productivity tends to be higher when workers are hired to produce high-quality, valuable products, rather than lower-cost bulk commodities). The ratio of labour costs to productivity is called **UNIT LABOUR COST**. It represents the amount that employers must pay their workers for each unit of output they produce.

Employers strive to minimize unit labour cost, and they do this by addressing both parts of the equation: reducing wages and boosting productivity. The following simple formula is a convenient way to summarize the various interactions between workers and employers – often conflictual, and occasionally harmonious.

$$\text{Unit labour cost} = \frac{\text{Compensation}}{\text{Productivity}} = \frac{\text{Compensation}}{\text{Intensity * Efficiency}}$$

To reduce unit labour costs, employers can try to cut compensation (wages and benefits) on the top of the equation, or they can try to increase productivity on the bottom of the equation. Remember, a 10 percent improvement in productivity is just as good for employers as a 10 percent reduction in compensation. And there are two distinct ways to boost productivity: by increasing labour intensity, or by increasing true efficiency. Table 8.1 summarizes these various strategies for reducing unit labour costs.

The more employers cut wages and benefits, the worse off workers are, so this is an obvious source of conflict between workers and their bosses. Increasing the intensity of work will also harm the quality (and sometimes the safety) of work life, so this is another obvious source of conflict. Improvements in the genuine efficiency of work are more complicated. Efficiency improvements can be attained in ways that are harmful, neutral, or even beneficial for workers. One example of a beneficial efficiency improvement is the use of ergonomic machinery that enhances output but also reduces workplace injuries (such as strain injuries from reaching or lifting).

Table 8.1 **Strategies to Reduce Unit Labour Costs**

$$\text{Unit labour cost} \quad = \quad \frac{\text{Compensation}}{\text{Intensity} * \text{Efficiency}}$$

Strategy	Impact on Workers
Reduce Compensation: • Cut wages or salaries • Cut fringe benefits (pensions, health benefits) • For "core" workers: reduce the hourly cost of benefits by lengthening the work day, utilize more overtime • For workers in precarious jobs: pay no benefits, utilize part-time labour • Outsource work to lower-cost suppliers or contractors	Negative
Increase Labour Intensity: • Speed up pace of work (e.g. faster assembly line) • Enhance supervision and monitoring to require faster work • Reduce paid lunch breaks and rest breaks • Reduce paid vacations and holidays • Require unpaid overtime from salaried workers • "Lean production": eliminate any idle time in the working day	Negative
Increase True Efficiency: • Introduce labour-saving equipment • Use new machinery to reduce lifting or reaching • Produce higher-quality, more unique products	Positive, Negative, or Neutral

Increases in efficiency or intensity can indirectly facilitate higher compensation, but only if workers have sufficient bargaining power to win a share of the higher productivity that results.

Moreover, higher productivity can translate indirectly into higher compensation for workers. There's nothing automatic about the link, but when productivity grows, workers (and their unions) can demand higher compensation without affecting the profit margins of their employers. (On the other hand, higher productivity can also translate into layoffs and unemployment, depending on what is happening in the broader economy – since employers now need fewer workers to produce a given amount of output.)

For this reason, workers and unions sometimes cooperate with employers to enhance efficiency, especially around initiatives that are deemed neutral or beneficial for workers. Even unpleasant increases in the intensity of work can be (at least partially) offset by higher compensation; this can be a way for employers to "buy off" workers into accepting (or at least tolerating) a more intense and disciplined workplace. Employers always use a carrot as well as a stick to maintain effective labour discipline; for this reason, they may not wish to drive down wages to the lowest level possible, but rather may prefer to keep them relatively "generous" as a way of eliciting more intensity and loyalty. In many ways, then, compensation and productivity can influence each other.

Let's sum up the different ways that employers and workers relate to each other. Employers want to pay less, and make jobs more intense. Workers want the opposite. That's why most of the unit labour cost-reducing initiatives in Table 8.1 are clearly negative for workers. But sometimes the interests of these two opposing sides can coincide (especially when productivity opens up economic space for higher compensation). When we study the impacts of competition in Chapter 11, we'll see other ways in which the interests of workers and their *specific* employer might further coincide: workers may feel a need to help their particular employer

succeed in competition with other firms. (This strategy might help some groups of workers, but it cannot help *all* workers.) Clever employers try to build this loyalty, using gimmicks like free turkeys at Christmas and token profit-sharing bonuses to promote a sense of togetherness. But these can only paper over the fundamental schisms between the two sides that result from the logic of private profit and wage labour.

The relationships between capitalists and workers, therefore, are complex and troubled. Like two spouses who squabble continuously but can't seem to break up, the two great classes of capitalism seem to need each other – yet they still haven't yet found a way to truly get along.

Unions and collective bargaining

We saw earlier that the employment relationship reflects an inherent asymmetry between workers and employers. Individual workers need a job to support themselves and their families. Their work choices may be limited by unemployment, labour market segmentation, or a lack of employment alternatives (especially in smaller communities). An employer, on the other hand, can easily replace any individual worker (unless they possess some very special skill). So at the individual level, workers need their employer a lot more than their employer needs them.

Collectively, however, employers depend on their workers to perform all or most of the labour required for a private company to operate and generate profits. Workers realized very early in the history of capitalism that they could win a better deal by joining forces to take advantage of their combined bargaining power, and negotiate collectively for better wages and working conditions. It is difficult (although not impossible) for an employer to replace their whole workforce at once. Therefore, workers have much more clout dealing with their employer collectively, rather than one at a time.

Early efforts to organize unions encountered ruthless, often violent opposition from employers, backed up in many cases by government and police measures to crush organizing campaigns or outlaw unions altogether. In the twentieth century, unions won more acceptance, for both economic and political reasons. Labour-friendly political parties gained influence, and sometimes power. And after World War II, business leaders felt more pressure to accommodate workers' demands (for better pay and labour rights). Initially, rapid productivity growth allowed companies to pay union-level wages while still generating strong profits. With the advent of neoliberalism, however, business returned to a more confrontational attitude, and has actively undermined union power ever since. The legal, economic, and cultural environment facing unions has become very hostile in most capitalist countries. The experience has been worst in the US, where unionization has been slipping steadily; unions there now represent barely one-tenth of the workforce, largely explaining why America's economy is now the most unequal of all developed countries.

The ability of unions to organize and bargain effectively depends on several factors:

- **The legal climate**   Specific laws regulating union organizing, bargaining rights, the right to strike, and other aspects of bargaining can alter union success in subtle but powerful ways.

- **The attitudes of workers**   Do workers demand better treatment from their employers, or have they been conditioned to accept their lot in life? Can they stick together in order to win things collectively? (Trade unionists call this *solidarity*.)

- **The cost of job loss**   The same factors that enforce labour discipline in the workplace also make it harder to organize unions. Higher unemployment, reduced social programs, precarious work, and sharper labour market segmentation all undermine union activity – not least because union sympathizers fear being fired for their activities.

- **Productivity**   If total productivity is growing rapidly, then workers can win higher compensation without harming profits or threatening their company's future. On the other hand, if higher productivity comes about mostly through greater labour intensity, then union activity and solidarity may be undermined in highly-disciplined workplaces.

- **Competition**   If competition between companies is very intense, then it is difficult for a union to make gains with one employer – since it may then experience higher costs, lower profits, and lower sales than its competitors. Competitive pressures have definitely become more intense in recent decades in most industries, and this has undermined union power. The alternative for unions is to organize and bargain for all workers across an industry at once (using sectoral or pattern bargaining techniques); this is more effective, but hard to attain.

Market forces will never guarantee workers a decent share of the wealth they produce – even under vibrant economic and productivity conditions. As we have seen, employers pay wages just high enough to elicit desired labour discipline from their workers. This level depends on factors such as workers' legal and union rights, labour market conditions (including unemployment and segmentation), and broader social policies (which influence how desperate workers are to keep their jobs).

No society without strong and effective unions and widespread collective bargaining has ever achieved mass prosperity, whereby most workers are able to attain decent living standards, security, and well-being – what is commonly (if misleadingly) called a "middle class" lifestyle. Indeed, it was the postwar expansion of unions and collective bargaining that created that "middle class" in the first place. Until then, there was no expectation that workers would experience anything other than near-poverty and perpetual insecurity. The degree of unionization is one of the most important factors determining wage levels, working conditions, hours of work, inequality, and poverty. In my view, the ability of workers to protect and strengthen their unions will be essential if they are to limit and eventually reverse the negative economic and social consequences of neoliberalism.

Play Nice

In capitalism, wages and working conditions are determined mostly by the brute economic strength of employers, relative to the generally weaker power of workers. Who is most desperate, who enjoys more flexibility, who has the most power to enforce a desired deal? It is little wonder, then, that living standards have stagnated under neoliberalism, as employers flex their pumped-up muscles.

Imagine, however, a totally different approach to managing the conflicting interests of workers and employers, rather than relying on pure economic power to see who wins. After all, in legal affairs, conflict resolution is generally guided by legal precedent, principles of natural justice, and other "more civilized" criteria. Disputes are not settled according to who is the biggest or strongest. Isn't it possible to govern work relationships through a similarly civilized "rule of law"?

That was exactly the dream of early social reformers in New Zealand at the dawn of the twentieth century. Disturbed by a wave of harsh, often violent strikes in the 1890s, they devised a brand new system of industrial conciliation and arbitration. It tried to replicate, in the realm of labour relations, the same methods of dispute settlement and rule of law that prevailed in other legal areas, with the goal of preventing violence and equitably solving disagreements. The idea was to explicitly benchmark wages, benefits, and working conditions on the basis of productivity, profitability, and social goals – instead of having those things determined by a never-ending power struggle between employers and workers. Court-like arbitration bodies were established to hear arguments from employers and unions, and then issue judgments that covered workers in each industry. A decade later a similar system was introduced in Australia. Strikes were rare; incomes rose steadily in line with productivity; and inequality was moderated. Indeed, by the 1970s New Zealand boasted one of the most egalitarian economies in the world, on par with the Nordic countries.

By the 1980s, however, employers rebelled against this system, demanding the same freedom to minimize labour costs and discipline workers as was being enjoyed by their emboldened counterparts in other Anglo-Saxon economies. The system was dismantled entirely in New Zealand, and only a remnant remains in Australia. When capitalists have the upper hand, it seems, they definitely prefer brute strength to rule of law.

9

Reproduction (for Economists!)

Where do people come from?

Economics is called the "dismal science," and that reputation is often well-deserved. Economists, it seems, can make anything dry and boring – even sex!

Whereas the rest of the world associates reproduction with love, commitment, fulfilment, and (of course) sex, economists view reproduction as a rather more dull undertaking. For them, reproduction is the *economic* re-creation of the human race. This includes the biological process of reproduction. But it also includes the sustenance, care, and training of people, so that they can lead fully productive economic lives. **REPRODUCTION**, therefore, is much more than making babies: it also means raising them, caring for them, and educating them. And it includes caring for the grown-ups, too: feeding them, providing them with rest and recreation, keeping them healthy and strong – and then sending them back to work, lunchbox packed, on Monday morning.

Most of the work that goes into reproduction occurs inside the home, away from the prying eyes of supply and demand. No money changes hands, no profits are made, and the value of output is not even counted in the GDP statistics. For this reason, most economists tend to ignore reproduction as a private, non-economic matter.

But this is a terrible mistake. The economics (and politics) of reproduction (broadly defined) have huge consequences for how the rest of the economy functions – everything from consumer spending to labour supply to education to pensions. The economics of reproduction are also essential to understanding economic inequality between men and women, and between different cultural and racialized groups.

Recall from earlier chapters that about 85 percent of households in developed capitalist economies depend on wage labour for their main livelihood over their lives. They own no economically meaningful property, and must sell their labour in a paid job to support themselves and their families. This means that most households in society are worker households. And for the most part, when households reproduce themselves, they reproduce *workers*. In this sense, households form a crucial link in the overall economic chain of capitalism. Production is where private businesses hire workers to produce goods and services for profit. Reproduction is where families buy back some of what they produce in order to reproduce the workers who produced it in the first place.

Indeed, when the classical economists were first studying wage determination in the new capitalist system, they thought of the household much like a worker-producing factory. For them, the "cost" of labour (its wage) should equal its cost of "production" – that is, the direct cost of feeding, clothing, and caring for workers, not to mention producing brand new little workers to eventually take their place on the assembly line. That's why the classical economists concluded that wages would settle at a level just high enough to cover workers' physical subsistence. Marx had a similar view, although he noted that social and political factors (not just the physiological requirements of subsistence) would also affect wage levels, by influencing the broad social understanding of what constitutes a minimum acceptable standard of living.

Today most workers (in the developed economies, at any rate) clearly earn more than what's required to stay alive. This can be understood in two alternative, equivalent ways: either the (social and cultural) definition of "subsistence" has expanded over time to reflect new standards of what is considered minimal (to include basic amenities like indoor toilets, television and internet, some vacation time, and so on), or else workers have successfully captured a share of the economic **SURPLUS** (thus allowing them a standard of living superior to minimum subsistence).

Either way, the economic reality is that most households still spend all their lifetime income on the goods and services which they and their families need to get by. While they don't live solely to reproduce themselves (and many people are not interested in having children, for various reasons), giving their children a good start in life is nevertheless a central, life-defining goal for most families. In this way, understanding the household as a "factory" which produces new workers may seem rather unromantic – but is probably not too far off the mark.

The economics of households

The work performed in households directly accounts for a significant share of all economic output (perhaps one-quarter in developed economies, and more than that in less developed countries). But since household output is not sold in a market, it is hard to value. Most household work involves caring for family members, cooking, cleaning, and other household tasks. Women do more than half of it. Indeed, reproductive work is a pivotal way that unequal economic roles for women and men are perpetuated.

Household work has changed dramatically over time, reflecting economic, technological, and cultural trends. Moreover, the boundaries which distinguish the household from the rest of the economy are fuzzy. For example, just like any workplace, capital equipment (tools) is used to perform household work faster and better. As income levels rise, families purchase more tools (dishwashers, vacuum cleaners, ovens, small appliances) to reduce their household labour. In this way, the purchase of manufactured goods (which are counted in GDP statistics) gradually replaces some unpaid labour (which is not counted in GDP).

Another way households (especially higher-income families) reduce their domestic labour is by hiring someone else to do it. This includes eating prepared meals from restaurants; hiring maids, gardeners, and other household labour; and hiring nannies to care for children. Thus some unpaid, uncounted household labour is replaced with marketed, paid labour (which, once again, is included in GDP). Usually that paid reproductive work is also performed by women, often from lower-income racialized groups.

Finally, governments have assumed some of the duties of reproduction through the expansion of public services like schools, child care centres, old age homes, and hospitals. These facilities perform services that were once delivered inside the home. Their public provision (also counted in GDP) generally leads to higher-quality services, more access to the services by lower-income people, relatively well-paid jobs (especially for women), and less burden on family members. Under neoliberalism and austerity, however, there has been some effort to shift caring work (such as child care and elder care) back to private households.

For all of these reasons – household industrialization, purchases of commercial household services, and the growth of public services – the importance of unpaid household labour to the overall economy has declined steadily in recent decades. Meanwhile, women have transferred more of their own work effort from the home to the paid labour market, even though they're still saddled with an unfair share of household duties when they get home from their paying jobs. Nevertheless, the unpaid work that goes on inside households is still very important to the overall economy.

Apart from their work and production, households perform other important economic functions. Most **CONSUMPTION** occurs within the household, through

---

You Write the Book: Stealing Your Time

There are only 24 hours in a day. Workers spend many of them in wage labour, trying to support themselves and their families. They spend several more caring for themselves – in essence, getting ready to go back to work the next day. And if they're lucky, they'll have a couple of hours left for relaxation and recreation.

So time is scarce and valuable. And businesses understand this. They try to reduce how much of your time they have to "pay for" – whether you are a worker, a customer, or an innocent bystander. In so doing, profit-seeking businesses "steal your time" … and thus steal part of your life.

In the workplace, for example, employers minimize any non-productive time they must pay for. So workers are usually required to travel to, prepare for, and clean up after work on their own time, not the boss's time. While they are on the payroll, every possible paid minute is monitored and dedicated to production. Outside of the workplace, businesses regularly waste the unpaid time of customers or potential customers: putting customers on hold for long periods of time, forcing customers to wait in line, selling products that require many hours to assemble, interrupting homelife with unsolicited phone calls. All this wasted time may be "free" from the perspective of a company, but it's invaluable to busy families. What would happen to capitalism if companies actually had to pay people for all the time they currently "steal" without payment?

Send an example of a company that wasted your time (as a worker, a consumer, or a bystander) to author@economicsforeveryone.com. We'll post the best examples at www.economicsforeveryone.com.

the many different goods and services which families buy and use. In developed capitalist economies, private consumption spending accounts for half or more of GDP. Most households spend essentially all their income on consumption, and hence their **SAVINGS** are non-existent. (In fact, more and more households go into debt to finance consumption.) This helps explain why (as indicated in Chapter 7) most families own little or no financial wealth.

The Company Store

"You load sixteen tons, what do you get?
Another day older, and deeper in debt.
Saint Peter don't you call me, 'cause I can't go.
I owe my soul to the company store."

Merle Travis, US country singer (1940s).

In capitalism, workers work for employers, who pay them a wage. Workers use that income to buy back from employers a share of what they produced: to stay alive, support their families, and come back to work the next day. The spending power of workers is thus an essential part of the market for their own output.

This circular process is especially obvious in remote towns, where an entire community may depend on one or a few major employers. Indeed, in traditional mining towns, the mining company itself would often own the local retail outlet, and even the very houses that miners lived in. This arrangement meant that workers were exploited twice: first while they laboured (in difficult and often unsafe conditions), and then again when they spent their money to buy essentials (at inflated prices). The lack of competing retail and housing opportunities in remote regions made matters all the worse. Employers could lock workers into a near-slavery relationship, by advancing credit for retail and housing that could never be repaid out of the miners' inadequate incomes – thus condemning the workers to ongoing servitude.

In bigger towns and cities workers have more choice about where to spend their hard-earned money, and hence this dual exploitation is less severe. However, the fundamental cycle of production and consumption is still the same: workers work, workers get paid – and then workers give their money right back to the "bosses" to pay for the essentials of their own subsistence.

Households are also in charge of **LABOUR SUPPLY**: deciding how many workers to provide to the formal labour market, for how many hours, and at what periods in their lives. Of course, labour supply decisions are always shaped by the essential, coercive challenge facing working-class households: they must find paid work to survive. Moreover, labour supply decisions are not independent from labour demand. Usually, jobs must be available before individuals bother seeking one (that's why labour supply tends to rise in good economic times, and fall during recessions). But household attitudes toward work and income can also exert independent influence over labour supply. If for cultural or other reasons households prefer to reduce their labour supply (by retiring earlier, staying home to raise children, or staying longer in college), then there will be fewer workers available, and the labour market pressures facing employers will be more binding. On the other hand, if households maximize labour supply – perhaps in order to afford the latest consumer goods (even working overtime or multiple jobs, and working later in life) – then employers benefit from a more abundant and available workforce.

Finally, most households also directly undertake one economically important type of INVESTMENT: in their own homes. If the household is viewed as a site of production, then the building where that production occurs is the household's most important (and expensive) capital asset. In the developed Anglo-Saxon economies, over two-thirds of households own their own home, and this proportion has grown over time. Apart from providing shelter, home-ownership also constitutes the major wealth owned by most families, and is thus an important feature of household finances. Unlike most consumer spending (which tends to be quite stable in relation to income levels), home purchases are less predictable. In response to changes in unemployment, interest rates, demographic trends, and other economic pressures, home values can fluctuate substantially. The resulting ups and downs of the home construction and renovation industry contribute to the ongoing roller-coaster pattern of capitalism.

Women, men, and work

The economic activities of the household are fundamentally tied up with different economic roles played by women and men. For starters, the division of unpaid labour within the home is very unequal: women do more of this work than men, they perform different types of unpaid work (more caring, cleaning, and cooking), and the work they do generally has lower "status" and recognition. This division of labour reflects outdated, sexist attitudes that women are "naturally" better-suited to caring work (based, in part, on the fact that they give birth to babies), and that men shouldn't have to do so much around the home since they work outside of the home. This sexism is reinforced by a complex mixture of tradition, religion, economic pressure – and all too often by violence.

The inequality of men's and women's labour market experience reinforces, and is reinforced by, the inequality of their economic position within the home. Women usually earn less than men, and so some families make a supposedly "rational" choice that the woman should stay home to care for children (since her foregone wages are less than the man's). The lack of affordable and quality child care services in most countries plays a negative role in these decisions, too. Then, because men work hard in their paid jobs, many refuse to do their share of work at home. (This argument doesn't seem to work for women: women with paid jobs still have to work their "double shift.") The fact that women's career paths are often interrupted by childbirth, child rearing, or other domestic duties (like caring for sick or elderly family members) further undermines their ability to advance their careers and earn higher wages, reinforcing all of the above trends.

There has been incremental progress toward greater economic equality for women in most developed economies, but it hasn't come easily. Most women now participate in paid work, and PARTICIPATION RATES (which measure the proportion of working-age persons in the paid labour market) for men and women are converging. As shown in Figure 9.1, this is partly because men's labour market participation declined somewhat under neoliberalism (due to deteriorating job conditions).

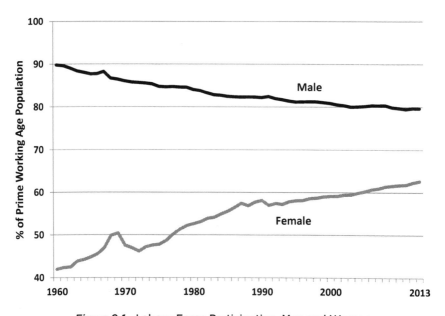

Figure 9.1 Labour Force Participation, Men and Women

OECD average, prime age 15–64 years old
Source: Labour Force Statistics.

The Nordic countries, which support women's paid work with extensive public services and labour rights, have achieved the highest levels of female labour force participation – as high as 80 percent of working-age women. Liberal social attitudes in the developed Anglo-Saxon economies have promoted relatively high female participation there, too. Continental European countries have lower female participation, reflecting a combination of outdated attitudes and unsupportive public programs. Women's growing paid work expands their personal incomes and enhances their power within the family. But since they are still required to do most household labour, this progress has come at a considerable cost of stress and exhaustion. In some countries (like the Netherlands), women are concentrated in part-time work; this undermines earnings equality, but may make it easier to juggle paid work and home responsibilities (especially if part-time jobs come with stable hours and fair compensation, including benefits and pensions).

There are three different reasons why women continue to earn much less than men in paid work, despite the gradual narrowing of the economic gender gap:

- Women still earn less than equally qualified men working in comparable jobs; this reflects both pure DISCRIMINATION, and the constraints placed on women's paid work opportunities by their domestic responsibilities (such as interrupted career paths, or the impossibility of working overtime).
- Women's employment is concentrated in jobs which tend to pay less; this reflects an intense LABOUR MARKET SEGMENTATION, sometimes called feminine "job ghettos." Women are disproportionately represented in lower-paying and PRECARIOUS jobs in service industries (such as retail work and personal services) and caring professions.
- Due to career interruptions and a greater reliance on part-time work, women work fewer hours in paid jobs than men (especially when measured on a lifetime basis).

Putting all these factors together, employed women in the developed economies earn around half as much as men over their paid working lives (and this doesn't consider women who do not perform paid work). As a result, women are much more likely to experience poverty than men. Poverty rates are especially high for two groups of single women: single mothers and single pensioners.

Further reducing the economic gaps between men and women will require several strategies to transfer more reproductive work to men and to public programs. Men must be challenged to pick up a larger share of unpaid domestic work, including child care. There is some evidence that this is starting to occur, but unevenly and inadequately. One interesting example was provided in France following the introduction of that country's 35-hour working week in the 1990s; surveys indicated that men's contribution to unpaid domestic labour grew significantly in subsequent years. Indeed, changes in paid employment practices will be important to allow both women and men to balance paid work with domestic responsibilities. It will take sustained pressure on private employers and governments to force them to pay more than lip service to the challenge of WORK-LIFE BALANCE. Finally, public services must be expanded, to take up more of the reproductive responsibilities that still fall on women's shoulders. The sorely inadequate state of child and elder care systems in most economies (with the exception of Nordic countries) are only one glaring example of this need. Working women, and working households more generally, will need to demand more support from both employers and governments in the always-challenging task of combining production and reproduction.

10

Closing the Little Circle

Meet the players

The previous chapters of Part Two introduced the major actors in the economy and their assigned tasks. This chapter now fits them all together in a circular loop that reflects the repeating cycle of the economy: work, production (using tools), income distribution, consumption, and reproduction. These are the core functions and relationships that make up capitalism. We'll even draw a simple map of this circular system. We'll call this map the "little circle." In later chapters, this map will get bigger as we consider more of capitalism's real-world complexity (including the roles of competition, the environment, banks, government, and globalization).

You can't tell the players without a program, so here's a handy listing of the key actors, what they do, and where they work and live:

- **Workers** These people (and their families) make up the vast majority of the population (around 85 percent) of advanced capitalist economies. They own no economically meaningful property (other than, for many, their own homes). To survive, they must sell their labour for wages and salaries to private companies, which they do not meaningfully own or control. At any point in time some workers are not working: they may be unemployed, supported by their families, receiving government income support, or retired. But even those who are not currently employed are still "workers", on the basis of their lifetime dependence on employment for their basic livelihood.

- **Capitalists** These people (and their families) make up only a couple of percent of the population of advanced capitalist economies. They own the clear majority of financial wealth (including most business wealth – via either direct ownership of companies, or large holdings of corporate shares). They also control the operation of large businesses, either directly as owner-managers or indirectly through their appointment of professional executives (who themselves own large stakes in the businesses they run). Hired employees do most of the work in these businesses. Capitalists do not need to work to survive, since their ownership of financial wealth generates sufficient income to live very comfortably. However, many do work (including as managers of their own firms), and that work is productive (unlike their status as owners – which is not, in and of itself, productive).

- **Small business owners and farmers**   These people (and their families) make up 10-15 percent of the population of advanced capitalist economies (and a larger share in less developed countries). They work, nominally for themselves, in small companies or farms, in which they (and often their family members) perform most of the work required for production. These small operations may sell goods and services to consumers (like a neighbourhood corner store) or to other, larger businesses (like a photocopy shop). Either way, they are always dependent on the more important, central "loop" of capitalism: namely, the decisions by larger businesses to invest, hire labour, and produce. The profits received by small business owners reflect a combination of hard work and their status as owners. But most can be safely ascribed to their work effort, since the average total incomes of small business owners (despite their long hours and high stress) are generally no higher than those of paid workers. (To keep our map simple, we don't draw small businesses directly, reflecting this subsidiary economic role.)
- **Worker households**   This is where wage-labourers live and reproduce themselves. They raise and educate children; feed, clothe, and care for each other (including sick and elderly family members); and spend essentially all of their wages and salaries to buy the consumer goods and services that they need to survive and enjoy life. A great deal of unpaid, unmarketed work occurs inside the household, most of it performed by women.
- **Capitalist households**   The capitalists live here, and in fine style. Like workers, they also buy goods and services for consumption: in greater quantities than workers, and higher quality. Some of their income (most of which comes from profits or their financial wealth) is saved – supposedly to be re-invested back into their companies (although in practice that does not necessarily occur).
- **Private companies**   Workers go here to perform their labour in return for wages and salaries. The capitalist (or a hired executive) also works here, to organize production and supervise and discipline the workers. The output of this labour is a good or service which the company then sells. Hopefully, the resulting revenue is sufficient to cover wages and salaries, the wear and tear of machinery, and any raw materials or inputs used in production. What's left is a bottom-line profit for the owner. The output from these companies is sold into three distinct markets. Worker households buy run-of-the-mill consumer goods. Capitalist households buy luxury consumption goods. And other companies buy things (like machinery, equipment, and supplies) needed for production. If for some reason the company can't sell its output, the capitalist will never see the hoped-for profits, and production will slow or stop altogether. (We will discuss how and why this actually happens in Chapter 25.)

Follow the money

We've introduced the main players. Now let's sit back and watch the show. Figure 10.1 illustrates how these players interact with each other, in a normal day (or year) of work.

In addition to the players and places introduced above, our map also illustrates the major flows of money resulting from their productive activity. We label these money flows with shorthand symbols commonly used in economics. Like a forensic accountant trying to solve a corporate fraud, following the trail of money around the circle is a good way to understand what actually happens as capitalism unfolds. In fact, there's a whole branch of economics – called CIRCUIT THEORY – which is based on "following the money" in this manner.

Let's discuss each flow of money, in the order in which it appears on the economic stage:

Step 1: **Investment (I)**   Before anything else happens in capitalism, the capitalist must decide to make an initial investment: establishing their company and starting production. This requires an initial expenditure on FIXED CAPITAL (including the workplace itself, and all the machinery and tools inside). The capitalist must also provide some WORKING CAPITAL, to pay the initial wages of the company's employees, buy raw materials and supplies, and meet other day-to-day expenses; hence the capitalist needs a certain revolving fund of cash to get production started. (After a full cycle of production has occurred, the company can use some of its revenues to pay for those expenses in the next production cycle.)

This initial investment creates new jobs in its own right (both inside the company itself, and in the companies which produce capital equipment, raw materials, and other inputs). Even more crucially, this initial investment pushes the "Start" button on the whole process of production. Investment is the most important form of spending required for the successful functioning of capitalism. When investment is strong, capitalism is vibrant and growing. When investment is weak, capitalism stagnates.

Where did the capitalist get the money to make this initial investment? We'll discuss this in Chapters 17–19, when we discuss money, banking, finance, and stock markets. For now, all we need to know is that the capitalist only needs a credible business plan and a bit of start-up EQUITY; they can then borrow all the additional funds they need, in one form or another, from the financial system. Importantly, the capitalist doesn't need to first *save* all this money, in order to *invest* it.

Step 2: **Wages (W)**   Once workers start their new jobs and perform their work, they begin to earn wages and salaries.

Figure 10.1   Economic Road Map: Little Circle

***Step 3*: Consumption (C)**   The take-home pay earned by workers doesn't gather dust. As soon as they get their first paycheques, workers begin spending it. (In fact, thanks to the magic of credit cards, workers can start spending even before that first paycheque arrives!) In aggregate, workers spend all their income on consumer goods and services, which are consumed inside the home to reproduce themselves and their families (and, hopefully, enjoy life a bit in the process). The money goes back to the private companies which produced those goods and services.

Workers' consumption is the largest single expenditure that occurs in the economy. But it is also the most predictable. In effect, "workers spend what they get," and hence worker consumption spending closely tracks employment and wage levels.

***Step 4*: Profit (Π)**   Assuming the private company successfully sells its output and generates enough revenue to cover its costs, it then pays a profit back to its owner (the capitalist). Indeed, the hunger for profit was the motive that got the whole ball rolling in the first place. (Capitalists certainly don't invest their own money as a public service.) The capitalist eventually expects to get back their initial investment, plus some profit margin on top of that (otherwise why would they bother?). The Greek letter *pi* (Π), is commonly used in economics to symbolize profit ... could that be because it resembles the ostentatious faux Greek pillars which some modern capitalists erect at the entrances to their mansions? If the capitalist borrowed some of the money for the initial investment, then some of the resulting profit must be paid back to the lender as interest.

What do capitalists do with their profit? Generally, it doesn't gather dust either. (If it does, then this economy will experience a recession.) Some of it is spent on the luxury consumption of capitalist households (we call that $C_{\diamond}$ on the map, with the luxury diamond subscript distinguishing it from workers' more humble consumption). The rest is set aside to be re-invested (in the next cycle) in the capitalist's business: both to replace the wear and tear of the company's capital assets, and perhaps to expand the company's total output.

For completeness, we could also draw smaller flows of profits going to small business owners, and smaller flows for their own consumer spending and investment. This would make our diagram very complicated. For now, just keep in mind that small businesses play a subsidiary role in capitalism; they depend on the larger flows of corporate investment and worker consumption that are shown in this map. Imagine a stereotypical small business, like a small retail shop: it depends on larger companies both to produce the goods which it sells, and to employ the workers who are its main customers. Like a small shop, most small business is just a "go-between": facilitating spending transactions and minor production functions that ultimately depend on the larger and more powerful forces driving the whole system.

Reading the map

This map is a vast simplification of how capitalism actually works. But we can already learn some very important lessons by studying it. First, there are two broad categories of arrows (or money flows) on the map: those which flow from companies to households (both worker households and capitalist households), and those which flow from households back to companies. The arrows flowing from companies to households represent flows of *income* (wages and profits). The arrows flowing back to companies represent forms of *expenditure* (mass consumption, luxury consumption, and spending on capital goods).

Ultimately, the total flow of income will equal the total flow of expenditure. We summarize this in Table 10.1.

Table 10.1   Income and Expenditure: Little Circle

Class	Income	Expenditure
Workers	Wages (W)	Worker Consumption (C)
Capitalists	+ Profits (Π)	+ Luxury Consumption ($C_\lozenge$)
		+ Investment (I)
	= Total Income	= Total Expenditure

The centre column of this table shows the total income of the economy. The right column shows total expenditure. These are in fact the two methods that statistical agencies use to add up the total value of GDP (which excludes, remember, the value of unpaid work inside the home). The "GDP by income" tables report labour income, profits (broken down into corporate profits, depreciation, investment income, and small business profits), and some other, smaller categories of income. The "GDP by expenditure" tables report consumption, investment, and other forms of spending (such as government programs and exports) that we haven't considered yet. (Visit www.economicsforeveryone.com for a "how-to" guide on reading and interpreting GDP statistics.)

Recall that we identified two broad kinds of consumption: workers' mass consumption (C) and capitalists' luxury consumption ($C_\lozenge$). Mass consumption (C) in the right column of Table 10.1 tends to equal workers' wages (W) in the centre. Unlike workers, however, capitalists have a meaningful choice regarding how to spend their income: on luxury consumption, or reinvesting in their businesses. How much they consume, and how much they invest, will influence how strong the economy is today, and how fast it grows in the future. In earlier times, frugal capitalists tended to reinvest most of their profits, and hence capitalism developed quickly.

Today, however, capitalists consume much of their profit (or find other unproductive uses for some of it, like financial speculation), and this has been associated with a visible slowing of business investment during the years of neoliberalism. Indeed, if the goal of neoliberalism was to strengthen investment and growth, then it has clearly failed: despite new powers and freedoms, the world's capitalists invest less of their profit than in previous epochs. We will discuss this problem further in Chapter 12.

Where's the work?

Our map locates the main players in the basic economic loop that is capitalism, and the major flows of money that link them. Don't forget, though, that it is ultimately work that explains production, not money. What actual work is performed in this system, and where?

We discussed the main forms of work that occur in capitalism in Chapter 5. The biggest share of work is performed by workers in private firms in return for wages and salaries. Their work is coordinated and supervised by owners and top managers … when they do any actual work, that is! Another large share of work is performed, without pay, inside households. Smaller amounts of work are performed in small businesses and farms.

Part Three

Capitalism as a System

11

Competition

Kill or be killed

Part Two of this book outlined the basic functions and relationships that define capitalism: between the owners of private companies (who invest in hopes of generating a profit), and the workers who perform most of the productive labour within those companies (in return for wages and salaries). The "little circle" we drew in Chapter 10 depicted the cycle of production, income distribution, and spending that links one particular firm, its owner, and its workers.

In the real world, however, there isn't just one company. There are many thousands of them. And they can't focus solely on keeping their own workers in line, extracting maximum work effort for minimum cost, selling their output, and making sure their operations are efficient and profitable. They also have to worry constantly about the threat posed by competing firms – who are also trying to maximize their profits.

Competition – ruthless, unforgiving, to-the-death competition – is a crucial feature of capitalism. It opens up new opportunities for individual firms: they can expand revenues and profits by winning a larger share of sales from competitors. But competition also poses new challenges, since other companies are trying to do exactly the same thing: namely, grow their own market share at the expense of their competitors. Therefore, it's not just *greed* that motivates company efforts to minimize costs and maximize profits; with competition, it's also *fear*. If a company can't stand up to the competition, it's not just that they won't make quite as much profit as other companies. Far worse, eventually they will be destroyed by these competing firms producing better products at lower cost.

For most people, fear is usually a more powerful motivator than greed, and this is true for companies, too. Most of the behaviours exhibited by companies in the modern economy – the good, the bad, and the ugly – are motivated, and indeed *enforced*, by competitive pressures from other companies. This pressure leads companies to do dramatic, innovative, often painful and even destructive things – not solely because their owners and executives are greedy, but because they desperately want to stay in business. Competition is thus the disciplining force that compels companies to act in particular ways. And in so doing, competition ensures that the whole system behaves in particular ways.

Locating competition: Y vs Z

Figure 11.1 reproduces our "little circle" map from the last chapter. But this time, there are two companies operating side by side in the middle of the circle, not one. Company Y and Company Z produce similar products – let's say they manufacture televisions – and they sell into the same general market (households who want a new TV). Both firms also hire their workers from the same general community of worker households. Each firm has its respective capitalist owner, and each wants to see their own firm succeed and the other firm fail. But each owner also measures the profit they earn from their company against the general rate of profit earned by other companies (including the competing television manufacturer).

Figure 11.1 therefore highlights three distinct places where the two companies confront each other. The most important is in the market for new TVs – or what economists call the PRODUCT MARKET. Here each company must convince customers that its TV offers superior quality for a lower price. If they can't do this, then they won't sell the televisions they have carefully produced, and the owner will never earn a profit.

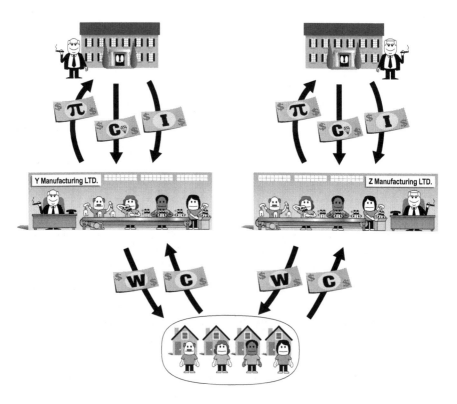

Figure 11.1 Economic Road Map: Competition

Companies Y and Z also compete in the labour market. In practice, the labour market rarely "runs out" of workers – that is, there is almost always a comfortable cushion of unemployment, from which companies can hire new workers when needed. Nevertheless, a company's ability to recruit, hire, and discipline new workers affects its overall performance. When companies must compete with other employers for labour, their power over their workers is somewhat reduced. (This is why large companies often locate major facilities in rural or semi-rural areas where they are the dominant employer; or concentrate hiring among particular neighbourhoods, demographic groups, or racialized communities.)

Finally, companies must also compete in capital markets. Again, as with labour, this is not to imply that there is a fixed amount of capital which must be allocated to one company or the other. In fact, new capital is actually *created* (through the banking and financial system) anytime a capitalist borrows money and invests it (we'll discuss this in detail in Part Four). But a company must still generate a competitive rate of profit for its owners, or else they will stop investing – and the firm will be unable to convince bankers to lend it money. And through incremental investment decisions, physical capital can eventually "move" from less profitable countries, industries, or companies toward more profitable ones. Indeed, one crucial outcome of competition is that it tends to *equalize* the rate of profit paid out across different firms or industries.

"Perfect competition" and real-world competition

Neoclassical economics relies heavily on a strange, idealized notion of competition, called PERFECT COMPETITION. Perfect competition is one of the most bizarre ideas in the whole of economics. It was not designed to explain reality: competition in capitalism has *never* resembled perfect competition. Instead, it was designed to provide intellectual justification for a theory: Walras' theory of GENERAL EQUILIBRIUM, which claims that free-market exchange is the best way to maximize human well-being. Without perfect competition, the Walrasian model cannot sustain this claim. (And as we saw in earlier chapters, there are many other logical failures in the theory, too.)

In perfect competition, individual firms are tiny. They cannot grow bigger, because neoclassical theory assumes that average production costs rise as they grow (due to a process called DIMINISHING RETURNS). This assumption is quite wrong. In reality, larger companies can actually produce most goods and services more cheaply. Every firm must pay for initial overhead costs (like factories, equipment, engineering, and marketing) before they produce their first unit of output. After that, average costs fall dramatically as the volume of output grows (since overhead expenses can be spread over a larger volume of output). Larger

Table 11.1 Economies of Scale: Hypothetical Television Manufacturer

Overhead Cost (Fixed Cost): $100 million
(capital equipment, engineering, marketing)

Extra Costs per Television (Variable Cost): $200
(materials, parts, labour)

Output	Fixed Cost	Variable Cost (output * $200)	Average Cost (per TV)
1	$100 million	$200	$100,000,200
1,000	$100 million	$200,000	$100,200
100,000	$100 million	$20 million	$1,200
1,000,000	$100 million	$200 million	$300
10,000,000	$100 million	$2 billion	$210

companies therefore can attain much lower average costs, and this is a powerful stimulus for companies to grow.

An example of this is provided in Table 11.1. To get into the television business in the first place, assume that Company Z must spend $100 million on capital equipment, engineering, and marketing. The very first TV set to come off the assembly line therefore costs over $100 million: the total overhead cost, plus the roughly $200 in materials and labour that are built into each TV set. Average costs then decline quickly, as output grows. By the time it produces 100,000 TVs, the company has reduced average costs to $1200 – but that's still too expensive. Imagine that the "going" price for a new TV is about $300. Company Z therefore must be able to produce (and sell) over a million units before it can hope to earn any profit at all. This example is quite realistic, and explains why there is only enough room, even in the global economy, for a very few television manufacturers. This powerful arithmetic also explains why small companies cannot compete in most industries, and why all companies constantly try to boost sales to make more efficient use of their fixed capacity. (This is exactly the opposite of the neoclassical theory, which concludes bizarrely that due to diminishing returns, companies don't actually want to grow!) Growing sales generate a double benefit for firms: higher revenues, along with lower average costs. An industry is said to demonstrate ECONOMIES OF SCALE when average production costs decline as the volume of output grows. Economies of scale are strong in most industries. They explain why enormous companies continue to emerge and dominate the market even in new industries (think of giant technology companies like Google, Apple, and Amazon), despite the highly competitive nature of the economy.

In addition to the false assumption that all firms are tiny, there are several other equally unrealistic aspects to the theory of perfect competition. Firms are assumed to produce completely identical products (so that consumers can't tell the difference between one variety of a product and another). Companies cannot influence market trends through advertising or other efforts. And they cannot try to anticipate or respond to the behaviour of their competitors. In this theory, competition is so intense and anonymous that it actually *eliminates* profits altogether: prices are driven to such a low level that companies can only just cover the costs of the inputs they hired (such as labour and borrowed capital), leaving no bottom-line profit whatsoever. Why any capitalist would bother investing in a private company in this environment is one of the great unanswered questions of neoclassical economics.

Real-world competition is very different from this strange theory – but it is still real, powerful, and unforgiving. Importantly, the fact that companies can be very large in no way implies that competition has become less intense. In fact, the incredible resources, technology, and managerial abilities that modern large corporations have at their disposal allow them to compete in ways, and in places, that were never before feasible.

Table 11.2 summarizes the key ways in which real-world competition differs from idealized neoclassical theory. The larger a company becomes, in general, the lower its production costs become (thanks to economies of scale). What prevents a single company from then taking over the whole market, on the basis of scale efficiencies? Sometimes this actually happens, but not usually. Consumers generally want some choice in their purchases (and hence will support competing brands for the sake of variety). Financial investors will recoil at the risks they would face if all their eggs, in any particular industry, had to be placed in just one company's basket. And if one company becomes too large (especially if it gets lazy, taking advantage of its dominant position), other companies will try to challenge (or "contest") the market with new products, technologies, or production methods. Even the *threat* of this occurring can be a powerful disciplining force on large companies. Finally, governments will usually intervene in cases of pure MONOPOLY to break up or regulate super-dominant firms.

Meanwhile, companies work continuously to create unique or novel features in their particular products. Sometimes this is done in genuine ways (with real technical innovations), sometimes in utterly phony ways (such as the billions of dollars spent on ads promoting the idea that one brand of jeans is sexier than others). Unique technologies, production methods, and cost savings can also give a firm a unique ability to earn profits (over and above "normal" returns). Those profits are what lure the corporate leaders; the threat of economic extinction motivates the followers.

Today enormous global companies can be driven from business if, for whatever reason, they lose the competitive battle. Think of General Motors, which for decades was the largest company in the world – but more recently experienced bankruptcy restructuring after years of losing sales and profits to other enormous corporations

Table 11.2 Contrasting Theories of Competition

Issue	Neoclassical "Perfect Competition"	Real-World Competition
Firm size	Firms are tiny, and there is an infinite number of them.	Firms can be very large; a few thousand dominate the world economy.
Impact of firm size on costs	Average production costs increase for bigger firms due to diminishing returns.	Average production costs decrease for bigger firms due to economies of scale.
Limit on size of firm	Diminishing returns, rising costs.	Consumers' desire for variety, increasing risk to investors, threat of entry by new firms.
Relationship to other firms	Firms cannot guess what other firms will do; competition is anonymous.	Firms observe and react to the actions of competing firms; competition is strategic.
Ability to influence market	Firms cannot influence prices or sales volumes.	Firms strive to influence prices and sales volumes.
Product differentiation	Consumers cannot tell the output of one firm from another; products are homogeneous.	Firms invest in research and advertising to distinguish their products; products are differentiated.
Competition and profits	Firms do not make any "pure" profits, over and above market payments to hired inputs (wages, interest).	Firms strive to earn "pure: profits with differentiated products, unique production methods, or unique cost advantages.

(like Toyota). And bankruptcy for smaller and medium-sized businesses is a frequent event. Meanwhile, footloose investors (utilizing new financial strategies, like PRIVATE EQUITY) can meaningfully threaten to enter any industry, in any country, to challenge market leaders by taking over and radically restructuring existing firms.

The largest companies are bigger than ever, they have unprecedented resources at their disposal, and incredible ability to reach into markets around the world. In large part *because* of this size, not *in spite* of it, there's no doubt that competition in capitalism is fiercer than ever. But is that a good thing?

The consequences of competition

Clearly there's nowhere to run, nowhere to hide, in the brave new world of uber-competition. If even the world's largest corporations aren't safe, who is? Neoclassical economists celebrate competition as an efficiency-enhancing force. Governments, more often than not, agree, and this has led them to enact laws promoting and enforcing competition. But is competition always a useful, beneficial force? Certainly not.

To be sure, the competitive struggle to survive elicits some forms of business behaviour that are genuinely efficient. These can translate into broad social benefits (assuming that new efficiency is shared, one way or another, with workers and consumers). Spurred by competition, managers will work hard to imagine ways of producing better products, and better ways of producing them. This spurs investment in both capital equipment and technology. Competition also allows consumers some degree of choice in their purchases. It thus imposes a particular form of accountability on companies to deliver high-quality, competitively-priced output. (Of course, all too often the range of "choice" provided by capitalist competition is rather monotonous. Competition in the fast food industry ensures that consumers can clog their arteries in several different, but equally unappetizing and unhealthy, ways!) Table 11.3 lists some of the positive responses to competitive pressure.

At the same time, however, competition also imposes many economic and social costs. We can't ignore these costs. Competition can lead to irrational or destructive outcomes for the whole system. Several downsides of competition are also summarized in Table 11.3. Some of the downsides are exactly opposite to the upsides, indicating the complex and often contradictory character of real-world competition.

Companies will respond to competition by cutting costs in any ways imaginable – including by reducing wages or intensifying work in socially damaging ways. They may even try to shift their costs onto others, through a phenomenon called EXTERNALITIES: if they can find ways (often underhanded or even illegal) to impose costs of their operations on innocent parties, then their own bottom line is strengthened. Ways of doing this include pollution, the sale of unsafe products, and forcing consumers of their products to bear hidden or unexpected costs. Remember that having a product that's differentiated in the minds of consumers is a key source of competitive profit. Companies try to create this differentiation in ways that are wasteful, useless, or even destructive: massive (and often misleading) advertising, excess packaging (to make products look "bigger"), and artificial obsolescence (where products are deliberately designed to wear out or become useless prematurely). Companies will not invest in innovations which they can't patent, for fear that competitors will simply copy them. For similar reasons, private firms consistently underinvest in on-the-job training and skills development for their workers, since they worry those trained workers may subsequently be hired away (or "poached") by competitors. Yet ironically, companies *will* spend money

Table 11.3   Competition: The Good, the Bad, and the Ugly

Positive Effects of Competition:

Innovation	Companies try to develop new products, and more efficient production systems.
Choice, accountability	Consumers can go to a competing firm if they are not satisfied with the price or quality of output.
Quality	Firms must try to improve the quality of their output or service, or else lose customers.
Investment	To earn more profit, some firms will invest in capital equipment and research & development.

Negative Effects of Competition:

Labour cost-cutting	Firms will try to cut wages and benefits, and increase the intensity of work, imposing costs on their workers.
Other cost-cutting	Large firms will also try to reduce the prices paid for other inputs and purchases, using their dominant position to squeeze smaller suppliers.
Externalize costs	Firms will shift their costs onto others if it improves their competitive position (example: pollution).
Wasteful differentiation	Firms spend vast amounts on advertising to differentiate their products; they also try to trick or fool consumers regarding the nature of their product.
Wasteful duplication	If competition is too intense then all companies in an industry may operate below efficient scale, resulting in wasteful duplication.
Inadequate profits	If competition is too intense, struggling companies will have inadequate profits to invest in innovation or improved quality.
Copying and poaching	Firms will be unwilling to invest in (non-patentable) innovation, or in training workers, for fear that competitors will copy or poach.
Battle costs	Firms invest in activities which are not efficient or productive, aimed solely at undermining competitors (for example, through negative marketing, diverting and disrupting consumers, or even sabotage).
Dislocation costs	When companies fail, owners lose vast sums of capital, workers lose their jobs, and communities suffer spin-off losses.

System-Wide Effects of Competition:

Profit equalization	Rates of profit tend to equalize across companies and industries (so long as new companies can enter an industry).
Herd mentality	Many companies follow each other's strategies, entering or exiting particular activities at the same time.
Cycles	The herd mentality of competing firms creates unplanned booms and busts in overall activity.
Uneven development	Competition has winners and losers, and they are distributed in "clumps" (not evenly); as a result, some companies, sectors, regions, and even entire countries grow and prosper, while others decline.
Divided labour	Workers who have much In common (and would benefit from joint efforts to improve their lot) see each other as threats because they work for competing employers.

---

on attempts to frustrate or undermine their competitors' strategies (for example, by spying, sabotaging, or disrupting competitors' businesses, or needlessly duplicating their capacity). This spending is utterly unproductive in economic terms. So is research and development aimed solely at copying products (from cookie recipes to prescription drugs) that have already been invented by another company; this activity may be privately profitable (for the company doing the copying), but it is socially useless (since no new knowledge was gained).

You Write the Book: Tweedledee and Tweedledum

Competition between private suppliers is supposed to promote efficiency, lower prices, higher quality, and greater choice. In practice it can lead to wasteful duplication, annoying and intrusive advertising, unacceptable product quality or side-effects, and a loss of true choice. Think of a real-world example of competition gone awry: that is, inter-capitalist competition which produces perverse or destructive outcomes. Send it to author@economicsforeveryone.com. We'll post your best examples at www.economicsforeveryone.com.

Competition can clearly be too intense. It may result in all companies in an industry operating below their normal efficient scale of production, imposing a wasteful duplication of excess capacity. It can drive profits too low, undermining the ability of firms to invest in new capital or research. Companies which are desperate just to survive will produce inferior products, simply because they cannot afford higher quality. If all companies in an industry suffer from the same over-competition, then the whole industry will be marked by shoddy, stagnant, even unsafe products. And when companies fail, both their owners and workers suffer massive economic losses. Competition is not, therefore, "free." It constantly imposes real and substantial costs on the economy, which must always be evaluated against its much-heralded benefits.

The politics of competition

In Chapter 8 we discussed the complicated economic relationships between owners and workers. The interests of these two great classes often conflict, but sometimes they can seem to converge. A private company's interest in maximizing profits gives it a powerful, ongoing incentive to minimize wages and maximize work intensity, at the expense of its workers. On the other hand, when productivity is growing then companies can "buy" the loyalty of workers (if they feel pressured to do so) by sharing that productivity dividend through higher wages, without undermining profits.

Just Buy a New One

Apple Inc. is the world's largest supplier of personal electronic devices – and the most valuable corporation on the planet (its stock market value surpassed US$700 billion in 2014). Every year Apple releases new versions of all of its popular phones, tablets, and pods. Certainly, each incarnation contains some novel technical features – but last year's edition still works. So how does Apple convince consumers to dispose of almost-new products, and shell out several hundred dollars for a "hot" new one?

Of course, perceived social status, cultivated through clever advertising, plays a key role (that strategy is common with all "trendy" products, from jeans to watches to cars). But Apple has also perfected a more nefarious corporate strategy, called "planned obsolescence," to boost sales even as its market becomes saturated. Planned obsolescence uses minor and artificial modifications to products, so that older vintages (with years of useful life ahead of them) become less desirable or even un-usable, and consumers are pressured to buy new ones. Updates to previously-purchased operating systems (which Apple automatically downloads to your device over internet and wireless connections) can cause older equipment to slow down dramatically. Batteries in Apple phones wear out after a few hundred charging cycles, but cannot be easily replaced. (In fact, the company uses unique proprietary screws and closures which prevent average consumers from even attempting simple repairs like changing the battery.) Repeated and inexplicable changes in peripheral devices and connectors (like power sockets and docking ports) further compel consumers to buy new equipment – but special programming chips prevent consumers from using cheaper peripherals made by other companies. Meanwhile, the careful integration and synchronization of proprietary programs and services (like calendars and contact lists, data storage, and music) discourages consumers from ever switching to alternative hardware. All this makes it all the more likely that consumers, confronting a dead battery or a slow application, resign themselves yet again to just buying a new one.

Capitalism has a "throw-away" mentality that pervades many industries, driven by the profit motive of private production. Globalization reinforces this wastefulness: manufacturers utilize ultra-cheap labour in poor countries to reduce prices for new products, making it economically unattractive to perform even simple repairs on existing equipment. Consumer frustration is not the only consequence of planned obsolescence; overflowing landfills is another.

Competition between firms adds another layer of complexity to these relationships. Now the workers at one particular company will be tempted to identify even further with their own employer, in the competitive battle against other companies. This commonality of interest doesn't go very deep. Workers as a whole still want better wages and safer, more enjoyable jobs; and employers as a whole still want lower wages and higher intensity. But when the choice seems to be between working harder for less money for your specific employer, or losing your job when that employer goes out of business altogether, then many workers will indeed start to identify with the employer.

It is the task of unions and political activists to try to convey a broader perspective on these trade-offs. Lower wages at one company will likely be copied at others, in which case they've had no impact at all on the balance of competition (all that has happened is that wages decline at *all* companies). And workers have a shared interest in shifting the overall balance of economic power in their favour (through government regulations and labour standards, union organizing, and other methods), regardless of the competitive strengths and weaknesses of any particular company.

The seemingly impersonal logic of competition has been "internalized" by many working people. Many will grudgingly accept painful changes – even the loss of their jobs – if they seem to be the result of competitive, impersonal "market forces." If a politician decided their factory should close, workers would immediately protest; but when so-called "markets" decide a factory should close, this is somehow accepted as legitimate. Individual workers rarely have any meaningful influence over the fate of the company they work for, so they shouldn't take its failures (or its successes, for that matter) personally. Nevertheless, the anonymous and seemingly neutral pressure of competition is an effective "screen" to justify incredible social pain and dislocation. If a company folds and all its workers lose their jobs, it's often accepted as fair because "they just couldn't compete." However, we should never forget that "market forces" are not anonymous or impersonal. This is just another name for the efforts of different companies (and their owners) to boost their profits at the expense of others. Competition is not a natural or inevitable force, it does not (in and of itself) justify anything, and people whose lives are damaged because of it should feel fully justified to complain and resist.

12

Business Investment

Investment, and why it matters

We learned in Part Two of this book that the initial decision by a capitalist to invest in a private profit-making business is the first and most important step in the cyclical process of production, income, and consumption. Without it, nothing else happens in capitalism.

When we speak of investment in this context, we are thinking of a real expenditure on buildings, machinery and equipment, or any other tools used in production. We are not thinking of a *financial* investment (like buying stocks, bonds, or other financial assets). We will discuss the (weak) relationship between finance and real investments in Chapters 17–19. In theory, financial investments are supposed to translate into real capital investments, but in practice it doesn't work that way.

Real investment comes in several different forms. The most common is private business investment in FIXED CAPITAL. The two major types of fixed capital are STRUCTURES (buildings, factories, offices, pipelines) and MACHINERY AND EQUIPMENT (machines and tools of all kinds, computers, telecommunications equipment, transportation equipment). Businesses also invest smaller amounts in WORKING CAPITAL to pay for day-to-day operating costs (including the initial wages of newly-hired workers, and the expense of raw materials, parts, and other inputs). Companies also invest in intangible capital assets (like scientific research or computer software). Governments also invest: in public INFRASTRUCTURE and capital associated with public enterprises (like utilities, hospitals, or schools). Meanwhile, individuals invest in their own homes. But of all these investment flows, business fixed investment is the largest; it is also the most important to the rise and fall of any capitalist economy.

Capitalists have a hot-cold relationship to investment. On the positive side is the hunger for additional profits that comes with a larger operation. Reinforcing this urge is the power of competition, which pushes companies to invest in new products or technology as a way of creating or maintaining a competitive edge.

At the same time, however, capitalists are very cautious about making new investments. They think carefully about the risk that they might not make a profit, or might lose their up-front investment altogether. Modern financial institutions (including pension funds and other "institutional" investors) strictly monitor corporate investment spending. If they don't think the expected profits are high enough, they will demand that companies cut back their investment spending. So there's never any guarantee that capitalists actually *want* to invest, even though it is their profit motive that drives the whole system. If they don't reinvest their profits, they can always spend them on other things (like luxury consumption or financial speculation), or just store them away as idle cash.

For the overall economy, however, there is no doubt that investment is a positive and hugely important economic force. Some of the broader economic benefits of strong investment include:

- **Spending power** Business investment spending is normally the most important source of new economic activity under capitalism. (It is supplemented by other expansionary forces, like exports, government spending, and housing construction, that we will discuss in later chapters.) When investment is strong, output and incomes grow. And the new spending sets off a chain-reaction of spending and job-creation in other sectors (including consumer goods and services, once newly-employed workers begin spending their new incomes).
- **Jobs and wages** The relationship between investment and jobs is complex, because sometimes new capital equipment can *replace* workers, resulting in a decrease in employment at a particular firm. The pace of *overall* job-creation, however, depends very positively on the overall level of business investment. In turn, rapid job-creation usually leads to rising wages, as workers take advantage of strong hiring to extract a better deal from employers. Table 12.1 reports several historical periods of strong private investment in various countries; periods of strong investment are usually associated with strong improvements in wages.

Table 12.1 Investment Booms and Workers

	Investment as Share of GDP	Annual Growth in Real Wages
US (1950s)	23%	2.5%
Europe (1960s)	25%	4%
Japan (1960s and 1970s)	32%	5%
Korea (1990s)	35%	5%
Canada (1960s and 1970s)	23%	3%
Australia (1960–75)	22%	3.5%
China (1995–present)	40%+	5–10%?

Source: Author's calculations from national sources, Organization for Economic Cooperation and Development.

- **Transformation** Economies don't just *expand*, they also *evolve* over time: adapting to new technology, new consumer preferences, new social and environmental challenges. Structural and technological changes don't occur seamlessly, however. New technologies, products, and ways of working must almost always be embodied in new capital (like equipment, buildings, and infrastructure). We need investment, therefore, to allow the economy to incorporate these innovations and changes.

- **Productivity** Employers can boost apparent productivity simply by intensifying work – forcing workers to work harder and faster. But that can only go so far. To improve true *efficiency* requires genuine enhancements in products and processes, and this requires investment. Statistical studies have proven that investment in new machinery and equipment is especially important to productivity growth.

- **Environment** We'll discuss environmental concerns in detail in Chapter 16. However, one way to reduce the environmental damage caused by the economy is through major investments in energy-efficient technologies and pollution abatement: high-tech heating and cooling systems, fuel-efficient vehicles, clean power generation, public transit, and more. Building a more sustainable economy will require massive investments in green technologies.

In general, because of all these positive "spin-offs" from investment spending, the broader economy has more at stake in strong business investment than business itself does. In economic language, the *social benefits* of investment spending are

---

Capitalism's Engine

"Investment in tangible assets is the most important source of economic growth in the G7 nations."

Dale Jorgenson, US economist (2007).

"Equipment [investment] appears to have a very high net social return – in the range of 20 percent per year; more than half of this comes from increased total factor productivity ... This suggests, significantly, large external benefits from equipment investment even in rich economies."

J. Bradford De Long and Lawrence Summers, US economists (1992).

"Each new machine produced and put into use is capable of changing the environment in which production takes place, so that learning takes place with continuous new stimuli."

Kenneth Arrow, US economist (1962).

greater than the *private benefits* (that is, the profits that private companies expect when they make an investment).

This is why governments regularly implement measures aimed at stimulating more business investment. Some of these measures have been more effective than others. Policies which reward savings and the financial industry in hopes of boosting real investment are generally very ineffective. On the other hand, policies which directly stimulate real capital spending by businesses (such as investment tax credits and targeted investment incentives) can be more effective. Simply fattening profit margins (for example, by cutting corporate income taxes – as most countries have done under neoliberalism) seldom works, either. Eventually, if efforts to entice more business spending are unsuccessful, governments and communities must learn to supplement or replace profit-driven business investment with other forms of investment (including through public and non-profit models for investing in infrastructure, service delivery, and even goods production, that we will discuss further in Chapter 29).

What determines investment?

At a basic level, investment is motivated by the expectation that a capitalist will earn back their money, plus a sufficient profit margin. Investment is therefore a *forward-looking* decision – and this is incredibly important to understanding its behaviour. Capitalists review current business conditions to judge whether an investment will be profitable in the future. But they always temper those judgements with additional information about how the business environment may change. Most investments, after all, are irreversible: once an investment is made in fixed capital, it is impossible to "take it back" for a refund. At best, purchased buildings and equipment can be sold for scrap or second-hand use (usually for a tiny fraction of the original purchase price). So the fact that investment involves long-term, irreversible commitments makes capitalists inherently cautious, and this makes business investment especially hard to predict.

Table 12.2 lists several of the factors influencing the expected profitability of a new investment, and hence influencing investment spending. Current profits are important, as an indication of future profits. Current profits also provide most of the funds for new business investment. Whether a company's existing facilities are being used to the utmost is another crucial factor; this is called CAPACITY UTILIZATION. Even if current profits are high, a company will not invest in new facilities if its existing facilities still have lots of spare room.

We know that investment causes economic growth. But it is also true that growth causes investment. If an economy is growing quickly, then companies are likely to expand their investment: they are more confident that they'll be able to sell their output, and it's less likely that they'll be stuck carrying excess capacity. Investment

152   Economics for Everyone

Table 12.2   Understanding Investment

Determinants of Amount of Investment:

Current profit	Affects expectations of future profit; provides cash to finance new investments.
Capacity utilization	If current capacity is tight, firms are more likely to invest; but if they have spare capacity, then they won't invest even if profits are high.
Current and expected growth	Firms must be confident that they can sell their output.
Interest rates	Low interest rates (and other finance costs) reduce the cost of borrowing, and reduce the appeal of non-productive "paper" investments.
Political, legal environment	Investors want certainty that their property is secure, and that policies will remain business-friendly.

Determinants of Location of Investment:

Unit labour costs	Companies seek places they can extract more labour effort and productivity, for less compensation.
Infrastructure	Companies need reliable infrastructure (such as electricity, transportation, and communications).
Taxes	Firms will be attracted to jurisdictions with lower taxes on profits, and/or which offer investment subsidies.
Transportation costs	A location must be near major suppliers and major markets; transportation must be reliable and affordable.
Supply chain	Companies must be able to purchase parts, raw materials, services, and other inputs reliably and affordably.
Local market	Firms often locate investments in locations where they also sell much of their output.
Trade policy	Tariffs and other trade policies can make it more or less profitable to produce and sell in a particular market.
Political, legal environment	Concerns over legal and political risks can easily overwhelm the appeal of low production costs.

---

and growth thus reinforce each other: more investment leads to more growth, which in turn leads to more investment (but only up to a point). Economists call this feedback effect the investment **ACCELERATOR**.

Because of this relationship between investment and growth, investors' collective attitudes can actually become self-fulfilling. If investors are optimistic about the future, they increase their investments. This stimulates growth, strong demand conditions, and healthy profits, thus validating their original optimism. When investors are pessimistic, they cut back their spending. But this undermines growth, sales, and profits – and ironically can actually leave companies worse off than they were *before* they cut back on spending. This self-fulfilling mechanism may help to explain the puzzling weakness of investment spending in most countries in recent years: companies worry about future economic problems (especially after the 2008–09 GLOBAL FINANCIAL CRISIS), and hence they are reluctant to commit to new projects. But that reluctance, and resulting weak investment spending, in turn undermines economic growth, reinforcing executives' original pessimism.

This general dependence of overall economic activity (and hence profits) on business investment was captured neatly in a phrase coined by the Polish economist Michal Kalecki: "Capitalists get what they spend." (Workers, in contrast, "spend what they get," reflecting their reliance on wage income to finance necessary consumption.) Pessimistic capitalists who fail to spend, won't generate strong profits either – precisely because of their own collective failure to set the wheels of capitalism into motion.

Interest rates (and financing costs more generally) also affect investment spending. When companies borrow external funds to pay for a new investment (because internal cash flow was insufficient), interest costs are a necessary deduction from revenues. Interest rates also indicate how much investors could earn by buying a purely financial asset (like a bond). If investors can earn high profits on paper assets (say, 8–10 percent per year), they are much less likely to take on the extra risk and trouble of investing in a real business. On the other hand, if purely financial returns are low (say, 4–5 percent), then companies will be more willing to put their money into motion in the real economy.

Finally, private investors will also take account of the broad political, economic, and legal climate before they commit funds for new investments. They worry about regulatory, tax, or policy changes that might undermine future profits. They worry about their ability to extract desired labour effort from paid workers, while minimizing their compensation costs. At times, they may worry more deeply about the stability of the whole arrangement called capitalism that affords them such unique economic power and prosperity in the first place.

The dependence of investment on broader socio-political factors has caused longer-run fluctuations in investment – like the 25-year postwar boom in private investment that drove the Golden Age expansion, and the subsequent downturn in investment spending that accompanied the turmoil and retrenchment of the 1970s and 1980s. It also poses a major hurdle for progressive efforts to challenge the dominance of private business over our economy and society. If it appears that a radical social change movement might be successful in a particular country, private investment spending will likely decline quickly. The economy then deteriorates before the challengers have even implemented their own policies. This is why many left-wing political leaders go out of their way to "reassure" investors of their non-threatening intentions long before ever getting elected. (Unfortunately, catering to business in this way creates its own political problems, by undermining the movement's subsequent ability to implement any change at all.)

Investment location

The preceding factors are all important in determining *whether* a company chooses to invest in a new project, or not. In many cases, the investing company then faces a second and largely separate decision: *where* should it make that investment? Some types of business (especially many service industries) must locate very near to their customers; these industries are called NON-TRADEABLE industries, because their product cannot be shipped long distances. These include retail, hospitality, and many business and personal services, as well as some kinds of perishable agriculture and manufacturing. Most goods-producing industries, however, and many service industries (including telecommunication, banking, and even some education and medical services) can transport or sell their output over long distances. These are called TRADEABLE sectors. In these cases companies can freely choose an investment location that maximizes their profit (depending, of course, on any legal or trade barriers affecting their businesses). When a company invests in a real business operation in another country, it is known as FOREIGN DIRECT INVESTMENT (FDI). The bottom of Table 12.2 lists several of the factors that influence this location decision.

Obviously, production costs will be a crucial influence on investment location. Labour costs are important here. Low wages will be appealing, but must be considered relative to the level of productivity (since, as discussed in Chapter 8, companies aim to minimize unit labour costs, not wages). Indeed, most low-wage countries are not very attractive to investors, because their ultra-low wages are associated with very poor productivity, poverty, and social and political instability. Other cost factors which enter the equation include the availability of reliable infrastructure (such as good electricity and telecommunications services); the availability of a reliable, high-quality supply chain (to supply parts and materials); the costs of shipping supplies and finished goods; and the level of taxes levied on company profits.

Major firms will often establish facilities in countries or regions where they also sell significant volumes of their output. This reduces transportation costs for their finished output, avoids tariffs and other trade barriers, and keeps companies in touch with local consumer tastes. Trade policy (the use of tariffs and other levers to enhance local investment and production) can reinforce this "local market effect" by making it more attractive to produce locally rather than importing.

Socio-political stability is a crucial determinant of investment location, too. Companies will not make expensive, long-term commitments in jurisdictions – even low-cost jurisdictions – where they fear for the basic security of their businesses. Competing efforts by countries around the world to make themselves more "investor-friendly" during the neoliberal era, promising long-term stability and business-friendly attitudes, have been a crucial factor behind changing global patterns of investment in recent decades. Nationalization and expropriation were real threats to investors in many parts of the world in the 1970s. Today this risk is rare; even left-wing governments are desperate to lay out the welcome mat to investors, in light of the importance of investment to overall job-creation and productivity.

Concerns and conflicts about investment location are understandably intense in a world that is desperate for investment and the benefits it brings. In higher-wage developed countries, workers fear a flight of investment to lower-cost jurisdictions. Developing countries, meanwhile, face an uphill challenge to win a larger share of investment – most of which is still concentrated in the advanced capitalist world. The simplistic fear that under globalization all investment will flow to low-wage countries is wrong. But the opposite claim that low wages always reflect low productivity, and hence pose no threat to higher-wage workers, is just as wrong. Modern factories in Mexico and China demonstrate productivity levels comparable to those in Europe or North America, yet labour costs are a small fraction of developed economies. No wonder global companies pour new FDI into China at a rate of over US$100 billion per year; Mexico (where wages are now lower than China's, due to harsh social and labour policies) attracts nearly US $40 billion per year.

The reality of investment mobility, then, is nuanced and complex. If a country can combine low wages, a disciplined and productive workforce, a decent infrastructure and supply network, and political stability, then investors will line up at the door. The long-term migration of investment to lower-cost, pro-business jurisdictions (like China and Mexico) proves that pro-business policies can have a dramatic impact on investment location. Incoming investment certainly generates some jobs and other benefits for working people in those jurisdictions (although their ability to capture a fair share of growing GDP is undermined by the same pro-business policies which attracted the investment in the first place). At the same time, economic pain is experienced in those jurisdictions which lose investment. Finding ways to manage the increasingly intense competition for investment, and to expand the total global amount of investment (thus making it easier for all jurisdictions to capture an adequate amount), will need to be a central component of any progressive global economic strategy.

Investment under neoliberalism

If investment depends on current and expected profits, and on the existence of a stable, business-friendly political and legal climate, then capitalists should be supercharging their investment effort under neoliberalism. Right? Wrong. Curiously, despite the dramatic pro-business shifts in laws, policies, and culture which have occurred in the last quarter-century, and the consequent rise in profits in most jurisdictions, business investment has actually remained quite sluggish.

Figure 12.1 illustrates that net investment spending (after paying off wear and tear on existing assets, known as DEPRECIATION) has markedly deteriorated under neoliberalism. Global investment slowed in the 1980s, as the system adjusted to the initial shock of neoliberal medicine: higher interest rates, cutbacks in government spending, and other tough-love measures. Even as the system adapted to new rules of the game, however, investors did not respond to a more favourable climate with a vigorous economic effort. Investment remains weaker, despite supposedly strong economic "fundamentals" and the economic and political dominance of business, than it was in the crisis-ridden 1970s. Largely because of this failure of the world's capitalists to reinvest their booming profits, average growth in productivity and incomes (other than in China and a few other booming developing countries) has been similarly unspectacular. Because new investment has lagged so far behind the impressive growth of business profits, companies accumulate large hoards of inactive cash, which undermines spending power and job-creation. So while neoliberalism has been successful in restoring business profitability and power, it has not led to stronger world growth.

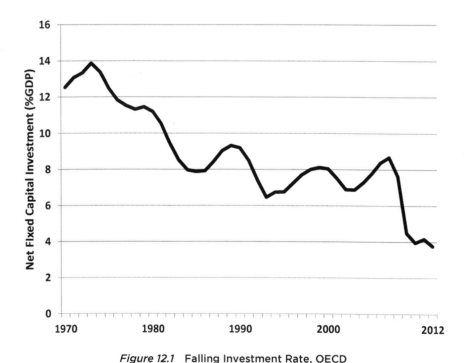

Figure 12.1 Falling Investment Rate, OECD

Source: OECD National Accounts Statistics, unweighted average of 26 countries.
Fixed capital formation net of fixed capital consumption.

Why has the big U-turn of neoliberalism not elicited a more energetic response from the world's capitalists? This is an unanswered puzzle. Even the International Monetary Fund and other mainstream institutions have admitted that global business investment has been disappointing, compared to the high level of business profits.

The intense but pointless hyperactivity of financial markets under neoliberalism has certainly diverted attention from real business investment. Perhaps investors also understand the strict limits that have been placed on global growth by CENTRAL BANK policies. After all, growth in modern capitalism is always kept on a tight leash, in order to prevent labour markets from "overheating" and keep workers perpetually insecure (as we'll discuss more in Chapter 18). Understanding this new regime, businesses may decide there's little point accelerating investment (even though the competitive urge for each individual company to grow at the expense of its competitors still exists).

Whatever the reason, it is clear that the link between current profits and future investment has been seriously weakened. This badly undermines the logic of "trickle-down" economics: namely, that enhancing the profits of companies and their owners will stimulate more investment, more jobs, and higher incomes throughout the economy. In fact, further increases in business profits will likely have little impact on investment at all, given the mountains of idle cash which corporations are already accumulating.

It may even be that many capitalists have lost the primal hunger to expand their wealth at all costs – and are instead content to sit back consuming a larger share of it (in luxurious style), or simply hoarding it away. Once upon a time, this hunger (which Keynes famously referred to as the "animal spirits" of capitalists) was the driving force that made capitalism a dynamic and creative system. If that hunger has indeed abated, then capitalism's fundamental legitimacy as an energetic and progressive force may be threatened. And an important opening will be created for alternative economic visions – offering more convincing ideas for how to mobilize investment to meet our many economic, social, and environmental needs.

Animal Spirits

"Our decisions to do something positive, the full consequences of which will be drawn out over many days to come, can only be taken as the result of animal spirits – a spontaneous urge to action rather than inaction, and not as the outcome of a weighted average of quantitative benefits multiplied by quantitative probabilities."

John Maynard Keynes, British economist (1936).

13

Employment and Unemployment

Supply and demand?

Based on the economic picture we have drawn so far, it is clear that the total level of employment is determined mostly by the decisions of employers and investors. Capitalists invest money in private businesses in search of profit. They hire workers to produce. Other jobs are created in companies which supply those businesses (with capital equipment, raw materials, and other inputs). More jobs still are created in companies which supply consumer goods and services to newly-employed workers (who quickly begin to spend their wages). The ultimate level of employment therefore depends on the initial amount of business investment, and on the extent to which it generates spin-off activities through both supply industries and consumer industries. In other words, total employment depends on the *demand* for labour from investing and producing businesses.

So far there is no reference at all in this story to the issue of labour *supply*: that is, how many workers are willing to offer their services in return for a wage or salary. We have only considered the demand side of the equation: that is, how many workers do employers need, given their investment and production plans. Indeed, there is no particular reason why employment (which depends on business output) should ever equal the number of people who wish to work. In other words, there is no reason to expect **FULL EMPLOYMENT** (see box). If there is not enough investment and production to usefully employ all willing workers, then unemployment will exist – and capitalism has no sure-fire internal mechanism to eliminate it.

Having large numbers of desperate people sitting around without work is a recipe for trouble, however – both economic and political. So there are various ways in which capitalism has tried to manage the problem of mass unemployment. One is through conscious efforts by governments to influence employment levels (using government spending, interest rates, and other tools to stimulate job creation when needed). But flexibility in labour supply is another important economic "shock absorber."

Labour supply tends to *follow* labour demand, and this helps to maintain some rough proportionality between the two sides of the market (although always with a comfortable "cushion" of unemployment). As capitalism was first being established, employers (helped by governments) consciously cultivated new supplies of

Measuring the Labour Market

Labour market statistics are among the most important economic data reported by statistical agencies. Their release (usually each month) is eagerly anticipated by economists, government officials, and financial traders, and they offer the most immediate and direct glimpse into broader economic trends. The key numbers reported include:

- **Working-age population** How many people are considered to be of "normal" working age: say, between the ages of 16 and 65? (The specific ages used in this definition vary from country to country.)
- **Labour force** How many working-age people are employed, or want to be employed (and are actively looking for a job)? These people are considered to be "in" the labour market.
- **Employment** How many people in the labour force are employed? This number can be subdivided into full-time and part-time employment; temporary and permanent; private sector and public sector; and self-employment and paid employment.
- **Unemployment** How many people want to work (and hence are in the labour force), but cannot find work? To count as officially "unemployed," a person must be actively seeking work. (Each country has its own definition of what qualifies as "actively" looking.) Ironically, unemployment can decline simply because unemployed people give up looking, and hence drop out of the labour market (these people are known as discouraged workers).

From these data, several key ratios are calculated. The PARTICIPATION RATE is the proportion of working-age population that officially "participates" in the labour market (by working or looking for work). The UNEMPLOYMENT RATE is the proportion of the labour force that can't find a job, despite actively looking for one. The EMPLOYMENT RATE is the proportion of the working-age population that is actually employed. The unemployment rate depends on whether non-employed individuals are actively seeking work (and hence counted in the labour force), but the employment rate does not. For that reason, the employment rate is usually a more accurate indicator of the true health of the labour market (especially during times of economic weakness, when many unemployed "disappear" from official statistics simply because they gave up looking).

landless workers to sweat and strain in the early factories. As capitalism expanded, a growing share of the population was recruited to wage labour (leaving their former, non-waged activities behind). It's important to remember that the demand for their labour always came first. This pattern of labour demand stimulating new sources of labour supply can still be seen in developing countries.

Even in modern times, it is clear that labour supply follows labour demand. When employment conditions are strong, more workers enter the labour market to search for a job – including women, older and younger workers, immigrants, and other "incremental" sources of labour supply. When demand is weak, many of these people are simply pushed back out of the market. Immigration can be reduced; women may be encouraged to abandon paying work (as they were in the years following World War II); early retirement options can be introduced.

It is certainly possible (although rare) that business could actually "run out" of workers. Capitalists feel this constraint via the pressure that labour shortages place on their profit margins. If unemployment is very low, workers (individually and collectively) feel confident to demand higher wages and better working conditions. Employers must pay them, in order to retain staff and maintain labour discipline. But they will complain loudly about this state of affairs, and pressure governments to develop and mobilize new, cheaper sources of labour supply (preferably lower-cost workers, like contract or agency employees, or temporary migrants from other countries who usually lack full legal protections). One way or another, unemployment never disappears.

Unemployment: "natural," and otherwise

Unemployment is thus a normal feature of the capitalist labour market. Neoclassical economists, who still accept the fiction of full employment, try to downplay the importance of the unemployment we see all around us. They pretend it represents only "frictional" effects (resulting from the time lags associated with seeking and finding a job), or even "voluntary" decisions by unemployed people to turn down available jobs (in favour of collecting unemployment benefits).

In reality, however, unemployment plays an ongoing and important role in the whole system of wage labour (as we discussed in Chapter 8). Employers need a believable threat of job loss to enforce labour discipline in their workplaces. If unemployment falls too low for the good of employers, CENTRAL BANKS will intervene: raising interest rates to re-establish enough unemployment to restrain wages and reinforce labour discipline (we discuss this strategy further in Chapter 18). Even if central banks didn't pro-actively manage this situation, however, investment and job creation would eventually falter as a result of diminishing profitability, until sufficient unemployment was automatically re-created.

Conventional economists have given a name to this ongoing unemployment. Monetarists like Milton Friedman misleadingly termed it the NATURAL RATE OF UNEMPLOYMENT: a term that deliberately reflects their bias that governments shouldn't do anything about it, since unemployment is only "natural". Somewhat less ideologically, other economists call it the NON-ACCELERATING INFLATION RATE OF UNEMPLOYMENT (or NAIRU, for short). The theory suggests that if unemployment falls below this threshold, wage pressures will be passed on by companies in the form of inflation. (In fact, while inflation is one possible

outcome of the tension between workers and employers in a low-unemployment environment, it is not the only possible outcome. And while wages that grow faster than productivity can be one source of inflation, they are not the only source of inflation, nor even the most important source.)

Many neoclassical economists have tried to identify the precise level of the NAIRU, using sophisticated statistical techniques. These efforts have failed, and it is now widely accepted that the NAIRU is neither constant nor measurable; its credibility as a guide for interest rate policy has evaporated. Today, modern central banks tend not to target a specific NAIRU in their efforts to regulate labour markets. But they still explicitly believe the system needs a certain degree of unemployment to restrain wages, and they act forcefully when needed (with higher interest rates) to maintain that cushion.

How much unemployment is needed to discipline labour will depend on various factors – most of which we introduced in Chapter 8, in our discussion of **LABOUR EXTRACTION**. If social benefits are generous, then unemployment is less painful (and hence less "effective" in disciplining workers). If workers enjoy extensive legal protections against arbitrary dismissal, then they will be less fearful of job loss. If unions are stronger, then workers can demand higher wages, even when unemployment is significant.

NAIRU advocates interpret all of these factors as sources of "inflexibility" in labour markets. They argue that weaker unions, workplace protections, and social benefits will allow labour markets to function more "efficiently" (that is, profitably) with a lower long-run level of unemployment. They have thus pushed strongly for policies to enhance what they call labour market "flexibility." This term is another deliberate, highly ideological misnomer. In fact, there are many ways in which a highly disciplined labour market is quite *inflexible*: for example, insecure workers are less likely to quit jobs they aren't well-suited for. The real issue is not flexibility (in the common-sense meaning of being able to adapt to change); the real issues are power and discipline.

There is statistical evidence that central banks permit lower interest rates in countries where workers are structurally disempowered (with weak unions, poor social benefits, and weak workplace protections). In this sense, the belief of central bankers that a "flexible" (that is, business-friendly) labour market can safely attain a lower long-run unemployment rate without threatening profits, becomes self-fulfilling. They then allow interest rates to fall, stimulating more investment (and other kinds of spending), and reducing unemployment. However, this is not the result of any automatic, market mechanism. It is, rather, the result of central banks' active and biased economic *management*.

Wages and employment

The argument is regularly made (by neoclassical economists, employers, and business-friendly politicians) that the unemployed could find work if they simply cut their wage demands and agreed to work for less. Following the same logic, these same powerful voices oppose minimum wages or any other measures (like collective bargaining) which increase wages. Higher minimum wages encourage more people to look for work, but discourage companies from offering employment. For both reasons, they argue, wage-boosting policies backfire, producing unemployment instead of higher living standards.

Many statistical studies, however, have shown that gradual changes in minimum wages have little if any impact on employment levels. More generally, there is no demonstrated statistical relationship between high wages and lower employment. This is because employment levels are not determined, primarily, in the labour market. As we have seen, employment mostly depends on how much private businesses want to *produce*, which in turn depends on how much output they think they can sell. The demand for labour is therefore derived from the demand for the things that labour produces. Wages can affect output levels (and hence employment), but the links are indirect, unpredictable, and relatively weak.

Table 13.1 lists several ways in which lower wages might stimulate higher employment (and higher wages might result in lower employment). But it also lists some other ways in which lower wages can actually lead to *lower* employment – so that wage cuts would be self-defeating.

Let's start with the ways lower wages could stimulate more jobs. Once companies decide how much they want to produce, they have a certain amount of leeway to choose *how* to produce it. In particular, there is limited flexibility in how they combine labour, capital, and other inputs to produce the desired output. In most industries, however, the ratios of capital and labour are fixed quite rigidly by technology. To competitively produce any modern, high-technology product, firms cannot utilize old-fashioned labour-intensive production methods (even if labour is cheap). They must use up-to-date technology and equipment. Occasionally, low wages might allow an employer to use a few extra workers instead of buying a new machine: imagine a landscaping company using ten low-paid workers to dig a ditch, instead of one bulldozer and a driver. These situations are rare, however, and the resulting "substitutability" between workers and machinery is never sufficient to automatically establish full employment. And for many other reasons, it is seldom desirable for economies to use backward, labour-intensive technologies (even if wages are low). So this link between wages and employment is very weak.

Table 13.1 Will Cutting Wages Save Your Job?

Effect	How it Works	Strength
Ways that Lower Wages Lead to MORE Jobs:		
Capital substitution	If wages fall, employers use more labour and less machinery.	Weak
Profit-investment link	Lower wages mean higher profit margins, encouraging capitalists to invest more.	Weak
Competition for jobs	Cutting your wages may attract jobs from other companies or countries.	Zero (net)
Central bank behaviour	Structural weakness in wage demands may "permit" lower interest rates.	Modest
Ways that Lower Wages Lead to FEWER Jobs:		
Consumer spending	Lower wages mean less worker consumption spending, hence less business sales and less production.	Modest
Labour discipline / "efficiency wages"	Reducing wages too low undermines labour effort, productivity, worker retention, and hence profits.	Weak

As discussed above, lower wages might also stimulate higher investment and hence job creation if they produce stronger business profits. This result depends on there being enough purchasing power in the economy, despite falling wages, to purchase all produced output and thus support strong profits. Even then, however, as we noted in Chapter 12, the relationship between profits and investment has been very weak in recent years: profits have increased in most countries, but business investment has actually slowed down. So this link between wage levels and employment is also weak.

From the perspective of an individual company, which competes against other firms, growth may be enhanced if its own *particular* labour costs are reduced. Its products can then be sold more competitively, and its market share will grow. Remember, however, that the growth of one company's market share produces offsetting contractions in output (and hence employment) for other suppliers – which lose sales as a result of their higher wages. On a net basis, cutting wages at one company cannot expand overall employment; at best it merely transfers employment from one firm to another. It is likely, moreover, that *other* competitors will respond by cutting their wages, too – in which case there is no impact on employment at all (or even a negative impact, if overall consumer spending falls as a result of lower wages). The same logic applies to trying to "steal" jobs from another region or country by cutting wages in order to stimulate exports; total global employment is unchanged, and other regions are likely to eventually respond by cutting their own wages.

Perhaps the most important economic link between lower wages and higher employment is the indirect, policy-driven relationship between wage trends and central bank behaviour discussed above. Central banks tightly control the pace of job-creation to keep a lid on wages and protect profit margins. If wage demands are weak, for whatever reason, then bankers may allow the economy to expand a bit further. This whole relationship is rooted in the belief of central bankers that wage pressures are the dominant source of inflation, as well as their assumption that there are no other possible ways of attaining low inflation and low unemployment at the same time.

We must also consider the ways in which lower wages could perversely translate into *less* employment. The most important of these is through the impact of lower wages on workers' consumption spending – which, remember, accounts for about half of GDP in the advanced countries. Workers tend to spend their whole income on household consumption (both goods and services). Lower wages mean less spending, and hence less demand for output. Unless this is more than offset by new investment or exports, total output will contract as a result of the wage cut, and employment will fall.

This relationship is the foundation for the argument, made by some trade unionists and labour advocates, that high wages can actually be "good for business."

The precedent set by Henry Ford in 1914, who offered his workers $5 per day (a very high wage at the time) so they could afford to buy some of the cars they made, is often invoked. There are indeed some situations in which the positive boost to spending power (and hence output) resulting from higher wages can outweigh the negative impacts of higher wages on profits, exports, and other sources of spending. Economists call this situation a WAGE-LED economy. Capitalism can be wage-led under particular conditions: usually when capacity utilization is very low, investment is relatively insensitive to profitability, and the leakage of workers' spending power on the purchase of imported products is limited. It is wrong to conclude, however, that merely raising wages, in and of itself, is generally sufficient to solve unemployment. Normally, higher wages must be supplemented by other measures to stimulate investment (and other forms of spending), to ensure that higher labour costs do not undermine investment and employment. The proposal outlined in Chapter 28 for a *high-investment, sustainable, full-employment economy* is one example of this sort of double-barrelled strategy.

Another factor to keep in mind is the necessity for employers to pay sufficiently high wages to elicit desired work effort from their workers. This is why many

---

Buy My Cars

"The commonest laborer who sweeps the floor shall receive his $5 per day. We believe in making 20,000 men prosperous and contented rather than follow the plan of making a few slave drivers in our establishment millionaires."

Henry Ford, US industrialist (1914).

Henry Ford's decision to pay assembly-line workers a relatively high wage is often interpreted as a symbol of "enlightened capitalism." But his strategy was really motivated more by sophisticated self-interest than by generosity: to attract and motivate high-quality workers, he paid what economists now call an "efficiency wage" – far higher than the "going rate" in the labour market. But wouldn't paying higher wages also help Ford sell more cars? Not directly: after all, only a tiny share of the total output from his fantastic new factories was purchased by people who actually worked there. Sadly, Ford's approach to labour relations has gone out of vogue as the US economy becomes steadily more desperate and unequal. Indeed, starting in 2007 the Ford company won agreement from its hard-pressed union to pay newly-hired autoworkers as little as US$14 per hour (or $112 for an eight-hour day). Incredibly, adjusted for 100 years of inflation, Ford's original $5 per day back in 1914 was a higher rate of real daily pay (now worth about $120 per day at today's prices). So despite incredible advances in technology and automation, today's newly-hired autoworkers make less than their counterparts did a century ago. And not many of them can afford to buy a new car.

companies (especially larger, sophisticated firms) will not cut wages even when high unemployment might allow them to. It is more important to their profitability to continue paying relatively high wages, as part of their effort to retain and discipline workers. (Some economists refer to this effect as EFFICIENCY WAGES.) If they did cut wages, employee morale and retention would deteriorate, and productivity and profitability would suffer – with negative long-run effects on the company's employment.

On the whole, in summary, fluctuations in wages have very little impact on employment. Wages cannot be so high that they unduly undermine profits and prevent adequate investment. They cannot be too low, either: they must provide for the reproduction of workers and their families, they must allow employers to elicit desired work effort and labour discipline, and they must support enough consumption spending by workers to absorb much of the nation's output. Between these two extremes is a wide range of possible wage levels. Where precisely wages settle will depend on a mix of structural, institutional, and political factors (such as the strength of trade unions), and broader economic conditions (most importantly, the level of output and hence the level of employment). At most, wage levels have a weak and ambiguous effect on employment.

You Write the Book: Who Really Works Hard?

A modern economy includes a huge variety of different jobs, offering different wages and working conditions. Neoclassical economists claim that all workers are paid according to their productivity; also, wage differentials should "compensate" workers for especially challenging or unpleasant work. In reality, however, workers who perform the most unpleasant, difficult, and challenging jobs also tend to be paid relatively low wages. The same power imbalances that push them into accepting the least desirable jobs, also constrain their ability to earn higher wages. Meanwhile, those with comfortable, rewarding jobs also tend to earn higher incomes – and none are higher than the salaries and bonuses received by top executives of companies. Think of a worker who performs a job that is dirty, difficult, or dangerous. Is their income higher, to compensate them for their challenging working conditions? How would you explain the difference between their income, and the income of chief executives? Is it due to productivity or difficulty? Or something else? Send your examples to author@economicsforeveryone.com. We'll post several at www.economicsforeveryone.com.

Demographics and labour supply

Most countries in the world are experiencing significant demographic shifts. Higher living standards have led to growing life expectancy and falling birth rates in most parts of the world, and hence to an increase in the proportion of the population that is elderly. This "problem" (most people would not consider living longer to be a problem at all!) is most acute in developed countries. But some developing countries (notably China) are also ageing rapidly.

This has sparked considerable concern among employers and some governments, who warn of an impending era of labour shortages. Employers worry about higher wages and difficulties in recruitment. Governments worry about paying for retirement benefits and health costs. Both concerns are exaggerated. And the main proposed "solution" – namely, encouraging or even forcing people to work longer in life – could be worse than the "problem."

We know from history that employers are very adept at identifying and recruiting new sources of labour supply whenever tight labour markets impinge on their profitability. There are plenty of potential new labour sources still available, without forcing older people to stay in the workforce – so long as employers are required to make those opportunities sufficiently appealing. For example, women's labour force participation is still lower than men's, and hence (with appropriate supports, such as child care services and family-friendly work schedules) more women could be encouraged to accept paid work.

Immigration is another tried-and-true source of "flexible" labour supply. Immigrant workers (especially workers on temporary visas, and "illegal" migrants) are an especially vulnerable workforce, and are exploited accordingly. More humane immigration programs (featuring good legal protections, training, and settlement supports) could expand labour supply in a manner that enhances, rather than undermines, labour standards.

Employers could also respond to a genuine labour shortage by investing in new capital and new skills. Labour would thus be transferred from menial, degrading, and unproductive work toward higher-value, better-paid occupations. But it is only when labour shortages really begin to "bite," impinging on profit margins, that employers will be forced to treat labour as a valuable and scarce commodity – and hence upgrade the quality and productivity of work. If central bankers clamp down on growth to ensure that labour remains "cheap," then this positive transformation of work will never occur.

It is always structural factors, more than "supply and demand," that ultimately determine the economic position of labour. Nevertheless, the coming demographic shifts may provide workers with some opportunity to enhance their economic and political position in society. But this will not happen if employers are permitted to re-create abundant supplies of cheap, desperate labour by exploiting vulnerable immigrants or compelling older workers to keep working.

14

Inequality and its Consequences

In its genes

Economics is the study of work: what we produce. But it is also the study of who gets what, and what we do with it. Production and distribution are closely linked, since what we produce, how much of it, and how we produce it all depend on the distribution and final use of that output. Some reformers concede that capitalism is efficient and productive, and limit their ambitions to redistributing some output in order to attain a decent society at the end of the day. But for both economic and political reasons, production and distribution cannot be separated so easily. Pure redistribution is unlikely to permanently succeed, so long as the prior, fundamental inequality in economic power at the point of production (between those who own most wealth, and those who are employed by them do the work) is unquestioned.

Deep inequality across individuals and groups in society is an inherent feature of capitalism. There are many different ways to measure that inequality: according to income, wealth, power, health, happiness, security, and more. We can consider inequality of opportunity: that is, differences in peoples' starting points in life, before they've even begun their education or their working lives. And we can consider inequality of outcome: the even bigger differences that emerge between peoples' economic trajectories over their lifetimes of work, production, and sacrifice. There are many reasons why inequality is created and re-created in society. It's not an accidental outcome: under capitalism, inequality is the normal state of affairs. In fact, there is mounting evidence that, without powerful interventions aimed at limiting and countering inequality, it tends to get worse over time, not better.

Understanding these polarizing forces within capitalism, and understanding the profound consequences of inequality for our individual and collective well-being, will be increasingly important in confronting the worst excesses of this economic system. Inequality strikes a deep moral chord among many people. Despite far-fetched arguments trying to justify the enormous gaps between rich and poor (advanced by economists, politicians, and the wealthy), most people instinctively recoil at the contrast between a luxuriously rich elite and everyone else struggling to get by. Indeed, outrage over inequality has fuelled some of the

---

It's Better

"I've been rich and I've been poor. Believe me, honey, rich is better."

Sophie Tucker, American vaudeville singer (c. 1930s).

---

most potent opposition to neoliberal policies and politics: like the worldwide "Occupy" movement which sprang up after the GLOBAL FINANCIAL CRISIS. And new scientific evidence about the far-reaching consequences of inequality for physical, emotional, and social well-being has reinforced this powerful critique of capitalism's yawning economic divide.

Dimensions of inequality: factors of production

There are two broad ways to think about the distribution of income: across the major FACTORS OF PRODUCTION (that is, comparing labour, capital, and other economic inputs), and across different individuals or households. These two approaches are related, of course, since what we call "factors" are actually economic resources that belong to different groups of *people* (as we learned in Chapter 7).

Income distribution across factors depends on the economic, political and social power of the owners of each factor. Under capitalism, as we have seen, employers pay wages and salaries on the basis of their need to attract and retain employees, and then extract desired labour effort and discipline. How much employers have to pay in this effort depends on many factors: including the level of unemployment, institutional constraints (like trade unionism, minimum wages, and labour regulations), workers' attitudes and expectations, and the nature of technology.

Profits are the residual remaining after wages and other input costs have been paid out of current production. (Remember, the costs of purchased inputs such as capital equipment, parts, and raw materials also embody a similar split between wages and profits. By calculating factor incomes generated at each stage of production, and then adding them up along the economy's entire "value chain," eventually we can calculate a wage-profit split for the whole economy.) Income received by small business owners and farmers, meanwhile, reflects a combination of their own personal labour, and the wealth embodied in their businesses.

These structural determinants of factor incomes evolve over time. Labour steadily increased its share of total income in the OECD economies during the Golden Age expansion – not because of "supply and demand" forces, but mostly because of steady improvements in labour's economic and political bargaining position. As indicated in Figure 14.1, however, since the early 1980s the shoe has been on capitalism's other foot, and labour's share of output has fallen steadily. Capital income has increased thanks to neoliberal economic and social policies which undermine labour and reinforce the power of businesses and their owners. Small business income, meanwhile, has stagnated or declined over time, reflecting agricultural depopulation and the marginalization of most non-farm small businesses.

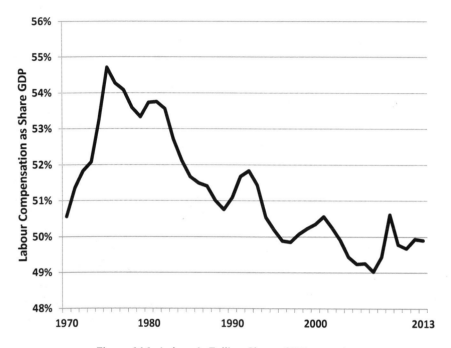

Figure 14.1 Labour's Falling Share, G7 Economies

OECD National Account Statistics, unweighted average seven largest economies.
Labour compensation (wages, salaries, and benefits) plus employer social security contributions.

Dimensions of inequality: households and individuals

The other way to understand inequality is to measure incomes across different individuals or households. Most individuals receive income from more than one source: from their own work, from government programs (like unemployment insurance, public pensions, or other TRANSFER PAYMENTS), and perhaps from investments. After totalling income from all these sources, how large are the income differences between individuals and households? (See box.)

Of course, investment income is concentrated among the wealthy households who own most financial wealth. Working households, on the other hand, receive most of their lifetime income from employment (supplemented, to varying degrees, by government income security programs). Thus there is a clear overlap between the distribution of income across factors, and the distribution of income across households – for the obvious reason that particular households rely on particular types of factor income. After all, economic classes exist precisely because identifiable groups of people play structurally different economic roles. Even among workers, however, inequality exists, and can rise or fall over time. Inequality between workers reflects differences in the degree of bargaining power which they wield in their respective efforts to attain work and negotiate decent wages, as well as the role of taxes and social programs in offsetting differences in household income between workers.

As the overall returns to capital have grown under neoliberalism, so too has the share of personal income captured by the very richest segment of society (namely, the ones who own most capital). This partly reflects direct capital incomes (like dividends, capital gains, and profits from privately-held businesses). But the super-sized compensation received by CEOs and other top executives is also, directly or indirectly, a payment to "capital" (even though it is usually counted as "labour income" in official economic statistics). After all, the most lucrative payments to executives are now stock options, equity grants, and other capital-related arrangements. And even when they are paid direct salary, multi-million-dollar CEO compensation is clearly driven by the overall profitability of the enterprise, not their personal "work". So for both the major owners of capital, and the hired top guns who manage their companies, the growth of capital income has been the key source of their rising personal income in recent decades. Moreover, thanks to the preferential tax treatment of capital income that prevails in most capitalist countries (whereby dividends and capital gains are taxed at lower rates, if at all), the growth of capital income has had an even larger impact on the distribution of after-tax income.

Because capital income is concentrated so precariously at the very top echelons of society, any increase in the relative importance of capital income will have an automatic polarizing effect on income distribution. Now a larger share of income is going to those who were already rich. If they, in turn, save and invest some of that higher income, then the tendency is reinforced. In this way, over time, changes in

Almost Inevitable

"When the rate of return on capital significantly exceeds the growth rate of the economy, ... then it logically follows that inherited wealth grows faster than output and income ... Under such conditions, it is almost inevitable that inherited wealth will dominate wealth amassed from a lifetime's labour by a wide margin, and the concentration of capital will attain remarkably high levels."

Thomas Piketty, French economist (2014).

Measuring Inequality

Here is a brief introduction to the various methods that economists and statisticians use to define and measure inequality.

First, we must decide what variable we are measuring. Income inequality measures differences in the amount of current income which individuals or households receive in a year. We can measure income for individuals, or for families. Some low-income individuals belong to families with high-income members, and hence their actual standard of living may be higher than their own personal income would allow. On the other hand, if high-income people tend to marry each other (as is often true), then inequality in family incomes can be greater than inequality across individuals.

Income can be measured before tax, or after tax. It can include TRANSFER PAYMENTS from governments (such as unemployment benefits or public pensions), or it might include only "market" incomes (such as wages, salaries, investment income, and small business income). *After*-tax income *including* transfer payments is much more equal than *before*-tax income *excluding* transfers. This is because high-income individuals in most countries pay more income tax, but low-income individuals receive more transfer payments. Across the OECD countries on average, the tax-and-transfer system reduces inequality by about one-quarter.*

Wealth inequality can also be measured. This compares the accumulated wealth of different households – including home-ownership, direct business wealth, and financial assets (such as stocks, bonds, and savings accounts). Wealth is distributed far more unequally than income. And financial wealth is distributed the most unequally of all (since the only significant form of wealth owned by most working people is non-financial: namely, the equity in

▸

---

the factor distribution of income (favouring capital) have cascading, concentrating effects on the personal distribution of income.

Neoliberalism and inequality

Rising inequality across most of the world has been closely associated with the policies and practices of neoliberalism. In fact, there is no better way to measure the motives for, and successes of, neoliberalism than by analyzing the evolving share of income received by the richest 1 percent of society. [As we noted in Chapter 7, the segment of society which owns and controls enough financial and business wealth to evade the compulsion to work for a living, is actually slightly over 2 percent – but zeroing in on the richest 1 percent is statistically convenient. And as the Occupy protestors showed, it certainly makes for a good political slogan!] The income share of the richest 1 percent declined steadily through the postwar Golden Age, but then recovered dramatically after the beginning of neoliberalism.

their own homes). As discussed in Chapter 7, business and financial wealth in advanced capitalist countries is owned by a surprisingly small and wealthy elite; in most countries a clear majority of financial and business wealth is owned by less than 10 percent of society, and the richest 1 percent typically owns one-third or more.

Once we decide which variable we are measuring, a convenient way must be selected to summarize inequality. One way is to compare the income or wealth of the top fifth (or tenth) of the population, to the bottom fifth (or tenth). These are called quintile (fifth) or decile (tenth) INCOME RATIOS. Another way is to calculate a statistic called a GINI COEFFICIENT. This statistic varies between 0 (a situation of perfect equality, where everyone has an equal share) and 1 (a situation of perfect inequality, where the richest person gets everything). A rise in the Gini coefficient indicates an increase in inequality.

In recent years, many researchers have concentrated their attention on TOP INCOME SHARES: measuring the share of total income received by the richest 1 percent, or 0.1 percent, or even 0.01 percent of households. It turns out that these small elites (which correspond closely to the class of "major owners and top managers" we defined in Chapter 7) have captured an enormous share of new income under neoliberalism – and this concentration of income at the top explains most of the overall growth in inequality. Moreover, official data on top income shares underestimate the true riches of these lucky people. It's very hard to gather accurate data on top incomes due to sampling errors (they constitute such a small portion of society they are never fully captured in statistical samples), evasion on tax returns, and incomplete measurement of capital gains and business income.

* Organization for Economic Cooperation and Development, *Economic Policy Reforms 2012: Going for Growth* (2012, p. 186).

Figure 14.2 illustrates this top income share for the US. The graph resembles a giant "U." The richest 1 percent of Americans took home an enormous share of total national income (as much as one-fifth) in the 1920s. This was the so-called "Gilded Age," when the economy was dominated by enormously powerful capitalists (like railway and petroleum magnates). Their share of the pie declined in the 1930s with the Great Depression, due to financial losses from the stock market crash and resulting stagnation. It declined further during World War II (as wartime production boosted incomes in the rest of society), and further still through the vibrant postwar expansion. In those years, most workers enjoyed rising living standards thanks to strong job-creation, confident unions, and a growing SOCIAL WAGE. Capital incomes, meanwhile, were squeezed by wages, by taxes (to pay for expanded public programs), and by lacklustre financial markets. By the mid-1970s, the richest 1 percent of US society was pocketing "only" around 8 percent of total national income. Pity the poor elite: they still took home 8 times more than a fair "share" of the pie, but that was a pale shadow of the treatment they enjoyed in earlier decades.

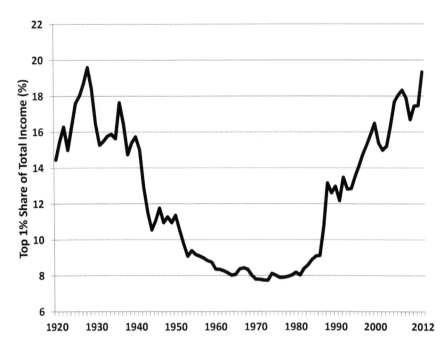

Figure 14.2   Top 1% Share of Total US Income

Source: World Top Incomes Database.

That's when the wealthy and powerful of society began to formulate a plan to turn things around. As we reviewed in Chapter 3, this consisted of multidimensional efforts to reinforce the power and freedom of private businesses, and the wealthy individuals who are their major owners. Strict monetary policy was used to reduce inflation and restore the sanctity of financial returns, and financial deregulation allowed those with wealth more leeway to play the paper casinos of the financial system. Tough labour policies undermined unions, reduced workers' expectations, and dampened wage pressures. Globalization further suppressed the bargaining power of labour (since workers everywhere now feared relocation of their work to somewhere cheaper), and opened up new profit-making terrain for the private sector. Finally, government tax and spending measures amplified the growing inequality in after-tax incomes. For example, average personal income tax rates on high-income individuals across the OECD countries declined by more than one-third in the first three decades of neoliberalism. Taxes on capital income (like dividends and capital gains) were reduced even further. At the same time, income support programs for lower-income people (especially those of working age) were ruthlessly suppressed.

All this translated into a dramatic rebound in the share of total income taken home by the richest part of society. This rebound was particularly dramatic in the US, where the richest 1 percent of society once again now receive as large a share of total income as in the 1920s. The huge stock market losses incurred by the wealthy during the 2008–09 financial crisis was only a temporary setback for this concentration of income. After 2010 (as stock markets bounced back, but labour markets remained mired in underemployment and austerity), the rich once again captured far more than their share of whatever new income was generated by an anaemic recovery. In fact, by some measures the richest 1 percent of Americans pocketed all of the personal income gains generated in the US economy in the first several years of recovery after the meltdown.

That's Why We Did It

"The overall dynamics of capitalism under neoliberalism, both nationally and internationally, were determined by new class objectives that worked to the benefit of the highest income brackets: capitalist owners and the upper fractions of management."

Gérard Duménil and Dominique Lévy, French economists (2011).

The extent to which the richest segments of society captured the lion's share of new incomes generated under neoliberalism is shocking. In the US, according to data compiled by the Organization for Economic Cooperation and Development, 47 percent of all new personal income generated between 1975 and 2007 was received by the richest 1 percent. In contrast, the bottom 90 percent of Americans took home just 18 cents of each dollar in new income over that generation. The US experience is the most extreme, but the very rich in other Anglo-Saxon countries also captured hugely disproportionate shares of new incomes under neoliberalism – including Canada (37 percent), the UK (24 percent), and Australia (23 percent). Even in more egalitarian countries like Sweden and Norway, the top 1 percent captured 10 percent of all new income.* (Feel sorry for the unfortunate elites of Denmark: they captured a mere 2.5 percent of all new income since 1975. Denmark is one of the only countries in the world where top income shares have declined in recent years.) Clearly, the whole idea of neoliberalism has been to make the rich richer – and by that simple standard, it has been very successful.

Poverty

One of the most glaring failures of capitalism is the continuing widespread existence of poverty – often extreme poverty. Even in the advanced economies,

---

* Organization for Economic Cooperation and Development, "Focus on Top Incomes and Taxation in OECD Countries" (May 2014).

many millions of people endure terrible economic and social deprivation, despite the incredible wealth all around them.

Even worse is the oppressive and grinding poverty that is so widespread in less developed countries: most of Africa, large parts of Asia and Latin America, and some former Communist countries in Eastern Europe. Indeed, the widest gaps in income in the world are the ones between richer and poorer countries. We will discuss these international dimensions of poverty and income distribution further in Chapter 23.

Poverty can be measured in different ways (see box). The extent of poverty varies greatly across the advanced economies. The US experiences the worst poverty among major developed economies, as summarized in Table 14.1. It has the weakest unions and labour market protections, and relies more on low-wage jobs. Not coincidentally, it also has the weakest social programs (to supplement low-wage incomes, and support those who are not employed). Anglo-Saxon economies (like Australia and Canada), Asian economies (Japan and Korea), and Mediterranean countries (like Spain and Greece) also have relatively high poverty rates.

Table 14.1 **Poverty Rates in Advanced Economies**

Country	Poverty Rate 2010 (%)*
United States	17.4
Japan	16.0
Spain	15.4
Korea	14.9
Australia	14.4
Greece	14.3
Italy	13.0
Canada	11.9
New Zealand	10.3
United Kingdom	10.0
Belgium	9.7
Switzerland	9.5
Sweden	9.1
Germany	8.8
Austria	8.1
France	7.9
Netherlands	7.5
Norway	7.5
Finland	7.3
Iceland	6.4
Denmark	6.0

* Poverty defined as individuals receiving less than 50% of median income after tax and after transfers, 2010 or most recent year.

Source: Organization for Economic Cooperation and Development, Income Distribution and Poverty Database.

In contrast, the Nordic and some continental European economies demonstrate much lower levels of poverty. Denmark has the lowest rate of poverty of any developed capitalist country, barely one-third the US rate. This indicates that there is nothing inevitable about poverty, despite the seeming universality of neoliberalism. Countries which invest in social programs, labour market supports, income security programs, and other proactive measures can continue to generate good jobs, protect those without work, and achieve very low rates of poverty.

Many economists and politicians prefer to blame poverty on the characteristics of poor people, rather than on the economy in which they live and work. They are urged to upgrade their skills, or improve their work ethic, or refine their job search strategies – often with trite advice like learning to prepare a more attractive resumé and develop better personal "networks". Obviously, learning new skills or improving one's job search can enhance the job chances for any particular *individual* – even someone from a relatively badly-off segment of the labour market. But this will never eliminate poverty in an economy with weak social programs and labour market supports, where concentrations of low-wage jobs (and low-wage workers to fill those jobs) are naturally *re-created* over time.

Suppose that every low-wage worker in the US (or any other highly unequal economy) graduated from college and prepared a sophisticated, modern resumé. Some would find better jobs. Yet the US economy would still need poor, desperate workers to fulfil the nastiest, worst-paid jobs in the system: washing dishes in restaurants, cleaning office towers at night, stocking cheap products at Wal-Mart. Moreover, the entire labour extraction strategy of employers depends in large part on the (highly visible) existence of poverty. It provides a constant reminder to employed low-wage workers of why they should follow the rules and work hard, despite lousy pay and working conditions. So new groups of workers would eventually be channelled into low-wage labour market segments, and poverty and inequality would be reproduced again.

Reducing poverty will ultimately require challenging these basic mechanisms of the capitalist labour market – rather than blaming or hectoring its most desperate victims.

The new science of inequality

In recent years, researchers from many disciplines have discovered surprising new evidence about the major economic, social, and even physiological costs of inequality and poverty. Moreover, they have shown that those costs are not just experienced by those who are poor; there are many ways in which non-poor people also suffer from poverty and inequality. This multi-disciplinary evidence

---

Measuring Poverty

Statisticians have long argued about the best way to measure poverty. The main debate is over whether to use absolute or relative indicators.

ABSOLUTE POVERTY measures whether an individual's material standard of living is lower than some arbitrary, fixed level. That benchmark is established at a certain point in time, based on the cost (at that time) of buying certain "necessities" of life (basic shelter, food, clothing, and other essentials). The cost of that bundle of basic goods usually grows over time (due to inflation), and the poverty threshold is adjusted accordingly.

The problem with this approach, however, is that it ignores the evolution of social standards regarding what constitutes a "minimum" acceptable standard of living. One hundred years ago, it was a luxury to have an indoor flush toilet. Today it is considered essential for decency and good health. An absolute poverty line established a century ago would therefore assume that people can still survive quite acceptably with outdoor facilities. The same goes for television sets, access to education and health care, transportation, internet connections, and other amenities once considered "luxuries" – but which are now clearly essential to an individual's health and participation in modern life.

For these reasons, most poverty experts prefer to use the concept of RELATIVE POVERTY. These determine whether someone is poor, in relation to typical income levels in the rest of society. If a person or household's income falls below some threshold relative to average incomes in broader society (perhaps half of average or median levels), then they are considered to be poor – even if their income might still be sufficient to meet the physiological

▶

---

strengthens the argument for reducing inequality, and suggests that doing so will be economically (as well as socially) beneficial.

For example, new medical research has documented numerous consequences of relative poverty for human health. Feeling that one is somehow inferior or short-changed relative to the rest of society produces significant stress (experienced physically as well as emotionally). This stress can be measured empirically (through tests for stress hormones, glucose, or white blood cells – all of which are released by the body in response to perceived threats). While these short-term stress responses (rooted in our evolutionary "fight or flight" instinct) help humans deal with immediate danger, long-run and chronic stress is damaging in many ways. It has been shown to cause heart disease, obesity, diabetes, mental illness, and many other health problems.

Health statisticians have known for years that these conditions are all strongly correlated with low income. But now we know this correlation is not primarily the result of the personal lifestyle choices or "bad habits" of poor people. A long-term self-conception as disadvantaged, inadequate, or underachieving compared to others (especially when experienced from an early age) can cause measurable health requirements of survival. This recognizes that whether or not a person "feels" poor depends on their relative position in society, not just on their absolute material standard of living. New scientific research on the physical and mental health consequences of inequality (summarized in this chapter) emphasizes the importance of these relative comparisons for a person's self-worth and well-being.

Different poverty measures produce very different estimates of poverty. The US government uses an absolute threshold for its official poverty statistics – one that has not been updated (other than for simple inflation) since 1964. By this measure, poverty in the US has been fairly steady over the past half-century, fluctuating between 12 percent and 15 percent (it increased to 15 percent after the 2008–09 recession). This implies that the absolute living standard of the poorest Americans has not changed at all in the 50 years since that benchmark was determined (a shocking result considering all the technological and productivity improvements experienced in that time). Using a relative poverty measure (such as the proportion of population receiving less than 50 percent of the median income – a common international standard), US poverty is even higher (17.4 percent in 2012). In 2012 an estimated 28 percent of employed Americans earned wages below the absolute poverty threshold for a family of four, so even among employed people poverty is a serious problem.*

Poverty measures must also be adjusted for other factors, including the number of individuals living in a household, and whether a household lives in a rural region or a (more expensive) urban location.

* Economic Policy Institute, *State of Working America* (2013).

damage – no matter how self-disciplined and nutrition-conscious an individual may be. The true culprit is an economic and social system which re-creates and glorifies wealth and conspicuous consumption, while simultaneously handicapping the self-worth of so many.

Partly through these negative impacts on physical and mental health, systemic inequality has many consequences for economic, fiscal, and social indicators. Poorer children experience worse education outcomes, for many reasons: they attend less resourced, less stable schools; they benefit from fewer emotional and financial resources at home; they experience poorer health and self-esteem. Poor education outcomes in turn are linked to criminality, incarceration, health problems, teenage pregnancy, and premature death. The concrete, measurable consequences of inequality are confirmed in many other indicators: including happiness, mental illness, infant mortality, homicide, and imprisonment.

This new research also confirms the enormous costs of inequality that are experienced more broadly by society and government – on top of the direct hardship experienced by poor people. For instance, since inequality is clearly bad for health, it also imposes major fiscal costs on governments, which must spend

---

Keeping Up With the Joneses

"The problems in rich countries are not caused by the society not being rich enough ... but by the scale of material differences between people within each society being too big. What matters is where we stand in relation to others in our own society."

Richard Wilkinson and Kate Pickett, UK epidemiologists (2009).

---

billions to treat preventable, inequality-related illnesses. The same goes for the immense public and private costs of crime and educational failure.

Meanwhile, even mainstream economists now recognize the myriad ways that inequality harms economic performance. An absence of trust and social cohesion, experienced most acutely in poor neighbourhoods (but spilling over throughout the economy), interferes with the ability to do business, settle contracts, and build partnerships and networks. Neoclassical economists call this effect SOCIAL CAPITAL: they say that a community's cumulative "investment" in mutual trust and cohesion pays off in enhanced productivity. This terminology is awkward: neoclassical writers are trying to fit a round peg (acknowledging the benefits of equality) into a square hole (their economic theory in which the pursuit of private wealth is the driving force of all efficiency and progress). The only way for them to understand the economic benefit of equality is to define it as somehow akin to a private "asset" – hence the odd term "social capital." But the mechanisms they have identified are undeniable: it is harder to undertake any kind of economic activity when you are distrustful, or even fearful, of those working with and around you.

Other economic studies have empirically linked widespread educational attainment and social inclusion to an economy's capacity to innovate and become more productive over time. In the stagnant macroeconomic conditions prevailing after the GLOBAL FINANCIAL CRISIS, the impact of growing inequality on consumer purchasing power is making things worse. Since high-income households save so much of their income (and, worse yet, invest some of those savings in unproductive financial speculation), the continuing redistribution of income toward the rich is persistently undermining economic recovery. Targeting working and poor households with more income (through wage-boosting institutions, transfer payments, and more) would therefore help to stimulate overall demand and job-creation.

Another dimension of recent inequality research has shown that inequality tends to become self-reinforcing over time, in the absence of countervailing efforts to reduce income gaps. The bigger are the differences between income groups, the more effort do higher-income people put into protecting their own privelege, and ensuring that their advantages are inherited by their children. These efforts (like building gated communities, or paying for private schools, or even voting against income support programs for poor people) may seem rational for well-off families. But they are unproductive (not to mention unethical) from the perspective of the whole economy. One immediate consequence of this perverse, self-reinforcing tendency is that poverty tends to become geographically concentrated (in very poor neighbourhoods) whenever inequality is worse. That makes it even worse for poor people, because now they must confront not only their own poverty – they must also grapple with the consequences of their neighbours' poverty (experienced through crime, disfunction, and social exclusion).

Precisely because of these barriers to social mobility (erected to protect privelege and keep the poor at a safe social and physical distance), the more unequal is a society, the less mobility there is between classes. For example, the income ratio between the richest and poorest segments of society in the US is more than three times larger than in Denmark. Correspondingly, the correlation between a parent's income and the income their child takes home later in life is also more than three times stronger in America than in Denmark (where a parent's income has only a minor impact on the income eventually earned by their children). Data from other countries confirms that very unequal societies experience much weaker social mobility.* This evidence completely refutes the "Horatio Alger" myth propagated in US culture, which pretends that any poor person with a good idea and strong work ethic can climb to the highest rungs of society. To the contrary, poor people (and their children) tend to stay poor, while rich people wastefully expend real economic resources to ensure that they (and their children) stay rich. This confirms that once inequality gets going, it will get worse over time – unless we consciously and deliberately stop it.

Fighting inequality

The causes of widening inequality in advanced capitalist economies in recent decades are hardly mysterious, and can be traced directly to the fundamental goals and tools of neoliberal economic policy. Governments and employers have worked systematically to weaken workers' institutional power and suppress wages. So incomes for the 85 percent of people who depend on wage labour to support themselves and their families have stagnated. Full employment was abandoned as a policy goal, with the economy deliberately managed to maintain enough unemployment to discipline workers and suppress wages. At the same time, FISCAL POLICY has reduced the extent of redistribution through the tax-and-transfer system (both by cutting taxes for businesses and high-income households, and by

---

* Miles Corak, "Inequality from Generation to Generation: The United States in Comparison." In Robert Rycroft, ed. *The Economics of Inequality, Poverty, and Discrimination in the 21st Century* (Santa Barbara: California: ABC-CLIO, 2013).

reducing transfer payments and income security programs). FINANCIALIZATION has enhanced the capacity of those with wealth to profit even further from that wealth – including through investments in ever-more elaborate (and destabilizing) securities, playing the markets anywhere in the world. So it's hardly surprising that inequality (driven by the concentration of income and wealth among the highest-income segments of society) has grown. To the contrary, that was largely the point of the whole exercise.

Reversing that unacceptable and economically damaging trend, therefore, requires confronting the major pillars of neoliberal policy – and the political assumptions and arguments that support it. Since most people depend on wage labour for their income, creating a lot more jobs would immediately and powerfully reduce inequality; that's why inequality fell so dramatically during World War II. Instead of suppressing wages, disempowering unions, and facilitating PRECARIOUS WORK, higher wages should become the goal of economic policy, attained through institutional measures like higher minimum wages, restored collective bargaining, and other tools. Targeted efforts must aim to overcome the barriers associated with LABOUR MARKET SEGMENTATION (described in the next chapter), so all workers can share in the benefits of a broad employment- and wage-led expansion. Fiscal and tax policies need to reemphasize redistributive goals, while raising the necessary funds for the ambitious expansion of public investment and public programs that will be part of the overall job-creation effort.

These are the obvious core elements of a progressive alternative to neoliberalism. Precisely how those goals can be formulated and implemented will be considered in the final part of this book. For now, we simply need to understand that if we want to challenge inequality in a serious and sustained way, we will need to tackle the whole direction of economic policy that's been engineered under neoliberalism.

15

Divide and Conquer

We're all workers, but ...

We have argued throughout this book that the vast majority of people in developed capitalist economies share one fundamental economic characteristic: they must work for someone else, to generate the income they need to support themselves and their families. They need to find a job, do what they're told ... and then hope that what they take home at the end of each month is enough to pay the bills. Today's economy includes an immense variety of jobs, in different industries, working under different conditions, requiring different levels and types of skills, and different kinds of mental and physical exertion. But all employment (or "wage labour") is similar in this essential way: an employee does the work, while the boss tells them what to do, pays them for it, owns their output, and decides when and where the workers' services are required. We estimated in Chapter 7 that around 85 percent of households in advanced capitalist societies support themselves over their lifetimes primarily through wage labour.

Not surprisingly, however, among such a large and diverse group of "workers," there are important differences in income, power, security, and status. Remember, income distribution in capitalism depends largely on the structural and institutional power of the various players in the game. That's why the overall share of GDP going to workers (in the form of wages, salaries, and non-wage benefits) fluctuates over time with the broad economic and political power of working people – and why that share has declined steadily under neoliberalism as employers consolidated their economic, political, and cultural power. For the same reason, wages earned in particular industries or occupations also reflect the specific bargaining power of workers in those different jobs. These job-specific determinants of bargaining power (and hence specific wage levels) include factors like:

- **Unionization** By negotiating collectively with employers over pay and conditions, workers can pressure employers for a better deal. Some industries have stronger unions than others.
- **Skills** Workers with unique or hard-to-replace skills enjoy a stronger bargaining position with their employers, since they are harder to replace. (This is quite different from the neoclassical explanation of the relationship

between skills and wages, which falsely assumes each worker is automatically paid according to productivity.)

- **Competition**   Employers in very competitive, dog-eat-dog industries will fiercely resist any pay increases, while those in more protected and profitable sectors might tolerate higher compensation. Public sector employers do not face the same competitive battle to the death, and hence in some cases provide better compensation and working conditions.
- **Productivity**   Higher output per worker (ultimately driven by technology, capital investment, and higher-value products) allows an employer to pay higher wages without pinching profit margins.
- **Other industry-specific institutions, practices, and norms**   Like pay grids, relative pay differentials, or minimum standards defined for some specific occupations.
- **Employer**   mobility The ability of employers in a particular industry to mobilize cheaper sources of labour can suppress wages. For example, if they can recruit lower-wage workers, or move the work to lower-wage regions or countries, then they are more able to resist wage demands.
- **Expectations and attitudes**   The expectations of workers about what is fair, and their own ability to move between jobs if they see a better offer somewhere else, will also influence wage offers.

Because of all these factors, otherwise identical workers will earn very different wages, and confront very different working conditions, reflecting the balance of power in their particular workplace or industry. This creates an economic basis for the persistence of clear differences between groups of workers. Some workers achieve relatively better and more secure positions, with higher wages. Others are channelled into occupations or industries with lower wages, few if any benefits, and PRECARIOUS WORK prospects.

Given these persistently unequal outcomes in labour markets, it is not surprising that capitalist society has found various ways to sort out (or "organize") the resulting inequality. It is also not surprising that competition and tensions would erupt between working people over access to whatever better-paid, more secure positions are available. The economy never randomly assigns individuals to better or worse jobs; nor does it allocate them on the basis of "neutral" criteria (like qualifications, performance, or seniority). Instead, formal and informal practices develop which provide certain groups with systematically better chances of capturing and keeping the better jobs. And those workers, in turn, are understandably anxious to protect their relatively lucky situation – and pass it along to their children, relatives, friends, and neighbours. (In fact, as we saw in the previous chapter, the greater is the level of inequality, the more resources are wastefully allocated to inhibiting mobility between different social groups.)

As a result, clear patterns and divisions within the labour market emerge over time. This outcome is known as **LABOUR MARKET SEGMENTATION**. There's not one unified labour market where employers and workers all meet to strike a fair deal (as assumed in neoclassical theories). Instead, workers are divided into different groups, and informally but effectively assigned to different categories of jobs. And arbitrary distinctions between groups of workers (such as gender, race, ethnicity, and language) come to be associated with those labour market divisions – even though they have no bearing on the ability of those workers to actually perform their assigned jobs. Racist and sexist attitudes about the supposed "suitability" of different types of people for different jobs emerge to reinforce and "justify" those divisions in jobs and incomes.

Neoclassical economists argue that anonymous competition between employers should automatically eliminate any unfair distinctions and prejudices in the labour market. Employers should be anxious to hire from any group of workers that is systematically underpaid, since employing them is super-profitable (they're as productive as other workers, but paid less); that drives up demand for the underpaid group until the wage gap disappears. But this theoretical faith in equality is not verified by real-world experience. In fact, far from equalizing outcomes and eliminating arbitrary divisions, employers actually appreciate these systematic fissures in the labour market, and work to preserve them. Economically, the existence of more desperate and hence cheaper pools of labour allows employers to exploit them more intensively: offering lower pay, demanding more discipline and work effort, and offering less security and stability. These vulnerable labour market segments also tend to experience the most precarious employment: last hired in an upswing, first fired in a downturn, denied the stability and predictability that comes from a permanent, regular job.

Politically, too, the existence of large divisions between workers allows employers to play one group against another, undermining worker solidarity (essential for winning better wages and conditions), and preventing the emergence of a more united workers' consciousness. In these ways, divisions among working people are reinforced by capitalism, and simultaneously help to reinforce capitalism.

For those lucky workers who benefit from better jobs and incomes, preserving and reinforcing their relatively privileged positions might seem logical. Professional and salaried workers might buy into the idea that they somehow "deserve" their better incomes and working conditions thanks to their "superior" skills – and hence try to suppress competition from more desperate groups of workers. Similarly, the mainly white, male workers who hold higher-income positions in core industries (like heavy manufacturing and construction) might be tempted to view marginalized labour segments as a threat, rather than a potential ally.

Thoughtful trade unionists will recognize, however, that relatively well-off workers can always be undercut by the systematic creation and recreation of pools

---

Division Comes Naturally

"The divide-and-conquer element of capitalism is not something that has to be introduced from outside of the system. It exists within the system."

Bill Fletcher Jr., US trade unionist (2004).

"Labor market segmentation arose and is perpetuated because it is functional – that is, it facilitates the operation of capitalist institutions .... Segmentation divides workers and forestalls potential movements uniting all workers against employers."

Michael Reich, David M. Gordon, and Richard C. Edwards, US economists (1973).

---

of especially desperate and exploited people. And all workers suffer from the loss of bargaining power that comes from division and segmentation. That's why fighting to reduce inequality between workers, and building solidarity between different segments of the workforce (including across gender, racial, ethnic, linguistic, sexual and gender identity, ability, and other lines), is a crucial priority for unions – just as important as fighting for a better overall deal between labour and capital as a whole.

Class and race

Workers can be divided from one another in any number of ways, always with the aim of undermining their power to wrest a better deal from capitalism. For example, we learned in Chapter 9 how women's role within families (and the unfair burden of unpaid reproductive work which they shoulder) overlaps with their particular exploitation in paid work, and helps to sustain artificial divisions between men and women in the labour market. Other groups of workers also face systematic barriers and inequalities as they strive to support themselves through paid employment: including workers from linguistic minorities, immigrants and migrant workers (who often lack the same legal protections as other workers), workers with disabilities, and workers with lesbian, gay, bisexual, transgendered, or queer (LGBTQ) identities.

One of the most pervasive and yet artificial divisions among workers is race. Racial and ethnic distinctions among workers are fluid and arbitrary, yet they are among the most powerful, persistent, and destructive of all dimensions of segmentation.

Geneticists, anthropologists, and sociologists alike agree that the very concept of "race" is an artificial and ideological category in the first place. There is no consistent scientific way to categorize the incredible physical and ethnic diversity of human beings into specific "races." In fact, the more we learn about human evolution and genetics, the more we understand our fundamental genetic similarity. Scientists can now trace the precise history of human migration around the world (starting with the first homo sapiens from East Africa), and locate the ancient heritage of each individual on the basis of the specific genetic code each of us carries. Through this lens, we are all "Africans."

What is commonly understood as "race" actually reflects a complex mixture of attitudes, privileges, and prejudices that emerges (and is deliberately fostered) over time through education, culture, politics … and economics. Since there is no empirical basis to racial categories, the definition of "races" (and the assignment of individuals to one category or another) must be socially constructed. Racial categories are invented, but racism is real – since enough people accept these artificial categories to maintain and reinforce the resulting differences in social and economic status (at the expense of those stuck on lower rungs in the racialized pecking order). And that process of defining, justifying, and reinforcing racial categories is always closely linked to economic inequality.

A similar process of social construction also applies to how we commonly understand gender. While there are obvious biological differences between the sexes, how society understands and responds to those differences, and assigns different roles, expectations, and powers (including economic power) to the genders, clearly reflects social and cultural processes – not biology. Feminists and trans-gender activists have worked diligently to expose the artificial, oppressive nature of those gender categories, and to advocate a world in which humans can fulfil any role in life (including any economic role) regardless of what sexual organs they happen to be born with. The same logic applies to understanding (and combatting) racism.

There are many historical examples of the social construction of arbitrary racial identities, and their intrinsic connection to economic exploitation and inequality. For example, the English once defined the Irish as a separate (and inferior) race, to try to justify the English invasion and occupation of that island. Similarly, elites in Japanese society invoked ideas of "race" to legitimize their own imperialism and exploitation – including occupations of Korea and China, whose residents were conveniently redefined as distinct (and inferior) races. The false idea of an African "race" was socially constructed coincident with the advent of the African slave trade, for obvious ideological reasons: how else could supposedly "civilized" European and American leaders justify the horrific violence and exploitation inflicted by that brutal practice? Even slave-owning whites in the US South once tried to define themselves as a separate race from northern whites, to buttress their arguments for the continuation of slavery. US government rules in the 1930s defined a person as "Native American" (hence entitling them to certain social benefits) only if they could prove they had at least "one quarter" native "blood". The most grotesque modern example of the social construction of race was the former practice of apartheid in South Africa: the whites-only government there tried to boil down the infinite diversity of human beings into four distinct categories, each with different legal rights and economic status, on the basis of far-fetched criteria such as whether a pencil could be stuck in someone's hair without falling out.

These arbitrary, fluid, and often-ridiculous definitions merely confirm that race cannot be empirically defined. Each arbitrary racial category must be created and re-created by social, cultural, and economic processes. And hence affected groups of people are said to have been RACIALIZED: that is, they weren't born into a specific "race." Rather, their status is deliberately created by ongoing social, cultural, and economic forces.

The history of racism is tied inextricably to the violent, ugly history of colonialism and imperialism. In their effort to conquer and subdue southern territories, European colonial powers invoked racialized arguments to justify their violent and exploitive acts. The coincidental fact that the new colonies were inhabited by people with different skin colour and physical characteristics facilitated this ideology – although, as we have seen, racial categories can always be invented (as they were in Ireland) even where none are visible to the naked eye! Racialized political, cultural, and legal concepts were wielded to justify the forcible seizure of territory and other assets from peoples who had inhabited their land for many thousands of years. The now-discredited legal doctrine of terra nullius (or "empty land") was applied in some colonies (such as Australia) to justify this theft; colonizers tried to rationalize expropriation on the racist assumption that the original inhabitants were somehow not "human." The slave trade dispersed Africans to work in colonies around the world under especially brutal economic and social conditions, and this history still explains the particular prejudice and exploitation their descendants face today. Colonialism also led to a flow of migration by colonized workers back toward the imperial homelands; those immigrants faced harsh conditions and were shunted into low-wage jobs and neighbourhoods, once again all justified with racialized ideology. In the settler colonies of North America and Australia, racist immigration laws (allowing only "white" workers to immigrate) reinforced the racialized pecking order already established by the initial capture of indigenous lands. In every case, a dominant and wealthy elite (usually, but not always, "white") invoked racist story-lines and ideologies to justify extreme and often violent exploitation of workers from other lands – whether within the colony, back in the land of the colonizer, or in a third country. This globalized history of racialization has been further reinforced during modern times by economic globalization, migration, war, and refugee flows.

The impact of race on peoples' day-to-day experiences reinforces the importance of racial and ethnic factors in their self-identities. In the US, for example, where racial identities (and racial divisions) are strong, researchers have noted that even "white" workers are more likely to define themselves according to their race, rather than their class – and hence are very susceptible to conservative messages disguised with racial cues and sub-texts. How convenient this is for an economic system which is organized, first and foremost, to sustain a deep structural inequality that is measured in dollar signs, not skin pigment.

Because racial and ethnic identities are so powerfully linked to economic inequality (indeed, that's largely why racial categories were invented in the first place), they hamper efforts by working people to win better jobs, security, and democracy. And racist ideas may be deliberately reinforced by employers who benefit from the resulting divisions among working people. Non-racialized (or "white") workers clearly enjoy some benefits as a result of racial and ethnic segmentation in the labour market; after all, they have a better chance at attaining whatever few decent jobs are actually generated in the economy. Hence some may accept arguments that racialized workers should be kept "in their place." When times are tough (such as during a long recession), right-wing forces deliberately foment racist responses, trying to divert workers' anger away from blaming capitalism, to blame racialized workers or immigrants instead.

Workers' movements must acknowledge and then confront the divisions that arise from racial and ethnic segmentation in the labour market, and in society. The more employers and conservatives succeed in turning worker against worker (no matter how arbitrary and artificial the reasons), the longer it will take for workers as a whole to build a united, effective movement against inequality in all its forms. This multi-racial unity can be built in many ways: by focusing union organizing efforts among immigrants and racialized workers; supporting employment equity and other programs to break down racial job barriers; fighting for fair treatment and full legal protections for migrant workers; incorporating anti-racist demands into all union campaigns and activities; nurturing and promoting racialized workers in leadership positions; and more. The most effective labour campaigns in recent history have placed great emphasis on this multi-racial dimension of political activism, in order to build enough unity and passion, from workers of all colours, to win real change. Working people didn't invent racism. But workers' movements must recognize it, understand its history and its effects, and put the struggle against racism at the core of our programme, if we are to win progress for workers of any colour.

Multiple oppressions

Social scientists and activists alike have devoted much effort in recent decades to better understanding the many ways people experience inequality, insecurity, prejudice, and violence in our society – and finding ways to forge those distinct experiences into a united movement for equality and inclusion. There are many different ways in which inequality and power imbalances are expressed in modern capitalism. Economic inequality (based on ownership of wealth, and its consequent impact on income distribution and the compulsion to work) is one fundamental dimension of inequality – but not the only one. Other dimensions of inequality overlap with, and shape, economic inequality, including gender, race, ethnicity, language, region, ability, sexual and gender identity, and more.

How any individual experiences economic inequality, therefore, is inevitably tied up with their personal situation regarding all these other schisms in society. Any dimension of inequality and injustice can exert a negative impact on someone's life chances, quite independently of whatever economic power they may possess. Imagine, for instance, a wealthy woman who faces violence at the hands of her husband, or a well-off racialized professional harassed by a racist police officer, or a queer politician attacked by a gang of homophobes. Each individual's self-identity (and political priorities) reflects the mixture of all those various characteristics shaping their life. Many people will mostly focus on their race or sexual identity or ethnic heritage – all the more so in a society which emphatically downplays the very idea of "class," and invests considerable resources in misleading people as to their class position.

Modern theories of **MULTIPLE OPPRESSION** attempt to explain how people simultaneously experience inequality and exploitation along more than one of these dimensions at the same time. This is a difficult theoretical task. There is no point trying to "rank" or "add" different forms of injustice: mostly this fosters divisive and unproductive debates over who in society is "most oppressed." And arguments that one form of exploitation somehow "trumps" all others have led to equally unpromising dead-ends.

The most important and successful social change movements in recent times have emphasized the commonalities between the many demands for equality, inclusion, and democracy. They work to link equity-seeking constituencies, arguing that each has a stake in building a more equal, inclusive, safe, and secure society. Victories attained on one issue strengthen other struggles: both by inspiring others to raise parallel demands, and by winning economic rights which in turn benefit everyone. For example, winning quality public child care is a clear victory for women (shifting some responsibility for child-rearing to the state). But it is also a victory for all working-class families, since their children can now benefit from quality early education which has been proven to enhance their long-run economic prospects. Similarly, research has shown conclusively that when investment and development aid are channelled toward women in developing economies, the entire community benefits from improved health and education outcomes. Likewise, statistics show that cities with a more visible and accepted LGBTQ community also demonstrate more diversity, better safety, stronger entrepreneurship, and other indications of urban well-being. In all these ways and more, a victory for one really is a victory for all.

> ## All Colors
>
> "All colors of hands gonna work together,
> All colors of eyes gonna laugh and shine,
> All colors of feet gonna dance together,
> When I bring my CIO to Caroline, Caroline."
>
> Woody Guthrie, US folk singer and activist (1947).
>
> Guthrie wrote this extra verse to his famous song, "You Gotta Go Down and Join the Union" as part of a union organizing and strike support initiative in North Carolina. The CIO was the Congress of Industrial Organizing, a new and more militant branch of the labour movement which worked hard after World War II to desegregate workplaces – and build a racially united labour movement.
>
> Source: Mark Allan Jackson, *Prophet Singer: The Voice and Vision of Woody Guthrie* (Jackson, MS: University Press of Mississippi, 2007, p. 248).

No society can be equal so long as 85 percent of its population faces an overarching and life-shaping economic disadvantage: namely, they must work for a wage, employed by others who own the workplace and the output, and as a result experience perpetual insecurity, disenfranchisement, and (often) poverty. So the demand for economic equality will always be central in any overall vision of equality, inclusion, and fairness. But the struggle for economic equality can only win if we recognize how deeply it is intertwined with race, gender, and other forms of injustice, and if we carefully build alliances that link good people fighting for fairness in all areas of life. Otherwise, the divide-and-conquer strategy which has been used so successfully against workers in the past, will continue to hold us back.

Precarious work

As we learned in Chapter 8, employers constantly seek ways to reduce what they pay for each bit of expended labour. This includes trying to escape any institutional constraints that limit employers' freedom to extract maximum labour effort for minimal cost. That endless quest is shaped by technology, legal and regulatory standards, and worker attitudes and expectations. Where it works to their advantage, employers will even fiddle with the very concept of what it means to have a "job." For example, in some industries, and using some technologies, it may be more profitable to pay someone for performed work on a piece-work or contract basis, rather than "hiring" them in a more conventional sense. This practice shifts various risks and costs from the employer to the worker. It is now the worker's problem if there isn't enough work to piece together a whole day's labour – rather than requiring the boss to pay a full day's pay even if there's not enough work to keep the worker busy. Contract workers also often cover the cost of their own tools, and may perform their labour in their own homes. They don't usually qualify for pensions, benefits, or any kind of security in event of accident or illness. But employers have to balance these advantages against various problems inherent with contract and piece-work arrangements. It can be more difficult in those situations to supervise work, meet quality standards, specify contractual terms, and achieve flexibility in tasks that are anything other than routine and predictable.

Examples of unconventional employment arrangements include "jobbing out" systems and home work (in garment production, for example, many workers perform piece work at home, using fabric provided and owned by the employer), or independent contractors in industries like transportation, forestry, and construction (where workers own and maintain their own equipment). One key motivation for employers' experimentation with new work arrangements is to evade standards on pay, benefits, and job security imposed by unions or governments. Employers claim that contractors are not actually "employees" (or at least not their employees), and hence they are not obliged to meet minimum legal employment standards. In some cases employers can find workers who work for free: like unpaid interns trying desperately to get their first opportunity in a depressed labour market.

But all these efforts to manipulate the specific legal form of the employment relationship cannot change the fundamental reality: these workers, whatever we call them, still work for someone else, who tells them what to do and owns their output, all in return for compensation (which the employer constantly strives to minimize). The compensation may now be paid by the job, rather than by the hour. And the worker may not know whether their services are required from one day to the next. But the core nature of the relationship is still clear: the boss decides whether, when, and how the work is to be performed. So the people expending the mental and physical labour that is the essential ingredient in all production are still clearly "workers."

In recent years, new technology, organizational innovations, and globalization have facilitated a dramatic expansion of new work arrangements that deviate even further from the traditional employment relationship. The goal in every case is to reduce unit labour cost (that is, the amount of compensation paid per unit of output), and minimize risks for the employer (including risks associated with hours of work, demand for the firm's product, the time it takes to complete a given task, and more). These new practices and relationships are called **PRECARIOUS WORK**. Examples of precarious work include:

- Variable part-time employment, where workers have fluctuating, unpredictable shifts – called into work only when the employer immediately needs them.
- Contract or temporary jobs, where workers are hired to perform a specific job, or for a certain period of time, with no guarantee of continuing employment.
- Nominal forms of self-employment, where the worker has a somewhat independent economic status (perhaps even constituting their own "company"), yet still labours directly for one or a handful of larger employers, often working out of their own homes.
- Home-work, jobbing out, and other systems whereby the worker performs the work away from a normal workplace, and with irregular hours.
- Specific jobs within a large worksite, where the worker is technically employed by an outside company or contractor of some kind, and typically receives a lower wage.
- Workers hired by employment agencies and then assigned to work for other companies; typically the agency creams off a significant share (so that workers receive only a portion of the wages they worked for).

Workers in precarious positions receive lower and more variable incomes, and face much more insecurity, than workers in standard jobs. They usually do not receive pensions, health insurance, or other fringe benefits. Research has shown that the chronic uncertainty of their position exacts a considerable toll in personal and family stress, health, and quality of life. Trade unions try to limit the use of precarious work strategies by employers: the exploitation of this insecure, lower-cost, just-in-time labour force obviously undermines the bargaining position of the firm's "core" paid workforce. Another way to limit precarious work is through stronger government regulations: such as requiring more severance notice (even for contract workers), setting minimum pay periods for part-time call-in (for example, requiring at least four hours' pay for any shift), mandating vacation and benefits for part-time workers, and limiting how much employment agencies can siphon from workers' wages.

To succeed, however, these efforts must resist and overcome the divisions between workers that are created by the precarious work strategy. Here, too, we see the divide-and-conquer imperative of capitalism. Workers in "core" positions may tacitly accept the outsourcing of some precarious jobs, so long as their own particular positions are not affected (at least not for now). And workers in precarious positions may understandably begrudge the superior incomes and stability enjoyed by the remaining "core" workforce. For both groups, however, the ultimate enemy is certainly not each other. Rather, they need to nurture solidarity, and build a common movement to limit the use of precarious work and improve the security of all jobs.

The reliance of employers on precarious work practices will certainly expand in coming years. Technological and organizational innovations reinforce the trend: for example, software companies now offer programs to allow employers to easily manage volatile shift schedules among part-time workers, and huge global employment agencies (like Manpower Group and Adecco Group) are allowing even large multinational companies to take advantage of precarious work. Weak labour market conditions further strengthen the hand of employers: when workers are desperate for any type of job, they will accept uncertain hours and security. In a stronger labour market, workers could demand more security, and precarious employment strategies would be less effective (since employers could no longer rely on a pool of always-available vulnerable workers). So addressing the inadequate quantity of jobs will also be a key part of our effort to lift the quality of work. Union and social justice campaigners will need to place great emphasis on restricting precarious work and improving the conditions faced by workers in precarious jobs, through a combination of regulatory reform, union organizing, and political action.

16

Capitalism and the Environment

Nature and the economy

From the outset of this book, we have identified "work" (human effort) as the driving force behind economic activity. Work is required to transform the materials we attain from nature into useful goods and services. All those goods and services, therefore, require two things: human work, and the essential resources, benefits, and services we obtain from nature. No production is possible without nature, which provides us with needed supplies and resources, a capacity to absorb (a certain amount of) pollution, and a healthy and pleasurable place to live and work.

Figure 16.1 presents our ongoing map of capitalism. (For simplicity, we return to portraying capitalists collectively as one big company, rather than breaking out the competition between firms.) This time the map adds in the natural environment as an explicit part of the economic system. Three broad links between nature and the economy are indicated:

- **Ecological benefits and services** Human beings need, and directly "consume," certain benefits from the natural environment: the air we breathe, the water we drink (hopefully after it's been purified!), the general quality of the environment in which we work and live, and the parks and other natural places where we enjoy some of our free time. The capacity of nature to cleanse and regenerate itself is also essential to our ability to work and live. Our map indicates this direct consumption of ecological benefits and services with an arrow running from nature to worker households (which is where most people live – but don't forget that capitalist and small business households also need and enjoy nature). The loss or degradation of those ecological benefits and services can seriously undermine the quality of life; it can also disrupt the other functions that occur in the economy.
- **Natural resources** Nature also provides many different material inputs to the production of private firms: agricultural output, minerals and resources, energy, timber, and land (for both agricultural and non-agricultural purposes). These inputs are illustrated on the map by an arrow running from nature to productive companies. The availability and quality of natural inputs affect the productivity and profitability of business production. If natural

resources become more costly to extract, decline in quality, or even "run out" altogether (this seldom occurs), then the productive capacity of private firms will suffer accordingly. Some economists refer to these inputs and supplies as "natural capital."

• **Pollution**   Unfortunately, most economic activities generate byproducts and waste that are dumped back into the natural environment. Both the quantity of this waste and the way it is managed affect the quality of the natural environment – and its ability to keep supplying us with needed benefits and supplies. The environment can absorb some pollution, but eventually it begins to deteriorate. In some cases that deterioration is experienced locally (such as garbage or industrial waste). In some cases it is experienced regionally (such as smog or water pollution). In some cases it is experienced globally (most dangerously as global climate change). Differences between where pollution originates and where it is experienced greatly complicate efforts to control pollution – especially when pollution crosses borders. Figure 16.1 indicates pollution as originating at the stage of production; it can also occur, however, when products are consumed (such as the pollution caused by the use of private automobiles). Either way, pollution is an unwanted side-effect of the basic economic cycle.

Economists, and the public as a whole, have been concerned with the relationship between the economy and the environment since the beginning of capitalism. For example, the classical economist David Ricardo worried deeply about the supply of arable land. He developed a whole theory of economic stagnation based on his belief that land would eventually "run out." Early neoclassical economists worried about shortages of coal. The appalling environmental consequences of early unplanned capitalist development motivated efforts to manage the environmental effects of growth – through urban zoning, garbage collection and sanitation, air and water pollution regulations, and conservation programs (protecting specified natural places from economic development).

In recent years, however, public concern with the environment has become very intense – and with good reason. And the most pressing environmental challenge of all is clearly the problem of CLIMATE CHANGE.

Because of massive fossil fuel consumption (coal, oil, and natural gas) over the past two centuries, emissions of carbon dioxide and other chemicals into the earth's atmosphere have grown dramatically, and the average concentration of these chemicals in the atmosphere is steadily rising (see Figure 16.2). The resulting concentration of these gases (called GREENHOUSE GASES because of their warming effect) causes the atmosphere to retain more heat energy from the sun, and has produced a visible increase in average global temperatures. Worldwide average temperatures have risen by a full degree Celsius over the last century (and

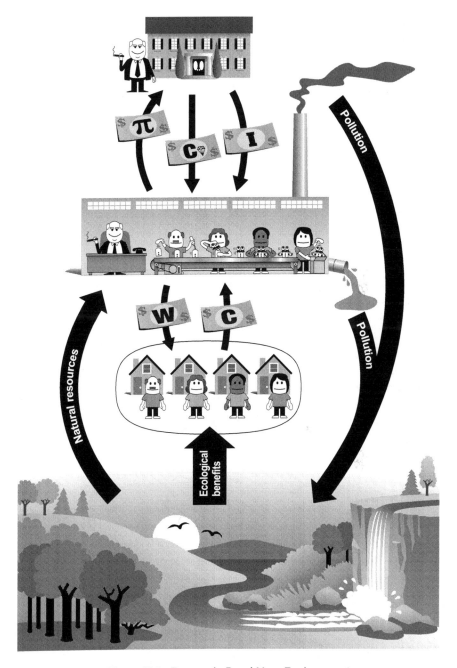

Figure 16.1 Economic Road Map: Environment

by more than that on land), enough already to cause dramatic changes in weather patterns, sea levels, and ecosystems. Unfortunately, this warming will continue for decades as a result of pollution that has *already* occurred. Scientists believe the concentration of carbon dioxide needs to be first stabilized and then reduced from current levels (around 400 parts per million) in order to avoid the most cataclysmic effects of climate change.

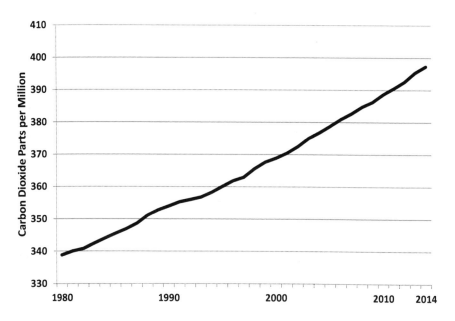

Figure 16.2 Global Atmospheric Carbon Dioxide Concentration

Source: US Oceanic and Atmospheric Administration.

The urgent challenge for humanity now is to quickly reduce greenhouse gas pollution, in order to stabilize carbon dioxide concentrations and slow down and eventually stop the rise in global temperatures as soon as possible. The implications of climate change for quality of life, settlement patterns, and geopolitical stability are potentially catastrophic. Consequences will include rising sea levels, drought, severe weather (including disastrous storms), mass dislocations of people, and the extinction of species that cannot adapt to rising temperatures. These terrible consequences, and the global scale of the problem, make climate change the most daunting environmental challenge humans have ever faced.

Aggressively reducing greenhouse gas emissions to avoid the worst effects of climate change will require powerful efforts to reduce fossil fuel use, and limit other sources of greenhouse gas pollution (such as methane gas and nitrous oxide emissions from agricultural and chemical industries). It is now clear that the

---

Can't Wait

"Continued emission of greenhouse gases will cause further warming and long-lasting changes in all components of the climate system, increasing the likelihood of severe, pervasive and irreversible impacts for people and ecosystems. Limiting climate change would require substantial and sustained reductions in greenhouse gas emissions which, together with adaptation, can limit climate change risks … Climate change will amplify existing risks and create new risks for natural and human systems. Risks are unevenly distributed and are generally greater for disadvantaged people and communities in countries at all levels of development."

Intergovernmental Panel on Climate Change (2014).

---

world will also have to invest heavily in *adapting* to warmer temperatures, and assisting the victims of climate change – including residents of low-lying regions facing rising sea levels, and those harmed by severe weather or dramatic changes in rainfall patterns. Those adaptation efforts will be economically important: they will cost trillions of dollars, with enormous employment and economic implications (including huge investments in construction, infrastructure, housing, and other priorities).

In addition to the incredible challenge of climate change, many other environmental problems also need attention, including:

- Controlling and reducing other kinds of pollution.
- Protecting important natural spaces (such as sensitive rainforests and marine areas), and the plants and animals that live there.
- Developing ways of harvesting timber, minerals, and other natural resources that do not degrade and disrupt ecosystems.
- Recycling materials used in the economy.
- Investing in systems to conserve and recycle water.
- Cleaning up and restoring past environmental damage, such as former industrial, mining, and toxic waste sites.

A key concept motivating all of these efforts is the goal of environmental SUSTAINABILITY. The general principle of sustainability is to manage interactions between the economy and the environment so that the economy can continue functioning *without* ongoing degradation of the environment. Sustainability for the environment is thus similar to reproduction for people (as we studied in Chapter 9): making sure that the planet (like the people who live on it) can continue to provide us with the ecological benefits and resource inputs we need to keep producing. Sustainability will require weaning the economy from non-renewable energy and minerals; extensive recycling of materials to reduce the need for resource extraction; aggressive protection of natural spaces and habitats; and strict limits on pollution of all kinds.

Environmental inequality

As with everything else under capitalism, poor people bear the worst costs of pollution. They have little power to prevent or avoid the garbage, polluted water, and filth that are the byproducts of unregulated capitalism. To confirm this, just take a walk through a poor neighbourhood in any Third World city, and consider the garbage and pollution that is all around you.

Well-off people, in contrast, can afford to live in more pleasant neighbourhoods, and to invest in mitigating many of the consequences of pollution – purified water, good trash collection, parks and other recreation facilities. They also enjoy more political clout to prohibit polluting activities in their own particular neighbourhoods. Economic studies have confirmed that pollution tends to be worse in poorer neighbourhoods and regions.

Perhaps the greatest environmental injustice of all is the distributional effect of climate change. The poor residents of low-lying tropical countries will bear the greatest costs of climate change, which was caused mostly by fossil fuel consumption in richer countries located thousands of miles away. Even in the developed countries, poor people suffer the worst consequences of environmental degradation – as illustrated by the horrifying impact of Hurricane Katrina on poor people in New Orleans in 2005. On the other hand, the horrifying effects of climate change cannot be limited to poor people alone. No-one will be able to fully escape the global and potentially catastrophic consequences of climate change – not even the wealthy.

Markets and the environment

Many economists argue that environmental problems reflect a "failure" or "imperfection" in the operation of free markets. The consumption of "free" natural resources, and the dumping of pollution (again for "free") back into the natural environment, both impose real costs on those who experience its negative effects. But those costs are not paid by the offending company. They can consume natural assets, or dump pollution into the environment, without charge – due to the absence of regulations and the inability of affected people to collect compensation for the real costs they experience. In economics, this is called a market EXTERNALITY. Producers are able to avoid, or "externalize," a real cost of their production, by treating the environment as a free source of materials and a free dumping ground.

Some environmentalists conclude, therefore, that the problem can be solved by correcting the market, and forcing companies to absorb (or "internalize") the costs of pollution and natural capital. One method for correcting the market might be to impose special fees (such as a **CARBON TAX** on greenhouse gas pollution) on environmentally damaging activities. Another approach, called **EMISSIONS TRADING**, would cap overall pollution and then rely on supply-and-demand forces to determine the "price" of pollution. Many economists believe this market-friendly approach is more effective than simply mandating resource conservation or lower pollution through direct government standards or regulations.

However, we should be careful not to place too much faith in the efficiency of markets and competition. In reality, price signals (even "corrected" ones, incorporating externalities) are not always effective in changing behaviour in desired ways. Think of alcohol consumption: even in countries with high alcohol taxes, people still drink a lot, and alcoholism is still a problem. Relying on the price mechanism to reduce pollution also has negative distributional effects: the burden falls disproportionately on lower-income households, whereas well-off people or profitable companies can keep "buying" as much pollution as they want. Stringent pollution fees could undermine profit rates in some industries, with consequent implications for business investment spending (although they would also stimulate new investment in some other industries, like green energy production). This doesn't worry free-market economists, who believe that market forces always automatically re-establish full employment and maximum prosperity; in the real world, however, demand-side problems like investment and unemployment are a constant concern.

Environmental taxes and other price mechanisms can surely play some role in encouraging energy conservation and other goals – not to mention raising valuable funds to pay for government-sponsored environmental investments. But these measures must be backed up with direct regulations and efficiency standards (which are more powerful than price signals in reducing pollution), with strict resource conservation rules, and with major environmental investments by businesses and governments.

Some environmentalists also hope that market forces will facilitate environmental progress through "green" choices by consumers. They urge consumers to purchase environmentally-friendly products – and assume that companies will respond to consumer opinion by improving their environmental performance. Some believe that consumers can also help by altering or "down-shifting" their lifestyles, spending and consuming less. All of these individual, personal decisions, presumably, will translate into a more sustainable economy.

Here, too, we must be cautious about crediting market mechanisms with more integrity and effectiveness than they deserve. Businesses shape consumer sentiment as much as they cater to it; they often respond to "green" consumerism with symbolic measures; many spend more money advertising the often-phony environmental virtues of their existing products, than investing in cleaner technologies. Sometimes consumers are presented with a genuine environmental choice: for example, buying an energy-efficient but more expensive home appliance. But most consumers will be attracted by a low up-front purchase price (often because of their limited income), rather than longer-term operating cost savings. Hence they will purchase the cheaper (but more polluting) product. This is why direct government energy efficiency regulations, which *force* industry to make less polluting products, are ultimately more effective.

As far as protecting the environment through reduced consumption, it is clearly unreasonable to ask most of the world's people (including people in low-income countries, and poor people in rich countries) to consume less. They deserve, and need, *more* goods and services, not less. The challenge is finding ways to meet those legitimate consumption needs without degrading the environment. And at any

---

A Green Way to Speculate

EMISSIONS TRADING (or "cap-and-trade") systems are favoured by neoclassical economists as a way to efficiently reduce pollution. The theory is elegant. First the government issues a limited number of pollution permits. The total permits issued equals the maximum amount of pollution that society is willing to tolerate. Permits may be given away or auctioned off to polluting companies. The total outstanding stock of permits might be reduced over time (to achieve gradual reductions in total pollution). Companies can then buy and sell the permits among themselves. The resulting market price for the permits supposedly represents the efficient "price" of pollution; in theory this should guide polluters in seeking the least expensive ways of reducing emissions.

The theory holds some promise, but there are many problems in practice – including that it allows companies to continue polluting so long as they're willing and able to "pay" for it. And like any other market in capitalism, there is no guarantee that the resulting price is either efficient or fair. The experience of the European Union's carbon dioxide emissions trading system (the world's largest) has not been encouraging. The "price" of EU permits has swung wildly: peaking at €30 per tonne in 2006, but then collapsing to near-zero in 2007, soaring back to €20 by 2011, and then plunging precipitously again (to under €3 by 2013). This hardly constitutes an "efficient guide" for long-run business decisions in capital investment and technology. And with the price so low, companies have almost no incentive to reduce emissions at all. Ironically, polluters in some other countries are now allowed to buy EU permits (at depressed prices) to validate their own excess emissions. Worst of all, wild price swings have spurred a whole new form of financial SPECULATION (we discuss speculation in more detail in Chapter 19). A new market in "carbon derivatives" has sprung up to allow speculators to place bets on future swings in carbon prices. Europe's environment would have been far better served by direct regulation of emissions in the most polluting industries (like coal-fired electricity plants), instead of undertaking this complicated, unsuccessful experiment in free-market engineering.

---

rate, if consumers ever did decide in sufficient numbers to significantly cut back overall spending in order to reduce their environmental footprint, the inadvertent outcome would likely be a recession. Consumer spending accounts for half of GDP in advanced economies. If we're going to have much less of it, then we'll need much more other spending (perhaps big increases in government spending on environmental programs or public services) or else we'll face a significant downturn in employment. However, that reallocation of spending (from more polluting to less polluting activities) won't happen automatically. It will require pro-active government planning and spending measures to sustain purchasing power and employment in the transition to a more sustainable economic structure.

So there are many reasons to be cautious about relying on market forces alone (even when they are "tweaked" with carbon taxes or similar corrections) to achieve a sustainable economy. Direct regulations and restrictions on pollution can achieve faster, more assured environmental gains. And whatever is done to rein in pollution, we will need aggressive investments (by governments and businesses alike) to ensure that enough new jobs are created in green industries, human services, and climate change adaptation to offset the potentially contractionary impact of environmental measures. Within the broad field of environmental economics, there is a wide range of views on these issues: some strongly favour market-based mechanisms (and oppose direct regulation), while others recognize the limits of free markets and support direct regulatory and demand-side environmental initiatives.

Is growth the culprit?

Many environmental activists blame economic growth for environmental problems, and it is certainly true that the dramatic expansion of global output (and more specifically the consumption of fossil fuels used to produce that output) over the last 200 years is the ultimate cause of climate change. An implication of this view (and sometimes its explicit conclusion) is that "growth" must be reduced or stopped to protect the environment. This suggests a conflict between economic activity and environmental protection, and leads many people to conclude (wrongly, in my view) that environmental sustainability can only be attained at the price of a reduced material standard of living.

This difficult discussion is complicated by a lack of clarity in terminology. As explained in Chapter 1, economists define "growth" simply as an increase in the real value of GDP (adjusted for inflation), which in turn represents the value of everything produced for money in the economy. This includes both goods and services, for consumption and investment, produced in the public sector as well as the private sector. So it is impossible to come to any general conclusions about the environmental consequences of growth, since "growth" consists of so many disparate activities. (Indeed, the only common ingredient in all the output included in GDP is work: productive human activity, in all its wondrous forms.) Growth for growth's sake is never our economic goal; there is never any guarantee that more output translates into a better life for the masses of humanity: it all depends on what is produced, who gets it, and how it is used. And under neoliberalism, growth has clearly not been the central economic goal. To the contrary, neoliberal policies have deliberately sacrificed growth in the interests of restoring business dominance and profits.

As human beings, it is clear we need to do more work, not less, to meet our many needs and solve the many problems we face: alleviating poverty, rebuilding troubled communities, providing necessary human services... and caring for

---

Think Big

"Changing the building blocks of our societies – the energy that powers our economies, how we move around, the designs of our major cities – is not about writing a few cheques. It requires bold long-term planning at every level of government, and a willingness to stand up to polluters whose actions put us all in danger. And that won't happen until the corporate liberation project that has shaped our political culture for three and a half decades is buried for good."

Naomi Klein, Canadian author and activist (2014).

---

the environment. The value of our work (other than what we do on a voluntary basis) shows up in GDP statistics, and hence it all contributes to "growth." But the environmental implications of our work depend completely on what we are doing, and why. Are we strip mining coal to generate highly-polluting electricity, or are we caring for children and elders in a neighbourhood community centre? Both are "work," and both are counted in GDP. So assuming that "growth" is bad for the environment is no more credible than assuming that "growth" enhances human well-being (a mistaken assumption we rejected in the first chapter of this book).

Some environmental problems clearly get better as economies develop and living standards improve. This is true for most localized forms of pollution – such as garbage, local air pollution, and polluted water – which are consistently worse in poor countries than in rich. People with higher incomes are more willing to devote resources to environmental protection in order to improve their quality of life. Moreover, advanced economies produce less polluting kinds of output (including more services), and use less polluting technologies and fuels. By the same token, poverty and desperation drive poor people to do many environmentally destructive things – like clear-cutting rainforests, using highly-polluting fuels (like wood and coal), or poaching endangered animals. For all these reasons, higher living standards (driven, in part, by economic growth) can contribute to the reduction of many kinds of pollution. In other ways, however, economies do more environmental harm as they get richer – especially by consuming more fossil fuels, and hence emitting more greenhouse gases.

It is very difficult, verging on impossible, for mass living standards to rise appreciably *without* economic growth (conventionally measured). And under capitalism, when growth *stops* (as during a recession), economic and political conditions change in ways that clearly undermine both the well-being of working people and prospects for environmental progress: mass unemployment, growing poverty, a "zero-sum" distributive struggle (in which one group's gain is necessarily another group's loss), and a desperate focus on meeting immediate income

Table 16.1 Work and the Environment

Work that Does Not Harm the Environment:
Improving the quality rather than the quantity of manufactured products.
Providing more child care, youth services, education, elder care, neighbourhood recreation, and other human services.
Production of many private services.

Work that Helps the Environment:
Building expanded public transportation.
Retro-fitting homes and buildings for energy efficiency.
Production of fuel-efficient and alternative-technology vehicles.
Investment in non-polluting machinery and equipment.
Investment in clean energy generation.
Cleaning up industrial waste sites.
Construction of new parks.

Improving Living Standards Without More Work:
Consume more "leisure" and less "stuff," by equitably reducing working hours (less hours per week, per year, or over a lifetime).

---

and consumption needs (rather than addressing longer-term challenges like sustainability).

Strictly speaking, the problem here is capitalism, not a lack of growth. It is possible to imagine a no-growth economy which avoids those negative outcomes (unemployment, poverty, and desperation), but it cannot be a capitalist one. As we have seen, capitalism relies on each firm's hunger for larger profits, enforced through competitive pressure, to motivate the business investment that drives the whole system. Therefore, growth is an inescapable feature of capitalism (although it is strictly and deliberately controlled under neoliberalism). So while we are working to manage capitalism in a more environmentally responsible manner, we must also think about alternative ways of organizing the economy to avoid a head-on collision with the environment (something we consider, tentatively, in Chapter 29).

Even under capitalism, however, there are clearly ways in which doing more work – on the right things – can help the environment, not harm it. Some of these are summarized in Table 16.1. One environmentally beneficial strategy is to produce higher-quality products, instead of larger quantities of low-quality products. For example, producing high-quality, long-lasting furniture (rather than cheap, assemble-it-yourself fixtures that fall apart in a couple of years) does not utilize any additional material inputs or cause any additional pollution. Yet the value-added (and hence GDP) associated with higher-quality furniture manufacturing could be three times as high as the cheap stuff. Of course, this depends on consumers being able to *afford* higher-quality goods – which is another reason why mass prosperity can help the environment, not hurt it.

Focusing on producing services instead of goods is another environmentally beneficial way to transform our work. In particular, a major expansion of public and caring services (like child care, education, elder care, and other life-affirming programs) would generate huge increases in employment and incomes (and hence in GDP), with virtually no impact on the environment. Even many private service industries – like restaurants, cultural facilities, household renovations, and personal services – have relatively minor environmental impacts.

Meanwhile, investing in environmental protection is itself a form of economic activity that obviously benefits the environment. After all, environmental investments create work, generate incomes, and contribute to GDP as surely as any strip mine or chemical factory. In this regard, there's no shortage of things to do. Trillions of dollars must be invested worldwide in coming years on energy-efficient transportation, clean energy technologies, energy-saving retro-fits of homes and buildings, the clean-up of waste sites, and the expansion of parks and conservation areas. These investments would generate massive, positive gains for workers and communities.

Of course, there are many forms of economic activity that clearly do damage the environment: activities that exploit and consume more natural resources, consume more fossil fuels, and emit more pollution. Our challenge is to close off profitable polluting activities (or else make them unprofitable), while simultaneously stimulating environmentally beneficial or benign activities. What statisticians ultimately report as GDP is in reality a composite of many different productive acts, mostly motivated by hunger for profit on the part of owners of private companies. In that context, we should be thoroughly agnostic about GDP growth: we cannot know whether growth is useful or destructive (environmentally or socially). And our main goal is not to get more growth (or less, for that matter). It's to organize and pay for a lot more work that lifts social and environmental standards, and a lot less that undermines them.

Declaring "war" on pollution

At the outset of World War II, the countries that fought fascism suddenly and dramatically invested huge resources in their military effort. These investments were not made because of a hunger for profit. They were made because of a deep, shared conviction that the battle against fascism had to be fought and won. These investments, therefore, sidestepped the usual motivation for work and production under capitalism. (Of course, private companies on both sides of the war profited mightily from military spending; but it was not the profit motive that elicited the spending in the first place.) These huge investments were financed in unusual ways: through massive government spending, large deficits, the issuance of "war bonds," and the direct creation of new money by government banks.

Notwithstanding the death and destruction experienced on the battlefields, the war produced nothing short of an economic miracle. Economies which had languished in deep depression for a decade, plagued by mass unemployment, poverty, and falling incomes, sprang suddenly to life. Full employment was quickly attained, and new sources of labour supply (such as women, recruited to the formal labour market in large numbers) were mobilized. Incredible innovation was demonstrated: not just in the technology of war, but in transportation, logistics, the organization of work, and even creative financial and social innovations to support the war effort. Incomes rose dramatically, and so did material living standards (despite wartime shortages of some goods). For those on the home front, nutrition, health, and life expectancy all improved. Workers became more confident and demanding, despite the wartime culture of mutual sacrifice; strikes were common, and unions grew. This wartime experience (along with other economic and political factors) left workers confident and empowered, and set the stage for them to demand and win mass prosperity during the postwar Golden Age.

Getting it Done

Scientists agree that global emissions of greenhouse gases must be reduced quickly and dramatically – cut 40 percent by 2030, according to the Intergovernmental Panel on Climate Change, to avoid the most catastrophic effects of climate change and eventually stabilize global temperatures. But this dramatic, essential shift need not imply a negative shock to employment and living standards. To the contrary, steady investments in energy efficiency and renewable energy generation would constitute a hugely beneficial economic engine. Robert Pollin, a US economist, has simulated a detailed plan to reach the 40 percent reduction for the American economy, based on publicly-supported investments of US$200 billion per year for 20 years (equal to just 1.2 percent of US GDP). The investments would be split between measures to reduce energy use, and stimulate clean renewable energy sources (including solar, wind, and geothermal). Thanks to the relatively labour-intensive nature of both energy efficiency and renewable energy initiatives, and their higher ratio of domestic content (as opposed to import-intensive fossil fuel industries), the program would generate a net increase of 2.7 million jobs per year in the US (even after considering the decline of employment in fossil fuel industries).* It's a plan that's good for the labour market – not just the climate.

* Robert Pollin, *Greening the Global Economy* (Cambridge, MA.: MIT Press, 2014).

How ironic that something as destructive and horrific as world war should generate such remarkable economic and social benefits – precisely because the usual incentives and constraints that constrain our collective work under capitalism were deliberately bypassed. And imagine if humanity could now mobilize both its collective willpower and its economic resources with just as much determination, but to an end purpose that is constructive rather than destructive.

Climate change likely poses a challenge to human well-being comparable to (if more gradual than) fascism in the 1930s and 1940s. It will take much more than fiddling with market mechanisms, or encouraging consumers to "think green," to arrest this fearsome process.

We should protect the environment by doing *more*, not by doing *less*. We should declare a peaceful "world war" on climate change, and mobilize large investments (significantly, though not exclusively, through government) in environmentally beneficial activities and socially sensitive adaptation. The resulting stimulus to spending power would offset any deterioration in profitability resulting from stricter environmental regulations, and would simultaneously open up profitable business opportunities in "green" industries (like building and installing energy-efficient machinery and clean-power systems).

Where consumption is actually reduced (in societies prosperous enough to do this), this could be attained through widespread and equitable reductions in working hours (shortening the working week; expanding holidays; and improving family leave, education leave, and early retirement opportunities). In this manner, the higher productivity generated by economic development would translate into greater opportunities for leisure – not just greater material consumption.

Like the war effort, this campaign against pollution would imply a significant expansion of government, public investment, and regulation – all justified by the urgent collective need to slow and stop climate change. But this would occur in a manner that enhances economic well-being (and actually boosts growth, properly defined), rather than undermining it.

Part Four

The Complexity of Capitalism

17

Money and Banking

A world of money

In this book, we've discussed the economy in very concrete, real terms. Production is how we make useful goods and services. Work is the human effort that goes into that production. Consumption is the use of some of those goods and services to keep us alive, and make life enjoyable. Investment is the use of some of that output as "tools," allowing us to produce even more output in the future. All of these things are *real*: they all consist of actual goods and services. None of them need be measured in terms of money. They're all real stuff.

But just look around at the actual economy: there are dollar signs *everywhere*. Prices in stores. Amounts in bank accounts. Values on stock markets. GDP in statistical reports. All measured in terms of money.

A visitor from Mars would quickly conclude that the economy is *totally* about money. Yet underneath, the economy is real and tangible. Underneath, the economy is ultimately about working to produce concrete goods and services, with the end goal of meeting concrete human needs.

Explaining money, and linking the real activities at the core of the economy with the monetary values that represent them (prices, income, wealth), has bedevilled economists for centuries. What is money, anyway? How are money prices determined? Why do they change over time? How does money (and the monetary system) affect real economic activity – for better and for worse? The next three chapters will start to answer these questions.

What is money? And what is it good for?

Very broadly, **MONEY** is anything that allows its holder to purchase other goods and services. In other words, money is purchasing power. Early forms of money were tangible objects with some perceived intrinsic value (such as trinkets or coins made from precious metal). Today, money is very different: it is usually intangible (in fact most money today consists of electronic entries in bank accounts), and its value depends completely on social convention and government pronouncement. What's more, in a modern economy money is constantly changing – driven mostly by the efforts of financial companies (like banks) to find more profitable financial

---

That's What I Want

"Your lovin' gives me such a thrill,
But your lovin' don't pay my bills.
Now give me money, that's what I want."

Berry Gordy and Janie Bradford, US songwriters (1960).

---

transactions and accumulate financial wealth. Indeed, in modern capitalism those private financial companies actually control the *creation* of money.

Modern money comes in different shapes and sizes:

- **Currency**   Currency is no longer minted from precious metal. Instead, currency consists of paper money and non-precious coins officially issued and sanctioned by the government. Most people still think of "money" as "currency." But in fact currency accounts for a very small share (as little as 2-3 percent) of total money outstanding in a modern economy.
- **Deposits**   Most people don't keep a lot of cash on hand. They deposit extra currency in the bank, so they don't lose it and can earn interest. But money in the bank is still money. And with modern electronic banking, deposits can quickly change hands, without ever touching hands. These deposits come in many different forms: standard savings and chequing deposits, term deposits, foreign currency deposits. Even some common, easily marketable financial investments (like short-term government bonds) are counted as "money" in official statistics.
- **Credit**   Today customers can make many purchases without paying anything at all – simply by promising to pay in the future. Think of a furniture store offering a great bargain on a new sofa: "Don't pay anything until next year!" Credit gives a person or company purchasing power, even when they don't yet own the funds to pay for their purchases. No longer does an individual have to save in advance in order to make a major purchase (like a sofa, a car, or a home). And no longer does a business have to save in advance (out of their past profits) before making a new investment. Instead, a bank or other financial institution provides the needed purchasing power: through a loan, a line of credit, a deposit into a chequing account, a bond, or the issuance of a credit card. In return, the borrower promises to pay the loan back later – with interest, of course.

Credit accounts for most new money creation in a modern capitalist economy. When a new loan is issued, the bank deposits the requested funds into the borrower's account, and – voila! – new money is born. But credit money doesn't live forever. When a loan is paid back (without a corresponding new loan being reissued), then money is destroyed. As we will see, banks (and other financial institutions, including investment dealers, mortgage brokers, and money markets) have the unique power to quite literally create new money out of thin air, each time they issue a new loan. Expanding credit (and hence creating new money) is crucial to the smooth functioning of the economy: without it, there wouldn't be enough purchasing power to buy all the goods and services we produce, and the economy would sink into depression. But in a private banking system, credit is controlled by private banks – which are, not surprisingly, concerned first and foremost with maximizing their own profits. Consequently, the monetary system operates in particular, peculiar, and sometimes damaging ways. Money can help build an efficient and prosperous real economy. But it can also disrupt and damage the real economy.

Money has several economic functions:

1. Money is a **means of payment**. It allows people to buy products or services. It also allows them to make other kinds of payments (like taxes or loan repayments).
2. Money is a **unit of account**. It provides a standardized way for companies, households, and governments to measure income and wealth, evaluate different products or assets, and determine whether a firm is profitable.
3. Money is a **store of value**. Money allows individuals or companies to store wealth in a flexible, convenient form. Few people get intrinsic pleasure from money, purely for its own sake. True, it must be thrilling for rich people to see all those zeros in their bank statements (just as kings and emperors in previous epochs enjoyed running their hands through piles of gold coins). But in general, money is useful only for what it can buy. When they can't find anything better to do with it, or when they fear losses on other types of assets, individuals or firms will simply set aside their money (in cash, bank accounts, or term deposits). Holding onto money in this way is called **HOARDING**, and it can cause major economic problems.
4. Thanks to its usefulness as both a means of payment and a store of value, money is necessary to **facilitate exchange** between different buyers and sellers. Without money, trade would have to occur on a **BARTER** basis – where one product or service is traded directly for another. This is tremendously inefficient: no deal can be made until a seller finds a buyer who has something to offer that the seller simultaneously wants. Imagine trying to sell a used car this way. You'd have to find someone who wanted to buy your used car, but who also wanted to part with something you wanted – like a month's rent on a vacation cottage, a large-screen television set, or whatever else you were interested in purchasing. It would be very hard to consummate such a deal. Money is thus essential for effective exchange.

Taking a Byte Out of the Monetary System

If banks can create money out of thin air (every time they issue a new loan), then why not dot.com entrepreneurs? That logic, combined with the technological wonders of the internet era, has sparked a flurry of VIRTUAL CURRENCIES that aim to challenge the dominance of state-backed currencies in economic affairs.

The largest of these currencies is Bitcoin, which began operations in 2009. But hundreds of others have also sprung up; most don't last long. Some on-line currencies have a central sponsor (who organizes trading and takes responsibility for managing accounts and guarantee-ing payments). But many (including Bitcoin) are decentralized: there is no one "in charge" of creating the money, handling transactions, or guaranteeing security. For this reason, virtual currencies appeal to anti-government libertarians, who want to circumvent what they see as the illegitimate authority of government institutions (like central banks). They also appeal to criminals of various kinds, who appreciate any opportunity to anonymously accumulate and transfer money, away from the prying eyes of police and regulators.

▶

Because of these obvious economic benefits, money has been used for thousands of years, in various forms. To be effective, it must be accepted as a valid form of payment by most participants in an economy. In this regard, money is a *social* institution. It requires the trust and faith of the people who use it. Anyone who accepts money payment for something must be confident they'll be able to spend that money when they want to buy something else.

More fundamentally, money is also a political institution. Its existence and value relies on the political and legal authority of the official body (usually a national government) that endorses it. Standardized, portable, widely accepted forms of money did not come into existence until powerful, centralized states emerged (starting with the first slave-owning empires around 5,000 years ago) to endorse and enforce the whole system. Money that is based on an arbitrary, state-enforced standard is known as **FIAT MONEY**. Whether it exists as printed currency or in an electronic account, fiat money has no intrinsic worth; instead, it requires the active endorsement and protection of the state for its survival and

The creation of new Bitcoin money is controlled through an odd system (called "mining") in which computer operators receive payment (in Bitcoins) for helping to create and manage the computer algorithms needed to keep Bitcoin accounts secure and confidential. (That's the theory, anyway: in practice, hackers have robbed many Bitcoin accounts.) Bitcoins can be exchanged for conventional currencies on open exchanges, but their value in those trades fluctuates wildly. That's mostly because speculators have seized on the Bitcoin market (like any other financial asset whose price fluctuates) as a new arena for making short-term trading profits. The inflexible supply of Bitcoins makes matters worse.

Do virtual currencies even count as "money," as conventionally understood? Not really. Their use as a means of exchange or unit of account is limited: few retailers accept Bitcoins, and those that do normally convert them into standard currencies (usually the US dollar) immediately, which means the Bitcoin has no stable value of its own. As a store of value, Bitcoins are also unreliable due to enormous, speculator-driven fluctuations in their exchange rate. For example, the US-dollar value of Bitcoins quintupled within a month late in 2013, but then crashed by more than half in the next four. Bitcoin prices are far more volatile than other speculative assets or commodities, largely due to uncertainty regarding the system's long-term viability (especially as financial regulators around the world start to crack down on illegal uses of virtual currencies).

The FIAT MONEY system ultimately depends on the active backing of state power. Government's ability to require its use (including to pay taxes!) is essential to its widespread and continuing acceptance. Virtual currencies have no such backing, which is why they are unlikely to ever amount to more than a passing fad among computer nerds, libertarians, and speculators.

stability. Indeed, the ultimate backstop to the value of money is the government's requirement that it be used to pay taxes; this forces all tax-paying entities (whether individuals or companies) to accumulate and use this particular form of money (thereby guaranteeing its widespread acceptance and value). True money, capable of fulfilling all four of the functions listed above, has never emerged spontaneously through mutual agreement among traders. Some modern-day computer geeks (many motivated by right-wing libertarian philosophies) have tried to create their own alternative internet-based currencies as a means of exchange (see box), but these are unlikely to become lasting features of the monetary system unless they receive active state backing.

Capitalism and money

While money has a very long history, under capitalism money takes on a new and particular importance, for three broad reasons:

1. For the first time in economic history, accumulating money becomes the *goal* of production. Companies initiate production in order to make a profit, and that profit is always measured in money.
2. In the act of initiating new production, companies actually *create* money. The financial system provides credit to companies to allow them to pay for capital investments, and for their initial purchases of labour and other inputs. Business credit is a crucial source of new money in capitalism, and that money is essential for stimulating production and job creation.
3. Private profit-seeking financial companies (like banks) oversee the creation and destruction of money through their lending (that is, credit-creating) activities. That causes the monetary system to behave in certain ways – sometimes helpful, ﹅ often disruptive and destructive.

For all these reasons, capitalism is an *inherently* monetary economy. It is impossible to imagine a capitalist economy in which money does not rule supreme. And thus, to understand how capitalism works, it is essential to understand money.

Controlling and creating money

In modern capitalism, credit is the main source of new money, and the crucial job of issuing new credit has been mostly handed over to banks and other private financial institutions. Hence they have replaced government as the most important players in the monetary system.

Of course, government's role is still essential. Government endorsement (including the requirement to pay taxes denominated in the official currency) is essential to the widespread acceptance and stability of any money. Governments closely control the printing and distribution of hard currency (supplied to the economy through the banking system) to prevent counterfeiting and other crimes. Governments and their agencies oversee the money-creating activities of private banks, providing extra funds when needed. In times of crisis, governments keep the whole, fragile system afloat (through enormous, extraordinary interventions). Even government FISCAL POLICY supports the monetary system, by providing government bonds and currency that are essential to the daily operations of private banks.

But despite all this government support, the day-to-day creation (and destruction) of money has become the domain of the private banks and other financial institutions which control credit. And their actions, in turn, are driven by the same motivating force that propels capitalism as a whole: namely, the pursuit of private profit.

Out of Thin Air

"Whenever a bank makes a loan, it simultaneously creates a matching deposit in the borrower's bank account, thereby creating new money."

Bank of England Quarterly Bulletin, 2014.

"The process by which banks create money is so simple that the mind is repelled."

John Kenneth Galbraith, Canadian-American economist (1975).

There is a popular myth that banks operate simply as a financial intermediary, or "middle-man." People who have thriftily saved their pennies deposit them in a bank for safe-keeping, earning a modest interest for their prudence. In turn, dynamic, growing companies borrow those funds from the bank to finance their productive new investments. Banks earn profits by charging more for the loans, than they pay on deposits. Clever banks can even lend out their deposits several times over (through a trick called **FRACTIONAL RESERVE BANKING**), on the assumption that not all depositors will ask for their money back at the same time. (If this happens, the result is a "run" on the bank, and the bank collapses.)

This old-fashioned vision of "savings and loan" banking was depicted memorably in the classic Disney film Mary Poppins. A young Michael Banks is encouraged by his father (a bank manager, accompanied by the bank's doddering president) to invest two pence in a bank account – thereby miraculously helping to finance enormous productive ventures like railways, canals, and tea plantations. When Michael refuses, other customers become worried and withdraw their deposits, and the bank fails.

In fact, this vision of productive financial intermediation is not (and has never been) an accurate description of how private banks actually operate. Banks do not passively wait for depositors to drop off their hard-earned pennies, which are then recycled as loans to growing, productive companies. Instead, banks lead the whole credit-creating process. They literally create new money with the stroke of a pen every time they issue a new loan. The new purchasing power transferred into the borrower's account is a liability for the bank; it is matched by a new asset, representing the borrower's promise to repay the loan.

But where do banks actually get the cold hard cash, once the borrower decides to spend that new credit? Banks are not allowed to print currency. (Only the government can do that.) But banks don't need that much actual cash to sustain this miraculous money-creating operation. Each bank requires a bit of currency for those of its customers (less common these days) who prefer to buy things with cash (rather than credit cards and electronic transfers). But the key test for banks comes at the end of each business day, when they calculate how much money left the bank (whether through cash withdrawals or electronic transfers), where that money ended up, and how much came back (in the form of new deposits by the bank's own customers). Remember, even when new credit is spent, it shows up somewhere in the banking system, in someone else's account (namely, whoever received the money spent by the original borrower). Credit money thus stays alive until the initial loan is repaid. Every bank therefore experiences many inflows and outflows each day, based on those customers who spent money, and those who received it (via expenditures made by borrowers at other banks). Each bank only worries about the net balance of those inflows and outflows; they are usually very small relative to the gross inflows and outflows experienced by each bank. Banks use a special overnight clearing-house system to settle their net balances every day. If more money left the bank than came in, the bank owes a net balance to the clearing-house, which it finances thanks to routine overnight loans from other banks (called INTERBANK LENDING). The opposite occurs when a bank draws in more money in a day than is transferred out; it then lends to other banks through the clearing-house.

The surprising result of this system is that banks do not actually need deposits to engage in money-creating lending. Every bank starts with an initial endowment of money (representing the initial equity investment of the bank's owners). It then must raise any additional money required to cover daily net balances with the rest of the banking system; there are several different ways to do this. Traditional "savings and loan" banks do indeed recruit deposits; they are a relatively low-cost source of funds to offset those day-to-day balances. But many financial institutions (like investment banks, and other near-bank institutions that make up what is known as the SHADOW BANKING system) don't bother with deposits at all. They tap other sources of money (such as short-term loans called "commercial paper") to cover the gaps between outgoing loans and incoming repayments. And at the end of the day (literally!), the interbank lending system reconciles any final money imbalances involving particular banks; for the banking system as a whole, the balances sum to zero. Interbank lending thus plays an essential role in lubricating the overall private credit system. If interbank lending freezes up for some reason (as it did during the 2008 GLOBAL FINANCIAL CRISIS), even enormous institutions can collapse as fast as the fictional bank in Mary Poppins. Indeed, modern bank runs are more likely to be sparked by problems in interbank lending, than by a mass exodus of mom-and-pop depositors.

The ultimate backstop for banks when things go badly is the government's CENTRAL BANK: a special bank owned by the government, with broader responsibilities for overseeing and stabilizing the operation of the whole banking system. Private bank borrowing from the central bank is also a daily occurrence, again normally in modest amounts. In some countries, private banks maintain ongoing reserve deposits with their central bank, typically in return for a low rate of interest. (These reserves were once required by government regulations, but those rules have been dismantled in most countries; today central bank deposits are usually voluntary.) Incremental increases or decreases in reserve deposits will reflect modest ongoing changes in a bank's overall net money balances. During times of severe uncertainty, however, the central bank backstop becomes a lifesaver for the private banks. In 2008 and 2009, for example, central banks around the world supplied trillions of dollars of emergency loans (at very low interest rates) to private banks, so they could meet their net money requirements (which suddenly surged, due to a freeze in interbank lending and money hoarding by worried customers). For this reason, central banks are called the "lender of last resort."

The interest rate charged by the central bank on its overnight loans to private banks, and the rate which banks then charge each other for interbank lending, ultimately determine interest rates on most other loans (including household mortgages, business lending, and more). Recent scandals have exposed efforts by private banks to manipulate those overnight benchmark interest rates, and further boost their own profits (see box).

Let's review how the private credit money system differs fundamentally from the Mary Poppins stereotype. Deposits are not required for a private bank to issue new loans. Rather, issuing new loans initiates a money-creating process that is eventually reflected in matching new deposits somewhere in the banking system. A new loan creates new purchasing power (reflected directly in a new deposit in the borrower's

---

Crooked as They Come

Financial insiders can manipulate the price of important "benchmark" indicators (like interest rates, foreign exchange rates, and bond prices) that in turn are reference points for the pricing of many other financial assets. One such benchmark is a special UK interest rate called the London Interbank Offered Rate (LIBOR) – which determines how much banks charge each other for routine overnight loans. Due to its broad economic importance, the LIBOR also affects the prices of trillions of dollars of other bonds, derivatives, and other securities. Inside traders can manipulate the published LIBOR, usually by moving large sums of money in or out of bond markets in the last moments of any trading day. If this shifts the final posted price, even by a miniscule amount, those traders can use other positions in DERIVATIVE markets to make enormous profits. A scandal involving widespread manipulation of LIBOR was exposed in 2012, and resulted in huge fines imposed on some of the world's biggest banks (including Barclay's Bank, whose CEO and chairman had to resign). But there is no doubt that this kind of insider manipulation continues on many key markets, including foreign exchange and stock market indices.

name). When that money is spent, it moves to other deposits, mostly in other banks. Each bank balances its cash position as needed through interbank borrowing or, if necessary, through loans from the central bank. It is thus possible for banks to create credit (that is, new money) without attracting any depositors at all.

Contrary to the stereotype, therefore, bank lending does not depend at all on the thriftiness of households and other savers. To the contrary, loans issued by banks, by generating new economic activity and income, are the initial step in an income-generating process that ultimately allows households to save. In short, borrowing creates saving – not the other way around. (This is an obvious parallel to our finding, in Chapter 12, that business investment, by creating jobs, starting production, and generating income, ultimately creates the savings required to pay for it.)

The macroeconomics of credit

Private companies must sell the goods and services they produce, or else production stops. For customers to buy that output, they need purchasing power. The private credit system is the dominant source of new purchasing power. So it's not surprising that the functioning of the credit system is crucial to the operation of the broader economy. The economy needs a steady flow of new money to facilitate production, income, and spending. Expansive credit (when consumers and businesses take out lots of new loans) is usually associated with robust purchasing power, job-creation, and income growth. But there's no guarantee that credit growth translates into a stronger real economy. If credit grows too quickly, or is used for the wrong reasons (such as bidding up the price of speculative assets, like stock markets and real estate, instead of buying real goods and services), then credit expansions can cause trouble. And when credit is not growing, or even shrinking (a condition called DELEVERAGING, with borrowers repaying more loans than they take out), the real economy suffers badly. That's why economists and policy-makers watch the pace of credit growth very closely, as a crucial indication of how the economy is performing – and is likely to perform in the future.

Given this systemic importance, it is useful to think of credit like a public utility, similar to other utilities (like the electricity service or the water system). Every business needs electricity to flow through the wires, and water through the plumbing, before any production can occur. In the same way, credit must flow steadily through the economy, or else the whole system grinds to a halt. Essential public utilities (like power, water, and roads) work better when they are publicly owned and managed; the consequences of service disruptions are too severe for the overall economy, and all of society should never be "hostage" to the greed of utility companies. In the case of credit, however, this essential "utility" is outsourced to private, for-profit companies. They generate enormous profits, based on their unique power to create money. But their private vested interests need to be balanced against the public's interest in a smooth, steady flow of credit, essential for production and employment. Those two interests (banks' interest in maximum profit, and society's interest in stable and productive credit) can diverge, causing big macroeconomic problems.

For example, private banking has shown a tendency to produce repeating (and damaging) cycles of over-expansion followed by contraction and retrenchment. Banks make their profit from new lending, and this self-interest drives new credit expansion. But they always measure the opportunity for profits against the risk that loans might not be repaid. Losses on bad loans can gobble up a bank's profits, and even its base of equity capital, very quickly. Private banking thus demonstrates a perpetual clash of personalities, as "greed" (for profits on loans) battles "fear" (that loans won't be paid back). When economic times are good, few borrowers go bankrupt, and banks become less sensitive to the risks of loan default. Their greed overwhelms their fear, and they push new loans aggressively – creating purchasing power and stimulating economic activity (or, less desirably, bubbles in stock markets and real estate prices). The reverse occurs when times turn bad, and their fear trumps their greed. Then banks become hyper-sensitive to loan defaults, and pull back their lending (even from reliable customers), causing a **CREDIT SQUEEZE** which reduces overall purchasing power and growth even further. Ironically, in tough times banks' *fear* of defaults can actually *cause* defaults – since lending restrictions produce economic stagnation and thus more bankruptcies (among both businesses and households). This cyclical, profit-driven roller coaster is called the **BANKING CYCLE**, and it is a major factor behind the boom-and-bust cycle of capitalism (that we will consider further in later chapters). The American economist Hyman Minsky was one of the first to explore the dynamics and importance of these repeating mood swings (see box).

Of course, it takes two to tango, and every loan needs two willing dancers: a borrower who wants to borrow, and a bank which is willing to lend. Banks can be quite aggressive in "pushing" loans into the economy – by reducing interest rates, or offering risky loans to marginal customers. But they can't *force* anyone to borrow. For credit to expand, borrowers (both businesses and households) must *want* to borrow. The desire to take on new credit will depend on the level of interest rates, and on borrowers' degree of confidence about their future. If businesses and consumers are very pessimistic about future economic prospects, then even very low interest rates might not stimulate new credit and spending. In these conditions, trying to increase borrowing by reducing interest rates is like pushing on a string.

Ultimately, then, the expansion of credit (and hence the supply of money) depends on the willingness of companies and consumers to borrow, combined with the willingness and ability of profit-maximizing private banks (and other financial institutions) to lend. Given this relationship, the total supply of credit to the economy cannot be directly controlled by government. This way of understanding

---

Stability is Destabilizing

Hyman Minsky was a US economist who analyzed the macroeconomic consequences of repeated mood swings in the financial industry. He noted that despite the obvious and painful history of financial booms and downturns, financiers have short memories: after a period of relative stability and profitability, they soon forget the last crisis and initiate another episode of aggressive, leveraged credit expansion. Moreover, competitive pressures among banks and near-banks force each lender to keep up with the rest of the financial pack. The career of any overly cautious banker, who limited their lending for fear of a future downturn, would be finished long before that downturn arrived - because their profits (during the upswing) would badly lag those of other, more aggressive lenders. Minsky identified three distinct "phases" in this mass mood swing. With initial, cautious borrowing (which he called "hedge" finance), both interest and principal on the debt could be repaid from current cash flows on investments. As both borrowers and lenders become more fearless, they move to "speculative" finance, in which current cash flow is only sufficient to pay interest charges; the principal of the debt must be rolled over continuously. In the final, most exuberant stage - "Ponzi finance" - investors don't even earn enough cash flow from existing investments to pay the interest on their debts. They are dependent on continuing asset price inflation (the speculative bubble) and even more borrowing just to meet their interest obligations. This is obviously unsustainable, and melts down into crisis once asset prices turn down. Like a lead actor in a Shakespearean tragedy, the banking industry seems incapable of changing its behaviour to avoid the next cyclical crisis. As Minsky wrote in 1975, "Stability - or tranquility - in a world with a cyclical past and capitalist financial institutions, is destabilizing."

---

the monetary system is called the theory of ENDOGENOUS MONEY, so named since the quantity of money circulating in the economy cannot be directly (or exogenously) controlled. Instead, it is determined endogenously by the lending and borrowing decisions of banks and borrowers.

The fragility of private banking

Private banks begin business with an initial investment of capital by their owners. Then they rely on a combination of deposits, commercial borrowing, interbank lending, and help from the central bank to finance their day-to-day money balances. But at any point in time, the total loans they have issued vastly exceed the money actually owned by the bank. The ratio of total outstanding loans, to a bank's internal capital, is called its LEVERAGE RATIO. ("Leverage" refers to the degree to which a business is financed with borrowed money.) At the peak of the financial expansion that preceded the 2008 global financial crisis, the leverage ratio of major global banks and shadow banks exceeded 50-to-1. In essence, every dollar actually owned by bank shareholders had been magnified 50 times over into a much larger amount of lending. In the wake of such aggressive leveraging, it wouldn't take many losses (from bad loans, stock market trading, or any other division of the bank's business) to wipe out the bank's initial capital, leaving it with no financial cushion – and that's exactly what happened. Confidence in the stability of hard-hit banks evaporated, depositors withdrew their funds, and other banks refused routine interbank loans. (We'll describe the 2008 crisis in more detail in Chapter 26.)

But even when leverage ratios are more "modest" (say, a mere 20-to-1, which is the leverage ceiling imposed by regulations in some countries), private banking is an inherently fragile business. The whole system always hangs on confidence: an awfully intangible, unstable foundation for such an important part of the economy. In response to widespread bank failures during the 1930s (and the immense economic and social damage they caused), government regulators instituted rules limiting how aggressively private banks can expand their lending. They required banks to keep cash (or deposits at the central bank) equivalent to a certain fraction (usually just a few percent) of their total liabilities, as protection against a rush of withdrawals or a spate of bad loans. Other rules prohibited commercial banks from participating directly in stock market trading and other risky activities, so that speculative losses would never jeopardize a bank's survival. In some countries governments also regulated the quality of loans (for example, establishing minimum down payments or maximum repayment periods on home mortgages) to further reduce the risk of loan losses and bank failure, and provided deposit insurance to settle the nerves of depositors and reduce the risk of bank runs. The power of central banks to act as lender of last resort was enhanced.

Hungry for more profits, however, banks chafed at those rules (although they always appreciate the government safety net whenever it is needed). In the 1980s and 1990s, the financial sector successfully lobbied for the relaxation or elimination of most of these safeguards, and the scope and profitability of financial activity expanded accordingly. Restrictions on speculative investments by commercial banks were ended. Investment banks and other "near-banks" undertook a broader range of lending and investing functions – eventually coming to form a parallel SHADOW BANKING SYSTEM that operated largely free from government regulations. Barriers to international financial flows were relaxed, allowing banks to seek profits anywhere in the world, but increasing the risk that financial crisis in one country could spread to others. Under an international system called the BASEL COMMITTEE, banks were still required to meet broad CAPITAL ADEQUACY targets, which specify a minimum cushion of internal resources (including the bank's own invested capital) as protection against any surge in withdrawals or loan losses. But as the meltdown of 2008 proved, the Basel rules were sadly inadequate to forestall a serious crisis of confidence. In the wake of that crisis, global regulations have been tightened somewhat, but have not fundamentally changed the inherent fragility of leveraged private banking.

It is important to recognize that the fundamental instability of our present banking system ultimately arises from its private, profit-driven, competitive nature. Private banks possess a unique and lucrative power: the ability to create money from nothing. But the way the private credit system operates (through the leveraged creation of credit, in a context of competition between private banks for market share) leaves any individual bank always vulnerable to loss of confidence, an exodus of cash, and ultimate collapse. This risk of sudden death is not an inherent characteristic of credit; but it is an inherent feature of leveraged, private, competitive banking. Making private banks smaller (as some reform proposals have suggested) does not solve the problem, and likely makes it worse (since smaller banks are more vulnerable to default, because their loans and assets are less diversified).

In contrast, a system of publicly-owned banks, ultimately reinforced by the money-creating authority of the state, would not face the same inherent risk of evaporating confidence and sudden collapse. To be sure, even in a well-managed public banking system some borrowers will occasionally default, and some loan losses will occur. But these losses need not threaten the survival of any particular bank, since all are protected by the stabilizing effect of public ownership and the state's ultimate power to create new purchasing power (offsetting loan losses) as needed. There would be no reason for depositors or other banks to suddenly withdraw their funds. More importantly, a public banking system would be mandated to provide the economy with a steady, healthy supply of new credit; its goal is no longer to maximize private profit, but instead to reliably facilitate productive economic activity. Loans could even be channeled deliberately to the most important and productive uses of new credit (including new capital investments, public infrastructure, community development, and others), rather than flowing willy nilly into whatever activity (productive or not) offers the highest short-term returns for private banks. Publicly owned banks, in other words, would function like a true public utility: meeting the broader economy's need for steady, productive credit. I believe that proposals for public and non-profit banking must be an important element of any vision for progressive economic change; we will discuss these possibilities further in the final section of this book.

The circuit of credit: lending to non-financial businesses

As we've seen, new money is created every time a new loan is issued. The borrower withdraws and spends the money, which in turn generates new revenues (and bank deposits) elsewhere in the economy. When the loan is eventually paid back, the money is destroyed and disappears from the system. Credit therefore has a "life cycle": it is born, it lives, and it dies. One life cycle of credit is called a "circuit"; a whole branch of heterodox economics (called CIRCUIT THEORY) focuses on describing the path traversed by money, and the economic consequences it leaves in its wake.

The economic effects of credit depend crucially on what the new money is used for. Many options are possible in this regard. Private banks issue new loans based on the probability of being paid back at a profitable rate of interest (protected, where possible, by collateral that can be seized in the event of non-payment). Beyond this, they are indifferent about the ultimate use of the credit they create. The borrowers can spend the money on whatever they choose.

One important outlet for lending is the provision of credit to non-financial businesses, for the purpose of financing capital investment and other expenses associated with initiating or expanding real production. We illustrate this circuit in Figure 17.1, which adds a financial sector to our previous road map of investment, production, and employment. We have positioned finance "above" the real economy; it does not undertake direct production, but rather provides an important input (credit) to companies which do produce useful goods and services. The bank provides purchasing power to capitalists, allowing them to purchase capital equipment, inputs, and raw materials, and to pay for the initial wages of newly-hired workers. This flow is labelled D (for debt) on the map. In return, the banks receive a share of profits flowing from real production in the form of interest (i) on the initial loan, on top of the eventual repayment of that loan. The remaining profit (net of interest) is retained by the owners of the productive, non-financial business.

Some important implications arise from even this very simple depiction of the financial system on our road map. Firstly, this circuit of credit leaves a real economic legacy, even after the loan is repaid (and the money is extinguished): the real productive capacity of the economy has grown thanks to the new capital investment. New capital equipment represents a lasting, real analogue to the financial capital created by the bank. And the real output produced thanks to that investment provides a source of new income, some of which must be repaid (as interest) to the banks which created the initial purchasing power.

Secondly, the financial system's ability to create credit for productive businesses, without requiring real savings to be set aside beforehand, allows the real economy to grow and change with tremendous speed and flexibility. If private businesses see an opportunity for new profit, they do not need to save up needed funds (from profits on existing operations) before springing into action. All they need is a convincing business plan and a willing banker. With the advent of credit, business

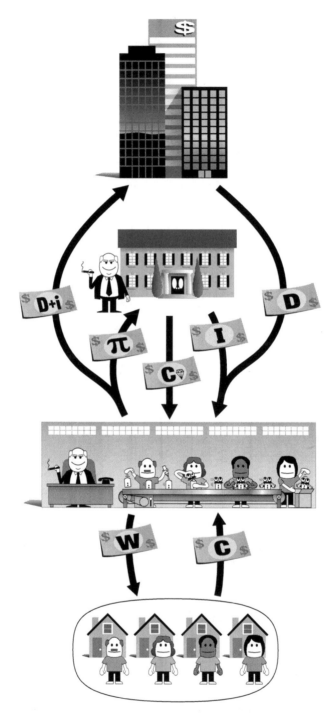

Figure 17.1 Economic Road Map: Banking (Lending to Non-Financial Business)

investment is "freed" from the constraint of past savings. When it works well, this use of credit explains how new industries (like the explosion of high-technology and internet firms in recent years) can spring out of nowhere to make important contributions to the economy. In a credit system, investment *leads* economic growth; savings, meanwhile, are *produced* by economic growth. By facilitating an investment-led expansion, credit can play an important and genuinely productive economic role.

A third implication of Figure 17.1 is that it creates a potential conflict of interest between the financial sector and capitalists in the "real" economy over how the profits from real production will be divided. If the banks' share becomes too large, then the incentive for companies to undertake real investment is reduced (since their bottom line profits, after paying back interest, are squeezed). On the other hand, both financiers and real capitalists have a shared interest in increasing the *total* return to capital. This explains why both have continued to strongly support the overall direction of neoliberal economic policy. Indeed, it was a coming together of financial interests (appalled at the losses experienced in the 1970s) and real businesses (fatigued at the difficulty of extracting work effort from an increasingly empowered and uppity workforce) that was the crucial precondition for the political triumph of neoliberalism at the end of the 1970s.

Bankers, like capitalists, live very comfortable lives, and a portion of their interest income (which was siphoned off from capitalists' profit income) is devoted to the same luxury consumption patterns as the capitalists they lend to. In fact, the salaries and bonuses earned by top financiers are larger than any other business executives (even running into the billions of dollars for CEOs of successful hedge funds and investment banks). However, to keep our road map simple, we do not separately show bankers' consumption spending in Figure 17.1.

Lending to productive non-financial businesses is likely the most useful and productive form of credit creation. New credit is linked closely to the expansion of production, employment, and income. There is no guarantee, of course, that real capitalists will indeed use the new purchasing power to expand their real operations; it is possible they could use new credit for less productive purposes (like speculating in financial markets, buying up and restructuring competing companies, financing additional luxury consumption, or even just paying off other debts). But when new credit is converted into expanded productive activity, the benefits of credit are enhanced, and the potential downsides minimized. The middle column of Table 17.1 summarizes the main features and outcomes of bank lending to productive businesses.

Ironically, however, this most productive use of credit has declined in importance during neoliberalism. Business profits have grown steadily as a share of GDP throughout the capitalist world since the 1980s – after all, that was the

Table 17.1   Contrasting Circuits of Credit

	Lending to Non-Financial Businesses	Lending to Households
Motive for Supplying Credit	Bank profit	Bank profit
Motive for Demanding Credit	To finance expanded production and generate business profit	To finance consumer purchases in excess of consumer income
Source of Income to Service and Repay Debt	New production and profit	Assumed future increases in labour income
Impact on Productive Capacity	Direct	Indirect (construction or consumer industries may expand to meet demand)
Potential to Fuel Speculative Activity	Modest	Strong
Source of Potential Default	Inability to realize profit on real production	Inability to service debt from future income

whole point of enhancing business freedom, restraining labour costs, and cutting business taxes. Yet real investment spending (as noted in Chapter 12) has not kept pace. In fact, as a share of GDP business capital spending has declined over the last three decades in the major developed economies. Since companies are taking in more profits, yet spending less on investment, their net credit needs have largely disappeared. To be sure, particular individual companies still require access to credit at different times (sometimes just a revolving line of credit to finance normal business expenses). But in most OECD countries the non-financial business sector as a whole no longer borrows on a net basis. Perversely, it has become a significant source of net lending back into the financial system, rather than the other way around. With non-financial companies taking in more money than they need to finance their own capital spending, excess funds are pumped back into banks (through debt repayment or the accumulation of financial assets). This saving by non-financial businesses is a new feature of capitalism under neoliberalism, and neoclassical economists have struggled to explain it; it does not fit with their assumption that investment and economic growth are led by the independent decisions of consumers to save (facilitated by efficient financial markets which transfer those savings to dynamic private businesses). At the macroeconomic level, meanwhile, money collected by capitalists, but not reinvested, now constitutes a chronic and significant drain on overall purchasing power and job-creation.

The circuit of credit: lending to households

With real businesses borrowing less, the banking industry has sought other profitable outlets for its credit-creating powers. Lending to households is another important and lucrative market. Of course, virtually every household experiences occasional needs for credit, and those needs evolve with the life-cycle of a family. Young families may take on significant debt to purchase a home, which is gradually extinguished as the mortgage is paid off. Later, in their prime earning years, some households manage to accumulate modest financial wealth – savings which are usually drawn down during retirement. As we learned in Chapter 7, the entire class of working households does not, in aggregate, save over time. On the whole, workers are largely propertyless: they own little more than the equity in their own homes, and depend on their capacity to work for others to support themselves over their life-cycles. At any point in time, therefore, the savings of some households are offset by new borrowing by others. The comparatively mundane work of managing household finances, and providing credit at key points of the family life-cycle, is an important but not especially lucrative component of basic "savings and loan" banking.

More recently, however, lending to households has taken on a more independent, volatile, and often dangerous nature. Profit-hungry banks began to compete more aggressively to issue more loans: taking advantage of relaxed regulations, offering innovative lending arrangements (with creative interest and repayment terms), and advancing credit to riskier, more marginal customers. At the same time, households became more willing to take on debt: not just to finance occasional major purchases, but seemingly to subsidize higher long-run levels of consumption than would otherwise be permitted by their actual incomes. Household debt, measured relative to household disposable incomes, grew dramatically in most advanced capitalist countries over the 1990s and 2000s.

This rise in household indebtedness has been the mirror image of declining borrowing by non-financial businesses. And both trends can be understood in part as a consequence of the significant redistribution of economic output that has occurred under neoliberalism. With wages stagnant, precarious work more common, and decent working class jobs harder to find, the only way many families could hope to achieve the "middle class dream" was through an ongoing increase in debt (through mortgages, credit cards, student loans, and other forms). If hard-pressed consumers are willing (or even desperate) to borrow, the financial industry is always willing to supply the needed funds.

Another factor behind sky-high personal debt levels has been the escalation of housing prices in many major cities. This has necessitated much larger mortgage borrowing by households. Worse yet, the interaction of easily available credit with real estate SPECULATION (whereby investors purchase properties not to personally live in, but rather to hold and resell for profit) can set off a self-reinforcing bubble in housing prices. In this case, rapid expansion of mortgage lending can fuel rising house prices which in turn forces even more borrowing by home buyers. Government subsidies for mortgage borrowing (such as tax preferences provided to home-owners and real estate investors in some countries) adds fuel to this speculative fire.

From a macroeconomic perspective, household borrowing can be "useful," to a point, by facilitating purchasing power and maintaining economic growth. More mortgage lending may translate into residential construction activity and employment (although some of the new money is always siphoned off into higher prices for existing properties, instead of new construction). Debt-financed consumer spending adds to demand for consumer goods and services (at least for as long as consumers keep borrowing), and this in turn can stimulate more production and employment. Many home-owners will even divert mortgage borrowing into consumer spending, by taking out second mortgages (which typically charge lower interest rates than credit cards) to finance non-real-estate purchases.

These macroeconomic spin-offs explain why central bankers and financial regulators have been reluctant to interfere with this long-term rise in personal indebtedness, despite rising concerns about the resulting financial instability of households (and potentially the whole banking system). If businesses are not borrowing to stimulate new demand, then perhaps households can fill the void – for a while. Moreover, growing household borrowing serves a political function, as well: it seemingly allows working people (again, for a while) to attain the promised good life, despite wage stagnation and unemployment. Debt-financed consumer spending can thus delay the economic slowdown that would otherwise result from weak business investment, the accumulation of cash by non-financial businesses, and weak labour incomes. But household debt burdens cannot grow forever. Sooner or later, if higher household debt is not matched by higher output and incomes (thus allowing households to service and eventually repay their debts), the long-run escalation in personal debt must eventually reach a ceiling. At that point economic crisis (featuring defaults and foreclosures among households, and spillover problems for the banks which lent to them) is likely to occur. This is exactly what occurred in the US beginning in 2008, when an enormous decades-long increase in household borrowing suddenly stopped (for reasons explained in detail in Chapter 26). American households then began to deleverage (that is, reduce their debts), and the resulting contraction in money and purchasing power led to several years of very weak macroeconomic conditions.

We illustrate this consumer-focused circuit of credit in Figure 17.2. Now new credit is advanced directly to working class households (reflected in an increase over time in personal indebtedness relative to income levels). This permits additional consumption expenditure, over and above what would normally be

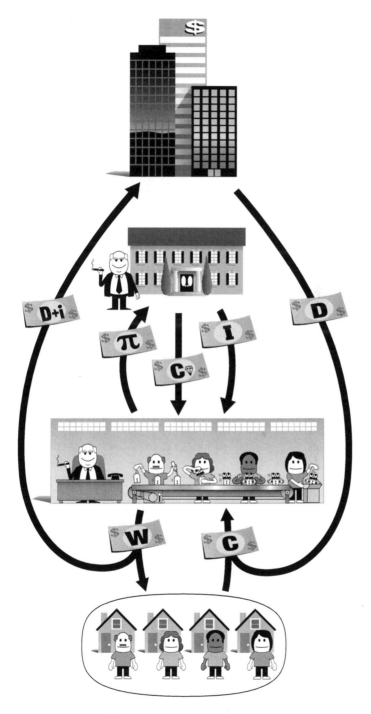

Figure 17.2 Economic Road Map: Banking (Lending to Consumers)

justified by labour incomes. Assuming that the new lending is not fully consumed by unproductive increases in real estate prices and other speculative assets, the new spending power can translate indirectly into new productive capacity – as businesses in the real economy mobilize to meet the growth in consumer demand. Eventually households must repay the debt to the banks with interest. Will future labour incomes after this consumption-led expansion be sufficient to justify, and reliably service, the higher levels of household debt required to set the process in motion? Not likely. Eventually there will be a day of reckoning for debt-laden consumers (and their banks). That moment of crisis could be sparked by anything which suddenly reveals that households are carrying more debt than they can afford (like an upward shift in interest rates, or a spike in unemployment, or a dip in real estate prices). Moreover, with the past expansion of credit having been used to finance consumption (instead of investment), the economy will not have benefited from a corresponding expansion in productive capacity. This circuit of credit thus demonstrates fewer benefits, and greater risks, than business-focused credit. The last column in Table 17.1 summarizes the different motives, and economic effects, of consumer credit.

For how long can capitalism be powered by credit-fueled consumer spending on the part of increasingly indebted households? Unless and until the fundamental engine of capitalist expansion kicks back into gear – namely, profit-seeking capital investments by non-financial companies, and the real production and employment that they generate – then this alternative circuit of credit can probably just delay the onset of bigger economic problems in the future.

Conclusion: money on the map

We have illustrated the two most important circuits of credit creation in modern capitalist economies: lending to non-financial businesses and to households. But these are not the only possible outlets for new credit. Banks can also advance credit to governments, to financial speculators, or to borrowers in foreign countries. And in addition to creating new credit, banks devote great energies to their own speculative trading in financial assets (a process we will consider further in Chapter 19).

Whether they are lending to businesses or households, banks are still positioned "above" the real economy on our road map. This position reflects both their unique power to create new money, and the fact that they do not directly produce useful goods and services which are the ultimate goal of economic activity.

18
Inflation, Central Banks, and Monetary Policy

Prices and inflation

Every marketed product has a money price, measured in units of some currency (dollars, pounds, euros). These prices help buyers to compare one commodity to another. When a shopper goes looking for a bargain, they compare prices of different brands to see which one offers (in their judgement) the best deal. When comparing prices of different commodities, we are examining their **RELATIVE PRICES**: that is, the price of one commodity compared to another. In this comparison, it doesn't really matter what currency is used, or whether we measure prices in dollars or cents. It is the *ratio* of prices, not the absolute prices themselves, that is most interesting. A bottle of fine sauvignon blanc costs three times as much as the cheap plonk; a passenger car costs 20 times as much as a high-definition TV; a detached home costs four times as much as a small condominium. For this purpose, you can choose any standard of measure.

Relative prices change over time, reflecting the changing conditions of production of different commodities. Technological breakthroughs which make it less costly to produce certain commodities usually lead to falling relative prices. For example, prices have declined quickly for personal computers and other electronic products for precisely this reason. Changes in the intensity of competition in particular industries can also change their relative prices, by affecting the "normal" rate of profit paid out in those industries.

In contrast, **ABSOLUTE PRICES** are simply the actual numbers attached to prices. And the **PRICE LEVEL** is the overall average level of absolute prices prevailing in an economy at any point in time. It is hypothetically possible for the absolute price level to change, without any change in relative prices. For example, suppose that suddenly, every store in the country began to label prices in cents (or pence), rather than dollars (or pounds or euros). Prices would suddenly *seem* 100 times higher. But at the same time everyone now receives their income in pennies. So their wages and salaries suddenly look much bigger, too.

Has anything changed? Not really. All relative prices are the same. And the purchasing power of wages and salaries hasn't changed. So people aren't any richer (by virtue of their "high" incomes), nor are they any poorer (because of "high" prices). But the absolute price level (quoted in cents now, rather than dollars) is 100 times higher than it used to be – since the absolute number describing each price is 100 times larger.

The most common reason for a change in the absolute price level is INFLATION. Inflation occurs when the overall level of prices in the economy increases over time. In real-world practice, as inflation occurs (and average prices increase over time), particular *relative* prices also change. Prices of some commodities increase more slowly than average (thus becoming less expensive in relative terms), while others increase more rapidly (becoming relatively more expensive). For a few commodities (like electronics), prices might decline in absolute terms despite the rise in the overall price level. These products thus become doubly inexpensive in relative terms – since their absolute prices are falling, even while most other prices are rising.

DEFLATION is also possible if the absolute price level *declines* over time. Deflation usually occurs during severe economic recession or crisis, when credit (and hence the money supply) is contracting, purchasing power is falling, and businesses become desperate to sell their products. If consumers think prices will be lower in the future, they will put off major purchases – and that makes the recession even worse. Deflation has disastrous consequences, including escalating debt burdens for households, businesses, and government.

Let's get real

The REAL PRICE of any commodity is its particular price expressed relative to the overall price level. A change in any commodity's real price, therefore, is the change in its particular price compared to the change in the general level of *all* prices. A commodity's real price goes up if its absolute price (measured in dollars) rises faster than the overall price level (and vice versa). If the cost of electricity, for example, rises 5 percent, while overall inflation is humming along at just 2 percent, then the real price of electricity has increased by about 3 percent. The real price of something therefore indicates its relative price, compared to the whole bundle of other prices in the economy (rather than comparing it to one other particular product).

Other economic variables can also be measured in real terms. For example, suppose that workers receive a 2 percent increase in their wages. But at the same time, suppose that overall consumer prices also grew by 2 percent. REAL WAGES – that is, the purchasing power of wages – haven't changed at all. Workers might feel 2 percent richer (a phenomenon that economists call "money illusion"), but in reality they are not. Wages measured in dollars (known as NOMINAL WAGES) must grow faster than consumer prices for workers to experience any improvement in real purchasing power. And if wages lag behind overall inflation, of course, then workers' real purchasing power declines.

Interest rates, too, can be measured in real terms, as the difference between the nominal interest rate (in percent) and the rate of inflation. If a bank charges 2 percent annual interest for a loan when overall prices are also growing at 2 percent, the bank's wealth doesn't change – because the loaned money, once repaid with interest, has no more purchasing power than it did when it was loaned out. If interest rates are *lower* than inflation, then the REAL INTEREST RATE is actually *negative*: the borrower, not the lender, is better off at the end of the loan because the money they pay back is worth less than the money they borrowed. The higher is inflation, therefore, the lower is the real interest rate. That's why financial institutions hate inflation with a passion.

The costs of inflation – and its benefits, too

Governments, financiers, businesses, and even ordinary citizens often wring their hands over inflation. And with the advent of neoliberalism, the never-ending fight to reduce and control inflation became the top economic priority: more important than reducing unemployment or alleviating poverty.

It is true that inflation can be painful. At very high levels, it can be downright destructive. But the social costs of inflation are often exaggerated by those (like bankers) who have vested interests in a low-inflation environment. And at moderate levels, inflation can actually be good for the economy – serving as a kind of lubricant to grease the economic wheels.

If every price and every flow of income experienced inflation at the same rate, it would have no real economic impact, and no winners or losers. This was true in the preceding hypothetical example of an economy which converted from dollars to cents. The absolute price level grew by 100 times, with no real effect whatsoever.

In real life, however, inflation is never so even-handed or predictable. Some prices rise faster than others. Some incomes keep up with inflation, or even surpass it; others lag behind. Inflation (or more precisely, a change in the rate of inflation) creates uncertainty in the minds of companies, investors, and households; this can be stressful, and in extreme cases can impede real investment.

Individuals or groups try to protect themselves against inflation by indexing their incomes to the price level. Labour contracts or social programs which provide for automatic cost-of-living adjustments are a common way to do this.

Some sectors of society, meanwhile, actually benefit from inflation (and from an increase in inflation). Borrowers are the biggest winners: the real burden of their loan is eaten away by higher prices. Governments are large borrowers, so in theory they should be relatively unconcerned about inflation. This makes it especially ironic that neoliberal governments pushed so hard for strict anti-inflation remedies in the 1980s and 1990s. A major side-effect of those measures (lower inflation and higher real interest rates) was a dramatic escalation in the real burden of their own debts.

Measuring Inflation

The most common measure of prices is the CONSUMER PRICE INDEX (CPI). This is a weighted index of inflation in all the things that consumers buy, including shelter, food, transportation, personal services, and household products and appliances. Statisticians gather detailed information (usually each month) on the prices of all products included in a specified "basket" of typical consumer purchases. Each product is then weighted according to its importance in overall consumer spending. The index is phrased in terms of prices in a certain base year (when the CPI is set to 100). Annual inflation in consumer prices then equals the percentage rise in the CPI index over one year. Since the CPI is based on the most detailed and frequent statistical research, and is widely reported in the media, it receives the most attention from policy-makers (including central banks).

There are other measures of inflation, too. Special price indices are calculated to measure average inflation in producer prices (like raw materials, parts, and other supplies), or commodities (such as oil, other forms of energy, minerals, and bulk foods). Many countries report a measure called CORE INFLATION, which strips out the effect of a few very volatile commodities (usually food and energy) from the overall CPI, and is believed to provide a more accurate indication of true underlying inflation. A somewhat different concept is the **GDP** DEFLATOR: this measures inflation as the difference between the increase in nominal GDP and the increase in real GDP (both of which are separately estimated by statistical agencies). Deflators can also be calculated for any particular component of spending in GDP (such as consumer spending, investment, and exports and imports).

On the other hand, some groups within society lose from inflation:

- Individuals who live on incomes that are fixed in nominal (or dollar) terms lose purchasing power when overall prices rise.
- Workers who are unable to win wage increases to keep up with inflation also lose real purchasing power.
- Lenders who loan money at a fixed rate of interest will see the real value of their loan (and future interest payments) reduced by inflation. It is possible to index loans to inflation, but this is rare.
- Owners of financial wealth lose some of their real wealth with every increase in prices.

These latter two sectors – financial institutions and wealth-owners – formed an immensely powerful and influential bloc in favour of reducing and tightly controlling inflation. Their negative experience during the 1970s, when accelerating inflation produced negative real interest rates and destroyed trillions of dollars of private wealth, led them to forcefully demand (and win) strict anti-inflation policies under neoliberalism.

In terms of the impact of inflation on overall economic performance (as opposed to its varying distributive impacts on different sectors of society), there's no conclusive evidence that moderate inflation undermines real investment, growth, or productivity. Higher rates of inflation can indeed cause significant economic and social stress, as individuals and companies take drastic measures (including the removal of capital from the country) to protect their incomes and wealth. And very high inflation (called HYPER-INFLATION) is usually associated with economic and political breakdown.

But there's no reliable evidence that single-digit inflation (under 10 percent per year) harms real economic progress. If anything, there seems to be a positive connection between modest inflation and growth: not because inflation *causes* higher growth, but simply because faster-growing economies tend to experience somewhat faster inflation. Considerable economic evidence suggests that modest inflation (perhaps 5 percent per year) is actually beneficial. It allows sellers of various commodities (including workers, who sell their labour) to reduce real prices when necessary (simply by lagging behind the pace of overall inflation), without actually cutting nominal prices (in dollars). Modest inflation thus lubricates the ongoing relative price adjustments that are necessary in any evolving economy. It is also useful in gradually reducing real debt burdens over time, thus enhancing purchasing power of households, governments, and other indebted sectors.

Another benefit of moderate inflation was discovered somewhat accidentally during the 2008–09 GLOBAL FINANCIAL CRISIS (GFC). Nominal interest rates cannot feasibly be reduced below zero (this would be equivalent to a bank paying its customers to borrow money). This problem is known as the ZERO LOWER BOUND; it limits a central bank's efforts to stimulate economic activity by cutting the interest rate. If inflation was very low (2 percent or even lower) before an economic slowdown begins, then nominal interest rates will have started from a relatively low level, and the central bank won't be able to reduce them very much before the nominal rate reaches zero. Indeed, within months of the onset of the GFC, nominal interest rates in most major capitalist countries hit the zero lower bound, forcing central banks to consider other unconventional ways of stimulating new lending (such as QUANTITATIVE EASING strategies, which will be explained in Chapter 26). If normal inflation had been running at a faster pace when the crisis hit, monetary policy could have responded to the downturn more effectively.

Beyond single-digits, however, there's no convincing evidence that higher inflation produces any economic benefits – and it can certainly cause economic harm. Very fast inflation creates widespread uncertainty, discourages long-term investments, and worsens the negative distributional effects (especially for those on fixed nominal incomes). In sum, it seems that a modest amount of inflation is useful as an economic lubricant. But too much of this lubricant (just like putting too much oil into your automobile's engine) can be harmful.

The causes of inflation

Inflation is a complex, unpredictable phenomenon. Over the years, many economists have developed one-size-fits-all theories of inflation, its causes, and its remedies. But these simplistic theories have all failed.

For example, the ultra-conservative MONETARISTS who became so influential with the advent of neoliberalism (led by MILTON FRIEDMAN) believed inflation was caused solely by an excess supply of money. This was proven wrong in the 1980s. Others argued inflation would take off whenever unemployment fell below its so-called "natural" rate. This was proven wrong in the 1990s. Today's central bankers have a more nuanced but still one-dimensional view: inflation results when overall spending exceeds the economy's vaguely-defined "potential output." Restraining spending (through higher interest rates, when needed) is the latest one-size-fits-all prescription for controlling inflation. But as we will see, this theory has been proven wrong, too.

In reality, there are many potential causes of inflation. Policy-makers should take a pragmatic, flexible, and balanced view of these various causes – because the appropriate cure for inflation (when one is deemed necessary) depends on its cause:

- Inflation can indeed result from excess spending; this is called "demand-pull inflation." If consumers and businesses are increasing spending too aggressively (fuelled, probably, by a rapid expansion of credit) relative to the quantity of goods and services available to purchase, then prices may be bid up as purchasers compete for whatever supplies are available at the time. This problem is more acute when demand surges are sudden (with no time for producers to respond with extra output) or regionally concentrated, and for commodities which are in fixed supply (like some natural resources or land and real estate). Curing this kind of inflation could involve reducing demand (through *higher* interest rates). But it could also involve stimulating additional supply (for example, encouraging more investment – which would require *lower* interest rates).
- Inflation can result from higher labour costs. If wages grow faster than productivity, then unit labour costs (the ratio of labour costs to productivity) will increase. Companies will try to pass on those higher production costs in higher prices. Depending on competitive conditions, they may or may not be able to do this. Potential responses to this kind of inflation include deliberately promoting unemployment (as neoliberal central banks have

done), finding ways to moderate wage increases when unemployment is low (perhaps through economy-wide bargaining arrangements, as exist in some European countries), or trying to prevent companies from passing on higher prices (through price controls, more competition, or increased imports).

* Higher profits can cause inflation, too – not just higher wages. If companies feel that they can increase prices without losing customers (perhaps due to a lack of competition, or a willingness of customers to tolerate higher prices), they will do so, whether or not there was any increase in their input costs. The steady rise in profit margins that businesses have enjoyed under neoliberalism have certainly, therefore, been an important factor in recent inflation.
* Another kind of inflation arises from increases in raw material prices, especially for crucial inputs that are used throughout the whole economy. Energy costs are an important example of this problem: higher oil prices were a major cause of the inflation of the 1970s. This type of inflation usually arises from sudden global shifts in commodity prices (often called "supply shocks").
* Inflation can become self-fuelling: once it starts, then the efforts of various economic players to protect themselves (such as companies passing on higher prices, or workers demanding cost-of-living adjustments) reinforce inflation at that rate. For this reason, inflation rates demonstrate a natural *inertia*: inflation next year will likely be similar to what it was this year, unless some significant change in economic conditions "knocks" the inflation rate off its mooring.

Real-world experience has indicated two additional insights regarding changes in the inflation rate:

* Reducing the inflation rate (called "disinflation") is a very painful process, usually involving recession, high unemployment, and lost economic opportunity. On one hand, this suggests extreme caution in deciding to reduce the inflation rate: the costs of doing so are very high, and the benefits (when inflation is moderate, anyway) are questionable. On the other hand, it also suggests caution in allowing inflation to increase – because the cost of bringing it back down, if that is ever deemed necessary, will be painful.
* Increases in employment and purchasing power can be associated with higher inflation, for obvious reasons. When more people are working, earning more money to spend, they willingly pay more for the things they buy, and companies willingly pump up prices. Experience has shown, however, that if economic expansion is gradual and steady, then the inflationary impacts of growth and employment are muted. Companies have time to respond to

strong purchasing power with more output, rather than higher prices, and competition will be more effective in restraining prices. Sudden surges in growth or employment, on the other hand, are more likely to lead to outbursts of inflation.

Central banks

CENTRAL BANKS are the most important single actors on the economic stage. They have the power to closely regulate everything from prices to job creation to incomes. And in most countries, central banks perform their duties without any direct accountability whatsoever to the broader population, or even to government … even though the central bank itself is a government agency!

The first central banks (like the Bank of England) were created in Europe in the early days of capitalism, to provide banking and credit services for national governments. In the twentieth century their role evolved, partly in response to problems in the private banking system. Central banks took on additional tasks: supervising private bank lending, imposing limits on risky bank activities, and stepping in during times of crisis and panic to provide emergency loans and forestall bank collapse. Because of this ability, the central bank is often called the "lender of last resort." The importance of this role was reinforced during the 2008–09 meltdown, when central banks around the world supplied trillions of dollars in emergency loans to prevent the outright collapse of major banks in the US, Europe and elsewhere.

Another crucial task of central banks is to regulate the "temperature" of the whole economy, through its control over interest rates. Central banks are in charge of MONETARY POLICY: using interest rates (and, occasionally, other policy instruments) to either stimulate or discourage spending and job creation. Low interest rates stimulate credit creation and spending across many sectors of the economy: including home-building and construction, cars and other major consumer purchases, business investment, and even exports (since low interest rates tend to reduce a country's exchange rate and thus stimulate more foreign sales). High interest rates have the opposite effect.

Central banks directly control interest rates on their own short-term loans to private banks (which, as we learned in the previous chapter, are a crucial part of normal day-to-day clearing-house operations in the banking system). In turn, private banks use this interest rate as a guide in setting the rates they charge customers for everything from home mortgages to business lines of credit. (Of course, the banks add a generous profit margin for themselves.) In turn, longer-term interest rates (like long-term bond rates) tend to follow the (longer-term) direction set by central banks. Central bank policy, therefore, is the crucial determinant of interest rates across the financial spectrum. In essence, the interest rate is a policy variable, set according to the priorities of government policy; under neoliberalism those priorities have emphasized boosting profits, protecting wealth, and disciplining workers. The amount of lending (and hence the supply of money) then adjusts to the prevailing interest rate, based on the demand for loans from consumers and businesses (as described in the theory of ENDOGENOUS MONEY).

This pragmatic understanding of interest rate determination is quite contrary to neoclassical theory, which pretends that the interest rate (like any other price in general equilibrium) reflects the forces of supply and demand (in this case, supply and demand for capital). Neoclassical writers even try to justify the payment of interest as ultimately reflecting the real "productivity" of capital; interest payments are supposedly the financial representation of the real profits paid out on real capital investments. As discussed in Chapter 6, this theory is untenable on theoretical grounds: capital itself is not productive (even though production methods which use more real capital can be). The neoclassical theory also fails as a description of how banking and investment actually works: in practice, interest rates are clearly a policy variable, they cannot be explained by changes in "supply and demand" (whether for money, or for real capital).

The impact of interest rates on economic growth is relatively slow to be felt: a change in interest rates can take up to two years to have full effect on spending. And monetary policy can be undermined or even overwhelmed by other factors – such as changes in consumer or investor sentiment, exchange rates, or government taxes and spending. In moments of severe crisis or uncertainty, shell-shocked businesses and consumers may not respond to lower interest rates at all, in which case monetary policy is totally ineffective: like pushing on a string (since there is no demand for loans, even at super-low interest rates). Furthermore, interest rates are a very blunt instrument: they're a one-size-fits-all policy tool, which can't take account of unique conditions or problems faced in specific regions or specific industries.

Nevertheless, interest rates are usually an important (if imperfect) tool for influencing the overall path of the economy. And the criteria on which central banks make their decisions are not "neutral" or "technical." They reflect central bankers' views of the economy, their ranking of the importance of different economic goals (holding inflation as more important than unemployment, poverty, and other problems), and their susceptibility to the influence of different sectors within society. In particular, central bankers are highly influenced by the attitudes and actions of the private financial industry: they meet regularly with financial executives, and constantly monitor feedback from financial markets. Central bankers like to pretend they are neutral technocrats, merely helping to guide the economy to some mythical point of maximum efficiency. This underpins the neoclassical claim that central bankers should be "independent" of elected government – that is, unfettered by any democratic pressure or oversight.

Yet in reality central banks are not independent at all. They are highly political institutions – and like other political institutions, their actions ultimately reflect the power differentials between various groups in society with competing interests and concerns regarding monetary policy.

Neoliberal monetary policy

During the long Golden Age expansion, central banks generally supported efforts to keep the economy as close to full employment as possible. However, both the direction of monetary policy and the ways in which it is implemented changed dramatically with the advent of neoliberalism. Indeed, the change in monetary policy that began in the late 1970s was the first and most important indicator of the dramatic U-turn being engineered at the economy's highest levels. And monetary policy remains one of the most powerful and entrenched features of the broader neoliberal agenda.

Initially, neoliberal monetary policy was heavily influenced by the MONETARIST ideas of Milton Friedman and other ultra-conservative economists. They weren't concerned with unemployment, arguing that it reflected laziness or the perverse impact of labour market "rigidities" (like unions, unemployment insurance, and minimum wages). In their extreme interpretation of neoclassical theory, the real forces of supply and demand automatically ensure an efficient full-employment equilibrium, and hence the only impact of money is to determine the absolute

---

Blood on the Floor

"The Federal Reserve had to show that when faced with the painful choice between maintaining a tight monetary policy to fight inflation and easing monetary policy to combat recession, it would choose to fight inflation. In other words, to establish its credibility, the Federal Reserve had to demonstrate its willingness to spill blood, lots of blood, other people's blood."

Michael Mussa, former Research Director, International Monetary Fund (1979), cited in Andrew Glyn, *Capitalism Unleashed: Finance, Globalization, and Welfare* (Oxford: Oxford University Press, 2006, p. 24).

"The Thatcher government never believed for a moment that [monetarism] was the correct way to bring down inflation. They did however see that this would be a very good way to raise unemployment. And raising unemployment was an extremely desirable way of reducing the strength of the working classes."

Alan Budd, chief economic advisor to then-UK Prime Minister Margaret Thatcher, cited in N. Cohen, "Gambling With our Future," *New Statesman* (January 13, 2003).

price level. Therefore, to control inflation, central banks simply had to strictly control the growth of the money supply. If they allowed an annual 5 percent increase in the total supply of money, and if they stuck to that rule for a long time, then inflation would eventually settle at 5 percent. Thus began an experiment in MONETARY TARGETING (trying to directly control the expansion of money) that was a colossal failure.

The severe global recession of 1981–82 was caused directly by monetarist policies. Their effort to link inflation to money supply growth failed for an obvious reason: in a credit banking system (with ENDOGENOUS MONEY) central banks *cannot* control money supply. Rather, money expansion is determined (as we explained in the last chapter) by the credit-creation activity of private banks, and by the willingness of borrowers to take on new loans.

However, that deliberate recession was successful in other important ways. It signaled a new era in global capitalism. It disposed of the notion that full employment was the top economic priority. And it began the long, painful process of ratcheting down popular expectations regarding what average people can (and can't) expect from the economy.

Since then, central banks have fine-tuned their approach to controlling inflation. Like the original monetarists, modern central bankers still believe the free-market economy is largely efficient and self-adjusting (see Table 18.1). In a stable macroeconomic context, real supply and demand forces should push the economy toward full-employment. The only long-run impact of monetary policy, they still believe, is on the rate of inflation; market forces determine real output, employment and productivity. And central banks should still have a myopic focus on one goal, and one goal alone: controlling inflation, ignoring other goals (like job creation).

However, modern central banks have altered their operational strategy for pursuing this single-minded vision they inherited from monetarism. They no longer try to control the money supply directly, recognizing that money expansion depends on the creation of credit. Instead, most central banks now try to manage inflation at a certain rate, or within a certain band. This approach is called INFLATION TARGETING. To attain the targeted inflation rate, central banks influence credit creation and hence spending through frequent adjustments to interest rates. It is clear that the fundamental assumptions of the monetarists have been inherited by today's central bankers, who can therefore be considered "quasi-monetarists." They still believe that controlling inflation is the central, even exclusive goal of central banking, and that if that effort is successful the real forces of supply and demand will ultimately take care of everything else. All that's changed is their view on how that goal should be best pursued.

Another important feature of neoliberal monetary policy has been an emphasis on entrenching the so-called "independence" of central banks. In most developed

Table 18.1 Monetarism and "Quasi-Monetarism"

Areas of Agreement:

Monetary policy should focus solely on controlling inflation, not reducing unemployment.

Apparent unemployment is temporary, voluntary (people who don't want to work), and/or reflects labour market frictions and rigidities.

The only long-term way to reduce unemployment is to make the labour market more "competitive" by reducing frictions and rigidities.

Low and stable inflation will assist the real economy to reach its natural full-employment equilibrium.

The central bank should be independent and "apolitical," free from political interference or democratic oversight, to insulate its inflation-controlling mandate from popular pressure.

Areas of Disagreement:

Monetarism *(Milton Friedman, 1980s)*	*Quasi-Monetarism* *(modern central banks)*
Inflation is caused by too much money.	Inflation is caused by too much spending (demand).
Central banks should directly control money supply.	Central banks should indirectly manage money supply via the interest rate.
Central banks should target growth in the money supply.	Central banks should target the inflation rate.
Economic fine-tuning doesn't work; government should stand back and let markets re-create full employment.	Constant fine-tuning of interest rates helps the economy reach its full-employment equilibrium.

---

countries, central banks have been granted day-to-day freedom to pursue their goals without oversight or interference from government. To varying degrees, national governments still participate in determining the banks' broader objectives – most importantly, formally establishing the inflation targets (where they exist). But in theory they are prohibited from influencing the banks' regular interest rate adjustments or other actions.

The deliberate goal of this supposed independence is to insulate the powerful, often painful interventions of central banks from popular opposition. But of course, central banks are not really "independent" at all: the elevation of inflation control to the top of the economic agenda, regardless of what else is sacrificed in the process, is a non-neutral and highly political choice that imposes uneven costs and benefits on different segments of society. The financial industry and owners of financial wealth have benefited most from neoliberal monetary policy. And they continue to have huge influence over the day-to-day actions of central banks. By erecting central banks as an independent, supposedly apolitical authority, elected governments pretend that choices regarding the fight against inflation are out of their hands.

Central bank "independence" is explicitly and deliberately anti-democratic. And it's utterly phony. It removes a crucial element of public economic policy from the realm of public deliberation and control. By pretending that monetary policy is a neutral, technical, and hence apolitical activity, governments hope that public debate over monetary policy will evaporate.

Evaluating neoliberal monetary policy

The dramatic shift in monetary policy in the late 1970s was the first sign that a new brand of capitalism was being born. The initial adjustment to this harsh new approach was painful: repeated recessions (in the early 1980s and again in the early 1990s), a sustained increase in unemployment, and a downward ratcheting of both inflation and worker expectations. After that painful adjustment, however, it seemed for a while that the system of "quasi-monetarism" and inflation targeting was working well. Global inflation rates subsided (see Figure 18.1), hovering at 2–3 percent throughout most of the developed capitalist world since the early 1990s. Later, despite a decline in official unemployment rates in the late 1990s and early 2000s, no major upsurge in inflation was detected (contrary to the now-discredited idea that higher inflation is an inevitable consequence of reducing unemployment "too far"). Major fluctuations in global energy and commodity prices were also absorbed by the system without setting off an inflationary spiral similar to that which followed the OPEC oil price shocks of the 1970s.

Politically, too, the new agenda seemed triumphant. The notion that interest rates should be used to control inflation, and nothing else, gained wide currency, even among centre-left political leaders (whose acceptance of this strict regime is usually motivated by a desire to impress powerful financial lobbyists). And the old-fashioned conviction that the economy can and should be managed to maintain full employment was thrown by the wayside. By early in the new century, mainstream economists arrogantly proclaimed a "new consensus in macroeconomics," pretending there was nothing left to debate in monetary policy. So long as independent central banks consistently and credibly target a stable rate of inflation, everything else in the macroeconomy will take care of itself.

Even before the breakdown of global finance in 2008, the totality of this triumph was never clear. Consumer price inflation certainly declined, but this was not solely due to monetary policy. Other factors – like shrinking unit labour costs, the expansion of low-cost imports from China, and new retail models (like Wal-Mart) which ratcheted down the price level – were also crucial. But while those other factors were helpful in reducing inflation rates for a time, they could

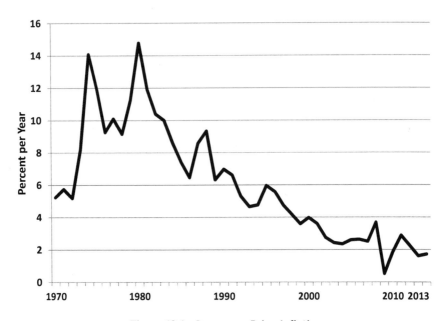

Figure 18.1 Consumer Price Inflation
OECD average
Source: OECD Main Economic Indicators.

not permanently reduce price pressures. Moreover, periodic bouts of inflation in asset prices (including unsustainable bubbles in stock markets and real estate) have been a regular and at times disastrous feature of life under quasi-monetarism. It is telling that orthodox monetary policy perceives wage and price inflation as a fundamental threat to economic stability, yet celebrates asset price inflation as a sign of investor confidence and optimism.

More fundamentally, the promised boost to real investment, growth, and productivity which was supposed to accompany low and stable inflation never arrived. GDP growth rates remained consistently slower than even in the latter, troubled years of the Golden Age expansion. As we noted in Chapter 12, real business investment has slowed noticeably – refuting the bizarre belief that "uncertainty" about future price levels somehow restrained capitalist expansion. (In reality, uncertainty about whether or not they can sell this year's output is a far greater constraint on business capital spending than whether long-run inflation will be 2 percent or 5 percent.) The failure of inflation targeting to stimulate any consistent improvement in real investment, growth, or productivity was the most glaring hole in the proclaimed triumph of quasi-monetarism.

In 1992, shortly after the collapse of Soviet communism, the US political scientist Francis Fukuyama wrote a now-infamous book proclaiming the "end of history." His claim quickly collapsed in the wake of the 9/11 terrorist attacks, the rise of China as an economic superpower, and other earth-shattering events. The neoclassical proclamation of a "new consensus" in macroeconomics was equivalently far-fetched – and equally short-lived. That phony consensus was finally buried during the collapse of global finance in 2008, as thoroughly as Fukuyama's prediction was discredited by the collapse of the twin towers in New York City.

Since the 2008–09 meltdown, neoliberal monetary policy has fallen somewhat into disarray, and the resulting intellectual and ideological confusion presents progressives with an important opportunity to challenge and change the orthodox monetary regime. Central banks around the world were forced to abandon or modify inflation targeting following the crisis. The new risk was that inflation would fall too low, even tipping into DEFLATION in some countries. Central banks' use of QUANTITATIVE EASING and other unconventional tools was an implicit admission that inflation targeting (and certainly the conventional ways it was operational-ized) was inadequate. And their key assumptions that excess aggregate demand is the only source of inflation, and that interest rate adjustments can powerfully and predictably fine-tune that demand, have both been disproven in real-world practice. Central bankers have also become more sensitive to the self-serving, fragile nature of leveraged private banking, and hence have accepted that financial stability (not just inflation control) must be one of their top goals. There is no doubt that central banks still serve the dominant interests of private banks and private wealth, and they still aim to manage the overall economy in a manner that deliberately constrains workers' power. But now they do this in the context of an ideological framework that is less certain, and more open to challenge, than before the meltdown. (We will discuss the causes, consequences, and responses to the GLOBAL FINANCIAL CRISIS in detail in Chapter 26.)

19

Paper Chase: Stock Markets, Financialization, and Pensions

Corporate finance: putting it all together

In Chapter 17 we described a simple process of business lending between a productive company and a bank. The bank creates credit – right out of thin air. The productive business uses this purchasing power to purchase capital goods and other inputs, hire workers, and expand production. This lending-and-investment process is essential to economic growth and job creation under capitalism.

In practice, however, companies have access to a wide range of financial resources to pay for their investments, not just bank loans. In fact, most established companies can usually pay for ongoing real investment needs internally (out of their profits on existing business), with no need for outside financing at all. Indeed, in recent years the business sector in advanced capitalist countries has generated far more profit than it needs to pay for new investments. As a result, a strange reversal of traditional financial channels has occurred: instead of turning to financial markets to finance new investment, companies now use financial institutions to recycle surplus cash.

Quickly-growing companies, however, do need outside help to pay for their growth and new investment. Troubled or loss-making companies, too, need to borrow – often as they struggle to turn around their operations. And all companies need access to routine financing (like lines of credit) to pay their day-to-day bills, while minimizing the idle cash they keep on hand.

The various financial resources available to productive companies include:

- **Bank loans** These are the simplest form of finance, but among the more expensive. Loans can be short term or long term, depending on how quickly the borrower must pay back the money (with interest, of course). Loans are usually backed up by some kind of real collateral from the borrowing company. If the company stops paying interest, then the bank gets that property as compensation.
- **Corporate bonds** These allow companies to borrow directly from financial investors, cutting out the bank as the "middleman." Like loans, companies must pay interest on a bond. The riskier is the business, the higher is the

interest rate it must pay on bonds. Very risky companies issue "junk" bonds, which pay interest several percentage points higher than normal loans. Even after a bond has been issued, its certificate can be bought and re-sold in special bond markets. Bond prices usually move inversely with the interest rate: lower interest rates mean higher bond prices (since an investor should now be willing to pay more money up-front for a given flow of interest income), and vice versa.

- **Equities**   Companies can also raise new funds by issuing small "pieces" of ownership, called equities, **SHARES**, or stocks. These assets do not normally pay interest, although special shares (called "preferred shares") may qualify for interest payments. And many companies pay cash dividends (usually every three months) to shareholders, which are similar to interest. But even if no interest is paid, issuing new equity is costly for a company. Administration costs (like brokerage fees) eat up a tenth or more of all new funds raised, and companies which issue shares must comply with complex regulations regarding financial disclosure, accounting procedures, and internal management practices. If a company goes bankrupt, shareholders are the last to receive any compensation from selling the company's remaining assets: this is the risk they must accept, by becoming part-owners of the company. Like bonds, company shares are also be bought and re-sold on special **STOCK MARKETS**.

Companies try to balance their financial needs across these different sources: loans, bonds, and equity. Interestingly, no corporate executive would ever claim (as conservative politicians do) that a company's debt should be eliminated altogether. Effectively used, debt allows a company's owners to enhance their own bottom-line profit. If the company's real investments generate a higher rate of profit than the interest paid on its debt, then the company can "magnify" its profit by increasing its debt. This strategy is called **LEVERAGE**: the company tries to "lever" greater profits for its owners through the use of borrowed funds. But big risks come with debt, too. In tough times, heavily-indebted companies face greater risk of outright bankruptcy (since they must keep paying interest on their loans, whether they have any profits or not). With little internal equity to fall back on as a cushion, an indebted firm might find itself unable to pay its interest costs – in which case it collapses.

Securitization and speculation

A loan represents an ongoing relationship between the lender and the borrower. The lender wants to make sure the loan is ultimately paid back, so it investigates the borrower's credit-worthiness before issuing the loan, and then monitors subsequent performance as the loan is gradually repaid. With bonds and equities, however, that ongoing relationship disappears. Now the loan itself becomes an asset, with a life of its own, that can be passed from one owner to another. This process is called SECURITIZATION, because it involves the creation of a new, tradeable financial asset (a security) to represent the money that has been advanced to the borrower. Unlike normal bank loans, securities are bought and sold on "second-hand" markets (like the bond market and the stock market). This secondary trading is supposed to serve a productive purpose: it makes it easier for companies to mobilize financial resources (from individual investors) for investment projects, and the ability to sell their holdings (and "get out") makes individual investors more willing to put their money in a company in the first place.

However, once they've been issued, the productive life of stocks and bonds is over. The borrowing company receives the initial finance, and (hopefully) does something useful with it. Subsequent secondary trading of its securities has no direct impact on the company which issued them. By buying a company's shares on the stock market, you are not giving your money to that company; rather, you are giving it to whoever owned the share before you. The company doesn't really care where its share certificate ends up (although corporate executives do watch share prices carefully, largely because their personal compensation is tied directly to getting it as high as possible). Almost all activity on stock and bond markets (over 99 percent) consists of buying and selling existing securities, not issuing new ones (and raising new funds in the process).

New issues of equities have become especially rare. Business investment has been sluggish, and hence cash-rich companies don't need much additional finance. Moreover, through SHARE BUY-BACKS, flush companies can repurchase some of their shares from investors (further boosting share prices, and further enriching the company's executives). In many countries, the total amount of outstanding corporate equity has actually declined in recent years, with the ongoing destruction of equity (through buy-backs and corporate mergers) outweighing the issue of new shares (see box). This confirms that the main purpose of stock markets is not "raising money for growing businesses," as is pompously claimed by the mission statements of stock exchanges. They have become, primarily, tax-subsidized casinos, whereby

Get Out While You Can

"In a paradoxical way, the function of equity markets today is not to enable savers to put money into companies. It's to enable them to get it out."

John Kay, head of UK government commission on stock markets (2013).

financial gamblers place bets on which way share prices will move in the next few hours or minutes.

This frenzied paper chase which occurs every day on the financial markets is largely divorced from the real day-to-day productive work of non-financial companies. Instead, financial traders are trying to make money through SPECULATION. Productive profit is generated when a company purchases inputs (including labour), produces a good or service, and sells it for more than it cost to produce. The pursuit of productive profit has many unfortunate side-effects that we have explored throughout this book – but at least it stimulates production and employment. Speculative profit, on the other hand, involves no production at all. It is guided by the age-old adage: "Buy low, and sell high." No jobs are created (except for the brokers who handle the trading, pocketing a lucrative commission on each sale). Investors simply buy an asset, and then hope that its price rises, allowing them to sell it for more than they paid. Speculation is the act of buying something purely in hopes of selling it later (for more than it cost).

Any asset can be bought and sold for speculative purposes: including tangible things like real estate, fine art, and commodities (like oil or pork bellies). But today financial assets (securities) are the major tool of the speculative trade. And the dramatic expansion of financial trading under neoliberalism – reflected in the variety of financial assets traded, the amount of selling that takes place, and the lightning speed with which they are bought and sold – means that financial speculation has come to play a dominant, wasteful, and often destructive role in the economy.

To make matters worse, clever financial experts are constantly developing new kinds of financial assets, and new ways of trading them for profit. Massive amounts of trading now occur in a broad class of securities called DERIVATIVES. These are securities whose price at any point in time depends, often in very complex ways, on the performance of *other* financial assets. Examples of derivatives include futures, options, and swaps. Through the clever use of derivatives, financial traders can place a bet on any expected change in the price of one or more other assets. A special derivative strategy called "shorting" actually allows speculators to profit from a fall in the price of another asset – thus reversing the traditional adage "buy low, sell high." (In contrast, short traders "buy high and sell low" to generate their speculative profit!) This is an especially dangerous activity, because it gives speculators a vested interest in the failure of the company they are shorting, and hence they may try to hasten its downfall (by spreading unfounded rumours, for example, or even engaging in financial sabotage). There are specialized derivative markets to bet on changes in the weather. Even money itself can be traded for speculative reasons, especially on foreign exchange markets (where one country's money is converted into another's). And whether it's stocks, bonds, or derivatives, every trade generates a juicy commission (typically 2 percent or 3 percent) for the brokers who conduct it – giving them a massive interest in frenetic trading for its own sake. The only thing speculators can't tolerate is stability: whether markets are rising or falling, they hunger for volatility and the trading opportunities that come with it.

Misplaced Creativity

"Speculators may do no harm as bubbles on a steady stream of enterprise. But the position is serious when enterprise becomes the bubble on a whirlpool of speculation. When the capital development of a country becomes a by-product of the activities of a casino, the job is likely to be ill-done."

John Maynard Keynes, British Economist (1936).

Financial institutions are very innovative, continually inventing new securities and new trading strategies – in many cases to sidestep the effect of financial regulations. Here are just a few of the complex financial products and practices which have contributed to the growing frenzy of the paper markets:

- **Mutual funds** Some investors prefer to buy a "bundle" of shares from different companies, to diversify their risks and profit from overall market trends (rather than tying their fortunes to any particular firm). Mutual funds are composed of the shares of many different companies, allowing an investor to efficiently buy a small bit of each of them. An infinite number of permutations and combinations of company shares can be assembled into mutual funds, and hence there are now far more of them available (each promising "superior" performance) than there are individual company shares trading on the stock market. Statistical research consistently shows that actively managed mutual funds (which pay professional "money managers" handsome sums to "pick winners" on the stock market) perform no better (and often worse) than the overall stock market.
- **Collateralized debt obligation (CDO)** Banks and other lenders found a clever way to reduce the risk that their loans may never be paid back. They convert a new loan (like a household mortgage) into a tradeable security (called a CDO), and then sell it to someone else (like an investment fund). The bank thus washes its hands of the responsibility of ensuring that the loan is ever repaid. The problems with this practice are obvious: mortgage lenders stop scrutinizing the credit-worthiness of their borrowers, and may not fully disclose (to purchasers of CDOs) the true risks buried deep within this new, complicated security. Risky and unethical CDOs played a major role in the US mortgage crisis that helped precipitate the global 2008–09 meltdown.
- **Credit default swap (CDS)** Another very risky practice is a special derivative called a CDS. The idea is that a lender can purchase a kind of insurance against the risk that their loan might not be paid back.

▶

Initially, derivatives were supposed to serve as a kind of "insurance" for companies who had some real connection to the industry in which the derivative was issued. For example, suppose an oil company wanted to protect itself against a possible future decline in the price of oil – or an oil consuming business wanted to protect against future price increases. They could "lock in" the current price, by selling

---

But this "insurance" takes the form of a tradeable security which itself can be sold to other investors (and whose price will fluctuate wildly in response to changes in interest rates, mortgage defaults, and other variables). Perversely, speculators can even take out "insurance" on the default of loans which they themselves have no connection to. This is akin to buying a life insurance package on your next-door neighbour: it creates a dangerous economic incentive for you to arrange their premature demise! In fact, CDSs have no real insurance value at all, because once defaults spread widely no market player has deep enough pockets to actually make good on the promised insurance. The best way to protect against default is through careful screening and scrutiny of borrowers, public insurance, and sensible macroeconomic policies that support the financial well-being of households and other borrowers. But hyperactive financial markets aren't interested in this kind of "prudence."

- **Structured investment vehicle (SIV)** Despite the overall deregulation of the financial industry under neoliberalism, banks must still meet minimal requirements regarding the safety of their lending – including capital adequacy rules (explained in Chapter 17) which require banks to keep a certain margin of money sitting (relatively unprofitably) in secure, low-yield investments. To get around this inconvenience, banks continually develop devious new strategies. For example, in the 2000s many banks developed a strategy called "structured investment vehicles" (SIV): special subsidiaries, typically headquartered in offshore tax havens, whose assets and liabilities were not reported on the bank's financial statements. SIVs used banks' safe capital to bankroll additional risky short-term investments, thus magnifying total lending and profits. But when those investments failed, it suddenly became clear that the banks didn't have as much "safe capital" as they seemed to; most SIVs collapsed, and this technique is no longer widely used. This cautionary tale illustrates the ability of major banks to sidestep regulation (and often taxes!) with their constant innovation. A better policy would be to ban commercial banks from financial trading and investment banking altogether.

Just imagine the immense intellectual creativity that has gone into developing these and other ingenious but wasteful and destructive products. And just imagine the potential benefits if the smartest people in society focused on finding a cure for cancer or a source of non-polluting energy – instead of seeking still more complicated ways to "buy low and sell high."

or buying future output on the oil futures market. However, the scale of genuine, insurance-driven trading in derivatives has been swamped by speculative activity: financial gamblers who use derivatives solely to try to "beat the market" and profit from changes in asset prices. Today, the vast majority of trading in oil and other commodities futures is undertaken by financial interests with no connection at all to using or producing the commodity in question. (One dramatic illustration of this was provided in November 2010, when the investment bank JP Morgan Chase single-handedly bought up over half the world's total inventory of copper: needless to say, the bank was not buying copper to fix up its own plumbing!)

Like any casino, financial speculation is a rigged game. Large institutions and professional traders have the best opportunity to learn about market-moving information (sometimes through illegal inside tips), move their own money around first, and even manipulate prices through their own trading. They can profit hugely from tiny misalignments in asset prices (often deliberately created), and by repeating miniscule speculative trades thousands of times over (see box).

Blink and You Miss It

Thanks to their inside information, their position at the epicentre of trading, and the vast sums of money which they can mobilize with the touch of a computer key, investment banks and brokerages have the best chance to profit from the constant volatility of paper markets. One technique used to great advantage is called HIGH FREQUENCY TRADING (HFT). Super-powered computers in brokerages scan multiple markets, looking for tiny price differentials or trends in share demand. Automated trading instructions then allow major players to exploit those differentials instantaneously, placing millions of different trading orders within seconds and beating other traders to the prize. High-frequency traders can even insert themselves as totally superfluous "middlemen" into trades that would have occurred anyway – creaming off a few pennies of extra profit on the resulting transaction. The profit on each transaction is small, but repeated millions of times over HFT still generates billions in profits. Other market participants (using traditional computer systems) don't even know what is happening. Apart from the obvious unfairness of this practice, it adds to the dangerous instability of electronic financial markets; automatic HFT instructions can spark cascading changes in asset prices that roil markets before any human being has even figured out what is happening.

In short, small personal investors have been deluded by financial advertising into believing they can play the markets just like the big boys: sitting at home on their PCs, reading investor reports, and executing day trades. But they are unwitting victims of a rigged game. The speculative self-interest of major traders, combined with their unique position in the middle of the fray, makes it no contest: like watching a basketball game between seven-foot-tall NBA champions and a pick-up team of school kids.

The development of secondary securities markets has thus opened up a Pandora's Box of speculative financial activity. Financial investors are less concerned with companies' real businesses, and more concerned with whether certain paper assets will be worth more tomorrow than they are today. And the profits from innovative financial "engineering" – developing and selling new types of paper assets – can be immense. Individuals and investors can become far wealthier, far faster, by playing the financial markets instead of undertaking the gradual, often boring work of building successful productive businesses.

Financialization and fragility

In many economies (especially those in the Anglo-Saxon world), this endless paper chase has come to dominate economic news and economic moods. It's assumed that if the stock market is rising, the economy must be healthy. Indeed, pompous executives commonly describe their efforts to boost shareholder wealth as the "creation of value." And miraculously, they can create billions of dollars of "value" overnight – so long as their company's shares catch a rising speculative tide. How utterly wonderful this must seem in contrast to the daily grind and drudge of average working people: the ones whose sweat and effort actually creates smaller bits of genuine value every day. But in concrete economic terms, there's no value at all in the hyperactive and pointless flight of paper assets around the markets.

This broad shift to an increasingly finance-dominated mode of economic development (and a finance-dominated culture) is called FINANCIALIZATION. Under neoliberalism, financial activity has become more intense and more profitable. Financial profits have increased as a share of total business profits (reaching almost half of all US business profits prior to the 2008–09 meltdown). Financial goals (like share prices, financial restructuring, and dividend payouts) have also become more important in determining the behaviour of non-financial corporations. Financial elites have become more influential in shaping economic and social policy, and their share of total income in the economy has grown enormously (contributing significantly to the growth in overall inequality). Indeed, financial occupations regularly attract the best and brightest (including recruits from non-financial fields like higher mathematics and quantum physics), because these jobs are so lucrative. For example, a study of the career paths of graduates from America's elite Harvard University showed that those working in the financial industry earned on average almost three times as much as those in all other fields (including professions like law and medicine, or executives of non-financial business).* Finance even dominates our culture: financial reports are a regular feature of every newscast, and even small mom-and-pop investors watch the stock

---

* Claudia Goldin and Lawrence F. Katz, "Transitions: Career and Family Life Cycles of the Educational Elite," *American Economic Review* 98(2), May (2008, pp. 363–9).

market tables with the same obsession as earlier generations followed sports scores – to see if their tiny nest eggs grew or shrank a bit in yesterday's trading.

You Write the Book: A Culture of Finance

Most financial wealth in capitalism is owned by a surprisingly small elite of very wealthy households – just a couple of percent of the total population. Yet to shore up political support for this unfair state of affairs, a pervasive ideology of financialization promotes the false idea that everyone can "play the markets." Think of an example where individuals are encouraged (by government, by the financial industry, or by economists) to believe that they, too, can use clever financial strategies to solve the problems in their lives – no matter how far-fetched the chances of success. Send your example to author@economicsforeveryone.com. We'll post your best ones at www. economicsforeveryone.com.

One simple way of measuring financialization is to contrast the value of financial assets and trading with the value of the real economic activity that ultimately underpins our collective prosperity. This provides a measure of the intensity of financial activity, relative to the production of real goods and services. Table 19.1 summarizes some broad indicators of the imbalance between financial and real activity. Across the global economy, there are now almost $4 in stocks and bonds for each dollar in real output. There are almost $10 in outstanding derivatives contracts for each dollar in GDP. And there are some $62 in foreign currency exchange, for every dollar worth of goods or services that crosses a national border.

Table 19.1 Financialization and the Real Economy

Indicator	Financial Value	Real Value	Ratio
Stocks and bonds	$274 trillion stocks, bonds, and bank assets	$72 trillion world GDP	$3.80-to-$1
Derivatives	$687 trillion outstanding contracts (including interest rate, commodity, equity, and other derivatives)	$72 trillion world GDP	$9.50-to-$1
Foreign exchange	$5.3 trillion per day foreign exchange transactions	$86 billion per day world trade in goods and services	$62-to-$1

Source: Author's calculations from Bank for International Settlements, International Monetary Fund, and World Trade Organization, end-2012.

Until the late 1970s, financial valuations rose broadly in tandem with the expansion of real output, real investment, and real trade. One could have some confidence that each financial asset was ultimately backed by something tangible and lasting, and each financial trade was connected somehow to a real economic transaction underneath. Table 19.1 confirms, however, that the relationship between financial and real economic activity has become precariously unbalanced. This reflects both the deliberate slowdown in real growth and capital accumulation that was engineered by neoliberal policy, and the explosion of financial activity and innovation that was permitted by deregulation and financialization. Clearly the financial tail has come to wag the economic dog. And we should all worry, quite rightly, about what, if anything, actually holds up the immense financial valuations that are now the Holy Grail of capitalism.

Financialization has added a new dimension of fragility to modern capitalism. One of the most dangerous manifestations of this hyperactive paper chase is the tendency of securities markets to produce repeating **SPECULATIVE BUBBLES**, in which the price of one or more assets rises spectacularly, sparking widespread frenzy among traders – but followed inevitably by downturn, panic, and collapse. A typical speculative bubble begins with the "discovery" of some new asset: perhaps a new product, a new technology, or even just some amazing new kind of financial derivative. In the 1600s, in one of capitalism's first speculative episodes, the initial spark was the discovery of tulip breeding. Dutch investors drove the price of stunning new breeds of tulips to astronomical highs – not because they wanted to plant them, but because they thought they could profit from re-selling them. Prices peaked in 1635 at several thousand Dutch florins for a single bulb (equivalent to as much as US$75,000 today). Initial investor interest, concentrated among insiders, gives the price of a speculative asset its initial upward momentum. But that's just the first step. Other investors see rising prices (and associated speculative profits), and rush in for a piece of the action. This drives prices even higher.

No matter how "rational" may have been the initial spark for the updraft in prices, it is soon overwhelmed by purely speculative pressure. Investors' hopes for quick trading profits become self-fulfilling, driving the price still higher ... for a while, anyway. The creation of new credit by the banking system, which gladly issues loans to speculators so long as the market is rising, is a crucial and dangerous ingredient in the bubble. If investors actually had to use their own money to place speculative bets, bubbles could never expand as far or as dangerously. The artificial purchasing power provided by credit (borrowed "on margin" by speculators at up to $50 for each dollar of their own money) is like an enormous hot air pump causing a balloon to expand and rise further and further. But eventually something shocks the confidence of investors. Insiders, smelling trouble, sell out first. That stalls the upward momentum, and soon the whole roller coaster turns downhill.

Suddenly greed turns to fear, and other investors sell the asset en masse. Once again, the herd mentality of investors becomes self-fulfilling – but this time in the other direction. When speculative bets were financed with borrowed money (as is usually the case), trading losses can cause gamblers to default on their loans, and this becomes a problem for the banks which lent to them in the first place. Bankrupt borrowers and banks alike sell off other assets to try to cover their losses, but that only drives down asset prices even faster. The bubble collapses, leaving a legacy of wasted energy and creativity, enormous losses (for those who didn't get to the exits on time), and shattered confidence.

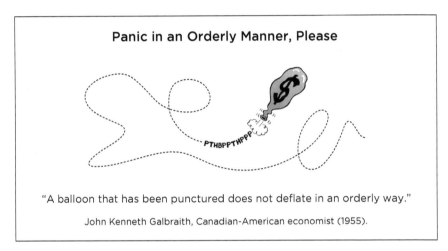

Panic in an Orderly Manner, Please

"A balloon that has been punctured does not deflate in an orderly way."

John Kenneth Galbraith, Canadian-American economist (1955).

Initially, a wave of speculative losses may have little impact on the real economy (which, after all, is a big step removed from the financial paper chase even at the best of times). But eventually a major financial downturn will spill over into real investment, production, and employment, via several possible channels:

- Companies worry about their ability to sell additional output in the future, and hence postpone planned investments.
- Banks suddenly become very worried about default risk, and pull back the amount of new credit on offer (even for routine business and consumer purchases), producing a CREDIT FREEZE that constrains spending, production, and employment.
- Consumers may become infected by negative headlines and postpone their own purchases (especially major, discretionary ones, like homes or cars).
- Real estate prices are particularly sensitive to the ups and downs of finance, and a sharp downturn in housing prices can cause a real contraction in the construction industry.

Any of these outcomes, if strong enough, could cause a recession in the real economy through spill-over effects described in more detail in Chapter 25. The global financial crisis of 2008–09 was a dramatic, but not unique, illustration of the pervasive fragility of this financialized house of cards.

Pensions and financialization

By allowing workers the opportunity to retire at a decent age and enjoy their last years in some comfort (free from the compulsion to work), pensions are an important component of quality of life. They reduce lifetime working hours and have helped reduce poverty among the elderly. For many workers, the hope that they will eventually qualify for a decent pension and retire in comfort is truly a "light at the end of the tunnel," helping them get through their long, hard work lives.

The first pensions were negotiated by unions at the workplace level. These workplace-based pensions are called **OCCUPATIONAL PENSION PLANS**. Later, workers fought for and (in most countries) won **PUBLIC PENSIONS**, paid by governments or government agencies. In some public programs, public pensions are universal, paid to all elderly citizens. In other programs, pensions are paid only to those who were employed for a sufficient number of years during their working lives. Employers and workers are usually required to contribute to public pensions via paycheque deductions.

Pensions can be financed in two main ways, and the choice has important consequences for financialization. A **PAY-AS-YOU-GO PENSION** (or "paygo")* is financed directly from the plan sponsor's ongoing current revenues. Most paygo systems are run by national governments. They allocate a share of ongoing tax revenues (including targeted pension premiums) to pay the benefits. This is the simplest way to organize a pension, with very low administration costs, and they do not significantly contribute to financialization (since current funds are transferred directly to pensioners, with little if any role for the financial industry). The stability of these plans, however, depends on the continuing economic viability of the sponsoring organization. This explains why they are used mostly by governments – since companies can't credibly promise that they'll stay in business forever, and hence be able to fund far-off pension benefits out of future revenues. Most public pensions in developed countries are organized on a paygo basis. In a few countries, such as parts of Europe, private companies also provide pensions on a paygo basis.

In contrast, in a **PRE-FUNDED PENSION** the plan sponsor accumulates financial wealth over time to pay promised pension benefits in the future. Typically, premiums are collected from plan members and/or their employers. These premiums are then invested in a range of financial assets (trying to maintain a

---

* Examples of this pay-as-you-go system are the US Social Security system, the Canada Pension Plan, the Basic State Pension and Second State Pension in the UK, and South Africa's Social Pension.

balance between high rates of return and low risk). On the basis of complex and uncertain actuarial forecasts (regarding everything from wage rates to interest rates to life expectancy), it is hoped that the plan will have enough disposable funds on hand to pay promised pensions when the time comes. Most occupational pensions are organized on a pre-funded basis, as are public pensions in some countries.

The advantage of a pre-funded pension is the somewhat greater certainty that a fund will be able to eventually pay its promised pension (although even pre-funded pensions are never truly secure – since financial markets can perform badly, and actuarial assumptions can miss the mark). This is essential with private companies, which can go bankrupt at any time. And if a plan sponsor (especially a government) is committed to investing pension monies according to some criteria other than maximum profits, the pool of capital created by pre-funding could potentially be a useful economic tool. The disadvantages of the pre-funding model include much higher administration costs (mostly for the well-paid professionals who manage the fund's investments), and the risk that the fund won't accumulate enough assets to pay out promised benefits. By transferring enormous funds to the financial industry for long-term investment and administration, pre-funded pensions have played an important role in financialization.

Pre-funded pensions, in turn, come in two main forms. DEFINED BENEFIT plans are group programs which specify the level of benefits to be paid, based on the number of years a retiree worked, their retirement age, and other factors. The onus then falls on the plan sponsor to ensure that sufficient funds are available to pay those benefits. DEFINED CONTRIBUTION plans, on the other hand, simply deposit a specified annual premium (typically shared between a worker and their employer) into personalized accounts for each worker. These accounts are then used to "buy" individual pensions for each worker when they retire. The pension received by each worker depends totally on how much was deposited into their account, how much profit the account earned while it was invested, the level of interest rates prevailing at the time they retired, and other variables completely beyond the worker's control. There's little difference between a defined contribution pension and an employer-subsidized personal savings account.

The choice between these two kinds of pre-funding mostly hinges on who should bear the risks related to investment returns, life expectancy, and other key variables. In a defined benefit plan, the sponsor bears the risk; under defined contribution rules, that risk is transferred to the individual pensioner. No wonder, then, that employers have pushed hard in recent years to eliminate defined benefit pension plans (or convert them into defined contribution schemes). And in some countries, such as Australia, defined benefit plans are almost unheard of. The downside of the shift away from defined benefit is that many pensioners will be left with inadequate pensions if their individual savings accounts should run out before they die.

The financial industry argues strongly that pre-funded pensions are superior to paygo plans, even for public pensions. However, they have a huge vested interest in moving to a pre-funded system: namely, the massive fees they collect for managing those funds, and investing them in various financial assets. From a broader economic perspective, pre-funding offers no benefits and many risks. It contributes significantly to the financialization of the economy, with all its associated waste and instability. For public pensions in particular, paygo systems are preferable. Concerns that these funds will be bankrupted by the ageing of the population have been deliberately exaggerated by the financial industry. In fact, while premium rates must be adjusted over time to reflect changing demographic trends, public paygo pension systems are clearly the most efficient and financially stable form of pensions in existence.

Most financial assets are owned by the small minority of very well-off households which composes the modern capitalist class. As discussed in Chapter 7, a clear majority of corporate wealth is owned by the very richest households in every leading capitalist economy. Financial wealth is especially concentrated at the top in the major Anglo-Saxon economies. However, one significant way that ordinary households participate in capital ownership (albeit indirectly) is through pension funds. Large pension funds (like the California public employees plan, CalPERS, with assets of US$275 billion) have been among the most active and sophisticated participants in the paper markets. Like other financial players, they are managed with the goal of maximizing financial wealth. Indeed, pension funds have perversely helped to impose a tighter degree of financial discipline over non-financial businesses, and hence reinforced the short-sighted emphasis of corporate executives on share prices rather than long-run real production. Pension funds, due to their concentrated influence, helped lead the "shareholder revolution" – compelling corporations to act more ruthlessly in the interests of their owners than ever. And the laser-like focus of executives on maximizing profits and share prices typically inspires intense emphasis on minimizing operating costs – including labour costs, through wage cuts, downsizing, outsourcing, and resistance to unionization. Pension funds' efforts to maximize financial returns, therefore, have undermined the immediate economic well-being of the very workers who pay into them.

Some have argued that the growth of pension funds could gradually "socialize" the ownership of business under capitalism. The potential for this positive outcome should not be exaggerated, however. Occupational pension plans (tied to particular workplaces or industries) are always governed with the goal of maximizing returns, since their top priority is to pay the promised pension benefits of plan members. Moreover, compared to the generally bloated financial sector, occupational funds have been shrinking in relative importance, mostly because fewer workers are covered by collective occupational pensions in the first place (thanks to deunionization and successful efforts by companies to shed their pension responsibilities). The equity holdings of the largest 300 occupational pension funds in the world in 2013 totalled some $4.5 trillion. That represents just 7 percent of the total equity value of world stock markets at that time.* So the idea that big pension funds somehow "control" the stock market is quite misplaced, notwithstanding the individual clout of certain large funds.

Government-run pension funds (associated with wholly or partially pre-funded public pension plans, like those in Japan, Norway, South Korea, and Canada) may have more long-run potential to consciously direct their investments toward meeting broader social or environmental priorities. These funds are one aspect of a broader trend called SOVEREIGN WEALTH (that is discussed further in Chapter 29). Pre-funded government pension funds are true behemoths, bigger than any of the large occupational plans. However, trying to wield this significant economic power in order to improve social or environmental outcomes (rather than just maximizing financial returns) raises many tricky political, economic, and legal issues. Sponsoring governments, generally neoliberal in outlook, are not interested in challenging the dominance of the business sector, even if they themselves have the power to do so. Moreover, their support for pre-funded public pensions is driven primarily by a rather conservative desire to reduce and control the future

---

*   Author's calculations from Towers Watson, "Pensions and Investment Towers Watson 300 Analysis" (2014), and World Federation of Exchanges, "2013 WFE Market Highlights" (2014). Excludes holdings of sovereign pension funds.

costs of public pensions – not by a desire to "socialize" economic decision-making. Nevertheless, in the context of a broader progressive shift in economic policy, large public pension funds could certainly play a supporting future role in building a more egalitarian and sustainable economy. Norway's huge Government Pension Fund has implemented some important rules regarding social and environmental standards in the private companies it invests in. This is a long way from achieving true social control over investment, but it is an avenue worthy of further exploration (as we discuss further in Part Five of this book).

20

The Conflicting Personalities
of Government

Does size matter?

Many political debates between "right" and "left" seem to be over the *size* of government. Conservatives want smaller government; they propose cutbacks in public programs, privatization of government agencies, and lower taxes. Progressives want bigger government; they demand more public programs, and higher taxes to pay for them. The main debate seems to be whether government should be "small" or "big."

Conservatives claim that governments over time have moved from "small" to "big," and that this is a major cause of poor economic performance. According to this storyline, capitalism supposedly began as an idealized, individualistic society, organized around self-governing free markets. But then governments began to disrupt that libertarian ideal – with taxes, regulations, public ownership, and other intrusions. These expanding intrusions supposedly undermined the efficiency of the market system, and conservatives have been fighting to roll back government ever since.

To support this argument, neoliberals invoke the writings of Adam Smith, the founder of classical economics (see Chapter 4). He argued that the state should play no economic role other than establishing a safe, secure framework for markets (by enforcing property rights; preventing individuals from stealing, or injuring others; and defending against internal or external threats). Everything else should be left up to markets, guided automatically by the self-interest of individual entrepreneurs. Today many neoclassical economists still adhere to that vision of minimalist government. And critics of that view are understandably tempted to distil their argument down to a demand for "bigger" (rather than "smaller") government.

The only problem is that capitalism *never* resembled that free-market, minimalist-state ideal – even during Adam Smith's day. And merely having a "bigger" government is no guarantee that capitalism will become fairer or more responsive to the needs of its citizens. Sex therapists have a motto: "It's not what you've got, it's how you use it." This motto could just as well apply to the economic role of government.

Taking care of business

Even in its early days – perhaps *especially* during its early days – capitalism was guided by a strong, focused, central government. In fact, the state played a crucial role in the very emergence of capitalism. It enhanced and protected the profits captured by the new class of capitalists, and provided essential functions and services without which capitalism could never have been born.

Recall that industrial capitalism emerged in Britain in the eighteenth century. Britain's relatively centralized and powerful state, willing and able to support private-sector investment and production, was a key reason capitalism began there – rather than in continental Europe, China, or India (which had comparable living standards at the time).

Britain's government created a unified market at home: breaking down barriers between feudal enclaves, standardizing weights and measures, and providing passable and safe transportation routes. It did the same thing globally: using military might and colonialism to forcibly access raw materials and markets. It provided early capitalists with tariff and patent protection. It helped to establish private ownership rights over agricultural land (through the ENCLOSURES process), thus creating a new class of landless, desperate workers to work in the new factories. And it facilitated that new form of work called wage labour, keeping workers in line and suppressing early efforts to form unions.

In short, far from reflecting the spontaneous energy of unplanned private enterprise, the early success of British capitalism couldn't have occurred *without* the state's active support. Measured as a share of GDP, the state's various and far-flung activities consumed about as much of Britain's total output then (around a third) as it does today.

And if anything, capitalism's subsequent expansion to other jurisdictions – first to continental Europe, then America, then around the world – was even more dependent on powerful state leadership. Governments in all these places used tariffs and trade policies, capital subsidies and public ownership, extensive regulations, aggressive labour market measures, and (surprisingly often) military force to foster the establishment and growth of capitalism. In Germany, deliberate state planning, public investment, and tariffs were essential to early industrialization. Early American capitalism relied on huge government investments in railroads and other infrastructure, enormous giveaways of public land and resources, and highly protectionist trade policy. American tariffs on imported industrial products remained extremely high (averaging nearly 50 percent) until World War II. In nineteenth-century Japan, to nurture early entrepreneurs, the government directly created new companies which were then (if they survived) handed over to private investors. Later, the Japanese pioneered state industrial planning, through which key industries were selected for targeted assistance and promotion. This recipe has been replicated with great success in Korea, China, and the other late-industrializing Asian economies.

This noble tradition of governments nurturing capitalists (like a nanny nurtures a baby) carries on, even in developed countries (see Table 20.1). Governments continue to intervene to regulate and create markets, support private investment,

---

The Long Arm of the Law

In the early days of capitalism, protecting the private property of wealthy investors was a fairly straightforward matter. Police kept the uncouth masses far away from the estates of the rich, protected banks and other stockpiles of financial wealth, and defended the capital equipment of factories (sometimes against the angry outbursts of their own workers).

As the system became more complex, however, private property became harder to define and protect. Now the law intrudes into our lives in new, far-reaching ways in order to protect the wealth of investors and companies:

- **Intellectual property** Complex laws and patents protect the monopoly powers of software companies, pharmaceutical firms, biotech companies, and other firms, regardless of the social benefits that could be generated by the wider distribution of those products. And governments devote vast resources to hunting down patent violators – hounding farmers who use privately-patented seeds, or health care providers distributing life-saving copycat drugs.
- **Financial property** In today's computerized financial system, "money" is a fluid, flexible, usually electronic commodity. And it's become harder and more expensive to prevent abuse or theft – such as white-collar crime, fraudulent investment schemes, and other financial shenanigans.
- [*] **Copyright** Governments will search far and wide to find and punish people who violate copyright rules on electronic code, entertainment, and other digital products. Individuals can even be arrested in one country and extradited to another for illegal downloads or copying.
- **Trade laws** Many modern free trade agreements grant special legal powers to companies to challenge government policies which hurt their profits, through a special quasi-judicial court system called INVESTOR-STATE DISPUTE SETTLEMENT.

It is very wrong, therefore, to conclude that the state has somehow become "powerless" under neoliberalism. In these and other ways, the modern capitalist state is as ambitious and active as ever in its efforts to protect private wealth.

You Write the Book: Open for Business

The unelected power of private businesses to determine the course of entire economies through investment and production decisions gives them tremendous influence over government policies, no matter which party is in power. The business community usually finds an understanding ear for its problems from political and government leaders. Think of an interesting example of a way that your government supports and promotes the interests of private business. Send it to author@economicsforeveryone.com. We'll post your best examples at www.economicsforeveryone.com.

---

protect private property, and facilitate the actions of capitalists in many different ways. Yet perversely, the capacity of government to serve this stabilizing, pro-business role may be simultaneously undermined by capitalists' unthinking pursuit of privatization and austerity – ideologies which have so dominated politics under neoliberalism. In this regard, the short-sighted greed of business may actually undermine its own long-term interests, by preventing the state from addressing fundamental challenges to capitalism (like financial instability or climate change).

Table 20.1 Whose Nanny State?
Ten Ways Governments Serve Business

Protect private property (including intangible property, like patents).	Pay for basic economic infrastructure (roads, communication, utilities).
Pay for essential training of workers.	Keep workers "in line" by managing and policing labour relations.
Maintain business-friendly macroeconomic conditions (low inflation, stable interest rates).	Enforce stable rules and standards (quality standards, competition laws, contracts).
Support business investment through tax incentives or subsidies.	Open up new markets for businesses (privatization, trade agreements).
Provide tax loopholes and subsidies to companies and the high-income individuals who own them.	Rescue businesses (especially financial companies) in times of crisis.

Whose economy? And whose government?

So the real question is not whether government should be big or small (although clearly, proposals for improved social programs and other progressive reforms would require more public funding and hence a "bigger" government). And there is no real debate over whether governments should "intervene" in the economy:

Trickle-Up

"The idea that conservatives trust the market while progressives want the government is a myth. Conservatives simply are not honest about the ways in which they want the government to intervene to distribute income upwards."

Dean Baker, US economist (2006).

---

they always have, and always will. The real questions are rather different. *How* does government intervene in the economy? And in *whose* interests?

We have learned throughout this book that the capitalist economy is a dramatically unequal place. The decisions by profit-seeking companies to invest in production are essential to setting the whole economic machine into motion. Without those decisions, the system grinds to a halt. All other economic actors (including workers, small businesses, and – yes – even governments) are fundamentally dependent on the continuing willingness and ability of capitalists to "do their thing." Meanwhile, ownership and control over wealth (and hence over investment) is concentrated among a surprisingly small and powerful elite.

This fundamental economic inequality naturally and inevitably translates into an equally fundamental, although partly disguised, political inequality. Because of their economic power, capitalists demand (and usually win) immediate attention from governments. Governments know they must cater to businesses' overall demand for a hospitable, profitable economic and social climate, or else businesses will stop investing and the economy will experience a crisis. Unless it is prepared to challenge the basic logic and structures of capitalism (by reorganizing the economy so it is no longer dependent on private investment), no government can risk that kind of crisis. Hence, when business talks, government – virtually regardless of its political stripe – listens. In this manner, businesses (and the individuals who own them) ensure that governments continue to play the proactive, supportive economic role described above.

In earlier eras, capitalist societies were not very democratic (in fact, only property owners had the right to vote), and the links between economic and political power were easier to see. In analyzing this relationship, Karl Marx described the role of the state under capitalism in broad, blunt terms: it was nothing more, he argued, than the "executive committee" of the ruling class, and he considered capitalism to be a dictatorship (even after nominally democratic institutions, like parliaments, were established).

Today, however, that simplistic stereotype is clearly wrong (in most countries, anyway). Thanks to centuries of popular struggle for fundamental rights (including the right to vote, to organize political parties, to form unions, and to go on strike), capitalism has become more democratic. Working people won the rights to vote and free speech – through those rights are often surprisingly fragile (see box). They usually therefore have considerable opportunity to air their views and concerns, and to demand that governments and businesses alike modify their actions and policies. To be sure, these efforts always face an uphill battle against the vested interests and economic power of private capital. But it is wrong to conclude that capitalists unilaterally call all the shots. When they are sufficiently motivated and organized, working people and their allies can clearly force governments to respond to *their* demands, too – not just those of business. After all, working people make up the vast majority of the population. If they can motivate and mobilize their majority power, important concessions can be won from governments and capitalists alike.

Democracy in Doubt

There is nothing inherently democratic about capitalism. In most places, the birth of capitalism occurred in the context of often-violent limits on the workplace and political rights of workers; only property owners were allowed to vote. Full voting rights were not granted for decades or even centuries, once capitalism was secure enough to make this concession. Women and members of racialized groups didn't win suffrage until well into the twentieth century. In Australia, aboriginal people did not win the full right to vote until 1967. In places where capitalism was introduced more recently (like post-Communist Russia), the initial establishment of private property and industry occurred on the basis of corruption, cronyism, and outright theft – not democratic choice. Even formal voting rights are still not secure. In the US, the effective franchise of black people in the southern US was undermined for a century after the Civil War by racist voting registration practices (like rigged "literacy" tests and identification tests that most black people could not pass), until the 1965 Voting Rights Act was passed by the US Congress. However, in 2013 the more conservative-minded US Supreme Court invalidated major portions of that Act; many Southern states have already begun reintroducing restrictions on effective access to voting rights.

In this regard, the state in modern developed capitalist economies demonstrates a kind of "split personality." Its natural tendency is to focus on the core function of protecting and promoting private wealth and business. And businesses (and the wealthy people who own them) have many sophisticated ways to ensure that governments continue to cater to their interests, despite the formal structures of democracy, including:

- Ownership and control over most of the mass media (and other cultural industries). This ensures that a broadly pro-business message is delivered constantly throughout society.
- Direct influence over the electoral process through candidate and campaign financing. Political candidates cannot succeed without massive financial resources; obviously this gives wealthy people (and their favoured candidates) a substantial headstart. For example, a right-wing political network founded by the billionaire Koch brothers in the US planned to raise and spend $900 million in the 2016 presidential elections – more than either of the major political parties.
- Structures and practices which discourage political participation by working and poor people – the ones who have the most to gain from political change. In the US, for example, less than half of people with income under $20,000 per year voted in the 2012 presidential election. But 80 percent of those with income over $150,000 voted.*
- Pro-business ideas are further strengthened through corporate and donor funding of think tanks, academic research, private schools, and other educational and ideological institutions.

When push comes to shove, businesses exert enormous political influence simply through their investment decisions. Investors and executives can "vote with their wallets" in response to unfavourable political or policy changes – cutting back investment (in what might be called a "capital strike" by business), and slowing down overall growth. This threat does not require any deliberate, planned "conspiracy." It can merely reflect the combined impact of many individual decisions to shift investment to other jurisdictions (or just hoard money, rather than re-investing it) until more business-friendly conditions emerge. In any event, the economic consequences of **DISINVESTMENT** are frightening, to both governments and voters. Usually the mere threat of disinvestment is sufficient to shift policy back onto a pro-business track. Indeed, to forestall this kind of problem, most left-wing political parties today (at least those with any realistic hope of winning an election) go out of their way to pacify business ahead of time – but then, perversely, this ties the hands of progressive governments even before they are elected.

This array of political weapons is intimidating, to say the least, and ensures that business interests remain predominant in most political debates and elections. But it's not a foregone conclusion. There are times when, thanks to popular pressure, a different personality of government can come to the fore. Popular pressure can force governments to use their power to enhance economic security and quality of life for the rest of society – namely, those who do not own companies or wealth,

* US Census Bureau, "Voting and Registration in the Election of November 2012" (2013).

and must work for a living. There are several different ways for working people and their allies to enforce their preferences on the actions of government:

- At the ballot box, by fighting to advance key issues during election campaigns, and supporting progressive political parties. Money carries disproportionate influence in elections, as discussed above. But by their sheer numbers (after all, wage-labourers and their families make up around 85 percent of the population of advanced capitalist countries), working people (if sufficiently organized and mobilized) can demand that their issues and concerns be addressed.
- Between elections, by campaigning for reforms through lobbying, pressure campaigns, advertising and information efforts, and protests.
- In the workplace, fighting for specific demands through collective bargaining and other union actions.
- Engaging in a longer-term "battle of ideas," to challenge the power of pro-business thinking. This requires the development of alternative media, cultural, and educational resources and activities. (Developing a more democratic, grass-roots approach to economics is one part of that ongoing battle of ideas.)

Democracy or dictatorship?

No capitalist country is truly democratic so long as those with wealth and power are able to exert such disproportionate influence over political decisions – hence ensuring that government policies continue to reflect the imperatives of private profit, regardless of which party is in power. Workers can try to level the democratic playing field by fighting for improvements in democracy (such as limits on private political financing, or the establishment of publicly-owned media outlets). And they will naturally use whatever democratic space they can carve out to advance their demands for a fairer economy and society.

In some countries, however, even these limited democratic levers are not available to workers. In these places, the state acts more directly and blatantly in the interests of wealth and business. Perhaps surprisingly, however, dictatorships (even pro-business ones) are not usually favoured by capitalists. They worry about long-run political instability, the arbitrary seizure of their property, bad publicity, and other risks. So in general, businesses prefer a modern, stable, liberal democracy as the most secure political context for their investments.

But capitalists are certainly not above partnering with dictators when they offer a stable, productive, pro-business climate. Corporations offered crucial support to past dictatorial regimes in places like Chile, South Korea, South Africa, and Indonesia. That deplorable pattern continues today in other countries (such as

---

How to Get Rid of a Prime Minister

Never mind the niceties of elections and formal democracy: every now and then the real decision-making process of capitalism is revealed through the decisive ability of corporations and the wealthy to shape government actions and policy. A startling example of this power was provided in Australia in 2010, when then-Prime Minister Kevin Rudd (leader of the Labor party) tried to impose a new corporate income tax on the highly profitable Australian mining industry. The tax was motivated in part to address budget deficits resulting from the government's successful effort to stimulate the economy and avoid being caught in the 2008–09 global recession. But mining executives reacted swiftly and effectively: they threatened disinvestment from Australia, warned of major layoffs and unemployment, and spent A$22 million in just two months on aggressive advertisements attacking the government. The industry also boosted funding for conservative opposition parties. Public opinion swung against the government, and within weeks Rudd was removed from office by his own party – and the tax was abandoned.

Saudi Arabia, Thailand, Colombia, Iraq, or Brunei) – where democratic rights range from shaky to non-existent, but where local and global companies alike are glad to scrabble for as much profit as they can get, while the getting's good.

Consider the massive foreign investments that flowed into China (over US$1.8 trillion worth from 2000 through 2013, including Hong Kong), undeterred by that country's democratic shortcomings. Low-cost, productive, regimented labour; powerful government support for technology and infrastructure; low business taxes; access to what will soon be the world's largest market – these advantages easily outweigh any concerns business executives might have over democratic rights. And corporate promises that foreign investments in China will leverage democratic reforms have proven hollow indeed. Instead, multinational companies have actually helped to *maintain* the current, immensely profitable state of affairs: for example, by opposing modest labour law reforms adopted in China in the late 2000s, and discouraging the democracy protests that erupted in Hong Kong in 2014.

So, contrary to the claims of philosophical libertarians like Milton Friedman (who equate "freedom" with the right to accumulate private wealth), there is no

---

Under the Bridge

"The law, in its majestic equality, forbids the rich as well as the poor to beg in the streets, steal bread, or sleep under a bridge."

Anatole France, French author (1894).

---

inherent link whatsoever between capitalism and democracy. Quite the reverse: capitalism demonstrates a natural anti-democratic streak by virtue of the inherent tendency for private wealth, and hence political influence, to be continually concentrated in the hands of a very small proportion of society. Therefore, fighting to protect and expand democratic rights, and rolling back the undue political influence of private wealth, must be an essential part of workers' broader struggles for a more just economic order.

The agenda, and the toolkit

If and when workers are able to force governments to protect and advance the interests of the "little people," rather than society's fat cats, there is a long list of *goals* which they will want to demand. And governments possess an equally diverse set of policy *tools* to use in order to pursue those goals.

Some of the economic and social goals that governments might pursue, when sufficiently pressured by the working majority of their population, include the following:

- **Redistribute income**, to partially offset the inequality that is the normal outcome of private markets, and establish minimum living standards for all citizens.
- **Stimulate employment and overall economic activity**, to offset cyclical downturns in private-sector activity, and resulting unemployment. (Issues related to recessions and depressions are discussed in detail in Chapter 25.)
- **Provide certain products** (mostly services) that private companies do not produce – often because they cannot be supplied profitably (due to flaws or quirks in private markets). Examples here include things that are useful to everyone in society, not just those who privately agree to pay for it – such as free radio and television broadcasts, safe streets, or national defence. Economists call these **PUBLIC GOODS**. Governments may also take charge of **NATURAL MONOPOLIES**: industries in which it is economically inefficient to have more than one producer (such as pipelines or electricity utilities).
- **Provide more equitable or efficient access to certain products** – even those that *could* be produced by private firms. For example, private firms can supply education and health care services (and in some countries, they dominate these industries). But governments can provide them more efficiently (for lower cost and/or higher quality), and make them more accessible to the whole population (rather than just higher-income households).
- **Regulate** the activities of private business. Some of the most damaging side-effects of private-sector production can be curtailed through government laws and regulations which set minimum standards for corporate behaviour.

Regulations can govern health and safety practices in workplaces, labour standards (such as hours of work or minimum pay), product safety, pollution, and other corporate sins. Businesses complain loudly about the burden of complying with all this "red tape." But in practice, many regulations are enforced weakly, if at all; most businesses are left essentially to self-regulate their behaviour.

While government action in all of these areas holds potential to improve the security and quality of life for working people, not all of these interventions would necessarily be *opposed* by business. In some cases, businesses might actually consider some of these goals beneficial. For various reasons, business might decide it is preferable to guarantee minimal living standards (*very* minimal), provide mass education, stabilize macroeconomic conditions, and equitably enforce regulations. So long as the essential prerequisites for successful capitalist production are maintained (including the ability to hire workers, and extract work effort from them, at acceptable labour costs, and the ability to sell their output for adequate profit), then businesses may grudgingly accept some intrusions into their realm. In other words, there is room to negotiate. But if government goes too far for the comfort of business, watch out: business will push back, and hard (as it did, successfully, in the latter years of the postwar Golden Age).

Governments have an array of tools at their disposal to try to attain whatever economic and social goals are ultimately impressed upon them by the ongoing political tussle between the wealthy and the majority. Several of the more important policy levers are listed below:

- **The legal system**   Basic personal security and property rights are protected through the operation of the police and legal system. Business laws (regarding patents, financial securities, liability, and related topics) can also have important economic effects.
- **Monetary policy**   This refers to adjustments in interest rates, and the use of regulations governing the financial system, to influence lending, the rate of inflation, and the level of overall economic activity (see Chapter 18).
- **Fiscal policy**   This refers to the spending and taxing functions of government (discussed further in the next chapter). How much tax is collected, and from whom? How are those revenues spent? Government spending includes both redistribution (through TRANSFER PAYMENTS) and the direct production by government of specific goods and services.
- **Public services**   High-quality human services (like education, child care, and health care) can promote stronger economic and social participation and achievement by all parts of society. They are especially important for

those who face limited employment and income opportunities (such as low-income households, women, immigrants, and racialized groups).

- **Labour market and social policy** Labour policies address the whole spectrum of employment conditions: minimum wages, trade unionization and collective bargaining, pay determination, income security, hours of work, employment security, training, and other aspects of employment. These policies determine whether the employment playing field tilts in favour of employers or in favour of workers. Social policies (such as family income supplements, child benefits, parenting supports, pensions, and disability insurance) also influence the labour market experience and income of specified groups – including women, seniors, and the disabled.

- **Competition policy** Most countries have rules aimed at fostering more competition between firms and preventing companies from abusing a dominant market position. As we saw in Chapter 11, competition can produce negative economic effects, as well as positive ones. In some industries, governments prefer to *limit* competition (to prevent economic damage resulting from excess supply and over-competition).

- **Technology policy** Most governments have developed special policies to foster innovation (such as research and development subsidies) and the adoption of new technology. The ultimate goal is to encourage productivity growth and competitiveness.

- **SECTOR DEVELOPMENT STRATEGIES** Sometimes called **INDUSTRIAL POLICY**, this refers to efforts by government to promote and nurture industries with particular importance to the overall economy. For example, many governments take special measures to stimulate investment and exports in high-tech industries such as auto, aerospace, biotechnology, defence, and computer technology.

- **Public ownership** In some cases (even beyond traditional public service delivery) government may directly undertake production – by nationalizing an existing private company, or building a publicly-owned company from the ground up. State-owned enterprises are used to pursue many different goals: to expand particular industries, to enhance domestic control, to capture a share of profits, to prevent private monopoly, to support employment, or to force companies to undertake activities that private owners reject. Public ownership expanded in most countries during the Golden Age, but has been dramatically scaled back under neoliberalism. The proportion of GDP produced by state-owned enterprises in the OECD countries has fallen steeply under neoliberalism, from around 10 percent in 1980 to well under 5 percent at present. There was a temporary rebound in public ownership after the global financial crisis of 2008–09, as many governments nationalized banks and some industrial firms (including General Motors in the US) to prevent their outright collapse. In many developing economies, however (including China, Brazil, and India), state-owned industrial firms remain very important. Many countries have accumulated **SOVEREIGN WEALTH** funds, which provide another vehicle for public ownership.

- **Foreign policy and trade policy** Managing economic and political relationships with other countries is an important government responsibility. Foreign policy (including military activity) can be important in opening or preserving international economic opportunities for domestic businesses. Trade policy is aimed at influencing exports, imports, and foreign investment flows (see Chapter 22).

These are some of the many ways in which government can influence economic and social conditions: how much is produced, what is produced, how it is produced, and how output is distributed and ultimately used. The policy challenge facing governments is to design and implement the right combination of these levers in order to attain the desired mix of outcomes. A rough rule of thumb suggests that each policy goal requires a distinct lever to make it happen. It is rare that multiple objectives can be satisfied simultaneously with a single policy instrument.

But for working and poor people, the *political* challenge is more daunting than the technical *policy* challenge. If government is willing to limit the power of private business and wealth, and enhance the well-being of the broader population, there are abundant tools in its toolkit to do the job. The big hurdle, however, is for working and poor people to organize enough power to force government to act that way. Unfortunately, it is on that score – with workers' collective strength and influence eroding substantially since the 1970s – that neoliberalism has been carrying the day.

21

Spending and Taxing

The fiscal role of the state

Conservatives often deride government as a "tax-and-spend" operation – implying that the goal of politicians is simply to find new ways to collect taxes from hard-working citizens, and then invent new (and presumably wasteful) projects to spend that money on. This stereotype is wrong on many counts.

First, no government (even "big-spending" ones) collects taxes just for the sake of collecting taxes. Taxes are raised to fund the complex mixture of activities and programs described in the previous chapter, with the nature of government activity shaped by the conflicting political pressures that confront it. If a government no longer feels compelled to provide a program, it stops – and then gives back the taxes. (In fact, some neoliberal governments actually cut taxes first, and *then* cut spending – using intervening deficits to politically justify the subsequent painful cuts.)

I prefer to reverse the order of the traditional conservative epithet. Government is actually in the business of spending and taxing. First it decides (in the context of conflicting and contradictory political pressures) what programs it must provide. Then it figures out how to fund those programs. This overall function of spending and taxing is called FISCAL POLICY.

Spending

Government expenditures contain many line items, which together may account for up to 50 percent (in highly developed welfare states) of a country's GDP. Several broad categories of spending can be defined (as illustrated in Figure 21.1).

- **Interest payments** Like businesses and consumers, most governments have debt (more on this below), and consequently they must make regular interest payments on that debt. On their own, interest costs serve no useful purpose; moreover, like other forms of investment income, interest payments disproportionately benefit wealthy households. These drawbacks must be weighed against the usefulness of the projects which were financed with borrowed money in the first place. If a debt-financed expenditure is

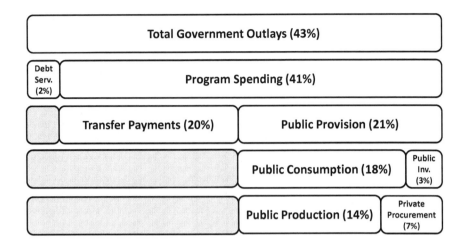

Figure 21.1 Composition of Government Spending, Shares of GDP

Source: Author's estimates from OECD data, 2012.

important, productive, or long-lasting, then interest payouts resulting from that debt (within limits) are sensible and justified.

- **Program spending**   All spending other than interest payments is known as PROGRAM SPENDING. Overall program spending, measured as a share of GDP, is a good indicator of the broad economic and social footprint of government. Program spending, in turn, can be divided into two major categories: TRANSFER PAYMENTS and PUBLIC PROVISION.

- **Transfer payments**   Many government programs involve collecting money (via taxes) with one hand, and then giving it back (to someone else) with the other. These programs are called transfer payments, since they involve no government function or expenditure other than shifting income from one group to another. Transfer payments can be made to individuals (via social programs like unemployment insurance, welfare benefits, and public pensions). Transfer payments can also be made to businesses (through business subsidies), or to other countries (as foreign aid).

- **Public provision**   A portion of government program spending involves government actually "doing" something – that is, arranging (and paying for) the production of some concrete function or service (rather than simply redistributing income). Some of this productive activity is organized directly by governments. Other functions are undertaken by independent or semi-independent agencies which receive most or all of their funding from governments (such as hospitals or school boards); together these agencies make up the broader public sector. Public provision can be further sub-divided, in two different ways: between consumption and investment, and between direct public production and private procurement.

- **Public consumption** Like private sector spending, public provision consists of both consumption and investment. Most government services are immediately used up (or "consumed") by the public: such as education, health care, recreation and culture, and more. These programs are economically equivalent to consumption, since they involve the use of output to meet a current human need or desire. But this consumption occurs in a public form: instead of buying it through their private purchasing power, the consumers of public services receive and consume those services by virtue of their status as citizens. In some cases, USER FEES are collected from service consumers (for public transit, some health care services, and others) to partially defray the costs of production; remaining costs are financed through government's general revenues.

- **Public investment** Not all public provision is consumed, however. Governments also dedicate resources to investment, in order to facilitate expanded public provision in future years. Governments allocate a portion of their revenues to long-lasting investments in infrastructure and other physical capital (like buildings, schools, hospitals, roads, machinery and equipment). PUBLIC INVESTMENT is an important contributor to broader economic growth and productivity. Unfortunately, however, public investment was scaled back substantially during the neoliberal era, and the public capital stock was badly run down in most countries – as evidenced by crumbling infrastructure, public buildings, facilities, and water systems. In many cases, the neoliberal policy-makers who starved public facilities of needed capital now point to their decrepit state as justification for further privatization.

- **Public production** Another way of categorizing public provision is according to how the actual production is undertaken. In many cases, government or public agencies themselves undertake to organize production, hire workers, and deliver the resulting good or service to its eventual users. Importantly, this real production – which contributes to GDP as surely as any private sector activity – occurs through a very different "chain of command" than for-profit production. This production occurs not because it will generate a profit for a private firm, but because a government (responding to political pressures in society) feels compelled to meet a perceived public need. Government-financed public production is the largest source of non-profit production in most capitalist countries (supplemented, to varying degrees, by production undertaken by state-owned enterprises, cooperatives, community associations, and other non-business entities).

- **Private procurement**   In some other cases, government provides a good or service by hiring a private firm to organize the required production. Political leaders can thus sidestep direct responsibility for organizing production, hiring workers, and the other minutae of public provision. The resulting public spending on **PROCUREMENT** constitutes an important market for private businesses. Under neoliberalism governments have faced strong pressure to shift (or "outsource") many public services from public production to private procurement, by contracting private firms to provide services once performed by public employees. Proponents of outsourcing boast of cost savings resulting from private delivery of public services; this is not always the case, and even when private delivery is less expensive it's usually because of lower compensation for those doing the work, reductions in quality and accessibility of the service, and other harmful strategies. At the extreme, a service may be fully privatized to market provision, in which private consumers (rather than a public funder) pay for its delivery.

Taxing

In order to pay for the programs and services which their voting constituents demand, governments collect revenues in a variety of ways.

- **Personal income taxes**   Individuals pay personal income taxes, as a proportion of their income from various sources (including labour income, investment income, small business income, and others), net of various allowable deductions. Most countries impose **PROGRESSIVE** personal income taxes, in which the rate of tax rises with a person's income. In this manner, well-off people pay a higher proportion of their income to support government programs. An alternative system, used in more conservative jurisdictions, is a **FLAT-RATE** personal income tax, which collects income tax at a constant rate (regardless of a person's income).
- **Corporate income taxes**   Businesses also pay tax on their net income, or profit, at a specified rate. Corporate income taxes are usually levied on a flat-rate basis, although very small businesses are often charged a lower percentage.
- **Sales taxes**   A growing share of total tax revenues in recent years has been provided by **SALES TAXES** (also known as value added, or indirect, taxes). Whenever a consumer makes a purchase, they pay a certain additional proportion in sales tax. Businesses may also have to pay sales taxes on their purchases; however, in most countries business sales tax payments are refunded (so that the full ultimate burden of the tax falls on the shoulders of consumers).

- **Payroll taxes**   Employment is also taxed, via PAYROLL TAXES imposed as a proportion of wages paid to an employee. The tax may be paid by the employer, by the employee, or shared between the two. Payroll tax revenues are often channeled to fund particular social programs – like pensions, health care, or unemployment insurance.
- **Wealth taxes**   Taxes can also be collected on the accumulated wealth of an individual or a business. This is morally appealing: a WEALTH TAX allows a government to target taxes at the most privileged members of society. However, they have fallen out of favour in recent years – mostly because wealthy people (whose political influence has grown under neoliberalism) strongly oppose them. Annual wealth taxes, inheritance taxes, land or property taxes, and capital taxes on business are all examples of wealth taxes.
- **Environmental taxes**   In recent years, new taxes have been proposed on the use of certain polluting inputs (like energy), or on the amount of pollution emitted. One example of an environmental tax is a CARBON TAX, which collects taxes on different types of energy according to their contribution to climate change.
- **Other revenues**   A share of government revenue is generated through non-tax measures. For example, many governments impose USER FEES for the use of certain programs and services (like public transit, garbage collection, or even health care). Governments also generate income from their own investments (such as interest on financial investments, rent and other income from government-owned properties, or the profits of state-owned enterprises), which can also make an important contribution to total government revenue.

Fiscal policy on the economic map

Government is a major player in the economy, largely (but not exclusively) because of its fiscal actions. Figure 21.2 presents the next incarnation of our economic map, this time including government.

Government collects taxes from various stakeholders, at various points in the economic chain. We have bundled all those taxes into two categories, depending on whether they are ultimately paid by either workers or capitalists. Income and other taxes paid by workers are labelled T. Taxes paid by capitalists are distinguished with the same subscript (a luxurious diamond!) that we used earlier in this book to identify their consumption: $T_\lozenge$. We assume that the burden of corporate income taxes is ultimately borne by the (mostly high-income) households who own those corporations.

Government uses this revenue to undertake many different functions, three of which are shown on our map. Transfer payments (TP) are given back to specified

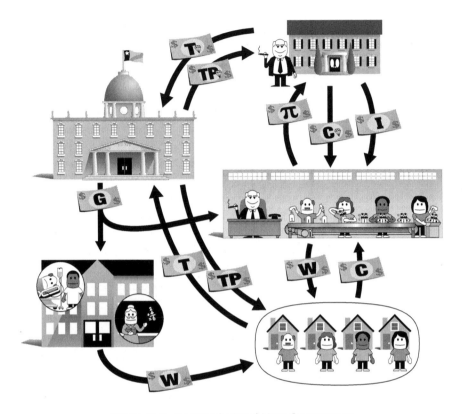

Figure 21.2 **Economic Road Map: Government**

households (as unemployment insurance, income security, and pensions). Most transfer payments go to worker households, but some are received by capitalists as well.

Meanwhile, public provision (G) involves the publicly-funded production of goods and services (mostly services). Some of that public provision is purchased from for-profit companies (through procurement, illustrated as P). This creates an additional sales channel for private businesses, who can now sell their output to government as well as to consumers or other businesses. Meanwhile, some public provision occurs via direct public production, undertaken by government and the broader public sector. Remember, public production constitutes a second, parallel channel of production in the economy. In addition to private, for-profit production, some production is now undertaken for other motives – namely, to meet a perceived public need (like education, health care, or infrastructure). Public production is illustrated in Figure 21.2 through the operation of a composite public service centre, and consumption of those services by members of the public.

Once again, this map is highly simplified, yet it still brings out some extremely important features. The fiscal actions of government alter the operation of the capitalist economy in several important ways:

- Taxes alter the economic incentives facing different economic players. Usually this isn't a major problem. But in terms of the system's overall energy level, the impact of taxes on the profitability of private investment and production is important. If taxes are too high on businesses, their investment spending may weaken (or be redirected to other, more business-friendly jurisdictions). Businesses have used this threat to lever down corporate income tax rates in most countries under neoliberalism.
- Worker households are no longer exclusively dependent on what they can earn through employment. Government transfer payments now offer workers a certain degree of economic independence. This can dramatically alter the economic and social relationships of capitalism. Not surprisingly, workers generally support strong transfer programs, while employers oppose them – especially social benefits for working-age adults (which make it harder for employers to suppress wage costs and enforce labour discipline, since workers now have something to fall back on if they lose their jobs). It has been a core priority of neoliberalism to reduce income supports for working-age adults, and thus reinforce the coercive "work or starve" logic that underpins wage labour.
- Direct public production establishes an entire, dual chain of economic output that supplements the productive activity of private companies. Society as a whole is now somewhat less dependent on private investors to set the whole economic cycle in motion. Moreover, public production helps to stabilize the economy in the face of fluctuations in private investment and production. In most developed countries, direct public production makes up a small share of total production (generally about 10–20 percent of GDP), and business lobbies hard to prevent the further expansion of the public sector. Nevertheless, the mere fact that production can and does occur successfully outside of the core profit relationship of capitalism opens up intriguing possibilities for future economic change.
- Another consequence of direct government production is that government itself becomes a major *employer*. A significant segment of workers (again, typically between 10 and 20 percent of the total labour force) is employed by public and non-profit providers, rather than private-sector employers. The nature of work in public-sector agencies is usually (although not always) better-paid and somewhat more secure than in private companies – since the employer (government) is not motivated by the same relentless pressures (the profit motive and competition) that drive private employers to cut costs.

At the same time, public-sector workers (and their unions) face a constant challenge to defend public services, working conditions, and compensation, and public-sector unions have historically played a crucial role in labour movements and other progressive struggles.

Deficits and debt

Fiscal debates in many countries in recent years have been dominated by concern – much of it exaggerated, but some of it legitimate – over big government deficits and rising government debt. Conservative politicians have seized on these concerns to justify painful cutbacks in public programs. Yet ironically, conservative governments often racked up the largest deficits of all. Indeed, the broad fiscal decline experienced in most developed economies during the 1980s and 1990s was clearly caused by neoliberal economic policies – especially by higher interest rates (which produced higher unemployment, slower growth, and higher debt-servicing

Do-It-Yourself Budgeting

Neoliberal governments around the world have dramatically reduced their financial support for key public programs, typically invoking fears about government deficits to justify the cuts. In Canada, a broad coalition of community and labour organizations developed a novel way to oppose the cuts, showing they were not at all "fiscally necessary." Through a project called the Alternative Federal Budget, they developed their own government budget, showing where they would collect the revenues necessary to maintain and even expand public programs. The alternative budget has now been produced for over 20 consecutive years.

You can try this, too. Consult with concerned groups and individuals in your city, region, or country. Identify the programs that are most important, and estimate their cost. Identify potential revenue sources. Show that the bottom line of your budget "adds up" – either to a balanced budget (that is, zero deficit), or to a bottom-line deficit that is consistent with your country's ability to stabilize and service its public debt.

Now you have proven that society does indeed have the capacity to provide public services and programs that improve the quality and security of life for all – so long as we are willing to allocate the resources necessary to pay for them. In most countries, it is not a shortage of economic resources that prevents governments from providing necessary services. It is a shortage of political will.

charges). Those neoliberal policies were far more damaging to governments' bottom line than public spending on social programs.

More recently, an even bigger blow to government finances was caused by the GLOBAL FINANCIAL CRISIS that erupted in 2008, sparking a worldwide recession from which the developed capitalist economies have still not fully recovered. That downturn hammered government budgets through multiple channels: tax revenues fell steeply (due to weak employment and consumer spending), the cost of income supports (like unemployment insurance) rose automatically, and the enormous cost of bailing out failed banks and other private companies added to the red ink. In some cases (especially peripheral European countries like Greece, Portugal, and Ireland) private bond markets began charging very high rates of interest for new lending – but soaring borrowing costs make the deficit even worse. This post-2008 eruption of public debt is also a legacy of neoliberalism (and the inherent financial instability it ingrained in the global economy). So the claim that modern right-wing governments are somehow more "fiscally prudent," compared to supposedly free-spending regimes of earlier years, is painfully false.

A government DEFICIT occurs when incoming tax revenues are insufficient to pay for outgoing expenses. A SURPLUS, on the other hand, occurs when tax revenues are larger than expenses. A BALANCED BUDGET is achieved when tax revenues perfectly match government spending.

It is normal for budgets to tend toward deficit when the economy experiences a slowdown or recession. This kind of deficit is called a CYCLICAL DEFICIT. Government revenues decline during a downturn (tax revenues shrink as workers lose their jobs and reduce their spending); meanwhile, expenses for unemployment insurance and other social programs automatically increase. Even without any change in policy, therefore, a recession makes a deficit worse. Likewise, strong economic growth automatically improves the government's budget balance. Tax and spending programs which produce this response to cyclical economic trends are called AUTOMATIC STABILIZERS.

A short-term deficit, especially one resulting from an economic downturn, is no cause for concern. In fact, cyclical deficits actually help the economy recover more quickly (by supporting spending despite the loss of jobs and private spending). Perversely, trying to eliminate a cyclical deficit through deliberate AUSTERITY (like spending cuts or tax increases) only makes the recession worse (by further undermining consumer and business spending).

On the other hand, large chronic deficits that persist year after year may be cause for more genuine concern. A STRUCTURAL DEFICIT reflects a deeper mismatch between revenues and expenditures, and persists even when the economy is relatively strong. Reducing a structural deficit requires discretionary measures to raise taxes or reduce spending, whereas cyclical deficits can be solved simply by boosting the level of economic activity and employment.

A deficit in any given year must be financed by government borrowing (which can occur in many different forms: issuing bonds to investors, borrowing from private banks, or even borrowing from the government's own central bank). A deficit, therefore, increases a government's outstanding DEBT, by the amount of the annual deficit each year. Large consecutive deficits produce an ongoing and rapid accumulation of public debt, which can have negative economic and financial consequences.

There is great controversy in economics regarding the appropriate level of public debt. Contrary to common knee-jerk criticisms of government debt from conservatives, public debt (and projects which are financed with that debt) can be positive and productive (see box). PUBLIC INVESTMENT enhances overall economic performance and business productivity, and can even stimulate stronger private investment (through an effect known as "crowding in"). There are financial benefits arising from a certain level of government debt, as well. Government bonds are typically the most stable and reliable financial assets – much safer than corporate shares or bonds. A sizeable stockpile of public debt (large, but not too large) can thus help to stabilize financial markets.

At the same time, there is a downside to public debt, too. The biggest is the burden of interest payments required to service the debt. If public debt is growing, then interest costs eat up a larger proportion of total government revenues.

Private Debt Good, Public Debt Bad

Conservative finance ministers regularly invoke a phony "kitchen-table" analogy, to justify the deep cuts in public programs they claim are essential for balancing the budget. "Mom and pop know they can't spend more than they take in," the minister gravely asserts. "And my government understands this, too. We have to run our government like mom and pop run their household. That's why we're eliminating your public programs."

First of all, the suggestion that moms and pops, planning household finances at the kitchen table, never spend more than they take in is factually ludicrous. Household borrowing (as we saw in Chapter 17) is an essential precondition for major household purchases (like homes and cars). Without it, the economy would be stuck in endless recession.

Businesses, too, borrow funds whenever required in order to finance essential investments. Any chief executive officer who proclaimed (as right-wing finance ministers regularly do) that their top priority is to eliminate debt, would be fired immediately as a superstitious incompetent. Financial analysts understand well that vast profits can be generated when businesses borrow to finance profitable investments (a strategy called LEVERAGING).

The same fundamental principle applies to public investments, too. If a public investment generates more incremental value (in jobs, incomes, or productivity) than the interest paid on the money borrowed to pay for it, then it is economically rational and legitimate to undertake the investment. Only a superstitious belief that "public debt is always bad" stands in the way of these opportunities to increase output and income through debt-financed public investment.

Interest payments play no productive economic or social role, and are received by financial investors who tend to be among society's richest households. Interest payments thus constitute a regressive redistribution (shifting resources from average taxpayers to well-off investors). If debt grows too quickly, or becomes too large, investor confidence in government bonds, or even in a country's currency, can become rattled. This produces financial and economic instability (including higher interest rates, exchange rate instability, and – in severe cases – an outflow of financial capital from the country).

But within limits, government debt is not just acceptable, it is desirable. The true constraint on public finance is not to balance the budget in any particular year (or even to balance it all), but rather to restrain debt from rising too far, too fast. The best way to measure the **DEBT BURDEN** in this context is as a proportion of nominal GDP – since government revenues derived from GDP determine a government's ability to service its debt. The European Union's Maastricht Treaty (signed in 1992) imposed a debt ceiling on countries joining the euro common currency zone. It was supposed to cap debt at a maximum of 60 percent of GDP

– but that rule was badly designed, weakly enforced, and became meaningless in the aftermath of the global crisis of 2008–09 (when debts in several EU countries soared past 100 percent of GDP). It is quite feasible for countries to take on larger public debts, but at the cost of higher debt-service charges. Very large public debts are more manageable when most of the debt is held domestically (rather than owed to foreign investors), when a country possesses its own national currency (giving it more flexibility in financing deficits), and when interest rates are lower. For all of these reasons, large debts incurred after the financial crisis in countries like Japan, the US, and the UK pose less of a problem than in countries like Greece, Portugal, or Italy (which lost their monetary and banking autonomy with the formation of the euro, and which face much higher interest rates because of their lack of monetary independence).

Counter-intuitively, a government can maintain a stable debt burden (measured as a share of GDP) while still incurring *annual* deficits. So long as GDP is growing, a government can experience a small deficit each year with no growth in the debt burden (measured as a share of GDP). The "allowable" deficit equals the rate of GDP growth times the desired, stable debt burden. For example, if nominal GDP grows at 5 percent per year, and the government wishes to maintain a stable debt burden equal to 60 percent of GDP, then it can safely budget for an annual deficit of 3 percent of GDP (60 percent times 5 percent). If the economy suffers a recession, however, then the debt burden will rise (due both to a larger deficit and to the decline in GDP). So to play it safe, government might aim to reduce the debt burden modestly during years of stronger growth, leaving room for an increase during years of economic slowdown; this would allow for a stable debt burden measured over the complete economic cycle. And again, if public debt is used to pay for productive investments that enhance the economy's productive capacity (by employing otherwise idle workers, and making their work more productive), then it is rational to incur more of it.

In sum, it is clear that conservative anti-deficit and anti-debt campaigns are motivated more by politics than economics. Neoliberals use fear of public debt to politically justify the elimination of public programs (like income security programs) which they want to get rid of anyway. They have used similar arguments to justify the stealthy privatization of public investment through **PUBLIC–PRIVATE PARTNERSHIPS**. These initiatives nominally transfer the responsibility for major public projects from government to private investors – yet governments (and taxpayers) are still left holding the bill for future, long-run interest costs (paying interest rates *higher* than the government would have paid to build the infrastructure itself). These so-called "partnerships" are in reality a taxpayer-funded giveaway to private investors, justified by a phony phobia of public debt that is itself the legacy of neoliberalism.

On the whole, it's usually best (barring national emergency) for governments to avoid increasing debt too rapidly. But government budgets do not need to be balanced every year (or even on average over periods of expansion and recession). Debts incurred to fund productive public investment, or to employ workers who would otherwise sit idle, can be economically efficient. And it is fundamentally wrong to assume that government debt is inherently "bad" and must be eliminated.

Fiscal policy under neoliberalism

As we saw in the previous chapter, even capitalists want a strong central state to perform many important functions – like protecting private property, managing income distribution, and paying for business-friendly government services (like training, roads, or utilities). These functions require money, and hence taxes, that can amount to a considerable portion of GDP. Even in the US (the role-model for many neoliberals), government activity consumes around one-third of GDP – and this figure hasn't declined under neoliberalism.

Nevertheless, a reorientation of fiscal policy has been an important part of the broader neoliberal agenda. And social struggles over those fiscal choices have been an important component of resistance to neoliberalism. Here are some of the key fiscal priorities that have been pursued by neoliberal governments:

- **Cutting income security programs**, especially for working-age adults. There is no more hated form of government spending, from an employers' perspective, than income security programs. They give working-age people a degree of independence from having to offer their labour for hire in the labour market. And across the capitalist world, income security programs for working-age adults – unemployment insurance, welfare benefits, even disability benefits – have borne the deepest proportionate spending cuts. The goal is to once again firmly compel people to work, work hard, and follow orders unquestioningly, on pain of costly job loss.
- **Privatizing once-public functions**   Privatization is doubly beneficial, in neoliberal eyes: it reduces government spending, and it opens potentially lucrative new terrain for private, profit-seeking investment.
- **Downplaying counter-cyclical fiscal policy**   In the initial post-war decades, fiscal policy was used more pro-actively to offset the ups and downs of the private sector economy: boosting spending in lean years, pulling back somewhat in better times. This counter-cyclical approach largely fell out of favour under neoliberalism: conservative governments seized on any excuse to ratchet down government spending, good times or bad. Meanwhile, neoclassical economists came to favour MONETARY POLICY as a more timely and flexible way to smooth out economic fluctuations. The downturn

that followed the global financial crisis was so severe, however, that even conservatives endorsed counter-cyclical spending – for a while, anyway. But soon the doctrine of **AUSTERITY** rose to the top of the neoliberal agenda again (as discussed further in Chapter 26).

- **Reducing income, wealth, and business taxes**   When fiscal conditions allow, and governments have sufficient funds to perform the functions that businesses support, neoliberal governments will happily cut taxes. In general, the first taxes cut are those which impose the maximum burden on businesses, and the well-off individuals who own them. Personal income taxes, wealth taxes, and corporate taxes of all kinds, have been reduced aggressively by neoliberal governments. Taxes on investment income (like dividends and capital gains) have been cut most of all. Sales taxes (which impose a slightly higher burden on lower-income households) have been maintained or even increased.

Spending, taxing, and redistribution

Despite these negative shifts in fiscal policy under neoliberalism, the spending and taxing activities of governments still have a broadly equalizing impact on the overall distribution of income and opportunity in capitalist societies. Despite neoliberal efforts, the overall tax system is still modestly **PROGRESSIVE**: that is, it imposes a relatively higher burden on higher-income individuals. (A **REGRESSIVE** tax, on the other hand, imposes a proportionately larger burden on lower-income individuals.)

Meanwhile, many forms of public spending make a significant contribution to the well-being of working and poor people. Of course, well-off people and businesses also benefit from government activities. But some programs (like income security transfers, and public health care and education) clearly benefit poor people proportionately more than rich people. Table 21.1 summarizes the distributional impact of different kinds of taxing and spending.

Assume for now that the overall tax system imposes a mildly progressive burden (with well-off people paying a proportionately higher share of their income in total taxes). Assume that transfer payments to individuals are also progressive: poor people definitely get more than "their share" of those payments. Finally, assume that all individuals consume, on average, an equal share of the value of government provision. These services add measurably to everyone's standard of living (supplementing the value of privately-purchased goods and services). But they make a *proportionately* larger contribution to the total standard of living

Table 21.1 Distributive Impacts of Spending and Taxing

Spending:	
Interest payments	Regressive
Transfer payments	
To individuals	Progressive
To others	Mixed
Government provision	
Health care	Progressive
Basic education	Progressive
Higher education	Mildly Progressive
Infrastructure	Neutral
Military and police	Mixed
Overall spending	**Mildly progressive**
Revenues:	
Income taxes	
Personal	Strongly progressive
Corporate	Strongly progressive
Sales taxes	Mildly regressive
Payroll taxes	Regressive
Wealth taxes	Strongly progressive
Other taxes	Mixed
User fees	Mildly regressive
Overall taxing	**Mildly progressive**

Class Warfare

"Through the tax code, there has been class warfare waged,
and my class has won. It's been a rout."

Warren Buffett, US Billionaire (2011).

Legendary financial manager Warren Buffett is one of the richest people in
the world, with an estimated fortune of US$73 billion in 2014. But most of his
income is generated by investments that are taxed at preferential rates. He
disclosed that in 2006 he paid a lower average rate of personal income tax
(17.7 percent) than his secretary (who paid 30 percent on a salary of about
US$60,000). To his credit, he called for changes in the tax code that would
impose minimum taxes on rich investors.

---

of lower-income people (since their private consumption possibilities are so
constrained by their incomes).

The overall impact of government spending and taxing on income distribution
can then be measured at three distinct stages, as follows:

1. **Market income**   If we consider only the total income (before tax) which
   individuals "earn" in the economy (including through employment, investment
   income, and other private sources of income – but excluding government
   transfers), the distribution of income in most capitalist countries is highly, and
   increasingly, unequal.
2. **After-tax-and-transfer income**   We then adjust each person's income for the
   taxes they pay and the personal transfer payments they receive from government
   (which were not counted in market income). Higher-income people pay more
   tax, and generally receive less transfer income. So the gap between rich and
   poor narrows significantly.
3. **Real consumption**   Next we adjust distribution to account for the
   consumption opportunities provided by direct public services (like health care,
   education, public facilities, and so on). These services supplement the standard
   of living possible for each household (above and beyond what they can buy
   with their money income). This further reduces the proportionate gap between
   the richest and poorest households.

Despite the regressive effect of neoliberal fiscal policies, therefore, the overall
spending and taxing activities of government continue to considerably narrow the
gaps between rich and poor under capitalism. The gap between the richest and
poorest households at stage 3 above, is much narrower than the initial difference

at stage 1. This positive distributional impact of government taxes and programs is not as strong as it used to be, nor as strong as it could be. But the positive distributional effect of government budgets is still very powerful, and it is important to understand the different ways in which it is felt. A strongly progressive public program will still have a net positive impact on society even if financed with a neutral or even mildly regressive tax. Hence the relative fairness of alternative taxes cannot be understood without taking into account the equality-enhancing value of the resulting programs. And arguments against "unfair" taxes (such as sales taxes) are often misused by conservatives whose true goal is to reduce all taxes (and, more importantly, the programs they fund). So our demands for a more progressive tax system must always be linked to our demands for a strong, accessible network of public programs and services that is funded by those taxes.

22

Globalization

Global, global, global

Globalization has been a core priority of neoliberal economic policy right from the beginning. Some of the greatest policy weapons in the neoliberal arsenal have been aimed at enhancing global economic linkages, and granting more global power and mobility to companies and investors. These include regional FREE TRADE AGREEMENTS; the unilateral opening of many countries (especially developing and former Communist countries) to international trade and foreign investment; and the creation in 1995 of the WORLD TRADE ORGANIZATION (WTO).

At the same time, some of the fiercest battles against neoliberalism have been waged by citizens concerned about the one-sided nature of those global policies and institutions. These include the youthful anti-globalization movement that sprang up at the turn of the century (sparked by the famous anti-WTO protests in Seattle in 1999), strong campaigns against particular free trade agreements (and some of their most nefarious features, like INVESTOR-STATE DISPUTE SETTLEMENT), and ongoing efforts to promote Third World debt relief and "fair trade."

To some extent, the preoccupation of both neoliberals and their opponents with globalization has been sensible and justified. Over the past quarter-century, changes in both the global economy and global economic policy have been massive. The economic and political power of businesses and investors has been strengthened immensely by globalization. And finding ways to manage the global economy differently will be crucial to any alternative, progressive economic vision.

At the same time, however, it is important to keep the "global" dimension in context. Many of the negative consequences of neoliberalism would clearly have occurred anyway, even without globalization. And we could conceivably dismantle specific aspects of globalization (for example, cancelling free-trade agreements, or even disbanding the WTO) without substantially altering the functioning of modern capitalism.

Try this: say the words "global, global, global" aloud to yourself several times, as fast as you can. You'll find yourself sounding like a turkey ("gobble, gobble, gobble").

We have to keep our eyes on the whole barnyard, not just the turkey; we can't become unduly obsessed with the global dimension of economics. The vast

Not So Global?

Table 22.1 How Big is Global?

Sector	Approximate Share Total GDP	Share Exported
Primary*	5%	Over half
Manufacturing	15%	Over half
Construction	5%	Almost none
Private services	60%	Under 10%
Public services	15%	Almost none
WEIGHTED AVERAGE	100%	Under 20%

* Primary includes agriculture, forestry, and minerals.

Misleading statistics can imply that international trade accounts for most or even all of a country's GDP. But in reality, foreign trade accounts for a small share of GDP – even in smaller, trade-dependent economies. We can see this by examining the sectoral composition of GDP, and considering how much of each sector's final output is actually exported. About 80 percent of GDP in a developed economy is produced by sectors (construction, private services, and public services) which experience very little foreign trade. Moreover, those NON-TRADEABLE sectors make up a growing share of total GDP – which means that the relative importance of foreign trade may *decline* over time.

majority of the goods and services produced in a modern economy never cross a national boundary (see box); these products are produced strictly by and for the residents of each country, and we can reform the conditions of their production without worrying much at all about global constraints on those reforms. Most of the decisions affecting how the economy evolves, for better or worse, are still made at home. Yes, globalization is a very important piece of the modern economic puzzle – but it is still just one piece.

Globalization: what's really new?

What's more, if we define globalization (at its simplest) as the expansion of economic linkages between countries, then it's not even *new*. People from different countries, even different continents, have been trading with each other for centuries. And capitalism has always had a global dimension. International trade in raw materials and finished products was important to early merchants and industrialists. Using brute global force to open captive, colonial markets allowed British capitalists to make the most of the awesome productivity of their new factories. And the inherent expansionary impulse arising from the drive to maximize profits spurred an ongoing global quest for markets and investment opportunities, right from the beginning of capitalism. By the turn of the twentieth century (before colonial rivalries exploded in World War I, and world trade subsequently declined), international trade and investment were probably nearly as important (relative to GDP) as they are today.

While globalization (in this concrete sense) has been around for a long time, it is certainly clear that there has been a dramatic, more recent shift in both the amount and the nature of international business. In 2012, some US$18 trillion worth of tangible merchandise crossed national borders – and merchandise trade has been growing faster than GDP since the end of World War II. Another US$4 trillion worth of services was sold across borders. Meanwhile, multinational corporations undertook US$1.5 trillion worth of new foreign direct investment projects in 2013 – and the accumulated stockpile of foreign direct investment that year exceeded US$25 trillion. The volume of cross-border financial flows is much larger: over US$5 trillion in foreign exchange transactions every business day.*

Many factors have contributed to the expansion of international business. Policy changes (like free-trade agreements) explain some of that growth, but not all. Other factors contributing to globalization include:

- **Communications technology** New computer and communications technologies have reduced the cost, and enhanced the capability, of global communications. Technology has opened up incredible possibilities for performing and coordinating work across long distances.
- **Transportation technology** Similarly, international transportation (including merchandise shipping and travel) has become easier and cheaper. This has also facilitated global business.
- **Improvements in management** Business executives have become more adept at identifying far-flung supply, production, and marketing opportunities; outsourcing particular functions to reliable suppliers (including those in far-off places); and implementing strategies to maximize global profits. This evolution in management capacity has been very important to the expansion of international commerce.
- **Unilateral opening** Quite apart from the impact of international agreements and institutions (like the WTO and regional free-trade agreements), many countries have unilaterally reduced policy barriers to foreign trade and investment during the neoliberal era. For various reasons – including the failure of previous, more inward-oriented economic strategies; pressure from international agencies like the **WORLD BANK** and

---

* Data from World Trade Organization, *World Trade Report* (2013); United Nations Commission on Trade and Development, *World Investment Report* (2014); and Bank for International Settlements, *Triennial Central Bank Survey* (2013).

the **International Monetary Fund** (IMF); and sheer desperation for investment – governments (especially in developing and formerly Communist countries) have dismantled regulations which once limited foreign trade and capital flows. This opened up lucrative new opportunities for global businesses to take advantage of the natural resources, labour, and markets of these countries.

- **Political "stability"** Companies once worried about investing in other countries (especially developing countries) because of potential political turmoil that could result in lost profits (and even, in many cases, lost businesses). Today, a pro-business welcome mat has been firmly laid out by almost all countries, and companies can globalize their operations with much less political risk.

- **Free trade agreements** The growth and deregulation of global commerce would have occurred anyway as a result of all these changes. But globalization has been mightily reinforced, and given a starkly pro-business character, by international agreements which cement free-trade rules and limit government powers to interfere with trade and capital flows. Some of these agreements are regional (like the European Union and the North American Free Trade Agreement); some are global (like the WTO). They promote freer trade in merchandise and services – for example, by eliminating **TARIFFS** (taxes imposed to limit imports) and other trade barriers. Less obvious, but ultimately more important, are provisions aimed at opening and protecting investment flows, granting special legal protections to foreign investors, and generally limiting government intrusions into the private sector. For example, the General Agreement on Trade in Services (GATS), which is a trade treaty overseen by the WTO, has a blanket provision curtailing governments' ability to regulate service industries – even services companies which do no exporting or importing at all.

All these factors have contributed to the growth of global commerce. However, it is clear that modern globalization is more than just the *quantitative* expansion of global linkages. Under neoliberalism, globalization has taken on a particular *qualitative* dimension. Yes, the global economy has become more integrated and connected – but in a very one-sided way, governed by a one-sided set of rules and practices. Trade and investment policies grant freedom and protection to companies and investors; they limit governments' ability to interfere with profit-maximizing business decisions; and they are virtually silent on protecting workers, regulatory powers, and the environment.

Free-trade advocates claim that globalization is "inevitable," and there is no point opposing it. Certainly, the fact that international commerce, communications, travel, and the transfer of knowledge are all faster and easier than ever is not something we can reverse – nor would we want to. There are many benefits from living in a more closely integrated world: for the economy, for culture, for global cooperation, for peace.

But the particular character of globalization under neoliberalism is not set in stone. Yes, countries will trade, capital will flow, and people will travel – exchanging ideas and knowledge in the process. But this does not have to occur under neoliberal rules – which grant unprecedented rights and security to businesses and investors, but no guarantees for anyone else. Working individually and multilaterally, countries have the power to change the current rules of the global game: balancing the interests of businesses and their owners against the need to promote employment, security, and sustainability. But this would require the citizens of the world to successfully demand a change of approach from their respective governments – and that, in turn, will require more of the energetic campaigns and protests like those we saw at the dawn of this century.

Forms of globalization

Economic activity can be conducted across a national border, and hence become international, in several different ways. Here are the major building blocks of global commerce:

- **Merchandise trade**   Tangible goods are the easiest thing to ship back and forth between countries, and international merchandise trade has been occurring for centuries. EXPORTS are products which are produced in one country and then sold in another; IMPORTS are products that are made elsewhere, but purchased and used at home.
- **Services trade**   It is not as easy to buy and sell services across a national border, because usually the service producer must be near to the service consumer. (It is hard to conduct international trade in haircuts, for example: that would require the hairstylist to have very long arms!) In some specialized service industries, however, international trade is important. Customers may purchase services from providers in another country, in order to access unique features or skills which can't be purchased closer to home. Service industries which sell their products internationally include higher-level financial and business services, cultural industries (like movies and music), higher education, and specialized health care. Technological changes are facilitating more international services trade, including many lower-wage functions (like telephone call centres). Tourism is another form of services trade: when a foreign tourist visits another country (spending money on travel, accommodation, and meals), it is equivalent to that country

"exporting" tourism services (since it is producing something, a nice vacation, that is purchased and consumed by someone from another country).

- **Foreign direct investment** A MULTINATIONAL CORPORATION is a company which operates productive facilities in more than one country.

Kangaroo Court

One of the most offensive aspects of modern trade agreements is the creation of INVESTOR-STATE DISPUTE SETTLEMENT (ISDS) systems. These quasi-judicial bodies give international businesses special legal powers to challenge unfavourable government policies.

One of the first examples of this system was Chapter 11 of the North American Free Trade Agreement (NAFTA), implemented in 1994. It created a new, parallel legal system – accessible only to businesses and their owners. If a NAFTA government implements a law or policy which reduces the profitability of a business investment, the owner can use this special court to sue the government for compensation. These kangaroo courts are operated by professional trade experts and arbitrators: unelected technocrats who fully embrace the flawed assumptions of free trade, and accept the anti-democratic nature of dispute settlement. Similar ISDS mechanisms have since been included in many other regional trade agreements and bilateral investment treaties.

In NAFTA's first two decades, 75 Chapter 11 claims were launched, challenging everything from limits on polluting additives in gasoline, to changes in pharmaceutical patent laws, to the operation of Canada's public post office. Total damages claimed in these suits exceeded US$40 billion – and companies have won enough judgements to force governments to take the process very seriously. Consequently, the ISDS system has had a chilling effect on all government policy-making: politicians fear that any policy that might harm corporate profits could spark yet another NAFTA lawsuit.

The spread of this practice to other trade agreements has sparked a worldwide surge in ISDS claims. From 2000 through 2013, a total of 530 ISDS claims were launched against governments around the world, and the rate of new claims has been accelerating (averaging over 50 per year since 2011). Complaining investors have been winning full or partial judgments in most of the cases they launch.

The widespread adoption of ISDS practices proves that modern globalization is not really about "promoting trade." The true goal is to construct and globally enforce a pro-business bias in all areas of government policy.

Source: Canadian Centre for Policy Alternatives, "NAFTA Chapter 11 Investor-State Disputes" (2014), and United Nations Conference on Trade and Development, "Recent Developments in Investor-State Dispute Settlement" (2014).

And the act of investing in those tangible foreign facilities is called FOREIGN
DIRECT INVESTMENT (FDI). Incoming FDI can be very useful to the receiving
(or "host") country: it supplements domestic investment spending, and the
multinational firm usually brings along some technological or managerial
advantages not possessed by domestic firms. For this reason, most countries
welcome FDI, and have reduced or eliminated barriers to incoming FDI. Many
countries retain restrictions on incoming FDI in some "strategic" industries –
like banking, non-renewable resources, or defense. The bigger concern now
for many countries is not trying to control incoming FDI, but rather trying to
limit *outgoing* investment flows – that is, to prevent or discourage capital from
heading to more profitable foreign jurisdictions (thus undermining domestic
investment, technological progress, and employment). Even incoming
FDI, however, comes with a price tag. Countries which are too reliant on
incoming FDI face many risks, including: a long-run outflow of profits from
a foreign-owned business back to its home base; the loss of head-office jobs
(like management, marketing, and engineering positions, which tend to be
clustered around a company's global headquarters); and the loss of domestic
control over major investment decisions.

- **International financial flows** The global flow of finance dwarfs
  international trade and real investment. Sophisticated financial institutions
  now operate 24 hours per day, using branch offices around the world,
  trading non-stop in an infinite variety of assets (currencies, stocks, bonds,
  and derivatives), and seeking to profit from short-term changes in prices and
  market sentiment. In most countries, investors can freely convert financial
  wealth from one currency into another; the "price" of buying another
  country's currency is its EXCHANGE RATE. Like other prices, a currency's
  exchange rate tends to rise (or "appreciate") when more people want to buy
  it; it falls ("depreciates") when people prefer other currencies. But the biggest
  buyers and sellers of currencies are not real exporters, multinational firms,
  or tourists; instead, most foreign exchange transactions are undertaken
  by financial institutions and speculators. This overdeveloped, hyperactive
  casino operates without much supervision or oversight. International
  institutions (like the INTERNATIONAL MONETARY FUND or the BANK FOR
  INTERNATIONAL SETTLEMENTS) try to impose certain rules on global
  finance; national financial regulators (like central banks) do the same, where
  possible. But the system is largely unregulated, and very prone to destructive
  mood swings on the part of global investors – who can do incredible
  economic damage to countries and continents.
- **Migration** Cross-border human flows, motivated by both economic and
  non-economic factors, have been important throughout human history.
  Workers move from one country to another in search of better employment

or income prospects. Capitalists may encourage those migrations when they face uncomfortably tight labour market conditions in particular countries (in which case inward immigration helps to keep a lid on wages). But migrant workers usually face difficult economic and social challenges in their new lives. Prejudice, racism, and LABOUR MARKET SEGMENTATION undermine their earning opportunities, and often prevent them from fully utilizing their skills and education. Migrants are treated as temporary, second-class citizens, often forced to return to their country of origin when their jobs are finished, and subjected to social and legal abuses in the interim. More often than other workers they are channeled into PRECARIOUS WORK. Their migration can also harm the countries they leave – especially since it is usually the best-educated, most capable people who get permission to immigrate to other, richer countries. Many migrants send regular remittance payments home to support their families; these payments are economically important to many developing countries.

• **International institutions** The globalization of governance and policy is another important dimension of the current world economy. And unfortunately, this area has been utterly dominated by neoliberal, pro-business ideas. At the conclusion of World War II, the leading capitalist economies, led by the US, established the IMF and the World Bank. The former was assigned to focus on stabilizing and freeing international financial flows; the latter's job was to assist poor countries with economic development. At the time, the British economist John Maynard Keynes argued for the IMF to function like a global CENTRAL BANK – supporting growth and employment, managing overall global purchasing power, and helping resolve trade imbalances. But Keynes' vision was rejected, and the IMF and the World Bank focused instead on imposing free-market, pro-business structures on the world economy. Both have used their financial leverage to force countries (especially desperate developing countries, but even richer economies at times – like hard-hit European nations after the GLOBAL FINANCIAL CRISIS) to follow the neoliberal recipe book. Using a strategy called CONDITIONALITY, they require countries to unilaterally open their markets, deregulate capital flows and labour markets, privatize industries, and cut back government spending – in return for short-term financial aid to survive economic and financial crises that were usually caused by neoliberal policies in the first place. Today even IMF and World Bank officials admit that many of those dictates were wrong – but that hasn't altered the strongly neoliberal direction of their policies. Meanwhile, the WTO, founded in 1995, became the third member of this global neoliberal trio. It has a special "dispute-settlement system" which can order countries to dismantle policies and programs which violate free-trade principles.

What's wrong with free trade, anyway?

Free-trade advocates claim that globalization is an unequivocally positive force. Freer global trade and investment flows will allow every country to specialize in what they do best. Efficiency and output will grow, and every country will benefit. They argue that globalization is especially beneficial for poor countries, which can finally escape their lower status and become full, prosperous players in a more inclusive global system.

Indeed, this faith in the automatic, mutual benefits of free trade has been a guiding principle of mainstream economics since the birth of capitalism. In the early nineteenth century, David Ricardo postulated his theory of **COMPARATIVE ADVANTAGE** to celebrate (and intellectually justify) the expansion of international trade. In fact, Ricardo was motivated less by economic theory and more by

---

Trade and the Environment

Free trade can be bad for the environment, too. In some polluting industries, companies may be lured to locate in countries with relatively weak environmental rules. This undermines global efforts to reduce pollution.

Also, the long-distance transportation associated with globalization consumes vast quantities of fossil fuels. Many products now consume more energy being transported to far-off markets, than in their actual production. Indeed, intercontinental ocean shipping, which relies on heavily-polluting bunker oil, is one of the most polluting industries on the planet. Ocean shipping produces about 3 percent of all global carbon dioxide emissions* – more than all but five entire countries (China, the US, India, Russia, and Japan). And because ocean shipping operates beyond the reach of national governments, it largely avoids environmental regulations. (For the same reason, labour standards in the shipping industry also tend to be horrendous.)

* International Maritime Organization, "Second IMO GHG Study" (2009).

---

pragmatic politics: freer trade would reduce labour costs (through imports of cheaper foodstuffs), supplement the profits of industrialists (who he viewed as the most dynamic force in society), and reduce the power of unproductive landlords.

But Ricardo developed an elegant economic theory to support the industrialists' demand for cheaper imported food. His theory of comparative advantage works like this: imagine two countries (he chose England and Portugal). Each can produce two products: wine and cloth. Suppose that Portugal can produce *both* wine and cloth more efficiently (that is, with fewer hours of required labour) than England. Portugal's advantage is greatest in wine – but even in cloth production it bests the English factories. England might fear that both its wine and cloth sectors would be wiped out by free trade with Portugal. But Ricardo showed that it was still better (under certain, restrictive conditions) for England to trade with Portugal (exporting English cloth, its *relatively* most efficient product, in return for Portuguese wine), than to try to produce both products itself. Portugal, too, is better-off to specialize in wine, and then exchange it for English cloth; this is more efficient for Portugal than making its own cloth.

This theory is much-beloved by economists, who enjoy expounding its counter-intuitive beauty at policy forums and cocktail parties alike. And the argument that international economic integration must always benefit both sides is still tremendously influential. Neoclassical economists adapted Ricardo's approach to fit their own, more complex GENERAL EQUILIBRIUM theories. They still argue that countries (even high-wage countries) have nothing to fear from expanded trade and investment with other countries (even low-wage countries). They have constructed computerized economic models to predict, in stunning detail, the economic gains from further globalization, and have used those predictions to support political campaigns to expand the WTO and implement more free-trade agreements.

There's only one problem: the theory is wrong. Even in theory, but especially in practice, the conditions and assumptions that must prevail in order for free trade to be *guaranteed* to benefit both sides, simply do not apply. In reality, free trade produces both winners and losers – just as capitalism itself produces winners and losers. There are several scenarios (summarized in Table 22.2) which disprove the conviction of Ricardo and his descendants that free trade necessarily benefits everyone involved:

Table 22.2 Six Ways Free Trade Can Do Damage

Unemployment: Trade will result in job losses when an economy's products are not competitive, and imports grow more quickly than exports.

Capital flows: If a country loses more investment than it gains under globalization, it will experience a slowdown or recession.

Transitional costs: The movement of labour from one industry to another is costly, and old capital is destroyed in the process. These costs can outweigh the efficiency benefits of trade.

Perverse specialization: Globalization can lead a country to specialize in less desirable, low-productivity industries.

Terms of trade: As a country produces more of a particular good under free trade, its world price can decline – offsetting the efficiency gains of specialization.

Distribution: A country's GDP may grow under free trade, but the incomes of particular groups (e.g. workers) may fall.

- Ricardo's model assumed a **SUPPLY-CONSTRAINED** system, in which all resources are used in production. In essence, everyone will be employed doing something after free trade, and market forces will then ensure they are employed doing what they do best. In reality, however, unemployment exists – in large numbers, and for long periods of time. If it leads to higher unemployment in a particular country or region, then free trade is clearly damaging.
- Ricardo also assumed that capital could not flow from one country to another. If capital was mobile, in his example, all investment would likely flow from England to Portugal (to take advantage of Portugal's superior productivity), thus devastating England's economy. In the real world, capital outflows can easily overwhelm efficiency gains from trade. Any country which loses investment spending as a result of globalization will experience major economic losses.
- When trade is opened up, market pressures will lead to a reallocation of capital and labour from one industry to another – reflecting a country's

specialization in its relatively most competitive industries. But that economic transition is not costless. Workers lose their jobs, may be unemployed for long periods of time, and may not earn as much even if they do find new jobs. And in most cases, it is not possible to physically shift real capital from one industry to another: capital in old industries is simply left to rust, while new investment gradually occurs in growing industries. This loss of capital in the old industry can also outweigh the efficiency benefits of trade.

• The issue of which countries get to specialize in which industries is very important in trade theory. Some industries (such as advanced manufacturing and higher-end services) are especially beneficial: they utilize cutting-edge technology, produce innovative products, and generate higher-than-average productivity and incomes. Other industries (such as many agricultural, minerals, and lower-technology manufactured goods) demonstrate stagnant technology and low productivity. If free trade pressures cause a country to abandon its foothold in more desirable, cutting-edge industries, in order to specialize in less appealing and dynamic sectors, then that country's long-run economic prospects will be undermined.

• Even when a country specializes in an industry with growing productivity, the efficiency gains from trade can be offset through a complex interaction involving the relative prices of a country's exports and imports (called the TERMS OF TRADE). A country (or countries) might specialize so much in producing a certain product, with so much added efficiency, that it can literally drive down the price of its own exports. As a result, the more the country produces, the lower the price falls – and the specialization is self-defeating. This risk is especially acute for agricultural and natural resource products.

• Finally, comparative advantage theory is all defined in terms of national economic benefits. It doesn't say anything about how the benefits of trade, even if they were realized, are *distributed* within a country. Even neoclassical models raise important distributional questions. For example, if a relatively high-wage economy opens trade with a relatively low-wage economy, wages in the richer economy should fall – even under neoclassical assumptions. (Curiously, even though this is a central finding of their own theory, neoclassical economists in rich countries still deny, for all sorts of invented reasons, that free trade would ever cause wages to fall.) The whole country may produce more GDP, but large groups within the country (namely, the workers) could still be worse off.

Honest neoclassical economists will admit that if any of these circumstances prevail then free trade can indeed be damaging. But free-trade conviction holds such a powerful sway over the economics profession that few are willing to explore the policy implications of those theoretical issues. And so the false impression persists that economists universally agree on the automatic virtues of free trade – even though actual economic theory (even *neoclassical* theory) indicates nothing of the sort.

At the same time, however, none of this implies that more trade is necessarily harmful, either. In reality, globalization introduces a combination of opportunities and threats to national economies (and to particular groups of people). New exports and incoming foreign direct investment can add positively to an economy's growth and employment prospects. The ability to produce specialized varieties of manufactured products for a larger international market can enhance productivity. But for every winner, there can also be a loser: an economy that loses production and employment as a result of a failure to compete internationally for market share and investment. Worst of all, the present (neoliberal) rules of globalization preclude governments from managing those trade and investment flows to enhance the broader benefits, and reduce the costs, of participation in the global economy.

Putting the world on the map

This core conclusion – that globalization introduces risks and costs, not just benefits, for any economy – can be illustrated with another edition of our economic map. Figure 22.1 adds the "world" to our economic map, and indicates (in highly simplified form) the different ways in which the domestic economic "circle" is now hooked into a global system.

Companies have an opportunity to sell some of their output as exports (X) into other countries' markets, to supplement what they are able to sell to their own consumers and domestic businesses. However, their own domestic sales (again, to both consumers and businesses) may now be undermined by imports (M) from other countries. There's an opportunity, but also a risk. If its imports are larger than its exports, the country experiences a trade deficit which undermines overall output and employment. (Figure 22.1 shows imports as entering the country through a private business, perhaps an import–export company.)

Total investment spending in the economy, meanwhile, may be amplified or reduced by cross-border flows of FDI. New incoming FDI can add to total investment and job-creation. But if more FDI leaves than enters, then investment spending is reduced by globalization. Once again, there's both an opportunity and a risk.

The overall prospects of the real economy, therefore, will be enhanced or hampered by globalization, depending on whether exports exceed imports, and on whether the inflow of FDI exceeds the outflow.

International financial linkages are also portrayed, symbolized by the diverse currency symbols linking domestic banks to their global counterparts. The

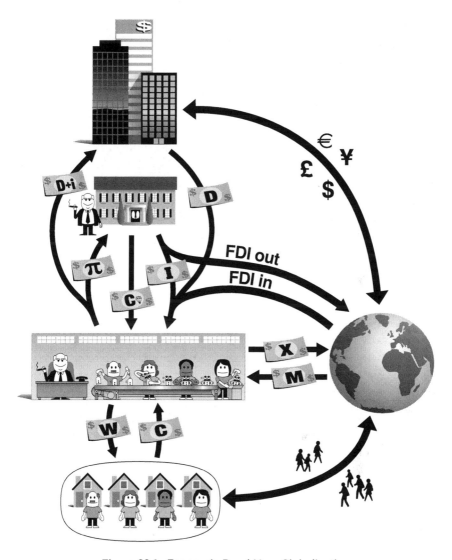

Figure 22.1 Economic Road Map: Globalization

potential benefit from these purely financial flows is harder to identify. In most countries, domestic banks are generally able to create all the purchasing power needed to finance real domestic investment; global linkages are not required for this. If an international financial flow helped to lubricate a real international trade or investment flow, then it could be genuinely useful. But most financial flows have nothing to do with real trade and investment, so their concrete value is not at all clear. On the other hand, global financial linkages clearly pose major risks: a large or sudden financial outflow can send an economy into crisis, and even large financial *inflows* can be damaging (causing the exchange rate to surge, or stimulating domestic inflation). International financial flows are thus the least beneficial, and most risky, of all the dimensions of international economic integration.

Finally, our global map also illustrates the cross-border flow of human beings: **MIGRATION**. People move from one country to another for both economic and non-economic reasons, on a temporary or a permanent basis. Many migrants are driven from their homelands by poverty, war, disaster, or oppression, and then face prejudice, racism, and difficult social and economic conditions in their new homes. Temporary migrants (or "guestworkers") face especially exploitive situations, because they are not generally covered by the same legal or union protections as other workers. On the other hand, migration can be a very positive economic and social force, if migrants are supported and integrated fairly and respectfully into their new societies – adding to the population, diversity, and spending power in their new communities.

Doing it differently

We have stressed in this chapter that under neoliberalism, what is called "globalization" has come to mean much more than just the expansion of economic linkages between countries. And while international travel, trade, and exchange will certainly continue to expand in the future, it is hardly inevitable that these linkages must retain the harshly pro-business bias reflected in the current global rules of the game. To the contrary: we can imagine ways to promote more international trade in goods and services, travel and migration, and even FDI – but without accepting the assumptions and dictates of neoliberal free trade policy (like full mobility of capital, investor-state dispute settlement, and constraints on national regulatory power).

There are even some real-world examples of trade agreements that break from the neoliberal free-trade mold. One interesting example is the Canada-US Auto Pact, signed in 1965. This trade deal eliminated tariffs on two-way trade in motor vehicles and auto parts, and facilitated a dramatic expansion of trade and efficiency in the continental auto industry. However, unlike modern FTAs, this trade deal came with "strings attached": companies which wanted the benefits of tariff-free trade had to pledge to maintain production facilities in each country in broad proportion to their sales in each country. This prevented the "race-to-the-bottom" competition to attract investment that typifies modern globalization, and ensured that each country retained a proportional share of total investment and employment in this strategically important industry. Despite its successes, however, the Auto Pact was abolished following a WTO order in 1999, precisely because of the restrictions it imposed on the location of foreign investment (a concept which has no place in a neoliberal framework).

A more far-reaching alternative to free trade is embodied in a new trade agreement called ALBA (which stands for Alianza Bolivariana para los pueblos de nuestra América). ALBA was founded by Venezuela and Cuba in 2004, but the agreement has since grown to include ten countries, including Ecuador, Bolivia, and Nicaragua. (Honduras was a member, but withdrew after a military coup deposed its elected President in 2009.) ALBA promotes greater regional trade, the development of a common alternative currency, and cooperation around development, ecological, and humanitarian priorities. Other alternative trade blocs in South America include Mercosur (with five member countries, including Brazil and Argentina, and five associates) and the Andean Community (with four countries). These trade blocs also promote greater regional trade, cooperation, and industrial cooperation – but without the blatantly pro-business and constitutional bias common to other "free trade" deals. Since Latin America is the continent which has so strongly rejected neoliberal assumptions in all areas of economic and social life, it is not surprising that this is where non-neoliberal trade practices have been most successful.

Progressive economists and activists around the world continue to develop ways in which global trade, investment, and development can be managed on non-neoliberal principles. Many have proposed detailed templates for trade negotiations that exclude investor-state dispute settlement, integrate human and democratic rights into trade policy, and balance the interests of global businesses with those of communities and the environment. Examples of "alter-globalization" proposals include initiatives like the International Forum on Globalization, the Trade Knowledge Network, and the Working Group on Investment of the Americas. They have proven that modern free trade agreements are not really about trade after all – and hence there is nothing inevitable about the one-sided vision of globalization embodied in modern "free trade" deals.

23

Development (and Otherwise)

A lopsided world

One of the most glaring inequalities in the global economy is that between the rich and poor countries. This schism is called the "North–South" gap – since most rich countries are located in the Northern hemisphere, and many poor countries in the Southern hemisphere. But the dividing line isn't based on geography: it's based on economic condition. Within many well-off Northern countries are pockets of poverty and exploitation more typical of the global South than an advanced economy. By the same token, rich and powerful elites in poor countries lead lives as privileged and luxurious as that of any Northern capitalist.

One third of the world's people live in economic conditions that can only be described as appalling. The **WORLD BANK** estimates that about 1 billion people live in "extreme poverty," surviving on less than US$1.25 of income per day. Another 1.2 billion people live in mere "moderate poverty," with just US$1.25–$2 of income per day. Over 30 percent of humanity therefore must support themselves on less income in a year than a chief executive officer earns in an hour – collectively consuming less than 2 percent of total global GDP. Close to 1 billion people are malnourished; even more lack access to safe water.*

Because of this deprivation, lives in the global South are both harsh and needlessly short. The World Health Organization estimates that over half of all childhood deaths in the world (more than 6 million children aged under five died in 2013) could be prevented with basic, very affordable interventions. On a more hopeful note, significant improvements in human condition have been achieved in many parts of the South, on the basis of medical and technological advances, modest international aid, and (in some countries) deliberate efforts by governments to make poverty-reduction a key economic and social priority. Worldwide, the under-5 mortality rate was cut in half from 1990 through 2013 – but it's still tragically high (at 46 deaths per 1000 live births). And much of the remaining hardship could be alleviated with a shockingly modest redirection of resources. For example, an international project called the Measles and Rubella Initiative oversaw a remarkable 80 percent reduction in worldwide deaths from measles

---

* World Bank, *World Development Indicators* (2014).

between 2000 and 2012, saving over 400,000 lives per year (mostly children) at a cost of just US$1 per vaccinated child. With continued attention, measles could conceivably be eradicated from the world by 2020 (on the other hand, poverty and ignorance could allow its quick resurgence, as demonstrated by recent outbreaks even in some rich countries). The cost of other life-enhancing initiatives is also tiny, relative to the world's overall economic resources.*

---

85 vs 3.5 Billion

The 85 richest billionaires in the world own combined wealth of almost $2 trillion. But most people in the global South own virtually no financial wealth. In fact, the global development organization Oxfam has estimated that the wealth of those 85 billionaires now exceeds the combined financial wealth of the poorest half of the world's population.

Forbes, "The World's Billionaires," 2014, and Oxfam, "Working for the Few," Briefing Paper 178 (2014).

Obviously, then, the immense and mind-numbing hardship that prevails across so much of the global South does not reflect any genuine economic *scarcity*. To the contrary, the world possesses ample resources, food, and know-how to immediately alleviate hardship and prevent most premature deaths. If the global economy is capable of installing a refrigerated soft-drink vending machine in a remote African village, it is also capable of supplying basic foods and medicines to that village – and every other community on the planet.

The problem is not scarcity; the problem is power. Who has the power (both economic and political) to demand that productive resources be devoted to *their* favoured uses? And who lacks this power? How else can we explain a world economy that allocates more resources to high fashion instead of basic children's clothing, video games instead of laptops for poor schoolkids, and medicines for erectile dysfunction instead of tuberculosis? The fact that this inequality is experienced via the supposedly "neutral" forces of supply and demand should not obscure the fact that it is still rooted in *power*: the power of some people to demand, and receive, so much more than others.

The nature of development

Poor countries face an overarching challenge to develop their economies. This process of **DEVELOPMENT** requires more than just increasing total GDP (although

---

* World Health Organization, "Children: Reducing Mortality," Fact Sheet #178 (2014); The Measles and Rubella Initiative, "Infographic" (2014).

that is certainly part of it). There are also many qualitative and structural changes that occur as an economy develops. These include:

- **Capital accumulation** An economy that uses more "tools," broadly defined, will be more productive, and capable of producing more goods and services. An increase in the stockpile of physical capital is a crucial indicator of development; successfully developing countries must attain a rapid rate of real investment.

- **Building knowledge, skills, and health** Productive economies need well-trained workers and managers, to make the most of the physical capital they are accumulating. Major investments in education – from early childhood through to post-graduate – are a prerequisite for successful development. In poor countries, improving health outcomes (again, starting with children) is also essential for improving human capacities and productivity.

- **Changing sectoral balance** As an economy develops, it experiences a series of important structural changes. Agriculture and other resource-based sectors tend to decline, sparking a population migration from rural areas to cities (which itself poses huge social and economic challenges). Manufacturing expands; exports may be particularly important at this stage. Eventually services production becomes dominant, and the economy gradually becomes more self-reliant. Throughout this process, there is normally a parallel expansion in the FORMAL sector of the economy (the portion that produces goods and services for money), and a decline of the INFORMAL sector (individuals producing food and other products in small quantities, largely for their own use).

- **Institutional development and stability** Improved institutional and political conditions are another key dimension of economic (and democratic) development. Institutions (including the legal system, regulatory agencies, and parliaments) need to become more developed, stable, and corruption-free. Investors, businesses, and individual households need certainty and confidence in the economic and political "rules of the game," so they will be more willing to make long-lived commitments to capital projects, education, home-ownership, and communities.

- **Rising incomes** If all of these ingredients come together, then productivity will improve, and GDP will expand – potentially quite quickly. Rapidly developing economies can attain real GDP growth rates of 10 percent per year, or more – sufficient to double total output every seven years. A healthy share of that new output must show up in rising personal incomes, to ensure that the bulk of the population shares in the gains of development.

In addition to meeting these broad qualitative prerequisites, every developing country must also confront an ongoing internal struggle regarding the direction of development, and who benefits from it. The outcome of that struggle will shape the pattern and effects of development. In many cases, wealthy elites in the South (whose power and privilege may have been initially garnered during colonial days) may not even be interested in fostering development – and they certainly don't worry whether its gains are widely shared. So economic development is never just a "technical" process: something that requires assembling the right ingredients and policies, and then unleashing the power of "progress." Rather, the struggle for inclusive, balanced, and sustainable development is inevitably and inherently political. Will economic development engage masses of poor farmers and workers? Or will it occur only within limited geographical and social "enclaves," marked by a widening chasm between so-called "modern" and "non-modern" spheres? Will the existing activities and assets of traditional producers be respected and nurtured as development proceeds? Or will they simply be pushed aside and left to fend for themselves, sideswiped by a rush to large-scale, profit-driven production and export? Will the state limit its ambitions to rolling out a welcome mat to multinational corporations and foreign investors, following their lead as to what sorts of investment and production are fostered? Or will it play a more pro-active and entrepreneurial role in stimulating all-around and self-reliant development?

In this regard, the issues and problems of economic development in the global South are not really that different from economic debates and conflicts in the North. As we learned early in this book, economics is never neutral or technical;

Table 23.1 United Nations Millennium Development Goals

In September 2000, 147 heads of state met in New York to sign the United Nations Millennium Declaration, which they hoped would symbolize a new commitment to reducing global poverty. The Declaration formulated eight broad goals to be met by 2015 (broken down into 18 specific quantitative targets). While progress has been made in a few areas, none of the goals has been met. And since the 2008–09 global financial crisis, many rich countries have reduced their participation and contributions. Clearly it will require more than well-meaning declarations to meet these reasonable goals. It will require a forceful, resourced commitment – just like a war. Ironically, this war (on global poverty) would actually cost much less than the real-world military conflicts which the world fights with depressing regularity.

1. Eradicate extreme poverty and hunger.
2. Achieve universal primary education.
3. Promote gender equality and empower women.
4. Reduce child mortality.
5. Improve maternal health.
6. Combat HIV/AIDS, malaria and other diseases.
7. Ensure environmental sustainability.
8. Develop a global partnership for development.

---

it is always political and contested. Who controls investment, production, and distribution? Who does the work, and who benefits from that work? And whose interests are served by the decisions that are made?

Development, undevelopment, and underdevelopment

In many ways, the plight of the global South is more sinister than just an absence or failure of development. To a large degree, the condition of the South is actually the *result* of the same economic processes which produced successful development in the North. In this view, it is not that poor countries failed to develop – rather, it's that global capitalism assigned them this particular, undesirable role. These countries, therefore, are not just undeveloped; they are *under*developed. They have not been "sidestepped" by growth and progress. In fact, they are an integral part of the global economy.

Several historical and economic factors help to explain underdevelopment – that is, the process through which the global economic system actually pushes poor countries backward:

- **Colonialism**   Strictly speaking, there are not many formal colonies left in the world (most of them small islands). But the violent and disruptive legacy of colonialism continues to undermine development in much of the South. Post-colonial national borders rarely reflect genuine cultural or linguistic realities, causing unending political and ethnic strife. Former colonial powers retain huge economic and political influence, allowing them to continue exploiting resources and labour in new ways. Many countries never had a chance to achieve stability or democracy, given the turmoil (and usually war) that accompanied decolonization.
- **Specialization in resources**   Another legacy of colonialism, reinforced after decolonization, has been the specialization of most poor countries in **PRIMARY PRODUCTS** (including agriculture, minerals, forestry, and other resource-based industries). The growth of primary industries can play a supporting role in kickstarting development. But there are drawbacks to relying too much on primary goods. In the long run, resource prices tend to decline (relative to manufactured goods and services); primary industries face risks of depletion and environmental degradation; primary industries have limited potential for productivity growth … and powerful developed countries have an annoying tendency to invade whenever the security of a key resource (like oil) is threatened!
- **FOREIGN DIRECT INVESTMENT**   Incoming FDI can provide a "host" country with capital investment, technological know-how, and management expertise. But here, again, too much of a good thing can become harmful.

Countries which are highly dependent on FDI suffer from a long-run failure to develop home-grown technological and managerial expertise. And they often end up paying more profit back to foreign investors than they received in incoming investment in the first place. Foreign debt is even worse: it carries an obligation to pay interest back to Northern lenders, but without any improvement in the borrowing country's productive capacity. Far from constituting a form of "assistance" to poor countries, foreign loans have been a massive economic dead weight around their necks.

- **Uneven development and cumulative causation** Free-market forces have an inherent tendency to imbalance that works against countries in the South – simply because they entered the development process later. The now-developed countries established an early lead in the production of more advanced products. That initial advantage was reinforced through ECONOMIES OF SCALE and other efficiency gains. The early leaders became more dominant through competition, making it even harder for newcomers to enter these industries. Unless Southern governments deliberately disrupt market forces in order to counter the North's advantage (through the use of interventionist investment and trade policies), free trade can "trap" Southern economies in a state of underdevelopment. Capitalism regularly displays this tendency to UNEVEN DEVELOPMENT: between companies, regions, and entire countries, reinforced by the logic of profit and competition. The North-South gap is one the most damaging examples of this process of "cumulative causation," whereby the rich get richer and the poor get poorer.

- **Neoliberal policy** One of the most important ways that globalization (as currently practiced, anyway) holds back the countries of the South is via the often-dictatorial advice given to poor countries by officials of the INTERNATIONAL MONETARY FUND and the WORLD BANK. In return for needed financial aid, these institutions have enforced a "hands-off" policy approach in most of the South: cementing free trade, free capital mobility, and government spending cuts. Unfortunately, this has generally made it even more difficult for these countries to escape underdevelopment. Perversely, developing countries which ignored or rejected those postulates (including China and much of Latin America) have been much more successful both in developing their economies, and ensuring that the benefits of development translate into reduced poverty.

For these reasons and more, poor countries face an uphill struggle to successfully launch the development process. Yes, wages are low in poor countries, and this can provide an incentive for Northern businesses to relocate some investment to the South (a process which evens out North–South differences somewhat – although at the expense of Northern workers). But this only occurs in certain conditions: if

Southern governments successfully establish the broader economic and political preconditions for productivity, profitability, and stability, and if political conditions within the Southern countries permit the broad sharing of economic gains throughout society. The South's poverty (which explains its low wages) is never, on its own, a recipe for *escaping* poverty.

Wrong Turn

"The application of mistaken economic theories would not be such a problem if the end of first colonialism and then communism had not given the IMF and the World Bank the opportunity to greatly expand their respective original mandates, to vastly extend their reach. Today these institutions have become dominant players in the world economy. Not only countries seeking their help but also those seeking their 'seal of approval' so that they can better access international financial markets must follow their economic prescriptions, which reflect their free-market ideologies and theories. The result for many people has been poverty and for many countries social and political chaos. The IMF has made mistakes in all areas it has been involved in."

Joseph Stiglitz, former Chief Economist of the World Bank (2003).

Recent development successes ... and failures

So in general, the economic deck is still stacked against poor countries. Assembling the right conditions and ingredients to launch development remains a daunting, often overwhelming task. The many advantages enjoyed by developed countries tend to strengthen their position in dealing with the global South, thus amplifying the grim inequality that already typifies the world economy.

But development is not impossible. A few countries have managed to do this in recent decades, proving that development can still occur under globalization (despite the roadblocks noted above). However, far from vindicating neoliberal policies, these success stories reflect a rather surprising departure from orthodox economic prescriptions.

By far the most important examples of successful development in recent years have been the East Asian economies. Japan's spectacular rise after World War II blazed the trail. Other regional economies followed suit (including Korea, Taiwan, Hong Kong, and Malaysia), each putting their own stamp on the recipe that Japan pioneered.

All of these countries relied on strong state intervention to guide the development process. (As we learned in Chapter 20, this was also true of Britain and the other early capitalist economies.) Very rapid investment was supported by government tax policy, capital subsidies, and financial regulations. Exports played a crucial role, but not in the manner imagined by neoclassical free-trade theory. Like the eighteenth-century Mercantilists, the Asian countries generated large trade surpluses through aggressive exports (reinforced by powerful constraints on imports). They welcomed foreign investment and foreign technology, but required that know-how be quickly transferred to domestic firms. Soon the imitators became the imitated, as Asian firms set global benchmarks for productivity, quality, and innovation. Incomes grew rapidly (for workers, too), thanks in part to a cautious, paternalistic form of CORPORATISM: a system in which income distribution is managed jointly by government, businesses, and unions.

The East Asian model is not without its problems. Attempts to regulate finance in order to accelerate real investment have been undermined by recurrent financial crises (such as Japan's decade-long real-estate meltdown that began in 1990, or the shorter-lived Asian financial crisis of 1997). Asia's export success, meanwhile, directly contributes to lost production and employment in its trading partners (whose chronic trade deficits are the other side of Asia's export-led coin). It is an open question how long those countries (especially the US) will tolerate huge trade deficits.

The history of this state-led development strategy is being rewritten, in very large font, by modern China. Beginning in the late 1980s, China's government reintroduced an explicitly capitalist economic policy in which growth is led by private investment (including both new domestic capitalists, and multinational companies lured by China's ultra-low labour costs and massive market). Like the East Asian economies which preceded it, China's strategy deviates fundamentally from the neoliberal vision of a minimalist state and free markets. Instead, the state is the very active conductor of the whole economic orchestra, wielding many active measures including:

- Channeling and regulating finance to support extremely rapid capital investment (amounting to 40 percent or more of GDP).
- Paying special attention to high-tech industries (including automotive, aerospace, electronics, and pharmaceuticals), and nurturing strong Chinese-owned export-oriented multinational companies.
- Welcoming foreign investment, but with strings attached – including the requirement to share technology with Chinese joint-venture partners.
- Investing massively in public infrastructure and services to meet growing needs for utilities, transportation, and skilled workers.
- Actively managing foreign trade to generate large, ongoing trade surpluses – including by controlling international financial flows and the EXCHANGE RATE.

- Tightly regulating labour relations (trade unionism is strong but politically restricted) to ensure discipline and productivity, and keep the growth of wages far below the growth of productivity.

China's economic transformation has had massive implications (economic, geopolitical, and environmental) for the entire planet. China has become, amazingly quickly, a focal point for global capitalism, and its economy continues to evolve in often-surprising ways. For example, while China continues to attract over US$100 billion per year in new inward foreign direct investment, this is now largely offset by outward FDI from Chinese-based multinationals (an outflow which by 2013 also surpassed US$100 billion per year). This structural change reflects, in part, the success of China's "national champions" strategy: a deliberate plan to foster large, innovative Chinese-based firms (most part-owned by the government) with the capacity to compete in global markets. It also reflects aggressive efforts by China to lock-in energy and other natural resource supplies from Africa, Canada, Australia, and elsewhere. Whereas much of the country's initial export growth was concentrated in low-wage lower-technology products, more recently Chinese industry has rapidly focused on higher-technology products and capacities. Chinese planners have also tried to rebalance macroeconomic demand away from exports (which were hurt by the recession experienced in most of the world in 2008–09), and toward domestic spending – including both growing consumer demand and huge public investments in infrastructure.

There is no doubt that hundreds of millions of Chinese have benefited substantially from this transformation. Indeed, China single-handedly accounts for most of the modest reduction in global poverty that has been achieved in the last quarter-century. On the other hand, the benefits of development have been poorly shared within China: shockingly, it is now one of the world's most unequal societies. The economic and political influence of China's nouveau-riche elite is growing, in often-perverse ways (including the emergence of a dangerous bubble in high-end private real estate that, at time of writing this book, loomed as a significant threat to China's future stability). And how long Chinese workers, and citizens in general, will tolerate suppression of their democratic and labour rights, even as the economy grows by leaps and bounds, is an open question. China's environmental record is also very poor (it is now the world's largest contributor to greenhouse gas pollution), although the country is now making enormous investments in green energy and pollution abatement.

Excluding China and the other East Asian economies, there are few examples of successful development during the neoliberal era. India is another enormous "emerging" economy, although it follows a more market-oriented, business-domi-nated strategy, and its economic and social progress has lagged far behind China's. Several countries in Latin America have made notable progress in recent years, also largely by rejecting the dictates of neoliberal policy. From renouncing foreign debt, to actively promoting state-owned enterprise, to huge investments in public infrastructure and public services, Latin America has provided more concrete proof that the starting point for successful development must involve active state management and heavy public investment.

Kicking Away the Ladder

"The developed countries used interventionist trade and industrial policies in order to promote their infant industries. The forms of these policies and the emphases among them may have been different across countries, but there is no denying that they actively used such policies. And ... many of them actually protected their industries a lot more heavily than what the currently developing countries have done. If this is the case, the current orthodoxy advocating free trade and *laissez-faire* industrial policies seems at odds with historical experience, and the developed countries that propagate such a view seem to be 'kicking away the ladder' that they used in order to climb up to where they are."

Ha-Joon Chang, Korean economist (2003).

China's dramatic and world-altering expansion, along with the successful development of some other large Southern economies, has sparked a certain rebalancing of global economic and political power. A loose coalition of major "emerging markets" took shape early in the century, called the **BRICS** (incorporating Brazil, Russia, India, China, and South Africa). These countries pushed back against the traditional dominance of northern countries in international institutions such as the IMF and the WTO. They even formed their own international bank in 2014, called the New Development Bank, to provide an alternative source of state-backed lending to the South. In varying and uneven ways, these emerging powers have rejected some assumptions and policies of neoliberalism; the continuing southward shift of economic power will surely have important implications for future global policies and politics. On the other hand, the BRICS' capacity (or even willingness) to resist the general dominance of neoliberal ideas, or challenge the power of private wealth, should not be overestimated – especially given the precarious inequality that persists within these emerging giants themselves.

Meanwhile, most of the global South remains mired in poverty, stagnation, and underdevelopment. Most Southern governments accepted the neoliberal advice of international institutions to the letter: unilaterally opening trade and finance to global markets, downsizing public programs and cutting taxes, and generally stepping back from an active role in directing development. That this advice has not worked (in glaring contrast to the East Asian and Latin American experience) still hasn't spurred a sufficient rethinking within those institutions – although there are intriguing cracks in the wall of orthodoxy. Even mainstream development economists now recognize that most neoliberal advice to poor countries has been misplaced and counterproductive.

Mix matters: the economics of industrial structure

The sectoral make-up of the economy, and changes in that composition over time, have important implications for economic policy and strategy – even in developed economies. In other words, even rich countries need to keep worrying about their continuing *qualitative* development.

In this context, let's define an overarching distinction between two broad categories of output. TRADEABLE goods and services are those which can be purchased by customers located far from their site of production. Tradeable products include most kinds of merchandise (with the exception of perishable food, some other non-durable goods, and a few very bulky products). Some services are also tradeable (high-end business, education, and health services; and a few lower-wage service functions, like call centres; and tourism). In contrast, NON-TRADEABLES are products which cannot be traded over long distances, and hence must be consumed near where they are produced. As discussed in the last chapter, non-tradeables include construction, most private services, and virtually all public services. (This distinction between tradeable and non-tradeable products roughly parallels the distinction between the FORMAL and INFORMAL sectors in a developing country.)

To successfully "pay its way" in global trade (and finance needed imports), every national or regional economy must be able to competitively produce a healthy range of tradeable products. And so having a core portfolio of tradeable industries, able to succeed in export markets, is a precondition for a region or country to have a successful economy. We'll refer to those core industries as a region's economic "base": they are the industries which generate initial production, employment, and income opportunities. Then, on the strength of that base, additional employment and income opportunities are generated as workers and capitalists alike spend and re-spend their incomes. Most of that "spin-off" activity occurs in non-tradeable sectors oriented around domestic consumers – like housing, private services (restaurants, retail, entertainment), and public services (paid for from taxes).

This relationship between a tradeable economic "base" and consequent spin-off jobs in non-tradeable sectors reflects the same circular pattern of income and expenditure described in our first economic map (back in Chapter 10). The initial export-oriented sales of the base industry play an economic role similar to an injection of investment in our simple economic "circle": they kick the economic ball into motion. Then, the subsequent spending and re-spending of that income by various players keeps it rolling – ultimately stimulating a multiplied volume of total production and income much larger than the initial expansion of the tradeable sector. The result is a **MULTIPLIER** effect similar to the spin-off benefits from business investment spending.

For this reason, policy-makers pay special attention to the success of "base" industries – even in developed countries. They don't normally worry about the viability of non-tradeable industries (although they need to consider ways of upgrading the quality of work and productivity in those industries). Indeed, it's rare that non-tradeable sectors themselves can lead job-creation and economic development. For example, the developer of a new shopping complex might claim the mall will create 500 new jobs, for people working in its shops. But that claim is false. Unless the earnings generated by the region's base industries are expanding at the same time, overall consumer spending in the region cannot grow. The new shopping complex might attract consumers away from existing retail facilities in the region – but ultimately every job in the new complex will be offset by a lost job somewhere else, unless the overall economic circle is expanding for other reasons.

Governments cannot expand output and employment by building shopping malls. More effective is ensuring that the economy's foundation of tradeable industries stays healthy – supported by pro-active policy, and public investments in infrastructure and public services.

SECTOR DEVELOPMENT STRATEGIES (sometimes called **INDUSTRIAL POLICIES**) refer to efforts to improve the sectoral mix of an economy, ensuring that a region or country has a strong mix of base industries that allow it to compete successfully in global trade, and support non-tradeable spin-offs. These strategies include tax, subsidy, trade, and technology policies, all aimed at attracting a greater portfolio of high-quality tradeable industries. Successful sector development strategies can strengthen productivity, incomes, trade performance, and even reduce inflation. Developed countries with a strong and diverse portfolio of high-quality tradeable industries (like Germany and Korea) tend to achieve stronger job-creation, incomes, and trade outcomes. For developing countries, too, the attainment of a beneficial sectoral mix is an important precondition for lasting development.

24

Closing the Big Circle

A complete system

In Part Two of this book, we described the basic capitalist "circle:" a cycle of income and expenditure that links capitalists who invest in a profit-making business, with the people who work for them. Our first economic map, in Chapter 10, described that circle and its main properties. Then, throughout Part Four, we've considered additional players and dimensions, one at a time: banks, governments, the global economy, and the environment. Now we'll add all of them into the picture – painting a composite portrait of the real-world economy, in all its complexity.

Figure 24.1 portrays the main players and sectors in the modern economy: capitalists, workers, the environment, banks, government, and the global economy. Still visible at the centre of the map is our core "little circle" that gives the system its distinctly capitalist character: profit-seeking investment, wage labour, production, profit, and reproduction.

Arranged around that core are the additional, complicating dimensions. Bankers may supply investment finance, and in turn siphon off a share of business profits. (Or they may push credit directly to consumers.) Public provision supplements the for-profit activity of capitalist enterprises, financed from the taxes (net of transfer payments) paid by workers and capitalists. Meanwhile, the global economy introduces new sources of potential demand (through exports), new competition (from imports), new investment (through FDI), new and unstable financial linkages, and new labour supply (through migration). Each of those global links can strengthen or weaken demand and activity; the net effect depends on the relative competitiveness of the economy to private capitalists, and its relative success in global commerce. Underlying the whole system is the natural environment, which supplies both directly-consumed natural goods (like fresh air, open spaces, and pleasant surroundings) and raw materials necessary for production.

Income and expenditure

As in our simpler circle, money flows in two directions around this system – representing the offsetting flows of income (received by the different players) and expenditure (spent by them). For the economy as a whole, those incoming and outgoing flows must balance. Table 24.1 reports those flows, organized by sector.

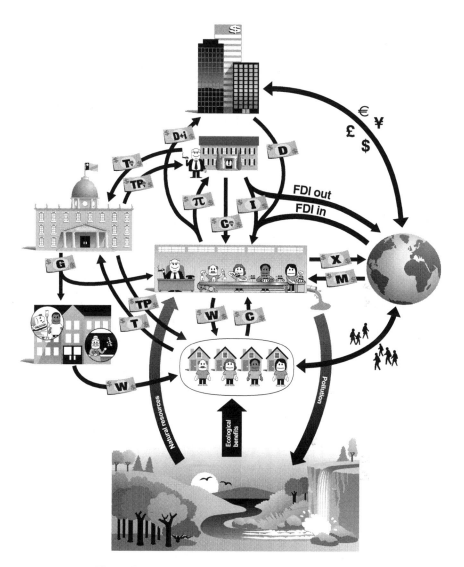

Figure 24.1 Economic Road Map: Complete System

Income flows are measured on the left side of the table. Workers' income equals wages (W), less their tax payments (T), supplemented by whatever transfer payments they receive back from government (TP). Capitalist income equals profits (Π), less their own tax payments, plus their own transfer payments; we distinguish capitalist taxes and transfers using the "luxury" diamond ($T_\Diamond$ and $TP_\Diamond$). A portion of profit income is diverted from capitalists to financiers, to pay interest on outstanding loans. The government's income, meanwhile, equals the total flow of taxes (from capitalists and workers, $T + T_\Diamond$), minus transfers paid back to the

---

Who's Who?

To help the audience make sense of the often-convoluted plot, opera companies always provide a handy synopsis that summarizes who everyone is, and what they do to each other. In the same spirit, here is a summary of the major actors who appear on our economic stage, and the major ways they relate:

Key Players

Workers Make up about 85 percent of society; perform labour for wages and salaries.

Capitalists Major owners and top managers of companies; constitute perhaps 2 percent of society, but own most real capital; initiate investment and organize production in pursuit of profit.

Environment Source of direct ecological benefits and natural resources; dumping ground for pollution.

Banks A special kind of private company that creates credit for business, and captures a portion of profit in return; may also create credit for other uses (like consumer spending or asset speculation).

Government Provides goods and services, financed with taxes received from workers and capitalists; some provision is procured from private businesses, while some is produced directly in public workplaces; government also redistributes income through transfer payments, and regulates production.

World Other countries linked to our economy via trade, investment, finance, and migration.

Key Flows

Investment (I) Spending on new real capital; sets production in motion.

Wages (W) Received by employees in return for work.

Profits (Π) The surplus received by capitalists after selling their output and paying their bills (including labour costs).

Consumption (C) Spending on goods and services needed for personal

▶

---

two classes of households. So the deduction of taxes from the worker and capitalist accounts is offset by their inclusion as income within the government account. For the economy as a whole, total income still equals simply the sum of *before-tax* wages and profits – and hence taxes net out (and disappear) from the bottom line of Table 24.1.

The right side of Table 24.1, meanwhile, measures expenditure flows. As before, workers "spend what they get": essentially all their wages (over their lifecycle) are devoted to mass consumption (C). Capitalists have more choice in spending their (much larger) incomes: on luxury consumption (C_0), or on re-investments in survival and well-being. Workers spend essentially all of their wages on mass consumption; capitalists spend some of their profits on luxury consumption (C_0).

Ecological Benefits   The essential and pleasurable things we derive directly from nature: fresh air, water, space.

Natural Resources   Products harvested from the natural environment for use in production.

Pollution   Wastes expelled back into the natural environment as a side-effect of economic activity.

Debt (D)   Banks create loans to allow real businesses to expand their operations, to allow consumers to spend more than their income, or to allow speculators to pay inflated prices for assets.

Interest (i)   Loans must be paid back with interest to the bank, siphoning off a share of business profits or household incomes.

Government Provision (G)   Governments finance the provision of certain goods and services to meet public demands.

Procurement (P)   Some government provision is "outsourced" to private firms through government procurement.

Taxes (T)   To pay for public services, governments collect taxes from workers (T) and capitalists (T_0).

Transfer Payments (TP)   Some tax revenues are paid back to both classes as transfer payments (TP and TP_0).

Exports (X)   A portion of our country's output is sold to purchasers in other countries.

Imports (M)   A portion of our country's spending buys products made in other countries.

Foreign Direct Investment (FDI)   Capitalists in one country may invest in a productive facility in another country; FDI can enter our country, or leave it.

International Financial Flows ($€£¥)   Banks lend to customers in other countries, and convert one country's money into another.

Migration   Workers cross national borders in search of employment.

their businesses (I). (As in Chapter 17, we have lumped bankers' consumption in with the capitalists'.) Government provision (G) provides an additional spending boost. Internationally, foreign purchases of domestic products (via exports, X) add to total expenditure. But this is offset by domestic purchases of foreign-made products (imports, M), which divert a share of domestic spending away from domestic production. The difference between the two (exports minus imports) equals the trade balance (also known as "net exports"). If the trade balance is positive (a trade surplus), then foreign trade enhances total expenditure on domestic production; if it is negative (a trade deficit), then foreign trade undermines domestic production.

Table 24.1 Income and Expenditure: Complete System

Class/Sector	Income	Expenditure
Workers	After-tax wages (W − T + TP)	Worker consumption (C)
Capitalists	+ After-tax profits ($\Pi - T_0 + TP_0$)	+ Luxury consumption (C_0) + Investment (I)
Government	+ Net taxes ($T + T_0 - TP - TP_0$)	+ Government provision (G)
Rest of world		+ Net exports (X − M)
	= Total income (W + Π)	= Total expenditure ($C + C_0 + I + G + X - M$)

At the end of the day, an economy's income (received by workers and capitalists) will be fully allocated to those four primary forms of expenditure: consumption, investment, government provision, and net exports. And these four categories of spending now constitute four distinct "markets" to which capitalists can now sell their output: to consumers, to other businesses (in capital goods, supplies, and other business inputs used in investment), to foreigners (through exports), and to government (through government procurement). Capitalists thus face a more diverse and flexible market environment (represented by the four different arrows pointing toward the workplace in Figure 24.1: I, C, X, and G) than in our original road map (which only featured I and C).

(Table 24.1 does not list any "income" received by the rest of the world. In practice, the rest of the world would need international borrowing of some form to finance any net purchases of our exports – that is, if they had a trade deficit. The reverse is true if they experienced a trade surplus. This international borrowing could occur through foreign direct investment, foreign loans, or other forms. To keep things simple, we have not shown this detail in Table 24.1.)

Surpluses and deficits

While the economy as a whole must maintain a broad balance between income and spending, any particular part of the economy may experience an imbalance (for a while, anyway). If one sector takes in more income than it spends, it generates a surplus. If it spends more than it takes in, it experiences a deficit. For the economic system as a whole, all these surpluses and deficits cancel each other out (since the whole economy's expenditure will equal its income).

Table 24.2 lists the same four major economic players: workers, capitalists (including bankers), government, and the rest of the world. Each player's potential deficit will equal the second column of Table 24.1 (its expenditure) minus the first column (its income).

We have generally assumed that workers can only spend as much on consumption as they earn in employment: that is, worker households "spend what they get." As explained in Chapter 17, however, if worker households are willing to go into debt (via credit cards, second mortgages, or loan sharks), and banks are willing to provide that debt, then workers can consume beyond their income. This creates household deficits, and growing consumer debt, which can help to support production and employment for a while. But it can also cause long-term financial problems, if consumer debt grows too large.

Table 24.2 Sectoral Deficits

Class/Sector	Deficit
Workers	Spend more than their wages.
Capitalists	Invest (and consume) more than their profits.
Government	Spends more than its tax revenues.
International	Imports more than it exports.
Total Economy	**Sum of all deficits = 0**

Other sectors may also experience deficits. The capitalist (or business) sector is in deficit when its new investment spending exceeds what it earns in profit (after deducting the costs of capitalist consumption). Government is in deficit when its spending (including transfer payments) exceeds its tax revenues. And any individual country experiences a trade deficit when it buys more imports than it exports. For the country as a whole, the deficits and surpluses must offset each other (unless the whole country goes into debt by borrowing from other countries).

As we discussed in Chapter 21, conservative commentators often argue that "deficits are always bad, and surpluses are always good." But Table 24.2 indicates that trying to reduce the government's deficit (or any other sector's deficit, for that matter) is likely to produce an offsetting reaction among other sectors, with very little impact on the overall economy. For example, consumers or businesses may end up taking on additional debt as an indirect, unintended consequence of tighter government fiscal policy.

It is impossible for *all* sectors in the economy to simultaneously reduce their deficits. If they tried to do so (perhaps following mistaken conservative advice), the end result would be a terrible recession (resulting from a broad decline in spending). Overall balance between income and expenditure would eventually be restored, but at a much lower level of income and employment. This self-defeating outcome is called the **PARADOX OF THRIFT**: economic players (whether consumers, businesses, or governments) who try to increase savings by cutting back spending can actually end up with *lower* savings – thanks to the economic slowdown which their spending cutbacks perversely caused.

Injections and leakages

There is still another way of understanding the relationships symbolized in our more complete map. Every economy needs some kind of initial spending push, just to get things going. In the simplest capitalist circle, that boost came from investment. It is the initial injection of spending power, which in turn generates additional income and spending (from suppliers, the company's workers, and consumer industries). The final amount of income and spending is much bigger than the initial injection of investment. This **MULTIPLIER** effect exists because workers can't spend anything until they get a job; new investment which creates new jobs thereby stimulates an ongoing chain of new spending (and matching production) that's several times larger than the initial investment. This is why investment is so important – and why governments, communities, and workers all have an interest in stimulating more of it.

In the more complex real-world economy, there are now other potential sources of initial spending power. The two most important come from government provision and exports. Decisions by government, or by foreign customers, to purchase domestic production can set off the same sort of economic chain-reaction caused by strong business investment. And these other forms of spending also support a total amount of economic activity far larger than the original injection (that is, multiplied).

Table 24.3 summarizes these three major forms of spending injections: business investment, government programs, and exports. They are the three key "engines" of economic progress for a modern capitalist economy; together they are essential to establish a basic level of vitality in the macro-economy. When these forms of spending are strong and growing, the overall condition of the economy is likely to be vibrant – via a multiplied impact on overall income and spending. Policy-makers concerned with stimulating more growth and employment, therefore, will want to focus on measures which stimulate investment, government provision, and exports.

How big is this multiplier effect? The final impact of an initial spending injection on total output, income, and employment depends on a number of factors. One is how quickly the initial injection of spending "leaks out" from the chain-reaction of spending and re-spending that it sparks. On the reasonable assumption that worker households continue to spend their full incomes on consumption, there are three broad sources of this leakage of spending power. Capitalists set aside some of their income as savings (in part to repay the loans they received from bankers), rather than re-investing it or spending it on consumption. Governments siphon off a share of the new income in net taxes – offsetting the cost of the programs which they provide. And all purchasers dedicate some of their spending towards imports. These three sources of leakage slow down (and eventually stop) the multiplier process. At a certain level of total output, the spending power lost to these leakages will perfectly offset the amount of spending power injected in the first place (by investors, governments, and exports).

What if the total GDP resulting from that balance of injections and leakages is too low, resulting in widespread unemployment? There is no reason to expect that this will not be the case; contrary to neoclassical theories, there are no automatic forces pushing the economy toward a FULL EMPLOYMENT resting place. To strengthen overall spending conditions when unemployment exists, Table 24.3 suggests two broad solutions: boost the injections, and reduce the leakages. First, overall output and employment will grow along with bigger spending injections: stronger investment, expanded government programs, or stronger exports. Policy-makers may invoke many different tools (from direct spending, to interest rate adjustments, to export promotion measures) to stimulate these injections.

Table 24.3 Injections and Leakages

Spending Injections	Unspent Leakages
Investment (I)	Capitalist savings ($\Pi - C_0$)
Government production (G)	Taxes ($T + T_0 - TP - TP_0$)
Exports (X)	Imports (M)
Total injections:	**Total leakages:**
Investment + government + exports	**Savings + taxes + imports**

Alternatively, the multiplier effect from a given set of injections will be stronger if leakages from subsequent spending can be minimized. Limiting import penetration in domestic consumer markets, reducing income taxes, and encouraging capitalists to spend more of their profits (rather than saving them) would all enhance the stimulative power of any initial injections. Of course, these measures to reduce leakages (especially for government and capitalists) must be balanced against the simultaneous need to maintain a stable financial balance within those sectors (so that neither government nor corporate debt becomes too large).

And while governments must be concerned with encouraging strong overall income and spending conditions (to promote a greater *quantity* of production), they must also aim to enhance the *quality* and efficiency of production. For that reason, policies to stimulate injections and limit leakages must be supplemented by policies that promote productivity, innovation, and high labour, social, and environmental standards.

Conclusion: a complex, flexible, but fragile system

Piece by piece, our economic map has become quite complicated. At the centre of the map are the core economic relationships that define capitalism: profit-seeking investment and wage labour. And the vitality of that core business-led "circle" still determines the rise or fall of the overall system.

In our more complex portrayal, however, that core mechanism operates in a broader and more diverse context. The actions of government, the financial system, and the global economy now tailor the actions of capitalists, and help determine the overall direction of the economy. These new elements can make the system stronger or weaker, depending on whether they support or undermine spending and production. However, they certainly help to diversify the economy: crucial spending decisions now come from a wider cast of characters (not just domestic capitalists), and there are new levers that can be used to adjust economic outcomes when needed. Meanwhile, the whole system operates in an environmental context, and ensuring the sustainability of our relationships with nature is an increasingly pressing priority in all economic policy decisions.

In this regard, modern capitalism (as portrayed in Figure 24.1) is more stable than the one-dimensional variety described in our earlier, simpler economic map. But at the same time, these other dimensions also introduce new sources of instability and even fragility into the system when they don't function well. The next chapter will consider the instability of capitalism in more detail.

25

The Ups and Downs of Capitalism

The never-ending rollercoaster

Economists have always been preoccupied with the boom-and-bust pattern of the capitalist economy. And with good reason. After all, the lost opportunity, human suffering, and political instability caused by recessions and depressions demand attention from economists, business executives, and politicians alike. At times, the economy is literally bursting at the seams: investment is booming, production is expanding, incomes are rising. Yet at other times, the economy is stuck in deep mud: weak spending, stagnant production, job loss, poverty, and pessimism.

What explains this rollercoaster, which has repeated itself many times through the history of capitalism? And what can be done to prevent these downturns and stabilize the economy around a path of steady job-creation and rising living standards?

A **RECESSION** occurs when a country's real GDP (adjusted for inflation) begins to shrink (see box). A very severe, long-lasting recession is called a **DEPRESSION**. Even a milder economic slowdown – in which GDP continues to grow, but very slowly – can produce unemployment and dislocation. A **RECOVERY** occurs when the economy stops contracting and starts growing again.

Recessions and subsequent recoveries have diverse causes and features; each one is unique. But this rollercoaster pattern is more than just a series of occasional, random events. There is clearly a *systemic* nature to economic cycles. Even a cursory review of economic history indicates that recessions and recoveries don't just "happen" because of random and seemingly unrelated "shocks." Instead, there are inherent forces within capitalism which create and re-create this cyclical pattern.

The boom-and-bust cycle of capitalism poses a special challenge to neoclassical free-market economists. Remember, neoclassical theory predicts that the operation of competitive markets will automatically ensure that all willing workers are employed, and that all available resources are fully utilized in production – so that the economy is ultimately **SUPPLY-CONSTRAINED**. This faith in the efficiency of self-adjusting markets is misplaced at the best of times. But the credibility of the whole theory is shaken to its core during deep recessions – when millions of workers sit idly by, capital is destroyed, and investment goes nowhere.

When is a Recession Really a Recession?

As a rule of thumb, economists In most countries define a recession as occurring when a country's real GDP declines for two straight quarters – that is, for at least six straight months. The US, however, has its own approach: there, a quasi-government body called the National Bureau of Economic Research judges when recessions begin and end, on the basis of a variety of economic variables (including GDP, employment, and incomes).

Either way, these official definitions are very arbitrary. More broadly, it's reasonable to define a recession as any economy-wide slowdown that results in higher unemployment and falling incomes. This can occur even if real GDP was still (slowly) expanding. Indeed, real GDP must grow at least as fast as the sum of population growth and productivity growth, or else the unemployment rate will rise. In most developed capitalist economies, this requires ongoing real GDP growth of at least 2–3 percent per year, just to keep unemployment from rising. If growth slows below this rate, then unemployment will rise and incomes will stagnate. It will "feel" like a recession, even if the economists haven't officially declared it so.

Free-market economists try to explain away recessions as resulting either from random "shocks" or else from the perverse economic interference of governments. But their explanations are not convincing. In reality, the economy has no automatic, internal ability to maintain full employment. Unemployment, as we have seen, is a normal feature of capitalism. And fluctuations in unemployment over time are also normal, reflecting the boom-and-bust tendency of an uncoordinated economy rooted in individualistic profit-seeking.

How a recession starts

A recession begins with a significant downturn in some part of the economy – within any one of the links described in the "big circle" portrayed in the last chapter. It could be a particular industry, or a particular region, or a particular type of spending (investment, consumer spending, government spending, or exports). Every recession starts with some negative event that reduces spending, production, and eventually employment in some part of the economy.

But this initial, focused contraction is seldom large enough to cause an all-out recession in its own right. After all, to reduce the entire GDP of a large economy would require a truly massive downturn within any single sector or region (since the other sectors, generally, should still be growing). Instead, it is a chain-reaction resulting from the initial problem that creates the wider economic crisis. The downturn spreads from one sector to another, following the links that connect different industries and different kinds of spending. If conditions are right, the initial downturn cascades into a broader decline in the total economy, far beyond the initial hard-hit sector – sometimes even spreading to other countries.

As a simple example, recall the simple investment-driven economy that was described in our first economic map (back in Chapter 10). That economy depended completely on new investment spending by profit-seeking capitalists. Investment generates new production and new employment. Workers get paid. They spend their earnings on consumer goods – and this, in turn, generates more production, more employment, and more investment.

Now suppose that something turns negative in those initial investment decisions. Companies might decide that profit rates no longer justify further investment. Or they may worry about political stability, labour peace, or other risk factors. Whatever their initial concern, investment spending declines.

What follows is an immediate contraction in industries which sell capital goods, spare parts, and other supplies to the companies which cut back investment. Eventually, those companies (along with the initial investing firm) fire unneeded workers. Now consumer spending begins to decline, too – since workers who are no longer earning are no longer spending, either. Thus the recession spreads into consumer goods industries. Consumer businesses then lay off their own workers. Total employment declines further, and consumer spending takes another hit. Meanwhile, as the recession deepens and spreads, companies become all the more pessimistic about their ability to sell new output. So investment declines even further (and not just from those companies whose initial pessimism sparked the downturn – now *every* company starts to fear the future), and the downturn is amplified.

This chain-reaction is illustrated in Figure 25.1. Because of the dependence of production on investment, the dependence of consumption spending on employment, and the uncoordinated nature of individual investment and

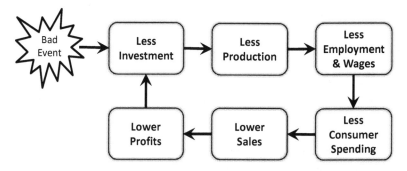

Figure 25.1 How a Recession Occurs

consumption decisions, a problem in one part of the economy – even a relatively small part of the economy – can spread and amplify until the entire economy is contracting. This whole contagious process is rooted in some essential features of capitalism:

- Profit-seeking investments by individual companies are required to set the economy in motion.
- Workers need a job to earn wages to pay for consumption.
- Each investment decision reflects the individual judgment of that particular capitalist about the balance of risk and opportunity that's best for their own company. There's no overall coordination of investment decisions across the economy.

Its interdependent yet decentralized nature, together with its structural reliance on profit-seeking business investment, explains why capitalism is inherently prone to boom-and-bust cycles. Other economic systems (including pre-capitalist systems and planned socialist economies) also experienced periods of good times and periods of bad times – depending on the state of agriculture, technological progress, political stability, and other factors. But these systems never demonstrated the same repeating, rollercoaster pattern as capitalism.

Causes of economic cycles

The preceding example describes a recession arising in an economy with only two kinds of spending: investment and consumption. In the real world, other sectors are also important – like government spending, finance, and exports. A sharp downturn in any type of spending, or in the banking and financial system, can spread into full-blown recession, thanks to the inherent instability of this decentralized, profit-driven economy. Here are some of the events that have been important in sparking past recessions:

- **Investment instability**   Business investment spending has more influence on the direction of the overall economy than any other category of spending. As we learned in Chapter 12, investment spending depends on a complex and unstable mixture of factors: current and expected profits, capacity utilization, interest rates, a variety of potential risks, and the relative attractiveness of competing jurisdictions. Negative developments in any of these variables, if experienced by enough businesses, can cause an investment-led downturn.
- **Consumer sentiment**   Consumer spending typically accounts for around half of total GDP. So by virtue of size alone, consumer spending plays an important role in the boom-and-bust cycle. However, since consumer

spending tends to follow employment and wage trends very closely (as opposed to leading those trends), it is rare that changes in consumer spending alone will actually *cause* a recession. However, an initial negative shock in any other part of the economy can quickly cause a subsequent downturn in consumer spending. If that consumer response is large, it will tip the economy into a full downturn. In rare cases, a sudden negative shift in consumer sentiment (perhaps because of the psychological response to a catastrophe, like a war or natural disaster) could be the initial cause of recession.

• **Supply shocks**   Major price increases or supply disruptions in key inputs used by many or most businesses may also induce an economic downturn, by disrupting supply chains, undermining profitability (and hence investment), and shocking business confidence. For example, disruptions in global oil supplies, and skyrocketing oil prices, contributed to the global recessions of the 1970s and 1980s. Dramatic agricultural problems can also cause recessions (although these are less frequent in modern developed economies).

Great Recessions of the Past

The Dirty Thirties   The 1920s, like the 1990s, were a wonderful time to play the stock market. Share prices boomed, and millions of average people gambled their life savings in hopes of winning a piece of the action. But like all speculative bubbles, this one collapsed – in 1929. That began a brutal decade-long recession that spread from North America to Europe and around the world. Unemployment rates reached as high as 30 percent. The downturn was made worse by perverse fiscal and monetary policies: ultra-orthodox central bankers and finance ministers were more worried about inflation and budget deficits than unemployment, and failed to take necessary measures to stop the decline and support recovery.

The Volcker Recession   Paul Volcker was appointed head of the US Federal Reserve in 1979. He immediately tightened bank lending and drove up interest rates in a battle to reduce inflation. This was a shocking change after 35 years of policies which emphasized full employment over inflation control. Volcker's appointment signalled the beginning of neoliberalism. It also resulted in a painful three-year recession – by far the worst since the Dirty Thirties – that spread from America through most of the world.

Japan's Lost Decade   Japan had one of the world's most vibrant economies in the 1970s and 1980s. But it ground to a sudden halt in 1990, following a stock market and real estate crash. Then followed a decade of recession and near-recession: real GDP growth was near-zero, and at times the country experienced outright deflation (falling average prices). Even gigantic increases in government spending and zero-percent interest rates couldn't end the stagnation.

- **Monetary policy** Several recessions, especially under neoliberalism, have been directly caused by overzealous monetary policy. Central banks, obsessed with controlling inflation, raise interest rates too far and too fast. The economy slows down too much, and may even tip into outright recession. The major global downturn of the early 1980s was caused by anti-inflation monetary policy (see box).

- **Banking cycles** As we learned in Chapter 17, private banks issue loans to businesses and households in order to profit from the resulting flow of interest payments. But banks must always balance the lure of interest income against the risk that borrowers may default. The creation of new credit by private banks is essential to growth under capitalism. Sometimes banks are confident, and happily issue loans to new customers, at relatively low interest rates. The result is strong spending and rapid growth. At other times, however, banks worry intensely about default. They quickly reduce new lending (causing a CREDIT SQUEEZE), and interest rates shoot up. This causes slower growth or recession. The inherent cause of this instability is the profit-driven nature of the private banking system.

- **Financialization** Speculative financial markets are inherently fragile, subject to episodes of panic, contraction, and even outright collapse. A dramatic financial downturn will quickly infect the real economy via contractions in credit, negative impacts on investor and consumer confidence, and other channels. In a globalized financial system, financial panic may also cause the sudden flight of short-term finance out of a country, called CAPITAL FLIGHT, further undermining banking and real production.

- **Real estate** Housing is an especially volatile component of the economy. The price of existing real estate can fluctuate dramatically (driven by population growth, consumer trends, fluctuations in credit and interest rates, and speculation). The level of employment and production in new home construction can also rise or fall rapidly, in response to the same trends. Financial instability is often transmitted through to the real economy through the construction sector.

- **Foreign trade** A recession can easily spread from one country to another via its impact on trade flows. Suppose one country suffers a major recession. If it has a trading partner which depends heavily on export sales to that country, it too may enter recession, as its exports decline. For example, consider the situation of Canada: its economy depends heavily on exports, almost 90 percent of which go to the US. A recession in the US, therefore, almost always causes a copycat recession in Canada, via its negative impact on American purchases of Canadian products. Imports can also cause a downturn. A major surge in import competition, if it damages too many domestic industries, can throw a trade-sensitive country into recession.

- **Government spending** A sudden downturn in government spending might also create the conditions for recession. This could result from some major change in government activity (such as the demobilization of military spending after a war), or from overly dramatic AUSTERITY aimed at eliminating a deficit. Ironically, aggressive fiscal restraint can backfire: the government's financial situation may be worse off because of a recession induced by spending cuts, than it was with the original deficit.

In summary, there are many different potential causes for a recession. What all recessions have in common, however, is that some initial downturn cascades through the consecutive links connecting companies, consumers, and industries. This is what ultimately creates the broader and more painful crisis.

Ending (and preventing) recessions

After a few months, or even years, of decline and contraction, the economy eventually shifts out of its doldrums, and growth commences once again. Various factors may contribute to the turnaround. Consumer spending may continue at some basic level, even if unemployment is high, as families dip into savings and other resources to meet basic consumption needs. Financial panics eventually run their course, allowing investors to pick up the pieces and start searching for bargains. Business costs may decline in the face of bankruptcies, unemployment, and excess inventories, and that may boost profit enough to spur new investment. In all of these cases, spending eventually begins to recover in at least one major part of the economy. This in turn creates positive spin-off benefits and spillovers that eventually spark a wider recovery. The same chain-reactions that caused the recession may now begin to operate in a positive direction.

This spontaneous recovery is slow and unreliable, however. So in modern times governments try to short-circuit recessions with proactive efforts to stop the contraction and spur recovery. These measures are called COUNTER-CYCLICAL POLICIES, because they represent a deliberate effort to interrupt the boom-and-bust cycle of the economy. And the use of counter-cyclical policies has continued under neoliberalism. In fact, if anything, these policies are more sophisticated and powerful than ever. No government is willing to tolerate the economic (and political) costs that come with prolonged recession, without at least trying to get the economy back on track.

The most common counter-cyclical tool used in modern capitalism is MONETARY POLICY. Central banks cut interest rates to speed up growth, and thus guide the economy back to a desired level of output and employment. (As we saw in Chapter 18, their goal is *not* full employment: central bankers prefer a certain, ongoing level of unemployment as a cushion against workers' wage demands.) Central bankers watch economic trends very closely, gathering vast amounts of data. And they move quickly when necessary to adjust interest rates, which in turn affect economic activity in many ways (via investment, consumer spending, and even exports). However, interest rates take a long time to have their full effect on spending power (generally about two years). And when confidence has been shattered by a severe crisis, and purchasing power has collapsed, then even interest rates of zero won't have much stimulative effect: when neither businesses nor consumers are confident enough to borrow and spend, cutting interest rates is like pushing on a string. Governments can use other financial tools, in addition to interest rate adjustments, to spur growth via the monetary system – such as adjustments in banking regulations, or issuing new credit directly from the central bank (a technique called QUANTITATIVE EASING).

The other main tool for smoothing out economic bumps is counter-cyclical FISCAL POLICY. Governments adjust their spending (and the taxes they collect to pay for that spending), in order to strengthen (or cool down) the economy. In a recession, governments can increase public spending to spur employment and production. It can also cut taxes to spur private spending – although tax cuts are indirect and less powerful (since consumers, especially higher-income households, don't fully or immediately spend their full tax savings). In contrast, if the economy is growing too quickly, then the government can reduce spending or raise taxes to cool off activity.

There are two broad types of counter-cyclical fiscal policy. DISCRETIONARY FISCAL POLICY consists of incremental, proactive programs or projects undertaken by government in response to a recession. On the other hand, AUTOMATIC STABILIZERS are fiscal tools which act immediately to smooth out cycles – without any deliberate action by governments at all. For example, income taxes are automatically stabilizing: when incomes fall, taxes automatically fall too, and this offsets some of the contraction in spending that would otherwise have occurred. Income security programs such as unemployment insurance and welfare benefits are also automatically stabilizing: they protect a portion of lost household income (and hence a proportion of consumer spending) during a downturn.

Merely having a relatively larger public sector in the first place can itself dampen economic cycles. Government programs such as education, health care, and other public services are not subject to the same profit motive, and hence the same boom-and-bust pattern, as private business production. The public sector thus tends to be an oasis of stability during recessions. It is much less vulnerable to contagious contraction than the private sector.

Unfortunately, some conservative politicians argue for measures that undermine the stabilizing power of government programs, and would in fact make government a *destabilizing* economic force. Neoliberal cutbacks to social programs (especially income security programs), and reductions in the taxes that once paid for those programs, have undermined the power of automatic stabilizers, leaving the economy more vulnerable to a chain-reaction recession. Even worse are **BALANCED BUDGET LAWS**, which require governments to keep their budgets in balance (with no deficit) – even during a recession. Under these laws, government must either increase taxes or cut spending during recession – either of which only makes the recession worse. Motivated by an ideological hatred of deficits, therefore, these policies have the perverse effect of *exaggerating* the economic swings that arise in the private sector.

Long waves

The preceding discussion has focused on relatively short-term ups and downs in economic performance – recessions that might last a year or two, followed by several years of growth, followed by another recession. Alongside these short-term fluctuations, however, a parallel cyclical pattern is also visible. Capitalism also demonstrates a pattern of very long-run cycles (or **LONG WAVES**), alternating extended episodes of relatively vibrant growth (lasting for several decades) with long periods of sluggishness and stagnation (if not outright recession).

The postwar Golden Age (1945–75) was one such sustained expansion. So was a 30-year period in the mid-nineteenth century, when growth was spurred by massive investments in railways. The early growth of heavy industry, and the early expansion of mass-production manufacturing, stimulated another sustained expansion during the 20 years prior to World War I. These vibrant periods alternated with extended periods of slow growth, recession, or even depression (as occurred in the 1930s).

The causes and patterns of these long waves are not fully understood by economists, although some key factors are visible in every long swing:

- **Technology** A clumping of fundamental (and profitable) technological innovations seems to be a common feature of most long upswings: railways in the 1850s; heavy industry and mass production in the early twentieth century; television, communication, and transportation in the postwar Golden Age.
- **Investment** Capitalism always depends on private investment. But investment spending is especially strong during these long upswings. This reflects an exuberant and long-lived conviction among capitalists that healthy profits are there for the making.
- **Politics** Every long upswing is also marked by a stable and well-functioning (from the perspective of capitalists, anyway) set of political institutions,

practices, and power relationships – both within individual countries, and internationally. These institutions are needed to control labour and manage income distribution (in a manner which keeps workers satisfied, but enriches capitalists), and also to manage overall economic affairs (including international trade).

The petering out of key innovations, a consequent slowdown in investment, and a breakdown of once-stable political relationships and structures, heralds the end of a long upswing and a slide into an intervening period of conflict, uncertainty, and stagnation. Economic and political stakeholders then cast about for another set of economic and political practices to allow a resumption of stable growth. When that recipe is found, then another long upswing may commence.

Where is capitalism positioned today with respect to this historical pattern of long waves? Clearly, the dynamism of the Golden Age had petered out by the 1970s; since then business and political elites have been trying to reconstitute the global economy on a harsher, neoliberal foundation. Has that effort succeeded, setting the stage for a new extended period of capitalist stability and expansion? Not likely. On one hand, breakthroughs in electronic technology (like the personal computer and the internet) have stimulated investment and productivity growth across a wide range of industries. And neoliberal policies clearly dominate the political arena, shifting the balance of economic power in favour of business and boosting profits accordingly. The geographical focus of expansion may have shifted somewhat – away from the industrialized countries, and toward China and other rapidly industrializing regions.

But on the other hand, there is plenty of evidence that neoliberalism has not truly achieved all the conditions needed for a new long upswing. Real investment spending by business is amazingly sluggish, considering strong profits and a solidly pro-business political and economic climate. International affairs continue to be disrupted by regional wars and massive trade imbalances. Environmental problems disrupt investment and undermine living standards. Perhaps most damagingly of all, hyperactive financial markets introduce regular episodes of panic and chaos into the global economy, and this is clearly inconsistent with long-run stability.

At any rate, even if neoliberalism is working profitably for capitalists, it has had negative impacts on the living standards of most people – and sooner or later, this will throw into question the long-run political stability of this new, "tough-love" regime. The jury is still out, therefore, on whether this modern incarnation of capitalism has really established the conditions for a longer-run winning streak.

26

Meltdown and Aftermath

This one was different

We have already learned about the inherent instability of capitalism: its ongoing boom and bust cycles. While every downward dip has its own particular precipitating factors, the fundamental source of the rollercoaster pattern lurks deep within capitalism's very DNA. Capitalism is an uncoordinated economic system guided by the profit-seeking decisions of individual firms (and the people who own those firms). Actions which may seem rational from the perspective of one company (like putting off investment projects because of worries about future economic conditions) can be irrational and destructive for the whole system. If too many investment projects are postponed, a recession will result, and the initial worries of individual capitalists become self-fulfilling.

In this regard, capitalism is always fragile: any shock to expectations or confidence or spending power could set off the cyclical chain-reactions that end in recession. The last chapter listed some of the factors which can push the system over the edge: the "bankers' cycle" in financial lending, overshooting in monetary policy (fluctuating between high and low interest rates), weak business investment, major swings in export conditions, and others.

In 2008 and 2009, however, the world economy slipped into a crisis unlike any it had experienced before. The **GLOBAL FINANCIAL CRISIS** (GFC) will have lasting and painful effects on billions of people: economic, political, even cultural. And it starkly exposed both the weaknesses, and the strengths, of the neoliberal order. To understand its causes and consequences, and ensure that we learn its lessons, this chapter will review the specific features of the 2008–09 GFC in detail.

This crisis was unique for several reasons:

- **Breadth and speed** The GFC started in the financial industry, and via global financial linkages it spread further and faster than any previous downturn. Most countries suffered a recession, and in most cases the decline of output and employment was steeper than any downturn since the 1930s. In fact, 2009 marked the first year since the end of World War II (when vast armies were decommissioned and war production scaled back) that total global GDP actually declined. (Previously, recessions occurred in a few

---

Three that Escaped

The 2008–09 crisis was unprecedented in its global scale. Most countries were dragged down by the spillover effects of financial chaos and collapse – but not all. A few countries managed to tiptoe through the economic destruction, and avoid recession altogether. It is insightful to study how they did it.

China (GDP growth in 2009: 9 percent): State management and planning still plays a leading role in China (as described in Chapter 23), despite the growing importance of private business. Strict regulation over international capital flows, interest rates, and exchange rates prevented contagion from the GFC from fully infecting China's economy. Realizing that Chinese exports to the US and other countries would be hammered by recession (exports did fall 25 percent in 2009), in late 2008 state planners quickly launched an enormous program to build infrastructure, financed mostly through loans from publicly-owned banks. This program was worth 12.5 percent of GDP, injected over two years; it was the biggest fiscal stimulus in the world. Huge investments were made in roads, railways, power grids, sewage, earthquake reconstruction, public facilities, and social housing. The fact that most banks in China are still publicly-owned helped greatly. First, they were in no danger of collapse from private speculation. Second, they continued to expand credit through the downturn (since their lending decisions are guided by ambitious state-determined lending targets, not by their own profit). Third, by keeping the flow of lending and repayment within the broad public sector, the impact of this massive spending on the deficit was muted (China's central budget deficit in 2009 was only 3 percent of GDP). However, after the GFC, China began to experience its own real estate bubble (concentrated largely in expensive properties purchased by China's wealthy new elite) that now poses a different danger to that country's future stability.

Australia (GDP growth in 2009: 1.5 percent): Australia was the only major developed capitalist country to escape recession in 2009. Part of it was

▶

---

countries at a time, but overall global GDP kept growing year after year.) Not everyone caught the bug: a few countries escaped contagion (see box). But the overall breadth and speed of the GFC dramatically illustrated the risks of globalized finance.

- **Length** A recession typically lasts for a few quarters, and then real GDP rebounds strongly – making up for lost time. No such bounceback happened this time. The initial frightening plunge in GDP was halted by mid-2009 in most places, thanks to aggressive FISCAL POLICY and MONETARY POLICY interventions. Beginning in 2009, then, most countries officially began their "recovery." (In some hard-hit countries, like Greece, GDP continued falling.) But the subsequent rebound was very slow, painful, and incomplete. The luck: China's continuing growth helped prop up Australia's economy (since Australia exports many minerals and agricultural products to China). But part of it was design. Australia's Labor Party held government when the recession hit, and it immediately organized major injections of spending to reinforce consumer confidence and employment. Measures included school construction, expanded social housing, energy efficiency, and accelerated infrastructure. The government also made special one-time cash payments of up to $950 per person to support consumer spending at the worst moment of the crisis. Australia's fiscal injection was more aggressive than those of many other industrial countries that faced much worse economic conditions; without it, Australia would have experienced a recession like other industrial countries.

Uruguay (GDP growth in 2009: 2 percent): Uruguay is a small country, but its economic and social achievements are attracting world attention. In 2005 a broad left coalition (called the Frente Amplio) took office, and began an ambitious program of massive investments in education, health care, and low-cost housing – including innovative measures like government-provided laptops for all school children. This stimulated strong job-creation which, combined with modest new taxes on the wealthy, kept the deficit in check. Strong social spending boosted employment and the economy right through the GFC, and the left-wing government was re-elected in 2010 and again in 2014. The poverty rate in Uruguay declined from over 30 percent in 2004 to 12 percent by 2012. Even the generally conservative *Economist* magazine named Uruguay its first-ever "country of the year" in 2013.

These three countries are very different, with very different economic and political features. But each of them, in their own way, made sure that real resources continued to be allocated to meeting social needs – even as the global financial system melted down around them. And in so doing, they avoided recession altogether. If they can do it, so can the rest of the world.

proportion of the working-age population employed fell dramatically across the OECD during the initial recession – and then stayed low for many years after the "recovery" commenced. Technically the recession was over. But for working people, it still felt like a recession. And the political and fiscal aftershocks of the crisis continued for years. In this regard, the years after the GFC were similar to the Great Depression of the 1930s: growth was never strong or sustained enough to truly repair the economic and social damage from the crisis.

- **Deficits and debt**   As discussed in Chapter 21, any recession automatically produces bigger government deficits. Some government programs (like unemployment insurance) get more expensive when a recession hits; at the same time, tax revenues fall. But the fallout for government finances was especially dramatic this time, for several reasons: the recession was very deep, recovery was very slow, and many governments faced enormous extra costs to bail-out private banks. Public debt grew rapidly, and this in turn sparked a whole second chapter of the crisis. In the **Euro** zone, plunging investor confidence, an inadequate response by European regulators, and speculative greed (many speculators placed bets against hard-hit governments by "shorting" their bonds, hoping to profit from the resulting crisis) all combined to throw Europe back into intermittent recession several times in the years after the crisis.

• **Politics**   It is now apparent that the GFC also altered the political balance of power across the industrial world. At first, it seemed this spectacular failure of globalized finance might spark a fundamental rethinking of key neoliberal ideas. Even mainstream economists, and international organizations like the **International Monetary Fund** and the **World Bank**, began to acknowledge the dangers of free-wheeling global finance. Demands for re-regulation of banks and other financial players were raised in many countries. However, neoliberalism didn't stay on the defensive for long. Once the financial system stabilized (despite the absence of real economic recovery), financial and business elites began to push back aggressively. They defeated (or watered down) regulatory attempts to interfere with their power and freedom. More dangerously, they seized on the problem of public debt to promote aggressive **austerity**, exploiting an atmosphere of crisis and confusion to attack public services and labour standards.

In short, the GFC was a uniquely dramatic and dangerous moment in the history of capitalism. Its consequences will continue to shape the economies and politics of many countries for years to come. On the other hand, despite these unique features, in many respects the GFC was entirely predictable – and its root causes readily visible in fundamental features of modern neoliberalism. Unregulated, profit-driven financial innovation led to financial products and practices that were unethical, unstable, and unsustainable. Government regulators failed to curb these practices, largely because of the concentrated political influence of the financial sector. The economy's vulnerability to financial excess was heightened by several other dangerous trends in the real economy under neoliberalism. Chief among these were the weak state of real business capital investment (and the corresponding accumulation of excess savings by non-financial firms), the rapid growth of household debt (reflecting, in part, the long stagnation of labour incomes), and the emergence of large and chronic international trade imbalances (including an enormous and persistent US trade deficit). As described in previous chapters, these outcomes were directly attributable to decades of neoliberal policies that emphasized profit over job-creation, and promoted the flexibility and freedom of business (both financial and non-financial) over broader goals like job-creation and stability. It was obvious that these and other underlying imbalances would someday erupt in breakdown – and a few progressive economists actually predicted this one.* From this perspective, then, the crisis of 2008–09, despite its unique and destructive dimensions, really represents "more of the same" from financialized, globalized capitalism.

Despite the mass human suffering and dislocation which the GFC caused, and its obvious connection to neoliberal policies and institutions, progressives in most countries were not ready to respond with a forceful, coherent, and convincing set of alternative policies. This is one reason why neoliberals managed to quickly recapture political leadership – even though the crisis, ironically, was clearly their own making. There were a few outstanding examples of popular resistance against the worst effects of the crisis (including the wave of austerity that was the second act of this painful drama), and a few progressive victories resulting from those campaigns. But in most places progressive movements were caught flat-footed by the conflagration, and have been on the political defensive since. This makes it all the more important to learn from what happened: so we can explain these dramatic events, and put forward better solutions to address the economic and human consequences of financial meltdown – before the next one occurs.

Countdown to collapse

Let's briefly review how the GFC unfolded with such drama and destruction. The crisis began with a downturn in US real estate. The US housing sector had expanded dramatically in the first part of the twenty-first century, aided by very low interest rates and lax lending by US banks and mortgage brokers. New construction boomed, and average housing prices across the US tripled between 1999 and 2006. But there was no fundamental economic foundation for such a dramatic upturn in housing. Seeing buoyant prices, speculators quickly got in on the action. They bought real estate not to live in, but to re-sell (or "flip") for speculative gain. More dangerously, they also bought complex financial **DERIVATIVES** related to real estate (such as securitized mortgage-backed bonds); this was an easier and more lucrative way to cash in on the housing bubble (while it lasted). As always, the whole upswing was fueled by an enormous expansion of credit. Profit-driven lending, when greed overpowers fear in the minds of bankers, is always the hot air that allows any speculative bubble to expand to such dangerous dimensions.

The downturn began when many US households (mostly lower-income families) began defaulting on their mortgages. This was partly due to unethical practices

---

* Notably including Dean Baker in the US and Steve Keen in Australia.

On the Edge

"As a scholar of the Great Depression, I honestly believe that September and October 2008 was the worst financial crisis in global history, including the Great Depression .... Out of ... 13 of the most important financial institutions in the United States, 12 were at risk of failure within a period of a week or two."

Ben Bernanke, then-Governor of the US Federal Reserve (2011).

---

by lenders, who issued loans to families who couldn't actually afford them, using manipulative contracts and ultra-low-interest "teaser" rates (which were soon ratcheted up to unaffordable levels). Normally, the risk of default would discourage mortgage lenders from issuing such risky loans. But **SECURITIZATION** allowed the original lenders to shift the risk to unknowing investors, in the form of tradeable securities like "collateralized debt obligations." These bonds were packaged to look virtually risk-free to financial investors, who were not necessarily aware that very risky mortgages were included in their portfolio. **CREDIT RATING AGENCIES** (like Standard and Poor's or Moody's, which are paid to evaluate the risk of different securities) either ignored these risks, or in some cases participated in the deception (lured by rich commissions from the issuers of the bonds they evaluate).

The first defaults turned into an avalanche, thanks to the collective irrationality of decentralized market decision-making. Banks ejected delinquent families from their homes, and then sold off foreclosed properties at fire sale prices. But this caused real estate prices in hard-hit markets to fall dramatically, which in turn caused more defaults. Entire neighbourhoods became ghost towns, as banks and sheriffs drove hundreds of thousands of families from their homes. Holders of mortgage-backed bonds, meanwhile, lost billions. Many of those investors were themselves banks (or **SHADOW BANKS**), and their growing losses caused panic on several fronts. Lending declined as banks conserved scarce resources to protect against loan losses. The **INTERBANK LENDING** system started to freeze up, as worried banks refused to lend to other banks (even just overnight). Several banks and shadow banks collapsed in this modern form of "bank run". Financial regulators (led by the US central bank, the **FEDERAL RESERVE**) jumped in to save some crumbling firms (including US insurance giant AIG, and the Bear Stearns investment conglomerate), using unusual tactics like forced mergers or temporary nationalization. After all, this is what central banks, as "lenders of last resort," are supposed to do during moments of crisis (as explained in Chapter 17). But regulators sent mixed messages, trying to preserve the polite fiction that underperforming banks should ultimately face collapse (as the ultimate form of "free-market" discipline), no matter the broader economic consequences.

This regulatory inconsistency culminated in the Federal Reserve's fateful decision on September 14, 2008 to allow the collapse of Lehman Brothers, a major investment bank – and that's when the damn broke and the full flood of the GFC was unleashed. Panic spread rapidly to financial centres around the world, banks stopped lending, anyone with cash held onto it, and the entire credit money system virtually ground to a halt. Banks in many countries collapsed in the following months: hardest hit were the US, the UK, and the Euro zone. The International Monetary Fund estimates the cumulative value of bank failures from 2008 through 2010 was \$2.3 trillion (not counting indirect macroeconomic costs).*

Even where no banks failed outright (like Canada and Australia), credit conditions became very tight, with a negative impact on lending, real investment, output, and employment. Stock markets plunged, too, erasing half or more of their paper value in just a few weeks, adding to the general sense of worldwide panic.

* International Monetary Fund, "Global Financial Stability Report: Meeting New Challenges to Stability and Building a Safer System" (2010).

This galloping financial crisis was transmitted into the real economy – the one that produces actual goods and services – through various channels. The first real industry to feel the pain was home construction in the US, which had swollen to unusual proportions during the real estate boom. Plunging house prices led to quick layoffs in construction. More broadly, investors and consumers were shocked by the dramatic events taking place in financial centres around the world. They immediately stopped making major purchases. Also, the collapse of several banks caused those still in business to become ultra-cautious in their own lending. The resulting credit freeze further curtailed money creation and new spending. Business capital investment fell sharply, as did consumer spending on durable goods (like motor vehicles). This is exactly like the chain-reaction (described in Chapter 25) that causes any recession in a capitalist economy – except this one was far bigger, and far faster, than normal.

Real GDP began shrinking in the US, Europe, and most of the world in the latter months of 2008. Output and employment fell dramatically for about 9 months. Real GDP across the entire OECD fell 3.5 percent in 2009 (and twice as much in some hard-hit countries). Financial regulators and political leaders alike worried where the system would "find bottom." In response, they organized an unprecedented and coordinated international STIMULUS effort. A once-obscure international body, the G20 (which includes the 20 largest economies in the world, together making up 85 percent of world GDP), became the leading forum for global leaders to plan this rescue. G20 heads of state met in Washington in November 2008, and agreed on aggressive increases in government spending, lower interest rates, and emergency life support for troubled banks. They also agreed to investigate new regulations to stabilize the financial system. Other bodies (including the World Bank, the International Monetary Fund, and the Bank for International Settlements) jumped into the effort. Partly through automatic programs (like unemployment insurance), and partly through pro-active spending initiatives, total government spending grew significantly. This helped stabilize purchasing power and prevent a deeper downturn. Governments also doled out trillions to bail-out or even take over failed financial institutions.

The combination of extra spending and falling tax revenues caused government deficits to balloon five-fold (on average) between 2007 and 2009. Particularly big deficits were incurred in the US (where the deficit reached 13 percent of GDP in 2009), the UK (11 percent), and Japan (9 percent). Some smaller countries were hit even harder, with deficits as big as 15 percent of GDP in places like Greece, Ireland, Portugal, and Spain. At that rate, public debt builds up rapidly. On their own, even very large deficits never posed the dire threat portrayed by conservative commentators. As we discussed in Chapter 21, government debts can be managed so long as the economy is growing (thus reducing the debt-to-GDP ratio), interest rates are reasonable, and government retains key financial powers. Many governments invoked emergency financial levers to get through these fiscal challenges.

In particular, an unusual policy called **QUANTITATIVE EASING** was used in the US, the UK, Japan, and Europe to stimulate spending and ease the pain of deficits. Central banks in those countries were empowered to directly buy financial assets (including government bonds, corporate bonds, and equities) with money created right from their own lending powers. (Remember, any bank creates money whenever it issues a loan; public banks can do this, too.) Mainstream economists traditionally frown on central bank financing of government debts, for fear it will facilitate fiscal irresponsibility by politicians and ignite rapid inflation; those fears were always exaggerated. But in the wake of the GFC, central bankers reconsidered the idea, since conventional **MONETARY POLICY** was not sufficient to the task at hand. In fact, interest rates in several countries had already been cut as low as they could go: namely, to zero (or what is known as the **ZERO LOWER BOUND**). Nominal interest rates cannot usually fall below zero (since that would imply a bank paying customers to borrow its money!). Since interest rates could not fall any further, central bankers sought other ways to try to pump monetary stimulus into the economy. Direct expansion of money through a central bank's asset purchases (funded through its own credit creation) is one way to do that. However, the specific quantitative easing technique used by central bankers (namely, buying financial securities, including those of government, on open markets) was indirect and needlessly diffuse. They thought that by driving up bond and stock prices, those credit-fueled central bank purchases would reduce interest rates and the cost of capital for businesses, thus stimulating more business lending and investment spending.

Central banks created over US$5 trillion in new money through quantitative easing in the first five years after the crisis; in the US the practice continued at the incredible pace of US$85 billion per month until 2014 (when the Federal Reserve phased out the injections). But the effects of this unprecedented strategy were indirect, and not as strong as they could have been (especially in Japan and Europe, where the economies remained mired in near-recession for years). Businesses and consumers remained pessimistic, and hence lower borrowing costs made little difference to their spending decisions. More effective would have been using central bank credit creation to directly finance real spending by government or other public bodies on tangible, useful projects. (China used its state-owned banks to stimulate real economic activity in this manner, with strong results; see box above.) Major infrastructure construction (such as public transit, low-cost housing, or green energy) would have been especially promising outlets for this kind of quantitative easing.

Despite its limitations, however, enormous quantitative easing has certainly (if inadvertently) undermined a core theme of neoliberal **AUSTERITY**: namely, the assumption that there is a deep shortage of resources in society, and thus everyone must tighten their belts. If money can be created out of thin air, by the government's own bank, to buy financial securities, why can't it be created out of thin air to do other things – like putting people back to work in real jobs? The answer is, "It can be." But that's a dangerous precedent. So arch-conservatives (both politicians and economists) hate quantitative easing, and have spoken passionately against it.

A long-term hangover

Historical experience suggests that downturns caused by financial crises tend to last longer than other recessions, and it's harder to repair the damage. Recovering from the after-effects of speculative bubbles involves a painful process called DELEVERAGING: instead of taking out new loans (and thus creating new money), companies and households now must reduce debt (and hence destroy money). This undermines purchasing power for years, unless offset by new borrowing and spending by other economic players (such as government). So it is not surprising that the recovery from this most spectacular failure of private finance would be especially slow and painful.

The world economy hit bottom in mid-2009, after which real GDP in most countries began growing again (the technical definition of "recovery"). But a genuine rebound in employment and output was very slow in coming. In fact, even five years after the official recovery began, there were few industrialized countries where real per capita GDP and the EMPLOYMENT RATE had regained their pre-recession levels. Chronic joblessness is experienced most acutely by young people and others on the margins of the labour market; in some European countries (like Spain and Greece) youth unemployment reached 50 percent, producing a lost generation of skilled youth with little hope of finding productive work. The social cost of unemployment was made all the worse by historic reductions in social security programs imposed by budget-cutting governments. Years into the official "recovery," GDP across the advanced capitalist economies remained at least 10 percent lower than its pre-crisis trend. In Europe, GDP languished closer to 20 percent below the pre-crisis trend – equivalent to the loss of as much combined output as the entire economy of Germany.

A sea change in the direction of government policy contributed to the stalling of the recovery. Instead of emphasizing stimulus and spending (as during the first months of the GFC), most governments began to promote AUSTERITY: reductions in government spending aimed at reducing deficits, downsizing government, and restoring normal "discipline" in the market economy. In reality, worries over deficits were not the most important reason for this shift to austerity. Conservatives in and out of government saw the supposed fiscal "crisis" as a tremendous opportunity to ratchet down social standards and expectations, and to dismantle public services which they dislike even at the best of times. This was the moment, with average citizens frightened and confused, to finally claw back public pensions, reduce income security (especially for working-age people), drive down wages (through a policy misleadingly titled "internal devaluation"), and privatize more public assets. Incredibly, conservatives even used the moment to fight for tax reductions (targeted at businesses and high-income households), on grounds that they were necessary to stimulate investment and productivity. (If you were really concerned about the deficit, you should favour tax increases, not tax cuts.)

Once again, the G20 played a key role in facilitating this policy turn: at a meeting in Toronto, Canada in July 2010 (just 20 months after the Washington summit), the G20 suddenly slammed on the fiscal brakes. The Toronto meeting's final communique stressed fiscal restraint, aiming to cut deficits in half by 2013, and begin reducing debt/GDP ratios no later than 2016. From that point on, fiscal policy in most countries was dominated by austerity and deficit reduction. However, dissenting voices (even including some mainstream economists) continued to warn that overzealous austerity would undermine the recovery.

Shock Doctrine

"Radical free-market transformations were not imposed democratically. Quite the opposite: ... the atmosphere of large-scale crisis produced the necessary pretext to overrule the expressed wishes of voters and to hand the country over to economic 'technocrats'."

Naomi Klein, Canadian author and activist (2007).

"The price of this financial crisis is being borne by people who absolutely did not cause it ... Now is the period when the cost is being paid, I'm surprised that the degree of public anger has not been greater than it is."

Mervyn King, then-Governor of the Bank of England (2011).

The worst-hit region during the second phase of the GFC was the **Euro** zone. To join the common European currency (launched in 1999), participating countries had to give up their own national money, as well as their ability to control and backstop their respective national banking systems. These powers were transferred to European monetary officials (centred at the **European Central Bank**, based in Frankfurt, Germany). But this continental integration of monetary affairs was not matched by a continental integration of fiscal or economic powers, and this proved to be a dangerous combination – all the more so because the ECB has been one of the most conservative and orthodox central banks in the world. It was slower than others to cut interest rates, it was late to adopt quantitative easing, and it remained strictly opposed to playing any role in helping member governments finance their large deficits.

Highly indebted countries (especially those on the poorer fringe of the Euro zone, like Greece, Italy, Spain, Portugal, and Ireland) were vulnerable to pressure from private bond markets – which was now the only place they could borrow money. In fact, sensing this weakness, sophisticated speculators actually targeted bonds of these countries, through a strategy called "shorting" which can generate speculative profits when bond prices fall. This SPECULATION drove up interest rates to unaffordable and economically destructive levels (10 percent or even higher). In contrast, in countries which kept their own currencies and central banks, governments could keep borrowing at near-zero interest rates. For example, Japan's cumulative debt was higher as a share of GDP, and grew faster during the crisis, than those of Greece, Portugal, or Italy – yet interest rates remained very low and no financial panic ensued. In short, the fallout from the GFC exposed deep flaws in the design of the Euro system, and raised the possibility that some countries might actually leave it (defaulting on their enormous debts in the process). It also highlighted the dangers of allowing speculative financial markets free reign to determine key economic variables (like the interest rate).

European austerity was imposed in a shockingly anti-democratic manner. To qualify for emergency loans from the ECB and the IMF, desperate countries (like Greece, Portugal, and Ireland) were forced to hand over decision-making power to an unelected "troika" of officials from three international agencies (the IMF, the ECB, and the European Commission). In every case the troika claimed to be "negotiating" reforms with the elected national government, but those negotiations (given the troika's threats to pull the plug on new lending, precipitating full financial collapse) were highly one-sided. The troika forced through a surprisingly aggressive agenda of so-called "structural reforms," affecting everything from trucking regulations to prescription drug policy to collective bargaining laws and minimum wages. The process was very reminiscent of the CONDITIONALITY imposed on developing countries over many years by the IMF and the World Bank (discussed in Chapter 23). Nevertheless, it was shocking to see such anti-democratic techniques used in developed capitalist countries; this is a reminder of how fragile democratic rights can be when the real power structure of capitalism is threatened. Moreover, the far-reaching nature of the troika's demands confirms that the true agenda of austerity is always to broadly reconstruct society in a business-friendly manner – never just to eliminate a deficit.

Of course, both the painful policies of austerity, and the anti-democratic manner in which they were imposed, sparked strong and lasting political opposition. In Europe the fightback challenged the social legitimacy of the troika system, and thus limited its more extreme demands. In some cases, troika demands were defeated or rolled back – such as the Irish labour movement's successful fight to reverse a troika-imposed cut in the minimum wage. Nevertheless, there is no doubt that the GFC and the resulting austerity have badly damaged Europe's reputation (never fully deserved) as a "kinder, gentler" variant of capitalism. Conservative forces within Europe have successfully capitalized on the crisis to engineer far-reaching and regressive changes in many aspects of economic and social policy – many of which have no direct connection to government deficits at all. The same trend is visible in other countries, where many cherished public programs and social protections have been sacrificed since the GFC in the name of deficit reduction.

Acknowledging the destructive role played by deregulated, speculative finance in causing and propagating the crisis, governments since 2009 have taken modest efforts to impose new regulations on the financial industry. New rules have been proposed and debated, and in some cases actually implemented, to address the glaring financial flaws which contributed to the meltdown: excess leverage, unethical lending and credit-rating, irrational and dangerous derivatives. Lenders are now supposed to be more honest in their approaches to prospective borrowers, and more cautious in assessing credit risks. Credit-rating agencies are supposed to be forthright about the kickbacks they receive from the companies whose securities they rate. Banks are supposed to meet stronger requirements regarding how much "safe" capital they keep on hand, and must conduct detailed simulation exercises (called "stress tests") to evaluate their vulnerability to loan defaults, shocks in derivatives markets, or other risks. Commercial banks are not supposed to participate so actively in speculative asset trading. Derivatives are supposed to be bought and sold through recognized public exchanges, rather than "over-the-counter" trades among financial players.

Will these measures be sufficient to prevent another financial crisis in the future? Certainly not. World capitalism has been wracked by periodic outbreaks of financial panic every few years for centuries. Under neoliberalism, with its overdeveloped and globalized financial industry, those crises have become more frequent, more contagious, and more dramatic. From the US Savings and Loans meltdown in the mid-1980s, to the Scandinavian crisis of the early 1990s, to the Mexican peso crisis of 1994, to the Asian financial crisis of 1997 and the Russian bond crisis a year later, to the meltdown of dot.com stocks in 2000, followed by the GFC just a few years afterward: global finance repeatedly reveals its fundamental, genetic instability. We don't know when, where, and precisely why the next financial crisis will erupt. But we know with certainty that it will occur – because the core behaviours and relationships that make the system unstable, are as powerful and uncontrollable as ever.

After all, the core features of global neoliberalism have not been altered by the piecemeal political and regulatory response to the dramatic events of the GFC. Banking is still a private, profit-driven activity. Even under modestly stronger global regulations, banks still create far more new money through lending (perhaps 30 times as much, instead of 50 times as much) than they have available in their own vaults; they are still precariously vulnerable to crises of confidence among depositors or (more likely) other banks. Speculators still have free reign to make enormous unproductive bets, using borrowed money, buying and selling derivatives that have no rational economic function other than gambling. Profit-driven innovation by financial players will find other ways to profit from asset trading (as distinct from lending to support real economic activity). And this entire hyperactive paper chase will continue to float above a real economy marked by grim stagnation and imbalance: slow capital spending, sluggish demand, widespread unemployment and underemployment, growing inequality, chronic international imbalances, and near-zero inflation.

In sum, the GFC cannot be blamed solely on its apparent immediate precipitating factors: fraudulent mortgage lending, corrupt bond rating agencies, and so on. Rather, the crisis has its ultimate roots in the core logic of financialized, globalized capitalism: the power of private profit-seeking financiers to create money, their power to decide where and how that money is used, and the failure of the whole system to promote real, stable, balanced economic activity. Those fundamental features of the neoliberal economy are as entrenched as ever. In fact, in some ways they are even stronger – thanks to the successful political counter-offensive of financiers and neoliberals after the GFC.

The GFC and the politics of neoliberalism

Indeed, it may be in the realm of politics, not economics, that the most lasting after-effects of the 2008–09 crisis will be noticed. After all, the initial financial and economic crisis was arrested – thanks to extraordinary government interventions (disproving once and for all the false stereotype that conservatives want "weak government"). The recovery has been painfully slow and incomplete, but in most places it is proceeding. Eventually it will pick up speed as the credit money-creating system kicks back into gear (until the next meltdown, anyway). In politics, however, things are still in flux years after the GFC – for better, and for worse.

In the early days of the GFC, there was widespread and often spontaneous public anger directed at the bankers and speculators whose actions brought the economy down. One influential example was the worldwide "Occupy" movement, which started when protestors took over a park in New York's Wall Street area – and then spread to hundreds of other cities around the world. These and other campaigns worked to educate people about the true causes of the GFC, strengthen their resistance to austerity, and mobilize demands for more fundamental changes. In some cases (such as Iceland – see box), these demands achieved important changes in government policy. Elsewhere, counter-movements against austerity, while not successful in winning government, certainly helped build a more aware and mobilized population. In some European countries (such as Spain and Greece), a new generation of radical political party has emerged out of this opposition. Where this happened, progressives were able to use the moment of the GFC to advance long-run prospects for progressive change.

Unfortunately, more often than not a different and more negative political outcome prevailed. Citizens' movements were caught largely flat-footed by the

Crisis on Ice

Tiny, remote Iceland was one of the hardest-hit countries during the GFC. Iceland's experience highlights both the worst of what neoliberal economics can do to a country – but also the potential that exists to reject neoliberal policies and ideas.

A right-wing government in Iceland privatized its formerly state-owned banks around the turn of the century. Those banks, run by new and cocky executives, jumped into the frothy business of leveraged global investment banking with gusto. They borrowed enormously from foreign lenders to finance domestic lending and international expansion. At peak the banks' foreign debts were several times larger than Iceland's GDP.

As global financial markets seized up in 2008, Iceland was hit hard: its exchange rate collapsed, the banks were unable to roll over (let alone repay) enormous foreign loans, and lenders and depositors alike began to flee. The three largest banks collapsed, and were taken over in late 2008. Iceland's GDP contracted 7 percent in 2009, and another 4 percent in 2010.

A scandalous sidebar to the Icelandic crisis was the unethical behaviour of leading economists, who advised Iceland's private banks and provided them with an undeserved intellectual seal of approval. Personal payments received by these so-called "experts" (creating an enormous conflict of interest) were not disclosed. This dishonest practice was exposed in the 2011 Academy Award-winning documentary *Inside Job* – which featured an unforgettable confrontation with Frederic Mishkin, a top neoliberal economist who had written a glowing review of Iceland's banking system (even as it was starting to crumble) in return for large payments (not disclosed at the time) from business groups.

The hopeful conclusion to this story is that the Icelandic people rebelled against this outrageous situation, and charted a very different response to the crisis than occurred elsewhere in Europe. Following mass street protests, a new left-wing government was elected. It retained public ownership of one of the rescued banks, and prosecuted the perpetrators of the crime – jailing former bank executives for fraud, and even convicting the former Prime Minister of a lesser charge. Since 2011 Iceland's economy, supported by partial mortgage debt write-offs and lower interest rates, has grown faster than Germany's. Most important, Icelanders showed that collective action can influence the course of economic and political events in important and hopeful ways.

crisis. Progressives were not ready to fill the void left by the sudden discrediting of neoliberal ideas, with our own progressive visions for reorganizing finance and the economy. Many hoped that neoliberalism would crumble spontaneously, under the sheer weight of its enormous failures and internal contradictions. But this was never going to happen, given the continuing ability of those with wealth and power to influence public discourse, "create" knowledge, manipulate politics, and wield powerful economic tools in their own interests. Spontaneous expressions of popular outrage must be converted into organized and lasting movements in order to achieve real change. The acceptance by most social-democratic parties of the underlying precepts of austerity, and their unwillingness to advocate more far-reaching policies (like the socialization of banks), left them mostly on the defensive when neoliberals regrouped and came charging. Politics in most countries (but not all) have become even more conservative than before the crisis hit; in some places (especially in hard-hit Europe), extreme right-wing parties (falsely blaming immigrants for the whole problem) have had more political success than progressive movements. It is perverse but possible that neoliberalism has actually been strengthened through a dramatic crisis of its own making.

The lessons of this irony are clear – and fully consistent with the core message of this book. Citizens and activists need to learn about economics. We must deconstruct the self-serving jargon of those in power (from the original phony arguments in favour of deregulating derivatives markets in the 1990s, to the current exaggerated phobias about government deficits), and expose who profits from speculation, globalization, and austerity. We must be able to define an alternative vision for harnessing our collective creativity, energy, and capacity to work, so that together we can build a better economy. Then we must mobilize ourselves, our workmates, and our communities into active campaigns to fight for that alternative vision. And so it is precisely to those tasks that the last part of this book now turns.

Part Five

Challenging Capitalism

27

Evaluating Capitalism

A report card

Back in Chapter 1, I proposed seven key criteria on which the success of any economy might be judged. Since then we've developed a comprehensive description of capitalism. Now let's go back to that initial list of criteria, and give capitalism a report card. How does modern capitalism rate, in terms of its ability to meet those seven goals? Of course, as we stressed in Chapter 1, evaluating an economy is inherently value-based and subjective; economics is never "neutral" or "objective," it is always value-laden and political. But since I am the author of this book, I can appoint myself the "teacher"! Here are the grades I give capitalism in each of those seven "subjects", on the basis of my proposed criteria and my own evaluation:

Prosperity: Uneven, Inadequate   When capitalism is growing vibrantly, it can lift material living standards for a significant portion of its population – although never for everyone, and never without a struggle. In the developed countries, most people (even workers) lead reasonably comfortable lives. But even there, many people have been left behind by the prosperity bus. Poverty is significant, and (in some countries) growing. Across the global South, meanwhile, capitalism has completely abandoned vast swaths of humanity. Many developing countries have failed to assemble the basic preconditions for development, let alone ensure that the proceeds of growth are widely shared. In both North and South, therefore, the prevalence and persistence of needless misery is proof positive that capitalism under-utilizes our collective capacity to provide for the material needs of humanity. Adherents claim that capitalism is naturally associated with "prosperity"; this claim is self-evidently false.

Security: Precarious   Even workers who have managed to win a decent material standard of living face a never-ending threat that everything could be lost in an instant – due to individual bad luck or broader economic failure. This chronic insecurity imposes real costs on working people and their families. Even if they never actually lose their job, their home, or their pension, the fear that they *could* lose those things significantly undermines their quality of life. More egalitarian economies (like the Nordic countries) provide comprehensive social security programs which remove much of that insecurity. But elsewhere, economic

Table 27.1 Capitalism's Report Card

Subject	Grade	Comments
Prosperity	Uneven, Inadequate	Student has produced significant progress for some groups, but left many others behind.
Security	Precarious	Even those with decent prosperity can lose it all in an instant.
Innovation	Energetic, but Misguided	Student innovates very well, but needs to apply talent to more important priorities.
Choice	Abundant, Often Superficial	Lots of stuff in the stores, but what about constrained life choices for billions?
Equality	Abysmal Failure	Student shows no interest whatsoever in this subject.
Sustainability	Short-Sighted, Passes the Buck	Failure to protect environment undermines future economic progress and threatens human welfare.
Democracy and Accountability	One-Sided and Incomplete	Corporations are governed effectively – but to what end? Economic inequality is deeply anti-democratic.
Overall	**Mediocre: Passes by Default**	Student consistently underperforms, wastes enormous economic and human potential.

downturn or personal misfortune ruin the life chances of millions. In the US, which lacks public health insurance, merely becoming seriously ill bankrupts an estimated 2 million Americans every year.*

Innovation: Energetic, but Misguided Innovation is definitely capitalism's best subject. The combination of the profit motive and competitive pressure leads companies to constantly seek new products, new ways of producing them, and new markets to sell them to. The only problem is that this innovation isn't always useful: many of the clever new ways firms devise to make money are wasteful, pointless, or destructive. Much of the system's innovative potential is misdirected to unproductive uses (from copycat prescription drugs which serve no medical purpose, to ever-more-complex financial derivatives, to annoying and intrusive new ways to advertise). But there's no denying capitalism's innovative impulse.

Choice: Abundant, Often Superficial Supermarkets and retail outlets, even in poor countries, are crammed with an incredible variety of products. When consumer demand exists, private companies fall over each other racing to satisfy

---

* Dan Mangan, "Medical Bills are the Biggest Cause of US Bankruptcies," *CNBC Online* (2013).

it with competing offerings. The only problem is that while companies offer a tremendous range of goods, a great many people can't afford to buy anything. This renders the glitzy "choice" of capitalist consumerism rather hollow. Unless you derive intrinsic pleasure from looking into store windows (and some people, indoctrinated into consumer culture, actually *do*), this kind of choice is painfully shallow. At the same time, we can't ignore the narrowing of life choices caused by the systemic inequality of capitalism. People with talent and ambition, who could make great economic contributions, are prevented from doing so by mass unemployment, and by artificial barriers of class, gender, race, or geography. This wasted opportunity and mass denial of true life choices is surely more important than the fact that the local supermarket sells a dozen different brands of toothpaste.

Equality: Abysmal Failure   Capitalism was simply not cut out to pass this subject. A deep and inherent inequality is hard-wired into the system's basic programming. The inequality between those who own business wealth and those who do not is stunning – and it's getting wider. Other forms of inequality are also generated by capitalism: between different groups of workers, different genders and races, different sectors, different regions, and different countries. What's more, competition tends to automatically *re-create* inequality over time. Only through deliberate and ongoing efforts to reduce inequality (through taxes, transfer payments, higher minimum wages, and other tools of redistribution) can the inherent inequality of capitalism be (partly) evened out.

Sustainability: Short-Sighted, Passes the Buck   The profit motive creates a strong incentive for private companies to "dump" environmental costs from their operations onto others, through pollution. Moreover, the hunger for profit also creates an inherent growth imperative within capitalism. Private companies need to grow continuously to keep investors happy, and keep competitors at bay; this makes it difficult for capitalism to adapt to the environmental constraints on extensive growth. At some times and in some places, popular concern and political pressure can push governments to protect the environment with regulations, environmental taxes, and other measures. But it's always an uphill struggle to rein in the environmental consequences of companies whose fundamental goal is to maximize private profit.

Democracy and Accountability: One-Sided and Incomplete   Capitalism has developed a very sophisticated, but peculiarly one-sided, method for governing its most important institutions: business corporations. An immense amount of energy and attention is devoted to governance structures, oversight and control, and overlapping checks and balances within corporations. They are all aimed at ensuring that firms act reliably and ruthlessly to maximize the wealth of the company's shareholders. In fact, corporate behaviour today is more directly and powerfully oriented toward the maximization of shareholder wealth than at any time in the history of capitalism. From the perspective of society, however, this vision of governance is distorted and inadequate. Most people are not shareholders, in any significant or meaningful sense. Why wouldn't we want the most powerful institutions in the economy to respect and work for all of us, not just shareholders? "One dollar, one vote" is hardly an inspiring view of democracy. Moreover, the fact that economic and social conditions depend so much on the investment decisions of an unelected economic elite, is itself immensely anti-democratic. Private wealth always exercises a highly disproportionate influence in formal politics.

Overall Grade: Mediocre, Passes by Default   In summary, I give modern capitalism a marginal passing grade. Its achievements should not be ignored; its flexibility and staying power should be respected. But its failings are obvious, numerous, and monumental. Indeed, millions of human beings die prematurely every year because of capitalism's failure to devote readily available resources to meet life-and-death human needs. And the future of the planetary ecosystem is in genuine jeopardy because of the system's short-sighted irresponsibility. Judged on its own merits, the system fails the test. The main reason it's still here is solely that humans haven't yet figured out how to replace it with something better.

You Write the Book: Report Card

Think back to Chapter 1, when you were asked to specify your own criteria for judging the effectiveness of an economic system. Remember, evaluating an economy is always subjective and value-laden; economic performance can never be measured "objectively." Now, using your chosen criteria, write capitalism a report card and give it a grade. How effectively does modern capitalism meet the criteria you have selected for a "good" economy? Send your report card to author@economicsforeveryone.com. We'll post your best examples at www.economicsforeveryone.com.

Mapping systemic instability

This unimpressive report card indicates that capitalism chronically underperforms in meeting the concrete needs of humanity for prosperity, security, equality, sustainability, and democracy. But what about the system's *own* internal staying power? Never mind its evident and immoral failure to satisfy the needs and desires of the planet's inhabitants. Is capitalism internally consistent and inherently stable? Or will it inevitably collapse under its own contradictions and fragilities – like the infamous Tacoma Narrows bridge in the US, which began swaying violently in the wind (due to faulty engineering) and eventually collapsed in a heap of rubble?

Let's go back to the composite economic map we developed in Part Four of this book. The core capitalist "circle" (investment, employment, production, profit, and reproduction) lies at the centre of the map. The other features of the economy (finance, government, global linkages, and the environment) are arrayed around it. Where (if anywhere) might the internal viability and stability of this complete system actually be in question?

The illustrated "explosions" in Figure 27.1 highlight what in my judgment are the main sites of potential systemic vulnerability. Of all the flows and relationships pictured, I believe that these five present meaningful risks to the continued viability of capitalism:

- **Financial fragility** Private finance always functions in an erratic, unpredictable, and potentially destructive manner. Financial assets are increasingly complex, interdependent, and unpredictable, and this creates (and re-creates) the possibility of financial collapse. The profit motive in private banking inspires financiers to periodically push gigantic sums of new, magically-created credit into the economy – regardless of whether it is used productively or not. The best use of credit is to finance real investments in private or public capital. More questionable is the use of credit to subsidize mass consumption and real estate purchases. Most dangerous is the role of credit in fueling dangerous bubbles in speculative asset markets. Episodes of exuberant credit expansion are inevitably followed by crises of confidence and panic that (as we learned again in 2008) can threaten the whole banking system. The modest strengthening of financial regulations and banking practices that has occurred since then has not remotely fixed the fundamental fragility of leveraged, profit-driven finance. Look for more crises, bigger and perhaps decisive, to occur in the future.

- **Global imbalance** Globalization can help or hurt particular national or regional economies, depending on whether they are competitive enough to capture positive net exports and a positive inflow of real investment spending. Corporations do not particularly care about the performance of particular national economies, so long as their global profitability remains healthy. Global imbalances have become larger as a result of shifts in regional competitiveness, combined with the unparalleled ability of corporations to take advantage of those shifts. Without the ability to manage imbalances globally (such as was proposed by Keynes in 1946), this form of globalization press-gangs all participants into a "beggar thy neighbour" battle for markets and FDI – but always won at the expense of other, less competitive countries. For countries which succeed in generating lasting trade surpluses and capital inflows (like Germany, China, and Korea), this unconstrained globalization seems to work. But for others it implies chronic trade deficits, growing international debt, and eventual financial and exchange rate instability.

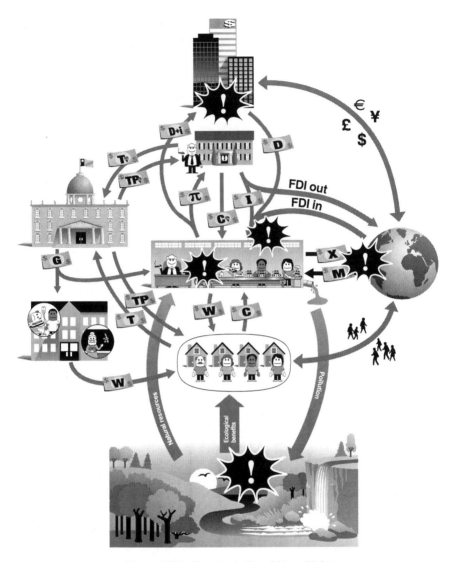

Figure 27.1   Economic Road Map: Risks

Meanwhile, across the whole system these rules of the game compel endless downward competition to curtail labour costs and environmental standards, taxes on business, and even domestic spending power (to suppress imports and boost trade surpluses). Big global imbalances (and the political resentment they spawn) cannot be sustained forever.

- **Environmental limits** There are several worrisome consequences of the economy's unsustainable relationship with the natural environment. First, the quality of life for many people is directly harmed by pollution, climate change, and the degradation of natural spaces. While deplorable, this in itself does not directly threaten capitalism, which is quite capable of tolerating human misery of any kind – unless and until that misery inspires serious political pressure. The economic costs of adjustment posed by environmental challenges are potentially more dangerous. In particular, global climate change will have huge economic effects: resulting from severe weather, rising sea levels, drought and desertification, the extinction of plant and animal species, and other catastrophic effects. Finally, the deterioration of the natural environment's capacity to supply needed resources and raw materials may also begin to constrain the economy. Potential energy shortages are one example of this risk. Oil prices have followed a dramatic roller-coaster in recent decades, reflecting swings in petroleum demand, war and geopolitical instability, and efforts by oil-exporting countries to control supply. However, the world economy can usually adapt to increases in resource prices (even big ones) by conserving consumption and developing alternative sources of supply (even for essential inputs like oil). So it is unlikely that either absolute resource shortages or declining environmental quality will ever, in and of themselves, threaten the continued viability of capitalism. The environment will not truly constrain capitalism so long as the citizens of the world tolerate deteriorating environmental quality, and the risk and disruption to their lives posed by climate change and other ecological problems. It is only when large numbers of people demand environmental change, that capitalism will finally be forced to pay serious attention to nature.

- **Stagnation**   One curious feature of the worldwide boom in corporate profits under neoliberalism has been the notable failure of private business to re-invest its abundant cash flow. Business capital spending in most locations has responded sluggishly, if at all, to the dramatic gains in profits resulting from painful neoliberal policies. The result has been a hoarding of corporate cash, a reduction in corporate debt, and an increase in speculative financial activity (as non-financial companies seek alternative outlets for their surplus funds). The gap between high profits and sluggish investment also imparts a tendency to stagnation and recession in the macroeconomy, since the accumulation of unspent profits is a chronic drain on spending power. Profit-seeking investment is the key driving force of capitalism. If investment does not respond well to the structural improvement in profitability that neoliberalism has successfully delivered, it could be symptomatic of an erosion in the underlying dynamism that gives capitalism its bragging rights. Some of the problem may reflect a geographical reallocation of investment (toward super-profitable China, for example – where investment remains incredibly robust). And even a more generalized weakness of investment does not necessarily threaten the continued survival of the system: so long as capitalists find *something* to spend their excess money on (like their own luxury consumption), then the economy can handle slower investment (and hence slower growth) without actually breaking down. However, if evidence continues to accumulate that the whole, painful neoliberal agenda has had no positive impact on real investment and economic performance, then political support for the system may be jeopardized.

• **Popular acquiescence**   Another core "achievement" of neoliberalism has been the re-creation of a more disciplined, compliant workforce. The reorientation of monetary policy (focusing on inflation control, rather than full employment), the clawback of social benefits (especially those aimed at working-age adults), and pro-employer shifts in labour standards

and industrial relations, were all aimed at restoring the conditions for successful labour extraction. Now employers get a lot more bang (in the form of work effort) for their labour cost buck. This strategy has transformed labour relations and reduced unit labour costs – but is it sustainable? This depends on how long workers remain willing to work, harder than ever, for a shrinking slice of the economic pie. Again, the constraint is more political than economic.

Don't hold your breath

There is no doubt that each of these five issues raises significant question marks regarding the long-term viability of global capitalism as we know it. The internal cohesion of the whole system could be shaken by financial panic, sudden global readjustment, environmental catastrophe, investment stagnation, and/or a breakdown in labour relations and social discipline.

What Economists Do

"This is what economics now does. It tells the young and susceptible (and also the old and vulnerable) that economic life has no content of power and politics because the firm is safely subordinate to the market and the state and for this reason it is safely at the command of the consumer and citizen. Such an economics is not neutral. It is the influential and invaluable ally of those whose exercise of power depends on an acquiescent public."

John Kenneth Galbraith, Canadian-American economist (1973).

But I would hesitate to conclude that any of these factors, at this point in history, poses a fundamental challenge to the whole system's continuing viability. Each one may be associated with widespread dislocation and misery. But none yet seems to fundamentally threaten the ability of capitalism to survive and re-create itself: that is, none jeopardizes the ability of private businesses to invest, to extract labour, to produce, to sell, and to make a profit. Even financial breakdown or environmental disaster, perhaps the most dramatic of the potential risks listed above, will not threaten capitalism's very existence – unless there is an informed, organized, and mobilized population to challenge the system's legitimacy and continuation. This is evidenced by the ultimately successful response of global capitalism to the breakdown of 2008–09. Despite enormous financial losses, despite an enormous blow to the credibility of the system and the elites that run it, despite moments when it seemed like outright collapse was possible, the system was rescued. It was stabilized through focused, biased interventions from pro-business governments (ultimately paid for by average working people through their tax payments and through subsequent **AUSTERITY**). Most perverse of all, capitalists actually attained a stronger economic and political position, in the wake of a global conflagration that they themselves precipitated. How did they manage such a feat? Largely because of the near-universal absence of any political challenge to their continued domination.

In other words, even for these five most fragile links in capitalism's economic chain, I do not see convincing evidence of imminent systemic vulnerability. The capitalist economy is unlikely to fall of its own accord – it must be pushed, by the collective will of many millions of human beings no longer willing to tolerate its excesses and abuses, and convinced that a better alternative is possible. Those of us hoping for change, therefore, cannot wait around for capitalism to self-destruct. The only factor that poses a true challenge to the current order is our shared willingness to reject the injustice and irrationality of this economy, and stand up to demand something better. Exactly what we might demand, both to incrementally improve capitalism and eventually to change it more fundamentally, is the focus of our final chapters.

28

Improving Capitalism

Room to improve

There are many obvious ways in which the economic and social performance of capitalism can and must be improved. Widespread poverty; environmental degradation; the underutilization of the talents and energies of billions of people; the misuse of so many resources. The current world economy fails the true test of efficiency (namely, does it permit us to work as much and as effectively as possible, so as to lift our living standards in an inclusive, sustainable manner?) in so many glaring ways, it's hard to know where to start fixing it up.

As we have emphasized from Part I of this book, capitalism is rooted in two crucial features: profit-seeking investment by private companies, and wage labour. The pursuit of private profit (and the economic, political, and social power of those who control and benefit from that profit) determines what is produced, and how. Meanwhile, wage labour is how most work gets done, and how most people in society support themselves. Is it possible to improve this system, while retaining these key defining characteristics: that is, the two things that make the economy "capitalist"? Absolutely. There are many obvious, incremental changes to make the economy more fair, efficient, and sustainable, without eliminating its essential capitalist character. To be sure, there are limits to our ability to improve and reform capitalism (limits that we will start to consider in the next chapter); the fact that most production depends on the willingness of wealthy business-owners to invest their own money in search of profit inevitably constrains our ambitions to reorganize the economy and attain more socially desirable outcomes. But those limits are not binding today; they clearly do not stop us from making capitalism incrementally better, in most countries and on most issues.

In other words, capitalism has lots of room to improve. We can verify this by simply comparing the differing characteristics of existing capitalist economies. Table 28.1 summarizes key economic and social indicators for one leading country from each of the four broad "varieties" of capitalism that we defined back in Chapter 3: Anglo-Saxon (US), Continental (Germany), Asian (Japan), and Nordic (Sweden). All these countries are capitalist. All depend on the continuing willingness of private businesses to invest in economic activity in search of profit. All rely on waged labour to perform most productive work. But clearly, some countries do much better than others in moderating the worst effects of capitalism, and achieving more desirable human, social, and environmental outcomes. The US demonstrates the highest level of GDP per capita (partly due to very long average hours of work). But the US reports much higher levels of poverty, inequality, pollution, incarceration, and premature death than other capitalist economies.

Table 28.1 **Take Your Pick: Performance of Selected Capitalist Countries**

Indicator	US	Germany	Japan	Sweden
GDP per capita (US$, 2013)	$53,081	$42,549	$36,317	$43,497
Hours worked per employee per year (2013)	1780	1388	1735	1607
Productivity per hour of work (US$, 2013)	$66.60	$60.20	$41.10	$55.60
Productivity growth (avg. % per year, 1994–2013)	1.8%	1.4%	1.5%	1.9%
Standardized unemployment rate (2013)	7.4%	5.3%	4.0%	8.0%
Poverty rate (% of population under half of median income, 2009–12)	17.4%	8.7%	16.0%	9.7%
Inequality (ratio of incomes of 90th to 10th percentile, 2011–13)	6.2	3.6	5.2	3.4
Motor vehicles per 1000 people (2009–13)	786	588	588	525
Carbon dioxide emissions per capita (tonnes, 2010)	17.6	9.1	9.2	5.6
Government program spending as share of GDP (2013)	36.7%	43.0%	42.2%	52.7%
Health system	Mostly private	Private/ public	Private/ public	Mostly public
Life expectancy at birth (years, 2013)	78.9	80.7	83.6	81.8
Infant mortality per 1,000 births (2012)	7	4	3	3
Incarceration rate per 100,000 people (2012–13)	716	79	51	67
Development aid (% gross national income, 2013)	0.19%	0.38%	0.23%	1.02%

Sources: United Nations Development Program; Organization for Economic Cooperation and Development; World Bank; United Nations Millenium Development Goals Indicators; International Centre for Prison Studies.

Fighting to make our respective countries more like the Nordic variant of capitalism and less like the Anglo-Saxon version (which reflects the worst social and environmental performance of any of those four broad categories) is a deserving and fitting challenge, that rightfully deserves our first attention. Whether those improvements to capitalism end up being sufficient, in the long run, to justify its continued existence is another question: one we should also pose in our ongoing research, education, policy experimentation, and activism. But in the interim, there is much that can and must be done to alleviate human suffering and injustice – right here, right now, within the framework of the economy we know: capitalism.

A progressive agenda, and how to win it

By now, every reader of this book should have compiled their own "shopping list" of key improvements which would make the economy more humane, stable, and environmentally sustainable:

1. Improving wages, benefits, and working conditions – especially for the lowest-paid workers. Strong unions and collective bargaining are critical for this goal.
2. Expanding overall employment and economic activity, to give unemployed and underemployed workers a chance to work, produce, and support themselves (not to mention pay their taxes!).
3. Strengthening the sectoral mix of the economy: enhancing the presence of high-technology, high-productivity tradeable industries, and lifting productivity and quality in non-tradeable industries. In developing countries, this is wrapped up with the broader challenge of successfully fostering economic development.
4. Regulating and stabilizing financial activity, and reducing the risk of financial crisis.
5. Moderating inequality between rich and poor, and across gender and racialized groups; and providing better economic security for people at all stages of their lives (including childhood, retirement, and periods of unemployment, ill health, or disability).
6. Providing high-quality, accessible public services like health care, education, and others. This enhances the quality of life for working people beyond the possibilities offered through private consumption alone.
7. Requiring businesses to reduce the environmental costs of their operations, and investing heavily in environmental protection, conservation, and repair. In particular, we need dramatic and quick action to reduce greenhouse gas emissions, and begin the long, costly process of humanely adapting to climate change.
8. Reforming governance of the global economy, to manage trade imbalances, stabilize financial flows, preserve the ability of national governments to regulate their economies in the public interest, and enhance development opportunities for poor countries.

This is a wish list of very big changes that would, if successfully attained, dramatically enhance the human and environmental performance of capitalism. And determined, worldwide campaigns by trade unions, social justice movements, and progressive political parties are fighting for change in each of these areas. Their efforts are aimed both at governments, demanding better policies, and directly at businesses, demanding better behaviour.

As we discussed in Chapter 20, governments possess an impressive toolbox of potential policies that could help to realize these and other goals (laws and regulations; spending and taxing power; control over interest rates and the financial system; and, when needed, the ability to step right in and do the job directly through public production). The attainment of any one of the major goals listed above would require the application of multiple policy initiatives. But as we also discussed in Chapter 20, the *political* challenge of forcing governments to use these tools in the interests of working and poor people (rather than protecting the interests solely of investors and businesses) is more daunting than the technical *policy* challenge of how to actually get the job done.

How do we mobilize politically to fight for improvements in capitalism, and force companies, governments, and other decision-makers to improve their practices? A good place to start is through issue-based campaigns for specific changes and reforms, that can be launched by unions, social movements, and any other group of concerned people. These efforts are best described by the old activists' credo: "Educate, Organize, Mobilize." First movements work to raise concern and awareness about some unacceptable failure of capitalism, and educate people about viable alternatives. Then they organize working people and others to work for change together, since their collective power is much greater than individual statements or actions. Finally, they mobilize the resulting movement to put focused pressure on governments, companies, and other targets. This activism can occur in workplaces and communities; locally, nationally, and even globally. Faced with concerted pressure from workers, consumers, students, and other citizens, companies and governments alike can be forced to accept (however grudgingly) many important and beneficial reforms.

This activism naturally extends into the arena of electoral politics, attempting to influence government policies through voting and elections. Remember, elections alone never truly determine the direction of society. The power of elected governments (even progressive ones) is always constrained by the structural power and vested interests of the small proportion of society which owns most wealth, and hence controls most investment and production. Nevertheless, social justice campaigners need to use the opportunity provided by parliamentary democracy to raise issues and demand change. Some of this happens automatically by virtue of their ongoing issue-based activism and campaigns. By fighting and hopefully winning the public debate over particular issues and problems (what might be called the "battle of ideas"), successful social movements can influence the positioning and platforms of all political parties. Even conservative, pro-business politicians, once they recognize that support for a progressive demand is widespread and strong, will adjust their platforms accordingly.

Campaigning around specific issues during election campaigns can also spill over to working to elect particular candidates or parties: namely, those who support the reform demands of unions and social movements. The relationship between progressive movements and progressive parties is always complicated, however, for many reasons. To be sure, electing progressive candidates and governments can be an important part of the struggle to improve capitalism – but activists must remember that true economic and social change requires far more than simply putting different people in charge. Progressive governments often abandon their reformist goals once elected, in the face of concerted opposition from businesses and the wealthy. Worse yet, some seemingly progressive parties actually become active leaders of painful neoliberal change. Indeed, perversely they may be more effective than right-wing parties at implementing austerity and other neoliberal measures: lingering loyalty to progressive politicians from unions and other activists may confuse and dilute their opposition to neoliberal policies, hence facilitating their successful implementation.

The strategy of incrementally reforming capitalism, while preserving the system's defining features, has traditionally been the ideological core of the SOCIAL-DEMOCRATIC movement. In many parts of the world, social-democrats still advance proposals for a more inclusive, sustainable capitalism – although the broad, holistic vision of systemic reform that once guided the most ambitious social-democratic parties (in places like Sweden, Australia, and France) has been largely abandoned in favour of piecemeal, ad-hoc policies. And the record of social-democrats in implementing and sustaining reforms to capitalism is very inconsistent. In some places, such as the Nordic countries and more recently in much of Latin America, social-democratic governments have managed to implement long-lasting and beneficial changes to capitalism. More often, however, elected social-democratic governments compromised or abandoned their reformist vision, focusing instead on trying to "manage" the economic problems and social tensions associated with neoliberalism. This nefarious influence has been especially visible in Europe, where some of the most painful and destructive attacks on income security, union power, and public ownership were implemented by social-democratic governments (including in the UK, Spain, and Greece). Support for social-democratic parties has consequently declined in most countries, partly due to this failed history, and partly to its failure to enunciate any comprehensive alternative to the social harm and polarization of neoliberalism. At the same time, however, new progressive and radical political parties have emerged to carry forward the demand for far-reaching economic and social changes in capitalism. This includes the rise of Green parties in many countries (some of which, although not all, advocate progressive economic and social policies in addition to environmental reforms), and militant new left-wing parties that have sprung up in several European and Latin American countries.

In sum, trade unionists, social change activists, and environmentalists will need to continue experimenting with new political strategies – both non-electoral and electoral – to win important reforms and concessions from capitalism. One key lesson guiding this work is the realization that winning power under capitalism is never synonymous with winning an election. Understanding the limits of electoral democracy, and the structural pressures that constrain the actions of elected officials of any stripe (due to the unelected and undemocratic power structure that governs capitalism all the time), will help these movements develop more comprehensive and ultimately more effective strategies.

Simply changing the individuals running government will not change the economy or society. But if an educated, organized, and mobilized population is ready and willing to demand concrete and progressive changes in the economy, then no politician or business executive will be able to stop them.

Footing the bill

The world's wealthy have made tremendous economic and political gains in the decades since neoliberalism took hold. They have increased their share of the economic pie. They have changed the rules of the economic game – enhancing their own freedom and security, and turning back most challenges from unions, progressive governments, and social change movements. They have consolidated their influence over politics and culture. Perhaps most importantly, they have reduced mass expectations, convincing most working and poor people that insecurity, inequality, and exploitation are inevitable facts of life (rather than injustices to be resisted and redressed).

On one hand, this constitutes a rather pessimistic scenario: efforts to reform capitalism confront the power of a well-entrenched, successful elite. But there's another way of viewing this situation. As a result of their own success, businesses have more ability to pay for the changes we are demanding of them, than at any time in recent decades. In other words, their pockets are deep.

Every trade unionist knows that an employer's ability to pay is a critical determinant of success in collective bargaining. A company rolling in profits is far more likely to (grudgingly) offer a wage increase than one racking up major losses. The same logic applies at the social level, too. It is easier to demand and win broader economic and social gains when the overall system is profitable. Profit rates have rebounded in most developed countries to post-war highs. As a share of GDP, business profits are at or near record levels in the US, Canada, Australia, and many other developed economies – despite the damage done by the 2008–09 financial crisis. Employers clearly have the capacity to improve wages, benefits, time off, and working conditions, without unduly harming their profitability or challenging their economic and cultural dominance. They can equally afford to invest in environmental protection – indeed, if done right, those investments would reinforce growth, productivity, and even profitbaility. In the realm of private business, therefore, there is ample economic room to meet the demands of trade unionists and social change advocates for higher standards.

Government is the other major target of our shared campaigns for economic and social progress. Can governments afford to invest the resources needed to improve income security, public services, and public and environmental infrastructure? As we emphasized in Chapter 20, even in a seemingly constrained fiscal environment every government budget reflects choices: namely, a government's choice whether to act primarily in the interests of the wealthy and powerful, or to pay more attention to the demands and needs of the rest of society. Of course, the mantra of deficit-reduction and balanced budgets is regularly invoked by conservatives to rebuff demands for expanded public programs, income security, and infrastructure. There are three broad arguments which progressives can use to counter these knee-jerk claims of fiscal poverty, and support their case for more government spending:

1. Tolerate larger deficits and a larger accumulation of public debt. As explained in Chapter 21, it is never essential for a government to balance its budget in any particular year, nor even on average over the business cycle. Public debt (within limits) has many useful functions, especially when used to pay for long-lived and productive public investment.

2. Shift consumption from the private to public spheres, financed by increased taxes. There is certainly economic room to raise taxes in most developed capitalist economies – although the political barriers to doing so can be daunting. Linking the call for selected tax increases to the concrete benefits arising from new public programs and investments (which those taxes would fund) is the most fruitful strategy in this regard. And targeting new taxes at the high-income households which have captured the lion's share of income growth under neoliberalism further enhances their political viability (although any truly comprehensive system of public programs and services requires everyone to pay significant taxes, not just the rich).

3. Link expanded public services and investments to an expansionary, full-employment macroeconomic strategy. By putting unemployed and underemployed people back to work, this strategy would automatically generate new tax revenues and validate expanded government. This is certainly the most painless way to strengthen the fiscal condition of government. Table 28.2 provides a simple numerical illustration of the fiscal benefits of full employment. In 2012

there were almost 50 million unemployed people across the OECD (and that doesn't count underemployed people working in part-time or marginal jobs, nor the millions who have abandoned the formal labour market due to the lack of job opportunities). Hiring those unemployed people, at prevailing productivity levels, would generate over US$4 trillion in new output and income. (In fact, this number is conservative, since average productivity tends to increase as the economy approaches full employment, since employers become compelled to conserve on labour and boost efficiency.) Even without hiking tax rates at all, therefore, this expansion would boost the flow of government revenues by an incredible US$1.5 trillion; that's enough to offset most existing deficits in the OECD, and allow for a substantial expansion of government spending.

Table 28.2   **Where To Find $1.5 Trillion**

OECD Unemployment	48 million
Average Productivity per Employee	US$85,000
New GDP from Eliminating Unemployment	US$4 trillion
Average Revenue Share of Government	37.5%
New Government Revenues	US$1.5 trillion

Source: Author's calculations from OECD statistics; 2012 data.

By using any (or all) of these three strategies, therefore, governments clearly have the capacity to mobilize needed fiscal resources, and pay for valuable services and infrastructure. The claim that governments simply cannot afford to respond to the urgent needs of their citizens is false. Conservative complaints that the "cupboard is bare" merely reflect their manipulative efforts to dampen the legitimate demands of the mass of society.

In sum, businesses and governments constitute the two major seats of power to which our shopping list of economic and social reforms must be presented. Precisely because it has taken so much from working and poor people, neoliberalism can certainly now afford to give something back.

One vision: a high-investment, sustainable, full-employment economy

The economy needs to be reformed. The government has the tools to do it. And ample resources can be mobilized (tapping into the rich profits of business, and the fiscal capacity of government – especially if unemployment is reduced) to pay for key improvements. So far, it looks like a "no-brainer." All we need to do is educate, organize, and mobilize enough people to demand the changes we need, and then go out and win them.

There is a drawback, however, to working through a whole shopping list of needed reforms, one item at a time – no matter how compelling the moral claims and economic evidence supporting each. As we have learned, capitalism is based on a certain logic: profit-seeking private investment sets economic resources into motion, creates jobs, and generates incomes. If our goal is to improve human and environmental conditions within the framework of capitalism, then we need to keep one eye on the vitality of that underlying economic engine: profit-driven investment. And even if our goal is to ultimately move beyond capitalism, understanding how business investment works will help us to better identify the limits to reform, and the specific ways in which the logic of a profit-driven economic system must ultimately be changed.

It may therefore be more convincing to assemble our "shopping list" into a more comprehensive and internally consistent package: one which directly addresses the underlying dynamism of investment that is so essential to overall economic activity under capitalism. Therefore, in addition to demanding policies which enhance social and environmental well-being (the traditional staples of the reformist vision), we must also propose measures to strengthen and stimulate investment spending (including public and non-profit investment, in addition to business investment). These deliberate efforts to strengthen investment will offset any negative side-effects of our reforms (such as pro-worker labour policies, which would likely increase unit labour costs) on traditional, profit-led channels of investment. And boosting investment (and hence job-creation) will generate additional incomes (including tax revenues) to help fund our progressive social and environmental reforms. So pairing our demands for specific labour, social, and environmental measures with a strategy to tackle the core challenge of the capitalist economy – namely, investment – produces a more well-rounded and convincing vision.

Ironically, as we saw in earlier chapters, neoliberalism itself has not done well at stimulating investment spending, despite the painful, business-friendly measures implemented since the early 1980s. Contrary to its rhetoric, neoliberalism is actually more concerned with redistributing the pie (in favour of business) than growing it. So there is a tremendous opportunity now to challenge this gritty, highly unequal incarnation of capitalism with a complete, internally consistent alternative: one that aims both to grow the pie (by eliciting more investment than has been forthcoming under neoliberalism) and to distribute it more fairly. The economic credibility of the current regime can thus be challenged on its own turf, with an agenda that reaches into the core of capitalism – the investment process – rather than limiting itself to smoothing some of the system's rougher edges. This alternative vision still depends on private investment, and takes seriously the need to keep that investment coming. But it supplements private investment with public and non-profit channels of economic activity that also contribute to job-creation

– and which may also gradually wean society from dependence on the profit motive to motivate economic activity in the first place. This strategy combines progressive redistributive reforms with stimulative, pro-investment policies to boost investment spending (despite other changes in the package which capitalists will undoubtedly find unappealing).

Table 28.3 summarizes the major elements of this alternative vision, which I call a *high-investment, sustainable, full-employment economy*. The term "high investment" highlights the importance of maintaining strong investment levels in order to enhance job-creation, incomes, productivity, and technological and structural change. Our goal will be to achieve higher investment rates (with total non-residential capital spending surpassing 20 percent of GDP) than are commonly attained under neoliberalism – but at the same time being much more deliberate in directing that investment to the most appropriate, beneficial uses. The term "sustainable" highlights the necessity of managing and directing investment to respect environmental constraints, and focus on enhancing the quality of output more than the quantity. Indeed, the urgent need to address climate change is itself a powerful argument in favour of investment: both to reduce greenhouse gas emissions (through green energy, public transit, energy conservation investments, and more) and to adapt to climate change (through enormous investments in infrastructure and resettlement). The term "full-employment" reflects the program's focus on tapping the unused potential of humans to work and produce: the one crucial ingredient, as we learned early in this book, that is essential to all "value-added" in the economy.

Private business investment spending remains at the core of the model. Aggressive measures are taken to elicit more real business capital spending, including favourable tax treatment of profits which are actually reinvested in new capital (rather than being hoarded or paid out to shareholders). Other supports for business investment could include targeted fiscal policies (like an investment tax credit, tied to new capital spending), and proactive, sector-specific industrial and trade policies to nurture key value-added sectors.

But public investment must play an increasing role in setting economic resources in motion, too. Major investments in tangible public infrastructure generate both short-term and long-term gains: stimulating work and income immediately, and boosting productivity and sustainability down the road. More spending on education, skills, and training is also needed to allow the economy to make the most of the growing stock of physical capital and evolving technology. More public and non-profit investment in direct production of goods and services (even intruding into some traditionally private-dominated industries like energy, transportation, and communications) further adds to the momentum of capital spending and the pace of job-creation. Throughout this ambitious pro-investment program, special emphasis is placed on environmental investments: including energy-saving

Table 28.3 A High-Investment, Sustainable, Full-Employment Economy

---

Investment Measures:

Business
- Spur private business spending on real capital equipment with tax measures, subsidies, expansionary macroeconomic policy, and other policies.
- Use targeted measures to support investment spending in strategically important tradeable industries.

Innovation
- Encourage more business R&D spending.
- Use public institutions (universities, research centres) to conduct R&D spending and supplement private innovation.
- Develop business–government programs for prototypes and commercialization of new technology.

Public
- Substantially increase public investment in infrastructure and public service facilities.

Human
- Expand public spending on education at all levels (including early childhood).
- Require employers to meet targeted spending levels for on-the-job training.
- Expand measures to improve lifelong learning and retraining opportunities for workers of all ages.

Environmental
- Spur private investment in environmentally advanced capital equipment.
- Establish very high environmental standards for new construction (private and public).
- Expand public investment in environmental protection, green energy, public transit, and climate change adaptation.

Overall Goal
- Increase non-residential capital investment spending to over 20% of GDP, supplemented by improved education and training.

Other Measures:

Monetary Policy
- Guide overall economy to near full-employment; maintain pressure on employers to upgrade work and incomes.

Labour and Social Policy
- Expand unionization and collective bargaining.
- Improve labour standards and protections (minimum wages, health and safety laws, limits on working time, protections for workers in precarious jobs).
- Work to improve pay, conditions, and productivity in lower-wage sectors (such as private services).
- Expand active labour supports to assist job-seekers with training, mobility, and job retention.
- Expand social and family programs to maximize labour force participation by women (child care, elder care, time off for family reasons).
- Centrally or sectorally negotiate wages to seek stable growth of real wages in line with productivity.

Fiscal Policy
- Run moderate annual deficits (including paying for public capital projects).
- Aim for long-run stability in public debt ratio (as share of GDP) over the business cycle.

Tax Policy
- Reform business taxes to reward real investment spending, and discourage corporate cash hoarding or dividend payouts.
- Eliminate favourable tax treatment for financial investments.
- Rely mostly on progressive personal income taxes, and other broad taxes, to fund public programs.

Trade Policy
- Manage international trade flows to limit trade imbalances and allow all countries to retain proportionate shares of employment and production, including in strategic sectors.
- Oversee incoming foreign direct investment to maximize domestic technology and job spin-offs.

Financial Markets
- Regulate financial activity to prevent irresponsible practices, stabilize credit creation.
- Eliminate favourable tax treatment for the financial industry.
- Establish or expand public or non-profit financial institutions with capacity to expand lending and direct it to most needed uses.

---

capital equipment, super-efficient construction and building improvements, major investments in green energy and public transit, and public investment in environmental clean-up, conservation, and climate change adaptation. In both public and private investment, an emphasis on innovation and technology is also important; public institutions can spur pure and applied research, and accelerate commercialization (sometimes in partnership with business).

In addition to this focus on boosting private and public investment, a whole program of supporting policies then aims to convert investment into better employment, distributional, environmental, and trade outcomes. These include measures to lift labour market standards (through collective bargaining and better labour regulations), redistribute incomes (through tax and fiscal measures), manage the global economy in a more stable and mutual manner, and closely regulate the financial sector to roll back financialization and improve financial stability.

This proposed high-investment, sustainable, full-employment economy includes several elements reminiscent of the Nordic version of capitalism – such as intensive public spending on education, health, and labour force mobility; generous redistributive programs, financed through personal taxes; moderate business taxes; and an overarching focus on R&D and innovation. Aspects of the model also reflect the successful experience of the Asian economic model – including important roles for proactive industrial policies supporting targeted industries, and active strategies to manage foreign trade and investment flows.

This proposal, then, is not utopian or untried: all its major elements are readily visible in the real-world experience of countries which have been relatively more successful at meeting social and environmental needs – while still respecting the imperative of private businesses to make a profit on their investments. For readers in the Anglo-Saxon world, this approach should be especially useful as a well-rounded, internally consistent alternative to the more extreme, unequal incarnation of capitalism which they presently confront.

29

Replacing Capitalism?

Socialism: what, and why?

The key decisions in capitalism are made by private investors who try to maximize the profitability of their businesses. In this regard, the whole system is driven by private greed. Good things can happen in the course of that pursuit – sometimes by design, sometimes by accident, sometimes through political pressure. But the core motive force driving the system is not a desire to improve the human condition. It is a desire to fatten someone's pocketbook.

A cursory look at the often-sorry state of our planet indicates vast unmet needs crying out for attention: the desperate plight of billions of people in the global South, the needless deprivation of hundreds of millions more in the North, and the ongoing degradation of the environment everywhere. Surely it is possible to devote economic resources directly to those problems – rather than crossing our fingers that they will be solved through the trickle-down benefits of profit-led growth. Just imagine if we took the economic resources at our disposal (our technology, our capital equipment, our skills, our work ethic) and directed them consciously to eliminating poverty, expanding human services, and protecting the environment – instead of using those same resources to produce video games, glossy advertising, and laser-guided weaponry, all in pursuit of maximum private profit.

This hope has led economists, and others, to imagine alternative, more humane economic systems, right from the earliest, dirtiest days of capitalism. The main alternative to capitalism in modern times is **SOCIALISM**. Under socialism, economic decisions are meant to be guided directly by the public interest, rather than the interests of private owners.

There have been many different theories about why socialism might be necessary, and just as many different ideas about how it could or should work. The earliest socialists were idealistic European reformers who tried building cooperative communities to improve humans' physical and moral condition. Later, Karl Marx predicted that socialism would inevitably arise due to endless class conflict between workers and capitalists, and perhaps also because of technological changes. John Maynard Keynes argued socialism would eventually be necessary to generate enough investment to keep everyone employed. His contemporary, Michal

---

He Was Pretty Smart ... and He Liked Socialism

"The real purpose of socialism is precisely to overcome and advance beyond the predatory phase of human development."

Albert Einstein, German-American physicist (1949).

On top of his many other scientific and humanitarian achievements, Albert Einstein was also a passionate socialist. In a famous 1949 essay in the journal *Monthly Review*, he explained his conclusion that socialism (including economic planning, public ownership, and a strong focus on public and civic education) was the only option to prevent war, unemployment, and poverty.

Kalecki, argued that only under socialism could full employment be attained in a sustainable and efficient manner.

Common to all of these visions for explicitly managing the economy in the interest of human needs is some combination of the following two features:

- **Widespread public or non-profit ownership of enterprises** Companies under socialism might be owned directly by the state. Or they might be owned through other non-profit or collective structures – like worker or consumer **COOPERATIVES**, community-owned enterprises, or non-profit agencies. In every case, the enterprises are owned in some collective or socialized form. And simply taking over private companies from capitalists, and then running them in the usual manner, is not enough: they must be publicly accountable, and managed to meet specified public goals (rather than just maximizing their own profit). Ultimately, in socialism publicly-owned enterprises would fulfil the same economic leadership demonstrated by private firms under capitalism: initiating investment, setting economic resources into motion, organizing production, and overseeing the efficiency and discipline of work. But now the *motive* for their activity has changed: to maximize public well-being, rather than private profit.

- **A larger role for economic planning** In most visions of socialism, many key economic decisions are made centrally by governments, rather than placed in the hands of individual firms. This allows the macro-economy to be consciously directed toward the fulfilment of human and social goals. Exercising collective, deliberate control over key aggregate variables (like investment, credit, the sectoral make-up of the economy, income distribution, inflation, and international trade) would help the economy meet social goals and targets. In contrast to capitalism's ongoing boom-and-bust instability, it should also help socialism attain more stable aggregate performance – achieving full employment, utilizing all available resources, and ensuring that growing production translates into rising mass incomes.

Along each of these two broad dimensions, differing "degrees" of socialism can be imagined. For example, public ownership could be expanded to take in virtually all companies, or it might be limited to just the largest, most important enterprises in key industries. Similarly, planners could set out detailed production plans and price schedules right down to the level of individual industries or companies. Or planning might be limited to broad economic aggregates (setting targets for total investment, consumer spending, wage increases, foreign trade, and other key variables), with detailed decisions left to individual firms. Different decision-making processes could also be used for economic planning, ranging from centralized government planning offices to more decentralized and participatory decision-making structures. In some proposals for socialism, markets (not planning) continue to determine the economy's overall direction (even though individual enterprises are publicly or cooperatively owned). This is called **MARKET SOCIALISM**; it was tried in a few countries, like the former Yugoslavia.

Socialism in practice: wha' 'appened?

The idea of socialism dates back two centuries. And many attempts have been made to implement that vision. Unfortunately, practical experience with socialism so far has not been very successful.

Two broad approaches have been tried in practice. First, a few very progressive **SOCIAL DEMOCRATIC** parties explicitly aimed to transform capitalism – not just incrementally reform it. Examples of social-democratic movements with a more ambitious, transformative vision include the early postwar Labour governments in Britain (which nationalized large segments of British industry), the French socialist government of the early 1980s (which nationalized most banks and many other large companies), Sweden (where a clever scheme, called the "Meidner Plan," was devised to gradually take over private business in the 1970s), and Australia (where the competitive labour market was replaced, for a while, with a centrally planned system of wage determination). In all of these cases, intense opposition from business interests, combined with unsatisfactory performance by publicly-owned enterprises, led these governments to abandon their more ambitious, socialist visions. Today there are no major social-democratic parties in the developed countries still committed to transforming capitalism; their only goal now is trying to *improve* capitalism (which is nevertheless, as discussed in the previous chapter, an important and legitimate priority).

The second broad experiment with socialism was undertaken by various communist-led governments, which implemented widespread state and collective ownership and CENTRAL PLANNING. There was a surprising diversity of experience within this category – ranging from all-encompassing central planning (usually implemented under very repressive political structures) to more decentralized, market-oriented systems. In every one of these countries, socialism came about in a context of war and violent upheaval, and this affected subsequent economic and democratic development. Nevertheless, central planning showed some initial promise and vitality, especially for poor countries trying to industrialize under difficult conditions. As late as the 1960s, when the USSR beat the US to put the first astronaut in space, central planning was genuinely challenging capitalism for global economic leadership. Subsequently, however, the planned communist economies gradually lost steam.

The collapse of the Soviet Union in 1991, and the adoption of pro-capitalist policies in China at about the same time, marked the end of this version of socialism. Its failure resulted from several weaknesses, including the anti-democratic nature of the communist political system, and difficulties in designing management and incentive structures to effectively guide the actions of state-owned enterprises. However, since the collapse of communism, human conditions in several former communist countries (including Russia) have visibly deteriorated (with declining life expectancy, growing poverty, and other negative indicators); this sobering experience certainly refutes any triumphalist notion that capitalism has now proven its "superiority."

Today there are only a handful of countries in the world today that can be called socialist – and even in those countries (like Cuba and Vietnam) the economic space occupied by private ownership and for-profit production is growing. Cuba's admirable social achievements (its education, health, and cultural indicators outrank most developing countries, and even many developed countries) demonstrate the potential of socialism to extract the maximum possible human well-being from a given amount of GDP. On the other hand, Cuba continues to grapple with the failure of state-run firms to develop adequate dynamism and productivity (the 50-year US economic blockade of the island hasn't helped), and continuing limits on democratic rights.

Governments in Venezuela, Bolivia, Ecuador, and Uruguay are now trying to build a new incarnation of socialism, based on the nationalization of key industries (especially natural resources), dramatic expansion of social benefits for poor people, and strong involvement by poor and working people in economic decision-making. These will be important experiments to watch and support – all the more so because they are occurring within a mostly peaceful, democratic political context. The waning of global US influence will hopefully give these and other countries more space to pursue their efforts, free from the political and military interference which undermined past peaceful reform efforts (like past governments in Chile, Honduras, Haiti, Iran, Indonesia, the Dominican Republic, and elsewhere, all defeated with the help of US-led intervention). Some equally interesting, smaller-scale experiments in non-profit economic management and development have occurred at the regional level – for example, in the Basque region of Spain, the Indian state of Kerala, or the Emilia-Romagna region in Italy. In these places extensive networks of collectively owned enterprises (including non-profit financial institutions) have demonstrated impressive productivity, innovation, and effectiveness.

Socializing ownership and production: ten paths

In the wake of decades of neoliberalism, and the widespread privatization of public assets, the mere idea of public or socialized ownership of business will strike many as a radical and far-fetched dream. But socializing investment, production, and ownership need not be a wide-eyed, utopian ideal. In modern capitalism, there are several points of "vulnerability" where private ownership is not working well at all – and hence where demands for socialized ownership can be advanced in concrete and pragmatic ways. Here are ten specific issues where the general assumption that "private is best" can be confronted and rolled back, and the credibility of not-for-profit production gradually rebuilt:

- **Resisting privatization**   Newly graduating doctors are required to take the Hippocratic Oath, which includes a promise "to abstain from doing harm." The same motto can apply to defending public or social ownership: we should stop governments from doing more harm, by resisting the direct sale or privatization of public assets, as well as stealthy or indirect privatization strategies like PUBLIC-PRIVATE PARTNERSHIPS. The successful defense of existing public enterprises can't be just a defense of the "status quo," since many people are disappointed with the performance and accountability of some public enterprises and public services. So efforts must be made to revitalize public understanding of the benefits of public ownership and a non-profit mandate, and to improve service quality and accountability in publicly-owned enterprises.
- **Remunicipalicization**   The flip side of resisting further privatization, is the effort to regain control of once-public operations that have already been privatized. This strategy is increasingly common at the municipal level, in response to the failure of many privatization experiments in municipal services like water, electric utilities, and waste collection. These remunici-

palization campaigns have been supported by broad political coalitions including consumers, community leaders, and unions. In Germany in recent years, for example, some 200 municipalities have bought back their local energy distribution utilities (privatized in the 1990s), in the face of political pressure from consumers and citizens concerned with poor service, high prices, and the poor environmental record of privatized utilities.

- **Strategic industries**   Conventional state ownership of major productive enterprises has declined sharply under neoliberalism, for many reasons: the hunger of private investors for more profit-making opportunities, the desire of governments to shed financial obligations and managerial responsibilities, and the failure of many of these firms to live up to their social mandate (thus undermining public support for the principle of public ownership). In many industries, however, a compelling case for public ownership of major companies can still be made. What is needed is a rationale as to why public ownership (combined with an explicit change in mandate, reorienting the company to pursue broader social or policy goals) would make a concrete difference to the company's behaviour and performance. This argument is especially appealing in cases of NATURAL MONOPOLY; industries which provide essential economy-wide services (like transportation, utilities, and communication); non-renewable resource extraction; and strategic high-value sectors where it is especially important to protect domestic capacity (like automobile, aerospace, defense, and computer companies).

- **Cooperatives**   Cooperatives have a long and important history as a "do-it-yourself" form of socialized ownership and governance. Cooperatives can be formed by both producers and consumers (see Table 29.1); they are governed on the basis of democratic voting by members. Cooperatives are most successful when they receive favourable fiscal supports from government (including subsidies and tax preferences); when their creation and operation is inspired by an overarching social or political vision (in some cases cooperatives were even inspired by religious communities); and when they reach a critical mass that allows them to establish strong financial and supplier linkages among themselves.

- **Green energy**   New green energy technologies are amenable to municipal or cooperative ownership structures, thanks to their small scale and decentralized structure. Cooperative enterprises in wind, solar, and geothermal energy production (called renewable energy source co-ops, or "resco-ops") have played a leading role in green energy production in several countries, including Denmark and Germany. In developing countries, too (such as Brazil, India, and the Philippines), local energy production cooperatives (using small-scale hydroelectric, biomass, and solar technologies) are important sources of energy supply and job-creation.

- **Socialized finance** We learned in Chapter 17 that the banking system enjoys the awesome (and highly profitable!) ability to create new money out of thin air. Harnessing that power to pursue deliberate social goals must be central in any strategy to challenge overall private domination of the economy. There are many different ways to socialize finance, including publicly-owned banks, **CREDIT UNIONS**, and other financial institutions with an explicit mandate to use the power of money for social and environmental benefit; several of these forms of socialized finance are listed in Table 29.1.

- **Housing** Housing is the most important consumer purchase for most families over their life-cycle. And private real estate is particularly susceptible to speculative swings and profit-taking (by home-builders and real estate speculators alike). So this is particularly promising terrain for proposing alternative ownership structures. Like other forms of socialized ownership, social housing comes in many shapes and sizes: including publicly owned housing developments (usually targeted at low-income families), housing cooperatives, and housing trusts which develop residential communities on a non-profit or low-profit basis. Proposing non-profit ownership structures to reduce housing costs and curtail speculative pressures in big cities is an especially promising progressive opportunity.

- **Food and health** Some of the most grotesque outcomes of for-profit production are found in the food industry. The profit motive produces damaging and horrifying impacts at all stages of the food supply chain, from factory farming (with terrible impacts on animal welfare and the environment) to manufacturing (widespread use of preservatives and hormones) to retailing and consumption (marked by excess packaging, lack of fresh produce, and a pervasive fast food culture). Growing awareness of the nutrition, health, and environmental consequences of corporate agriculture and food industries is sparking a willingness to look for alternatives. Agricultural cooperatives, farmers' markets, urban and community gardens, and collective kitchens are all gaining popularity; together they constitute a loose but hopeful "food movement" that challenges, in its own way, the logic of profit. In health care, too, the profit motive misallocates vast resources: spending enormous sums on administration, marketing, and duplication, and not nearly enough on developing the most-needed medicines, or providing treatment to those who need it. There are many potential applications for non-profit enterprise in health care, from operating more efficient community clinics (with an emphasis on prevention) to publicly-funded pharmaceutical research.

- **Non-marketed production** As discussed in Part I of this book, GDP statistics include the value of all goods and services produced for money in the formal economy. But they exclude many important flows of work and production: namely, goods and services that are produced but not sold, yet which contribute meaningfully to quality of life, community well-being, and consumption. There are many opportunities to expand and develop non-marketed (and hence non-capitalist) production, especially at times when the flow of money (and the purchasing power it represents) is limited by recession or financial crisis. Local exchanges and barter systems, do-it-yourself circles, and shared community projects are examples of this approach. Alternative currency schemes (which facilitate barter between small local producers) are another way to stimulate local work and production, especially when conventional money is scarce. Internet technology could potentially foster more of this non-traded production and exchange – although many on-line schemes have their own problems. Opportunities for non-marketed production are especially important in developing countries, and in poor regions and neighbourhoods in rich countries.

- **Education, training, and labour force development** Of course, all production depends on the application of work – productive human effort – to the resources and supplies we harvest from nature. But with the growing complexity and specialization of skills required by modern technology, the task of placing particular workers in particular jobs is more difficult than ever – and there is ample evidence that conventional market mechanisms are not up to the task. Most young workers now make a multi-year investment in college, university, or trades education before starting work. And separately, employers increasingly prefer to hire workers with full, specialized skill sets (rather than doling their own on-the-job training within the firm). The result is that it's harder for job-seekers to find a position that matches their talents and interests, even in times when unemployment is relatively low. Public recruitment and labour market information systems, skills inventories, and labour market planning (to help students pick a vocation that will land them a job when they graduate) would be far more efficient than the current unplanned hodgepodge of labour market services that exists in most countries. Best of all, public job placement services could replace the private temporary employment agencies that have become such an important, negative feature of modern labour markets. Community-based employment boards could even be given responsibility and authority to ensure that available workers in each community (especially young job seekers) are successfully matched with gainful opportunities. Germany's apprenticeship system (which links colleges with employers through intensive planning and job placement support) is an interesting example of the value of publicly-managed labour market planning.

These are just a few of the economic "flash points," where the efficiency and credibility of private ownership is particularly questionable. In any of these cases, therefore, arguments for public or socialized enterprise will have special resonance. And in each case, there are several different particular institutional forms which socialized ownership can take: outright public ownership, cooperatives, and more. Table 29.1 catalogues several of the specific structures through which the goal of socialized ownership (whether in direct production or in finance) could be realized.

Corporations: socialism in disguise?

Contrary to the common stereotype, capitalism is not an *individualistic* system. The economy is not composed of entrepreneurial "Lone Rangers": profit-hungry individuals using their personal talents and energies to invent, produce, and sell exciting new products. The most important players in the economy, rather, are large, bureaucratic institutions: big global corporations. It is their actions and decisions that dominate economic affairs. Moreover, corporations are carefully *planned* organizations. Indeed, if communist central planners could have organized the economy with as much detail, precision, and flexibility as a modern-day Toyota or Wal-Mart, communism would probably still exist! So it may seem counter-intuitive, but corporations are actually *social* institutions.

From the perspective of business owners, the corporation was a remarkable and successful institutional invention. It allows large numbers of people to work together in pursuit of a clearly-defined goal. It allows owners to invest and disinvest from companies easily, without dirtying their hands with day-to-day management responsibilities. But the company's owners still have clear and strong powers to ensure the corporation does what it's supposed to. The big problem with corporations has more to do with their goal – namely, the ruthless maximization of profit and shareholder wealth – than with the institution itself.

The challenge of corporate governance has preoccupied executives, shareholders, accountants, and economists for years. In earlier decades, many economists and business analysts worried that corporations would become powers unto themselves: self-interested empires governed by megalomaniac CEOs, obsessed with their own power and glory. But with the "shareholder revolution" under neoliberalism, those worries have largely been set aside. Now corporations are tightly disciplined to focus on the goal of maximum private profit, with the use of a range of disciplinary tools (including equity-based compensation for CEOs, powerful boards of directors, constant oversight by outside financial analysts, and the threat of hostile takeover for companies which stray from the path of wealth maximization). That's how shareholders ensure that these large bureaucracies act reliably and effectively in their own interests.

But the very success of capitalist corporate governance begs another question. If a large institution, usually owned by people who don't even work there, can be managed in such a disciplined and focused way (from the perspective of its

Table 29.1 Institutional Forms of Public and Social Ownership

Forms of Socialized Production*

Method	How it Works	Successful Examples
State-owned enterprises (SOEs)	Corporations are owned directly by a government (national or sub-national), and operate according to a mandate that may include social criteria.	In advanced capitalist countries many SOEs have been privatized under neoliberalism. But many still operate successfully (in diverse industries including manufacturing, communications, transportation, utilities, and resources), accounting for up to 5% of total GDP in some OECD countries. Examples of successful wholly or partly-owned SOEs include Volkswagen (Germany), StatOil (Norway), EDF Group (France), and Metsähallitus (Finland). In many developing and former communist countries (including China, Brazil, Russia, and Vietnam) SOEs are much more important.
Producer cooperatives	A producer cooperative is owned collectively and equally by the people who work in it, and is usually governed according to "one person one vote."	Cooperatives are one of the most common forms of non-profit enterprise. There are hundreds of thousands of cooperatives in the world; the United Nations estimates that half the world's population are members or customers of a cooperative. Examples of successful producer cooperatives include Fonterra (New Zealand's largest dairy producer), the ReWe Group (a major tourism company in Germany), Huawei (a giant Chinese electronics manufacturer, 99% owned by its workers), and Japan's farm sector (where over 90% of farmers belong to cooperatives). Strong networks of producer cooperatives are the dominant economic structure in Spain's Mondragon region and Italy's Emilia-Romagna region.
Consumer cooperatives	A consumer cooperative is owned collectively and equally by the people who buy its products, and is usually governed according to "one person, one vote."	Many retail cooperatives are formed to help consumers obtain lower prices and challenge the market power of private retailers. In Denmark over one-third of all retail sales are conducted through cooperatives. The E.Leclerc cooperative operates over 500 supermarkets in France. Canada's Mountain Equipment Co-op runs the country's largest retail network for outdoor recreation products.
"Recovered" companies	Workers in a bankrupt company effectively expropriate the enterprise and attempt to keep it in business.	In the years after the 2001 financial crisis in Argentina, over 200 bankrupt factories were taken over by their workers, who continued to operate them (with some government support for refinancing). A 2013 law in Bolivia gives workers the explicit legal authority to take over failed firms.

Method	How it Works	Successful Examples
Community trusts	A community trust is a non-profit corporation, usually exempt from normal business taxes, created to purchase and develop land, housing, and other community assets.	There are over 250 community land trusts operating in the US, with the explicit mission to undertake affordable housing development, environmental conservation, and local job-creation on lands that they own. Governance is based on a shared model that includes lessees and elected local representatives.
Benefit corporations	A benefit corporation is owned by private shareholders, but obliged by its charter to pursue social and environmental goals in addition to profit.	"B Lab" is an association which publishes an annual global ranking of successful benefit corporations. Recent recognized firms include Échele! a tu casa (a benefit corporation based in Mexico City which develops low-cost housing for residents of poor neighbourhoods), and Give Something Back (a major office supply company in California with a community development mandate).
Community and non-profit enterprise	Jobs in especially hard-hit regions and communities can be created by non-profit community development agencies, drawing on local resources including training, housing, and alternative finance.	Community economic development (CED) is an "up-by-the-bootstraps" effort to mobilize local resources that would otherwise sit idle, providing local services, developing infrastructure, and providing unemployed people with job experience and training. Decentralized CED initiatives can be important in many developing economies, and in poor or remote regions of developed countries. Some entire communities have been founded and sustained on cooperative principles in many countries.

Forms of Socialized Finance

Method	How it Works	Successful Examples
Public banks	Public banks are owned by national or sub-national levels of government; they take deposits, issue loans (create credit), and facilitate financial transactions.	Public banking is widespread in many parts of the world. Countries in which publicly-owned banks play a major role include Japan (the Japan Post Bank is the largest savings bank in the world), Germany (with two parallel networks of public banks: Sparkassen and Landesbanken), New Zealand (the Kiwi Bank is the largest domestically owned bank), Costa Rica (4 public banks, one of them governed by elected worker representatives, control 75% of banking), and China (where the state-owned banking system helped China completely avoid the 2008–09 world recession).
Credit unions and cooperative banks	Credit unions and other cooperative banks are owned by their members, and governed according to "one person, one vote."	There are at least 60,000 credit unions and cooperative banks in the world, with trillions of dollars in combined assets; they are the most developed and powerful form of cooperative enterprise. Large credit unions are important financial players in many countries, including: Netherlands (the huge Rabobank has 60,000 employees and €750 billion in assets), France (three major cooperative bank federations account for almost half of all consumer banking), Sweden (the JAK Bank makes loans without charging interest at all), and Canada (the Desjardins credit union movement is the largest financial institution in Quebec).

Table 29.1 (continued) Institutional Forms of Public and Social Ownership

Forms of Socialized Finance (continued)

Method	How it Works	Successful Examples
Investment and development banks	Publicly-owned investment banks specialize in targeted lending and investing in key companies (including private companies) with strategic economic importance.	State-owned investment or development banks play an important role in SECTOR DEVELOPMENT POLICY in many countries, including France, the Nordic countries, Japan, and Brazil. Singapore's Temasek Holdings was established to foster broad economic and industrial development there; it partially owns over 50 companies, and is consistently profitable.
Social investment funds and foundations	These financial funds are mandated to make investments in various firms or social enterprises, in accordance with a broader social mandate, while still earning an adequate or target rate of return.	The Solidarity Fund is a C$10 billion investment fund established by the Quebec Federation of Labour in Canada to invest in businesses which contribute to Quebec's economic and social development. RSF Social Finance is a non-profit financial institution (founded in 1936) focused on lending to non-profit and social enterprises in the US. Oxfam UK has started an Enterprise Development Program to channel financial investments to social enterprises in 20 developing countries. Alaska Native Corporations are collectively owned entities founded with native resource revenues, to invest in a range of businesses and development projects; their collective revenues exceed $10 billion per year.
Sovereign wealth	These funds are owned by a national government, funded with state revenues (often from resource production); they invest in strategic businesses and/or generate future investment income to fund public pensions and other public programs.	Sovereign wealth has grown rapidly in recent years, and now totals over US$5 trillion in investments. Petroleum producing countries have been most aggressive in creating these funds (to save non-renewable wealth for future uses), but some non-petroleum countries have established sovereign funds as well (such as Korea, China, and Singapore). The largest fund is Norway's Government Pension Fund, with assets approaching US$1 trillion; it single-handedly owns about 2% of all European corporate shares.
Micro-credit	Micro lending is undertaken on a non-profit or cost-recovery basis, with a focus on small loans to households and small producers (usually in developing countries or poor neighbourhoods).	The most famous micro-credit institution is the Grameen Bank in Bangladesh, owned cooperatively by its borrowers; it extends small low-interest loans (mostly to women) through a participatory loan management system (in which groups of borrowers collectively determine who receives new loans, and collectively ensure the loans are repaid). Similar systems have been introduced in other poor countries, and in some regions or neighbourhoods of rich countries.

* Excluding traditional public service delivery (such as health care, education, etc.).

shareholders), couldn't society develop economic institutions that pursued alternative goals with equal focus and efficiency? Wouldn't it be possible to devise a "social corporation", with the mandate to maximize social well-being (whether that be measured by job-creation or investment or community welfare) with just as much discipline and accountability as private corporations pursue profit? Perhaps socialists could learn from the institutional success of corporations, to improve our own efforts to organize public economic activity in an efficient but socially directed manner.

Some socially-minded business experts have proposed an alternative legal structure, in hopes of directing the economic power of a corporation toward specified public goals instead of just private profit. Many US states, for example, now permit an alternative corporate structure called a **BENEFIT CORPORATION** (or "B Corporation"). These companies have shareholders and boards of directors, just like regular corporations. And they still aim to make a profit from their operations. But their corporate charter also explicitly mandates the directors to pursue social and environmental goals. (In contrast, directors of traditional corporations are actually legally prohibited from pursuing broader goals other than the financial benefit of the shareholders, through a legal concept called "fiduciary responsibility.") So benefit corporations have not fully broken with the logic of capitalism (and they still face competitive pressure from traditional companies); but they have been partially reoriented around an alternative, broader set of criteria. A similar "hybrid" form of corporation exists in Germany, where companies are legally obliged to include workers and other stakeholders in decision-making (through a system called "codetermination"). Some major companies there are owned by non-profit foundations, with an explicit mandate to enhance social welfare. In this context, the social nature of corporations (as a productive, collective economic institution beholden to all of society, not just its owners) is more visible.

Perhaps the seeds of a deeper transformation are lurking in these and similar experiments: perhaps the institutional efficiency of the corporation could indeed be harnessed and explicitly redirected toward broader social goals. Even if this worked, however, changes in economic governance at the macroeconomic level would still be needed to guide the economy toward full employment and healthy distributional outcomes. Merely changing the marching orders of individual corporations will not, on its own, attain an egalitarian and democratic economy, unless the other rules of the game are changed, too.

More broadly, progressives need to seriously tackle the problems of institutional governance in socialized enterprises. Publicly-owned enterprises have a bad reputation (deserved in some cases, not in others) for operating in inefficient, uncreative, or even corrupt ways. Developing ways to define clear goals, create effective incentives, inspire innovation, impose checks and balances, and enforce accountability from public managers, constitutes in my view a central problem holding back the successful expansion of public and non-profit enterprise. Studying the experience of successful and efficient public enterprises, learning from the experience of private-sector corporate governance, and experimenting with new forms of social and non-profit entrepreneurship, will all help to set the stage for a revitalization of social ownership.

Nurturing a socialist ecology

Socialism cannot emerge out of abstract, idealistic dreaming, imposed on society by someone who thinks they've discovered the "true" plan. Socialism must arise in response to concrete human problems, and our concrete efforts to solve those problems. As long as humans continue to suffer needless deprivation, hardship, and exploitation, people in large numbers will continue to fight for a better deal. And as long as capitalism remains unable or unwilling to meet those demands, then socialism will exist as a potential solution.

Dream Together

"A dream you dream alone is only a dream.
A dream you dream together is reality."

Yoko Ono and John Lennon, pop personalities (1980).

In Chapter 28, we identified a long list of specific reforms that we can demand and win, even within an economy that retains its fundamentally "capitalist" character. And in this chapter, we compiled an equally long list of cases where the demand for public or socialized production may have special resonance. We also catalogued (in Table 29.1) an impressive variety of forms through which public or socialized ownership can take shape (both in direct production, and in the realm of finance). In short, all of the ingredients are there for an impressive kaleidoscope of movements and campaigns to challenge the failures of for-profit production, and build alternative economic vehicles that can meet human needs more effectively and sustainably. This is how socialists can nurture a diverse and creative culture that challenges the core ideological claim of capitalism: namely, that private for-profit production is the best way to organize economic activity.

Even where capitalism is strongest, it is never 100 percent pure "capitalist." There are always significant spaces in economic and social life where the dominance of private ownership and markets is not accepted (including the public sector, state-owned enterprises, non-profit and cooperative enterprise, and unpaid work inside the household). And there is always tension regarding where to draw the precise dividing line between the capitalist and non-capitalist spheres of life. So

You Write the Book: Doing It Ourselves

Neoclassical economics assumes that the profit motive, combined with the disciplining power of private markets, always ensures the most efficient and responsive economic management. But in reality there are many ways to organize economic activity, including various structures of public or non-profit ownership and management where work is directed explicitly to meeting a human or social goal (rather than maximizing private profit). Think of an example in your community where work occurs in a non-profit setting, and is both efficient and socially useful. Send it to author@economicsforeveryone. com. We'll post your best examples at www.economicsforeveryone.com.

we can push back at the edges of capitalism in many different ways: by resisting and reversing privatization; defending non-market, public, and social spaces and functions; and formulating pragmatic, creative proposals to expand non-profit enterprise. All of these efforts constrain the power of business and wealth, and challenge the assumption that private ownership is the only way to efficiently organize an economy.

We can also think bigger: Imagine a society which gradually accumulates experience with public or socialized ownership in many areas of the economy, through the incremental development of not-for-profit activities and enterprises. It would build strong linkages between those socialized and not-for-profit parts of the economy: for example, connecting socialized financial institutions (like credit unions), with public or cooperative productive enterprises, and cooperative retail networks. (This model of interlocking cross-sectoral non-profit activity exists in places like Mondragon, Spain; Kerala, India; and the Emilia Romagna region of Italy.) In this manner, a vibrant "ecology" of diverse, complementary non-capitalist ownership and production emerges. Like a natural ecology, this one is healthiest when there's a wide diversity of institutional forms and strategies at play; this permits maximum flexibility, adaptability, and successful evolution. As the concept of socialized investment and production becomes more commonplace and acceptable, enterprising and passionate people will be drawn to the task of building more non-profit and public enterprises. Each successful experiment, in other words, opens up new ideas, opportunities, and possibilities for expanding the realm of public and social enterprise – until it becomes part of the economic "common sense" possessed by society as a whole.

All this incremental progress, united and guided by an overarching determination to challenge the dominance of private wealth and profit, would gradually transform society. There's no "magic bullet," no centralized "seizure of power," and no detailed blueprint to follow. What's needed is a broad, lasting social and political movement, centred around the core determination to use our productive capacities – our brains and our brawn, our creativity and productivity, and the natural environment

---

It Worked for Them. It Could Work for Us, Too

"Only a crisis actual or perceived produces real change. When that crisis occurs, the actions that are taken depend on the ideas that are lying around. That, I believe, is our basic function: to develop alternatives to existing policies, to keep them alive and available until the politically impossible becomes politically inevitable."

Milton Friedman, US economist and intellectual father of neoliberalism (1982).

– to directly enhance the quality of life for the masses of people. And one day, that's how capitalism might end.

We conclude with a lesson from Milton Friedman, one of the intellectual founders of neoliberalism. For many years during the postwar Golden Age, he was a marginal outsider, his seemingly extreme ideas shunned by those who believed that some quasi-Keynesian fine-tuning had perfected capitalism. He kept working, however, to challenge the underlying assumptions of that postwar economic establishment, and flesh out his aggressive pro-business alternative. He was motivated by faith that when a moment of crisis arrived, he would have a complete alternative program to present and implement (see box). Tragically, the first appropriate crisis was the military coup and CIA intervention in Chile in 1973, which overthrew the elected socialist government of Salvador Allende; Chile thus became the first country in the world to experiment with full-on neoliberal economics (imposed, in this case, alongside the assassination and imprisonment of tens of thousands of socialists). Soon Friedman's program was being adopted in countries around the world.

Progressives need our own alternative program, fleshed out and ready to go, and a similar willingness to think big. And where possible, we should start implementing it: with concrete experiments in non-profit ownership, production, and governance, supplemented by complementary macroeconomic, labour market, and environmental policies. That way, the next time a crisis hits capitalism (and that will happen, potentially sooner than later), we will have an alternative vision ready to go. We didn't have one during the 2008–09 global financial crisis, and that permitted capitalism to emerge from that crisis politically stronger than it went in. Unlike Friedman, of course, we dream of a humane, egalitarian, and sustainable economy. But we should be at least as ambitious as he was, and we should get ready to make our dream a reality.

Conclusion

A Baker's Dozen:
Key Things to Remember

Congratulations! You've learned how capitalism works – from a critical, grass-roots perspective. Even though we've promised to keep things simple, the system we describe is not. And the economic map we've built, one step at a time, has now become rather impressive. It portrays an economy that is complex, diverse, flexible, and (in some ways) fragile.

You'll never remember everything in this book, as you carry on with your work, your life, and (hopefully) your contributions to economic and social justice.

But there are a few crucial lessons to keep in mind. These key themes will help you analyze specific economic issues and controversies as they come up. They are core principles to sort out what's important in the real economy, from what's not – to distinguish reality from ideology.

So here are 13 big things (a so-called "baker's dozen") to remember about economics:

1. **The economy depends on social relationships, not just technical relationships, and (like society) it evolves and changes over time**. There is no "natural" order to the economy. There are no inherent, unchanging laws governing its behaviour. What we call the "economy" is simply the way human beings work together, to produce goods and services, and then decide what to do with what we produce. And there's nothing permanent about it. Everything about the economy – technology, social relationships, the location and composition of output, and more – changes over time.

2. **Economics is an inherently subjective, value-laden, political discipline**. The economy is not natural, unchanging, or objective. And the study of the economy – what we call economics – is just as subjective and impermanent. The economy embodies conflicting interests between different groups; and clashing tendencies within the economics profession closely reflect those conflicting interests. No school of economic thought can claim to be neutral or objective. Different approaches to economics rise and fall, depending on the course of economic (and political) debates and conflicts. Every approach to economics combines an analysis of how the economy works, with a set of values and assumptions regarding how it *should* work (and in *whose* interests).

Beware of economists bearing free advice – especially if that economist claims to be "objective" or "scientific."

3. **Productive human activity is the only force that adds value to the wealth we were given by nature**. "Work," broadly defined, includes all forms of productive human effort – including paid employment, unpaid work within households, and even the managerial work of business executives. Without work, nothing happens in the economy. All work must start with the essential inputs and resources we receive from nature (including land to live on, air to breathe, and water to drink). Everything else in the economy then involves the application of work to transform those resources and materials into all the goods and services we need to survive and thrive.

4. **Using tools makes work more productive**. Humans discovered very quickly that it is much better to work with tools than with our bare hands. The invention, production, and accumulation of "tools" (defined broadly to include machinery, structures, infrastructure, and other kinds of physical capital) has been the central feature of economic development through human history. Developing and accumulating more advanced tools, and training people to use them effectively, is the key source of rising productivity. However, tools themselves are *not* productive: it is the *know-how* embodied in those tools (that is, knowing to make tools first, and then use them to produce the goods and services we actually want) that is productive. Merely owning a tool is not, in itself, a productive act.

5. **In capitalism, most work consists of employment**. Employment is work that is performed for someone else, and with its output owned by someone else, in return for the payment of wages and salaries. About 85 percent of households in developed capitalist economies rely on employment as their dominant source of income over their lives. Managing the employment relationship is a central aspect of capitalism. Employers face a complicated challenge to try to minimize their labour costs, while simultaneously maximizing the effort and discipline of their employees. This relationship introduces an inherent but complex conflict of interest between workers and capitalists.

6. **Unpaid work is also important**. A great deal of productive, necessary work occurs inside the household: out of sight, behind closed doors, and generally without pay. Most of that work is performed by women, whose opportunities in the "outside" economic world are constrained accordingly. Remembering that this work needs to be performed, analyzing how and by whom it is performed, and making changes to it over time, are central issues in economics.

7. **Competition is a central feature of capitalism, and forces companies to behave in certain ways**. Capitalists aim to maximize the profits on their investments; one way to do that is by poaching customers, workers, resources,

and capital from other capitalists. Competition therefore introduces new constraints on the behaviour of individual capitalists. It's no longer just greed that motivates them, it's also fear. That fear (of being driven out of business by more successful competitors) forces capitalists to behave in certain ways, regardless of their personal preferences or values. Competition has become more intense over time, not less (thanks to technology, globalization, privatization, and improved management skills). Even very large global companies are disciplined by competition that is unforgiving and ruthless.

8. **The condition of the natural environment is crucial to our prosperity**. The environment is both a source of direct ecological benefit (fresh air, open spaces, recreation, and so on) and a source of raw materials for production. The economy cannot continually run down the quality of the environment without society eventually paying an enormous economic (and human) price. Developing sustainable practices (to stabilize and preserve environmental quality) is a central economic priority. Most pressing is the urgent global need to reduce greenhouse gas emissions and adapt to climate change.

9. **The financial industry is not, in itself, productive**. Producing credit out of thin air, and buying financial assets solely in hopes of selling them later for a profit, are not concretely productive acts. Financial institutions can play a useful role in facilitating investment and production by companies in the real economy. And the creation of credit is an essential lubricant for production and spending – if it is used wisely and productively. But this useful function may be overwhelmed by pointless, wasteful, or downright destructive financial activity. The profit motive in private banking causes the financial system to behave in unproductive and destabilizing ways, erupting in regular crises and panics.

10. **Government has played a central, supporting role since the beginning of capitalism**. Government is not the "enemy" of free-market capitalism. In fact, without government capitalism wouldn't exist at all. Government actions and programs have tended to reinforce and stabilize the basic relationships of capitalism: guaranteeing private property rights, supplying business with needed inputs (like reliable infrastructure and skilled, disciplined workers), expanding markets, and managing social relationships to promote both stability and profitability. At the same time, working people – thanks to their sheer numbers – can use democratic openings to force governments to respond to *their* needs and priorities, but only when they are sufficiently motivated and well-organized.

11. **Globalization and "free trade" as we know it are one-sided and damaging**. Globalization in the generic sense is not new, and concrete linkages between countries (including trade, travel, and exchange of knowledge) are important

and beneficial. But modern globalization is institutionally biased in favour of corporations and the people who own them. Free-trade agreements and other global practices and institutions give them more mobility and more power, while limiting the ability of national governments to regulate international flows of goods and capital. In contrast to free-trade theory (which claims globalization should benefit everyone who participates), globalization may strengthen or weaken a national economy. It can increase or decrease demand for a country's products (via the trade balance), and it can strengthen or weaken investment (via capital flows). A country's competitiveness determines whether globalization leads to more output and employment, or less. But in all regions, under the current "rules of the game" globalization has sparked a damaging, beggar-thy-neighbour competition to suppress living standards and provide endless favours to business.

12. **Repeating boom-and-bust cycles are not accidents or "shocks," they are created (and recreated) by the core mechanisms of capitalism.** Capitalism is fundamentally unstable: there is no way (outside of government planning) to coordinate the individual spending decisions that set the economy in motion, and self-interested actions by individuals (such as a simultaneous desire to all save money) can be collectively irrational and self-defeating. Periodic crises are a fact of life of this system, and financialization and globalization have only heightened the risk. Recognizing this systemic failing, and responding to it with demands for planning and social security (instead of self-blame and austerity), can empower working people to protect themselves when the next crisis hits – as it certainly will,

13. **Workers and poor people get only as much from the economy as they are able to demand, fight for, and win.** There is no reason to believe that the success of capitalists will ever automatically "trickle-down" into improved living standards for the bulk of humanity. Neoclassical theories which claim everyone gets paid according to their productivity are theoretically inconsistent and empirically false. Income distribution is determined by power, more than markets. Demanding a fairer deal from the system, and building the organizational and political power to back up that demand (through unions, community organizations, and other social justice movements), is the only way to redivide the pie. And if those demands come up against a hard limit in the form of the system's unwillingness or inability to meet them, then the time will have come to look at alternatives.

On that note, this is a good time to put down this book, put on your boots – and go out to organize for a fairer share of the pie that you work so hard to produce.

Index

Terms highlighted in SMALL CAPITAL LETTERS are defined in the online glossary downloadable at www.economicsforeveryone.com.